About the Au

Born on the Wirral and educated at Birkenhead School, young Ken Senar joined the Combined Cadet Force and enjoyed 'air experience' flights with the RAF. After passing his School Certificate exams he left school and spent a year living-in 'below stairs' on a Shropshire farm. There, he gained a grounding in agriculture before joining the Royal Air Force for National Service. Enjoying the life, he 'signed on' and became a pilot. This book tells his RAF story.

On being invalided out of the RAF in 1958, a sick man, he joined his father's engineering business in Birkenhead. He became a director and served on the boards of the Wirral and Merseyside Chambers of Commerce.

After the business was sold, and after having stayed for a time with its new owners, Ken became a special projects manager and technical author for a GEC subsidiary. In retirement he continued his engineering interests in his home workshop making live-steam, passenger-hauling, model locomotives. This ceased when a long-standing injury to his hand caused too much trouble. As a necessary therapy he continued with Meccano modelling, a life-long hobby, producing models to international prize-winning standards. His other interests covered building a light hovercraft, genealogy, world-wide travel, researching and writing up his family's story, and serving in official capacities in his local village church. He likes to be busy.

Dedication

To the memory of all the friends I made in the Royal Air Force.

100% of author's profits from sales of this book will be donated to the Royal Air Forces Association which does so much good work tending to the welfare of members of the RAF Family who are in need.

KENNETH B. SENAR

I'll Call You Pod

Cold War Recollections of a
Low Level Pilot
1951–1958

AUSTIN MACAULEY PUBLISHERS™

LONDON • CAMBRIDGE • NEW YORK • SHARJAH

A CIP catalogue record for this title is available from the British Library.

ISBN 978-1-78710-196-8 (Paperback)
ISBN 978-1-78710-197-5 (Hardback)
ISBN 978-1-78710-198-4 (E-Book)
www.austinmacauley.com

First Published (2018)
Austin Macauley Publishers Ltd.
25 Canada Square
Canary Wharf
London
E14 5LQ

Acknowledgments

I wish to pass my grateful thanks to the following organisations and people:

To the Royal Air Force Museum at Hendon for demonstrating the need for me to write this piece.

To the Royal Air Force Air Defence Radar Museum for its help and encouragement.

To ex 93 Squadron pilot Tom Balfour for the loan of photographs.

To ex 93 Squadron pilot Eric Pigdon for his encouragement and the freedom with which he reactivated my memories of events at Jever.

To ex 93 Squadron pilot Mick Ryan, the Web Master of the RAF Jever website, from which I was able to download pictures and confirm dates of events at Jever. I also thank him for his willingness to publish this document on the website.

To many friends who loaned me pictures and cuttings, and for their encouragement.

To my wife Margaret for her patience and muted exasperation at me for spending so much time on my computer. And for her checking my initial typescripts, prompting me with grammar, and leaving me alone when I needed moments of deep thought. God bless her.

The author, then and now.

Contents

PROLOGUE

I T WAS SUGGESTED TO me some years ago by one of the curators at the Royal Air Force Museum at Hendon that I should record my experiences in the RAF. He emphasised that the 1950s period of the Cold War would never appear in the annals of the RAF unless people like me wrote down everything we could remember. After much consideration and thought, bearing in mind both what had been suggested to me, and my fading memory, I eventually decided, before it was too late, to record what I could. What follows is the result.

I have set out my narrative from an entirely personal viewpoint, telling what happened to me and what I did, mostly from memory yet supported by entries recorded in my two Log Books. Some additional dates, however, were extracted from official service documents relating to my first tour in Germany.

I apologise in advance for any errors, both of fact and time, which I may have made, as everything I have written about dates back to over half a century ago.

I have presented my experiences in what I hope will be regarded as a logical format, although several sets of events did run concurrently and have therefore had to be described in separate chapters. This is particularly the case in Part Three.

Undoubtedly there will be inaccuracies. Please excuse me for these, but I thought it better to record what I could recollect rather than nothing at all. There are also some outspoken views expressed, as well as incidents of an extremely vulgar nature, for this is the way life was. Times change, and I hope these incidents do not offend. They were typical of parts of Service life and behaviour in a mostly all male environment.

To readers who can recall some of the happenings of which I tell, please remember that in a very few years there will only be people reading this who are younger (as there are today) who have never experienced what we did, and who have very little concept of what Service life was like. This is why I have explained some things more fully than if they were being read solely by ex-RAF personnel of my age.

To my critics, and there will probably be many, I say this: none of us knows everything; we all make mistakes, therefore if you know better or more than me, don't contact me and expect a rewrite. That won't happen. Write your own stories yourselves and lodge them in appropriate places, as have I. Only by your contributions can future generations have a wider view of the 1950s Cold War as far as it concerned those of us in the Royal Air Force serving as a part of the 2nd Allied Tactical Air Force in Germany.

Part 1

TRAINING

1. Awakening Interest

AIRCRAFT HAVE FASCINATED ME ever since, as a very small child, I saw biplanes and autogyros flying over our garden at Upton, Wirral, when Cobham's Air Circus put on a show in a field not far from home. That was probably in 1935. Three years later I was taken to RAF Sealand to see the displays on Empire Air Day. I watched the tied-together aerobatics with wonder, and was equally fascinated watching a machine-gun firing through the propeller of an aircraft in the butts.[1] Memories of the noise and smells remain with me.

I was at school during the war. Living close to Merseyside I saw and experienced many air raids and became fairly competent at aircraft recognition. I could certainly tell 'theirs' from 'ours'. I then became aware of radar as a result of listening to news broadcasts on BBC radio and, just occasionally, seeing guarded glimpses of it on newsreels at the Tatler News Theatre in Liverpool, one of the few buildings that somehow survived the bombing of the city centre. I had no idea what radar really was but guessed it was a series of radio rays of some sort which frightened away enemy aircraft because we knew where they were. This, I reasoned, was why the bombers stopped coming over to bomb the Liverpool and Birkenhead docks, not far from where I lived.

Aerial activity diminished with the cessation of hostilities, but the matter of the supposed all-seeing eye of radar intrigued me, as did the thought of my possibly going up in an aeroplane someday. To actually fly one was just a pipe dream.

My first sight of radar masts was not until immediately after the war when on holiday with my parents near Salcombe, South Devon. We stayed at the Bolt Head Hotel, just up the hill from South Sands, on

---

1   For many years one of the clips that held the belt of ammunition together during that demonstration was kept on the mantelpiece at home.

the side of a sort of bluff or promontory and cosily sheltered by the lush vegetation of the area. Within a few miles of our hotel I remember seeing several (I think there might have been four) tall wooden towers with short side arms and with wires strung from and between them in a geometrical fashion. These, I was told, were radar masts. There were some wooden 'army' huts close by, but I had seen so many military camps during the war that I took very little notice of them.[2]

From one of the rooms in the hotel I could see a dish, rather like an oversize circular electric fire, which sometimes swivelled slowly on the top of a tall lattice tower. The lower part of the tower was hidden from view, yet it must have been within a mile or so away. My father asked Norman Long, the hotel owner, what it was.[3] He said that "They (whomsoever 'they' were) were looking across the sea towards Start Point." Mother thought it looked spooky, so did I. More than half a dozen years would pass before I discovered the truth.

I joined the Junior Training Corps (JTC) at an early age and later transferred to the RAF Section of the newly formed Combined Cadet Force (CCF) at school, and it was when, as part of our training, pictures were shown to me of radar 'heads' that I began to understand what I had seen at Salcombe.[4]

This picture was taken by a school pal and is dated 3rd March 1949 when I was in the Junior Training Corps, before I transferred to the CCF, RAF Section.

2   Probably at either West Prawle or Start Point.

3   Norman Long had been a much loved BBC wartime radio entertainer and, on the cessation of hostilities, had bought the hotel and ran it as his 'retirement' occupation.

4   CCF: Sometimes mockingly referred to as 'Compound Cooking Fat', a product made available to housewives during the strict rationing regime then in force.

My interest in aircraft was undiminished and, on family visits to the annual SBAC Farnborough Air Show, I watched many impressive flying displays by the Senior Test Pilots of the day and wondered, too, at the very different radar equipment rotating out on the airfield.[5] The aircraft fascinated me much more. Apart from using radios in the CCF and building a one-valve medium-wave wireless set from Government Surplus items, an interest I had had in electrical matters began to fade.

As a CCF Cadet I was to gain 'Air Experience' as a passenger, flying three times in RAF Ansons, from RAF Hooton Park, RAF Sealand, and RAF Hawarden. During one of those flights I was asked by the pilot to wind the handle behind his seat so as to lower the undercarriage for landing. That was exciting stuff; I actually helped operate the aircraft! As a result of practice at the school rifle range, and later on the Sealand Open Range on Burton Marshes, I earned my Marksman badge and became a good shot.[6]

That was the limit of my knowledge of the RAF until the 1950s when National Service came along.

---

5 SBAC = Society of British Aircraft Constructors of which there were many members at the time.

6 The school rifles were .22" calibre, whereas those we used at Sealand ranges were .303".

2. Into Uniform

I WAS 'CALLED UP' to start my 2 year National Service on the 13th of November, 1951, aged 18. I arrived at RAF Padgate in civilian clothes, carrying a small suitcase and, like others of my 'intake', with a slightly heavy heart.

It was fortunate for me, because of my earlier flying experience, that I had been accepted into the Royal Air Force as potential aircrew material. As such, I was allocated a bed in a hut in which there were a number of other somewhat apprehensive and intimidated young civilians. Collectively we were referred to as 'Static Aircrew', part of Padgate's No.3 Squadron, and designated Intake 46. At an early stage on the day of arrival we were issued with the standard necessities of knife, fork, mug, and spoon so that we could eat in the Airmens Mess.

Few of us ate much that day. Some of our number were in tears, others cursed and swore profusely – particularly on being marshalled by a well-meaning Corporal to the Bedding Store in misty drizzle to collect our pillows, blankets, and sheets for the night. Two of our number were detailed to attend to the stove in the middle of the hut. Lighting it proved a problem but was solved somehow. That evening, when most were either sobbing quietly or busily writing first letters to girlfriends and mums back home, I took a more adventurous approach and decided carefully to explore my wider surroundings. Time was on my hands and I had until 'Lights Out' at 22.00 hours to fill. I somehow found the Station Cinema and decided to watch the evening programme, the main feature film of which was 'Coastal Command'. For me, it was the best thing I could have done. I was now in the Royal Air Force (just), and it put me perfectly in the right frame of mind for what was to come. I slept reasonably well that night, but finding one's way in the dark to the outside latrines was not the most congenial of occupations, particularly in the rain.

During the next few days we completed many forms, were Attested, kitted out, and made to send all civilian kit (except shaving gear, handkerchiefs, and writing materials) back home. After this we all looked the same in our AC2 uniforms and had quickly to learn to recognise our associates by means other than the civilian clothes we had been

Taken about 2 days after being kitted out at Padgate and in front of just about the only greenery on the camp.

wearing. We were interviewed by various 'Bods', allocated our Service Numbers, and given medicals of varying degrees of severity. During one of these we all had, individually, to enter a room, drop our trousers, and present our rear orifices to the Medical Officer. He was thereafter referred to as the "Arsehole Inspector", and there was much conjecture as to how many he saw in a week. No-one envied him his job.

The FFI inspection sticks in my mind because of the circumstances in which it was conducted.[1] Following lunch we were 'marched', or rather shambled, back to our hut and told that an MO, as we had now learned to call uniformed doctors, would be with us in five minutes. In preparation we were ordered to strip naked and stand in a line, side by side, down the centre of the hut. No sooner done than the MO appeared, but not before one of our group raised an erection and started giggling uncontrollably, and several more became similarly afflicted. Even the Corporal started to smile in spite of his attempts to call us to order. The MO commenced his inspection of our private parts and, having seen it all before, quickly dismantled any priapism with a sharp flick of his pencil, carried out his examination, and passed on to the next recruit without saying a word.

Immediately after this episode we were sent to the coal dump to fill buckets for empty huts in our area of the camp in readiness for the next intake of recruits. Surprisingly, some of the bigger chaps proved to be weaklings. Personally I had no problem as I had, for the previous year, been involved with heavy agricultural work and was very fit.

During the next two or three days we, our numbers now reduced as a result of interviews and medical failures, were instructed in the rudiments of drill by some most unpleasant characters called DIs.[2] I had no problem with this because of previous CCF experience, but a good half of those present literally didn't know their left from their right when ordered to turn. This was bad enough when not on the march, but when marching caused absolute chaos and much use of insulting and intimidating Air Force vernacular from whomsoever was in charge of us at the time.

We quickly learned to treat with caution anyone wearing any badge of rank, particularly DIs, or indeed anyone wearing a blue blancoed webbing belt.

---

1   FFI = Freedom From Infection (Venereal Disease).
2   DI = Drill Instructor. Usually regarded as the lowest form of life.

One morning we remaining 'Static Aircrew' (pronounced 'Urcrew' at Padgate), now only half a hut full in all, were assembled and told that we would be leaving the camp temporarily to undergo more tests at the Aircrew Selection Centre at Hornchurch, the old Battle of Britain airfield in Essex on the outskirts of London.

After having returned our bedding to the Bedding Store we were duly ordered to 'Get fell in' and assembled in three ranks with packs and kit bags shouldered, to board a bus to take us to Warrington station for our journey south. A Corporal was in charge of us and held our collective Travel Warrant. This, I discovered later, was in case any of us was tempted to abscond and go AWOL, as it was our first venture in uniform into the outside world.[3]

The bus made its way to the Guardroom and there, at the side of the road, the notice which read proudly 'Welcome to the Royal Air Force' as one approached from 'civvy street', had on its back scrawled the words 'Now try and get out again'. I was reminded of this some years later by an RAF Padre who had done a stint at Padgate at about the same time that I was there.

---

3   AWOL = Absent Without Leave.

3. More Tests

ON ARRIVAL AT RAF Hornchurch we were allocated beds in a brick, pre-war style, two storey barrack block – luxury after a cold wooden hut. Better still, the latrines were in the same building. We quickly realised, also, that there were civilians staying downstairs. They were to undergo similar tests straight from civvy street and were mostly 'University Types' toying with the idea of becoming aircrew but, if they failed acceptance, they could opt out, because of their qualifications, or reserved occupations. These well-dressed lads looked up to us because we were in uniform!

Discipline on the camp was gentle but firm because of the civvy element present. We had originally thought we were going to be on a flying station and were disappointed when we found that houses and park land had taken the place of the airfield.

We went through stringent medical tests covering general fitness, hearing, eyesight, touch, breathing, manual dexterity, reaction speeds and hand-eye co-ordination. We were interviewed as to our medical history, backgrounds, academic skills, and future plans. We also took aptitude and intelligence tests. I was fortunate and passed them all and was declared fit for any aircrew duty except that of Air Gunner because, at 6'4½" tall, I wouldn't fit into a turret. I wasn't sorry! For some reason I was one of the first in our group to finish the tests and to get my results; therefore, with time to spare, I was allocated to an office to work for a day. A kindly Sergeant was in charge and I passed the day folding paper and stuffing envelopes. All the time he was passing on hints and tips as to how I should deal with situations in my future RAF life.

Tests over, a check between ourselves revealed that only about half of us were passed fit for aircrew training in any category. Only four of us were passed for pilot training; the remainder were to be trained as navigators.

We returned to Padgate and were split up; those who had failed were transferred straight away to square-bashing training in another Padgate Squadron or posted elsewhere. Those of us who had passed were put with others from other huts who had also passed, to await the next stage of our enlightenment. In the meantime we were all learning more about service life, what the different uniforms and badges meant, and how to address people who were senior to us, namely everyone else in the RAF at that time. Within days our block posting came through.

4. Grading

ON NOVEMBER 30TH, WITH kit packed again, we made our way once more to Warrington station, this time for our rail journey to Lincolnshire. Our destination was No.2 I.T.S., G.W. at Digby, a flying station, just north of Sleaford.[1] Now we could see real aeroplanes, close to, not as spectators. Little did we know it then but life was going to get tough.

We were allocated beds in a wooden hut at the edge of the grass airfield, exposed to all that the weather could throw at it. It had the same sort of stoves, same sort of beds down each side and the same type of outside latrines as at Padgate. We were only four weeks off Christmas and winter weather had begun to set in.

Flying clothing was issued – fur-lined boots, a 'Sidcot' kapok-lined inner suit and heavy canvas Sidcot outer suit, goggles, oxygen mask (with microphone), leather helmet, leather gauntlets, and silk inner gloves – all to be toted about in a second kit bag. We were given leather patches to sew above the left breast pocket on our No.2 Home Dress after our names had been clearly written on them.[2] We also wore white plastic discs behind the badges on our berets, these latter to distinguish us from other Airmen on the Station and elsewhere. Although still earning the same £1 a week we were now known as Officer Cadets, for at that time all new aircrew were being commissioned in the RAF.[3]

---

1   No.2 Initial Training School, Grading Wing.

2   This was our working uniform. No.1 Home Dress was known as 'Best Blue' and was usually worn on parades and when off camp for any time.

3   The RAF is unique in the British Armed Forces as, save for the RAF. Regiment, it is only the Officers who do the fighting. This was not the case before the 1950s but became the norm thenafter.

One of our group, now called a Flight, at Digby was an old hand who fancied his chance at becoming a pilot. The fact that he did not succeed was of no concern to us, but while he was with us he taught us much barrack room lore and how to bull-up and arrange kit for inspections. His knowledge was invaluable to us, even to showing us how to 'bone-up' the toecaps on our Army Pattern boots and shoes. We spent many evening and weekend hours doing this, sitting on our beds, building up a shine good enough to see your face in and to satisfy stringent inspections.

Our Flight was the newest of a series of Flights being processed through training at Digby. There was also a contingent of Cadets from the nearby RAF College at Cranwell stationed there. When they passed out, they would be awarded permanent commissions, and were undergoing a wholly different training regime to us. As chance would have it, one of the Cranwell Cadets was an old acquaintance of mine from Birkenhead. Class distinction on the camp was such that we had to be careful not to be seen speaking to each other; something we only managed to do a couple of times during the eight weeks I was there.

Our training at No.2 Initial Training School, Digby, was split between ground school studies and flight experience. This combination was designed to teach us the rudiments of aviation, RAF life, drill, and to sort through us once again to weed out those of us who failed hopelessly in the air or were airsick, and those who could not absorb the ground school training sufficiently quickly; also to eliminate those without the necessary 'personal qualities' who were not considered to be 'Officer Material'. We were also shown VD films, so detailed as to make some Cadets queasy. We were treated as students and were watched closely, hence our having to wear our names on our uniforms. Flt.Lt. Sinclair was Officer i/c our Flight and was ably assisted by Fg. Off. 'Jumbo' Cuthill. They shared the bulk of our ground school instruction. I was to meet Jumbo again later in my RAF career.

Corporal Brown was in charge of us, taught us drill, and showed us how to prepare and properly to lay out kit for inspection, and other barrack duties. He also marched us between the old Bellman hangars and hutted classrooms. After a fortnight of being in the wooden huts we were transferred into more comfortable permanent pre-war brick barrack blocks. Bull nights and kit inspections took place weekly. We quickly learned to get things right – that is precisely right, no less – so as to avoid adverse comments being written in our personal course assessments.

We had to buy our own Blanco, Brasso, and shoe polish from the NAAFI, and we paid for our own haircuts.[4] This drained our scant finances, especially when, occasionally, we were still hungry after a strenuous day and the meal in the Mess hadn't satisfied us. A helping of beans on toast, mugs of NAAFI tea, and occasional phone calls home, or the cost of writing paper, envelopes and stamps, left us with little or nothing by next Pay Parade.

If you were slow eating in the Mess, or a late arrival, the shout 'Last five' would go out and there would be a rush to gobble your food so as not to be one of the last five Cadets in the room, and thus have to clean-up after everyone else.

Phone calls home were made in the evening from a Public Call Box outside the local shop and Post Office some couple of hundred yards outside the main gate. There were no lights, and the kiosk was unlit. Usually there would be a queue waiting to use the phone, all standing there patiently, shivering in the pitch black December night air. It wasn't unusual to have to wait an hour or more to be given the chance to ask the operator to connect you to the number you wanted, and having done that, having to keep the call short because you were parting with valuable pennies as you spoke.

Not long after arriving at Digby we were taken by truck one afternoon to somewhere near Metheringham airfield and told to find our own way back, on foot. Not one of us was familiar with the area which was criss-crossed by drainage channels. Some of us were given maps, so we formed ourselves into groups, each having a map. The wide ditches posed a problem. Had they not been there we would have been able to get back to Digby within an hour. The maps were clear enough to show footpaths and probable bridges over the watercourses. Any attempt to find these bridges was doomed to failure because they had fallen into disrepair, collapsed, or been removed. We walked seemingly miles trying to find the shortest way, but with the bridges gone, we found we had to keep to the roads. We were actually further away from Digby than when we started out and it took us hours to get back. In fact we missed tea and didn't return until well after dark. Our feet were covered

---

4   NAAFI = Navy Army Air Force Institutes.

with blisters from our new boots and, next morning, we sought permission to be 'excused boots' and were excused marching for three days as well.[5]

We were only shown and allowed to watch the aircraft during the first weeks because the course ahead of us was doing its flying while we concentrated on ground school work, all the time making sure that we passed the regular progress tests so that we would have the chance to fly ourselves. Those who failed were 'chopped' from the course and were posted away at the same time as we were given a few days' leave, our first, over the Christmas period. We were issued with Travel Warrants to get home and back by rail. My own journey took me from Digby station to Lincoln, then to Sheffield, Manchester, and Liverpool, changing trains at each place. I had to save hard to pay for my own fare from Liverpool (Mersey Ferry and Corporation Bus) to home on the Wirral. We were undergoing initiative tests, but getting home by the most expeditious route in the minimum of time, and back again, proved equally taxing. I even managed the journey one weekend on a 36 hour pass. The effort was worthwhile because I came back to camp with two pounds in my pocket from my father. That helped ease my financial straits. Most other Cadets sought, and were given, similar parental assistance. On the evening of our return one of the Cadets, Pete Deuchar (son of a whisky distillery executive) brought a bottle which was shared round the barrack room (quite illegally) and drunk from our pint mugs.

Drill instruction was always carried out late in the afternoon, before tea. At that time of year it was dusk if not dark. Our 'parade ground' was between two hangars which, to some extent, sheltered us from the wind but created echoes through which we had to interpret Cpl. Brown's orders.[6] I have to say that towards the end of the course he was actually giving us praise for our proficiency – a rare accolade indeed.

Wednesday afternoons were devoted to sport and physical exercise. It was at Digby that I played my first game of hockey in the RAF. It was more of a shambles than a game and had the Flt.Sgt. PTI in fits of laughter at our antics.[7] He soon brought us to order and taught us how properly to play the game.

---

5   We all had RAF issue black shoes which we wore instead.

6   The Station parade ground was used by the Cranwell Cadets.

7   Flight Sergeant Physical Training Instructor.

The weather that January was bitterly cold with a sharp wind across the Lincolnshire plain when we started flying. The planes were nothing more modern than De Havilland DH82a Tiger Moths, two-seater, open cockpit biplanes. Our instructors were civilian ex-RAF pilots, and their job was to assess our airborne capabilities. Two of our number were always airsick, so they got the chop from the course. Others, even though they had passed the tests at Hornchurch, had no spatial awareness so they got the chop, too. I enjoyed my flying and learned fairly quickly, but not as quickly as others, the primary and secondary effect

After a freezing cold afternoon flight in January.

27

of controls, the art of stall recovery, and made several attempts at landing – with increasing degrees of success. Mr Unger was my instructor and seeing that I had no real problems in the air decided, one trip, to throw the aircraft about. Hanging from your straps when flying inverted for the first time in an open cockpit plane is something you never forget. Even though he had said "I have control" I made an instinctive grab for the stick. I let go immediately when told over the intercom "Let go of the stick you're not climbing a bloody tree!" It was during the same flight that I had control for the approach to land. I came in too low and landed somewhat short of the proper place. On debriefing me afterwards Mr Unger said aloud so that all present in the crew room could hear "You came in that low even the bloody pigs on the bloody pig farm next to the airfield had to duck!" On another flight there was a brief spell of formation flying alongside another aircraft – pre-briefed of course. Mr Unger couldn't understand why he had a job to keep station and had a tendency to drop back unless he pushed the throttle fully open. He didn't realise that, with me being so tall, I was acting as an effective air brake because my head and shoulders were so far out of the cockpit into the slip stream! In all I flew, dual, some 12 hours on type, over that freezing featureless landscape, sometimes when light snow was falling. A memorable experience, indeed, if only because of the cold.

Somehow I scraped through the course with average marks. I was wiser, I knew more about RAF life, flying, and what was to be expected of me in the future as an Officer, yet what lay ahead of us all were 3 months of solid, high pressure ground school work at our next destination, RAF Kirton-in-Lindsey.

5. No.2 I.T.S. Kirton-In-Lindsey

IF SOME OF US thought our course at Digby was hard, then at No.2 I.T.S. Kirton-in-Lindsey (an old fighter airfield) we were in for a shock.[1] There was fierce competition between the four courses undergoing training there in sequence. There was no flying. Lessons were more detailed; there were punishing cross-country runs, we were constantly watched by our superiors, and examinations, drill, and inspections were just about as tough as they could get. There was much emphasis on discipline, aerodynamics, physics, aviation law, mechanics, meteorology, aviation medicine, initiative training, and learning how to conduct oneself as an Officer. We also had to keep personal diaries which were examined each week. There was an emphasis on physical training, with particular importance attached to 'dry swim' parachute landing techniques and in how to fall properly without injury.

As can be imagined there were times when tensions ran high. Wednesdays were sports afternoons, Thursday night was bull night, Friday morning was full kit inspection, and on Saturday mornings we were on CO's Parade. We were housed in pre-war, two storey, H-style barrack blocks, one Squad to a room, two Squads to a Flight, two Flights to a course. Except in the evenings, Saturday afternoons, and Sundays, we marched everywhere. We removed the RAF 'Eagle' shoulder flashes from our uniforms to further distinguish us from the permanent staff, and we were issued with Lee Enfield rifles and bayonets for drill purposes.[2]

---

1   No.2 Initial Training School. This course was for budding pilots and navigators and was equivalent to, but stricter than, that at an O.C.T.U. (Officer Cadet Training Unit) attended by Cadets of other trades.

2   The eagle emblems on our shoulder flashes were known, in RAF vernacular, as 'Shite Hawks'.

Henceforth we were addressed as 'Sir', often in various sarcastic or insinuating tones by NCOs and permanent staff, particularly when found to be ignorant of a matter, or missing the obvious in certain situations. Officers called us by our surnames. There was no escape other than to be chopped.

There were times when some Cadets would lay out the kit on their beds, and that remaining in and on their lockers, for inspection late on Thursday night and, rather than disturb it or have to get up very early next morning (which most of us did), they would sleep on the hard linoleum floor of their bed spaces. A few Cadets became fanatical and even pressed creases in their pyjama trousers. One lad had his hair cut each week so that it stood up in 1" bristles – he was nicknamed 'Bog Brush'.

If we thought bull nights at Digby were tedious, those at Kirton were arduous. They are worthy of further description.

All beds and lockers had to be moved, the entire floor swept, black boot marks removed, polish applied and 'bumpered' in to bring all to a high shine.[3] As this progressed the windows were cleaned streak-free and the brass window handles polished. Light shades and the tops of doors received due attention; trouble would ensue if dust was found on them during inspection the following morning. Beds and furniture were then put back at uniform distances apart to the nearest inch. Lockers were dusted all round and realigned perfectly. Everyone slithered around on pads under their feet so as further to polish the floor, and keep it polished. These pads (known to all Airmen throughout the RAF) were pieces of old blanket torn into rough 12" by 6" pieces. Pads were issued but we provided our own dusters. Communal passages had to receive similar but not so stringent attention. It was only after this routine was completed that we could turn our attention to our personal kit.

Large and small packs had to be blancoed, 'squared off' with pieces of stiff cardboard placed inside, and precisely positioned on top of our lockers. Our webbing belts, gaiters, and rifle slings were blancoed each night as they were wont to get shiny during daily use. Sometimes a drop of water would remove the shine, but you could only risk getting away with that once. All badges and brassware were polished, as was

---

3   Bumpers were heavy metal blocks pivoted on the end of long handles and used, with pads underneath, to polish our brown linoleum floors. Much energy was expended when doing this.

all footwear. On the morning of inspection we usually rose very early, performed our personal ablutions, and quickly turned our attention to our kit layout. Non-issue personal items were first placed under the mattress. A blanket was spread smoothly and tucked in evenly all round. Other bedding was precisely folded and stacked sheet-blanket-sheet and wrapped round with the third blanket, ends underneath, and the pillow smoothed out and placed on top at the head of the bed. The remaining area of the bed was used for displaying one's kit and accoutrements to a precise pattern. The contents of lockers had to be immaculately displayed therein. Only after this was done did we go to breakfast, although if things went wrong breakfast would have to be missed. We then dashed back to our barrack rooms, checked everything over, and readied ourselves for parade.

Kit inspection would follow. "Stand by your beds. Room Atten – shun". To get to our bed spaces we could not help but scuff the floor with our boots, for the pads would already be hidden away. This, super-careful as we were, effectively meant that, regardless of pads, the floor had to be repolished next bull night. The inspection would commence. If the CO was present he would lead his entourage: Sqn. Ldr. Garner i/c Training Wing, our Flight Commander, the Station Adjutant, the Station Warrant Officer, and the course SNCO – in that order. Any dirty mug was smashed on the floor, any improperly laid out kit and the bed would be tipped up on its side. Black marks were awarded for such misdemeanours. Serious breaches would involve a charge sheet being made out (Form 252) and the culprit being put on a 'Fizzer'. Culprits were usually awarded 2 days CB.[4]

Our personal appearance was of the utmost importance at all times. Uniforms had to be pressed into sharp creases. This was done by taking it in turns to use the barrack room iron and ironing board. Haircuts had to be frequent and we used the barber down in the town who, fortunately for us, was usually very quiet on Saturday afternoons.[5]

There is always one chap who tries to rock the boat. That character in our barrack room was one John Roberts from Blackpool. If we weren't careful (and he caught all of us at some time or other) he would, after a barrack inspection, remove all the keys from our locker doors and put

---

4 CB = Confined to Barracks, sometimes referred to as 'Jankers', which involved parading at the Guardroom at inconvenient hours in full kit for inspection by the Orderly Officer.

5 As recently as 2003 the same barber's shop was still in business.

them in his mess tin. The swearing and clamour this created can only be imagined. After he had played us up for a while he would calmly, provided we remained quiet, remove one key at a time, and give it to the rightful owner, until all the keys were returned. He never made a mistake. How he managed to do it remained a mystery, for he would never explain.

The Chief Drill Instructor was Flight Sergeant Brown and one of his juniors was Corporal Grey who had an evil attitude to any Cadets. Flt.Sgt. Brown, although a thoroughly strict disciplinarian, in fairness, gave us many hints and a good deal of advice as to how to overcome various problems. As an instance, he told us that the best way to get tea stains out of a mug was to pick up a weed with soil on its roots and rub it round inside, using the soil as a scouring powder, before rinsing it out. He also showed us how to prevent fainting on parade, and much else. Cpl. Grey was always referred to as 'That bastard'. As an example, he would turn up in a barrack room precisely at Reveille and, if he found anyone failing to put their feet on the floor after three minutes he would charge them, under Section 40 of the Air Force Act, with 'Conduct prejudicial to good order and discipline'. Many times, after some altercation or other, was it threatened that, if the opportunity arose, he would be met on a dark night and made to suffer the consequences of his actions. I was never aware of this actually happening but it came close more than once. Fortunately our other Drill Instructors were of less vicious temperament.

There was a roster for barrack latrine cleaning. These were kept immaculate, and were subject to inspection at almost any time. I remember an instance when, during a snap inspection immediately after someone had used a toilet, a mark was found in the back of the pan. The roster was consulted and the duty cleaner was put on a charge. Our Flight Commander took the charge and, in evidence, it was stated that the toilet had been improperly cleaned "...because the shite 'ad an 'igh glaze on it". The poor Cadet was awarded 3 days CB. That was the sort of situation we endured, unfairly biased as it was at times.

There were pranks and dodges. The standard cross-country run was twice round the airfield. After enduring this ordeal we quickly found that no-one checked our progress, but someone always watched our barrack block for skivers returning early or after only one circuit. Those of us not so keen on running, after one lap, hid in the Works

Department compound where only sympathetic civvies worked. We waited there until we had word that the leaders were returning to barracks and followed them in.

There was one night when an unpopular Cadet, who happened to be a heavy sleeper, awoke one morning in his bed, clothes locker alongside, in the middle of the parade ground. The authorities ignored this, but he modified his attitude to others markedly thereafter.

We had another cadet who was regarded as dirty. He was told about it but did nothing. He, in due time, was forcibly undressed and frog-marched to the showers where he was scrubbed red raw, with particular attention to his nether regions.

One of the initiative exercises involved us being taken, together with some doors, planks, rope, and oil drums, to one of the nearby drainage canals. We were given a limited time in which to get ourselves – all of us – to the other side of the canal and back again. No one said we actually had to build a raft but we did try, and it capsized. By this time a crowd of civvies had gathered to watch our antics. We failed at a second attempt. By now thoroughly soaked we gave

Full of confidence – before our raft turned turtle and pitched us into the icy water.

up the raft idea, stripped off, and swam naked in the freezing water (it was March) to the other side, and back again. One of our number missed his footing when climbing out and had another go at a different part of the bank. When he got out he found two leeches, one attached to his leg, the other to his foreskin. A lighted cigarette end (applied with great caution) soon removed them.

Another leadership exercise involved our travelling to the nearby derelict domestic site on the disused Hibaldstow airfield. Once there, the task allotted was to form a team and build a tower at least ten feet tall, on top of which three of our number were to stand. In order to achieve this we searched for, and wrenched off, a suitable number of doors from within the huts. With these we built our tower in the manner of erecting a house of cards. One Cadet stayed on top while I (being the tallest) was given the task of passing the doors up to him and steadying them while he leaned them together in the form of inverted 'V's. Five feet high was achieved easily using only five doors, but things got much more complicated when the next storey came to be added. The original first storey had to be extended and a double layer of doors added flat on top. With the base for the second storey now more secure, its construction commenced in like manner. But there was only one man up there and he was atop this flimsy structure. To get another two up there to join him involved building a human tower alongside. The lightest Cadets were chosen to go aloft. The first made it but on attempting to raise the second the whole doings collapsed, fortunately without injury. Time was running short. At the next attempt, when the tower was put up again, we lifted the second man into place at first floor level, then the two of them rebuilt the second floor and somehow scrambled on top – without any sideways stability to help them. This done, the third man was stood on a door flat on the ground and hoisted by several of us to above head height from which precariously wobbly base, accompanied by much very bad language and contrastingly gentle assistance from above, he carefully climbed aboard to complete our task – with just five minutes to spare.

There were moments of relief. Occasionally, on a late afternoon, some of us found a few minutes to walk to the western edge of the airfield and look across the main road which ran along the top edge of a steep escarpment. From there we watched the columnar clouds rising above the flat land beyond. We were learning meteorology and these clouds were perfect, beautiful examples of 'clouds of marked vertical development' actually growing in an otherwise stable atmosphere above some artificial man-made heat source such as a power station. The last rays of sunlight shining from behind them created a perfect picture.

When we had time the films at the Astra Cinema distracted us for an evening.[6] One night a stage show was put on by the permanent staff. Mike and Bernie Winters were stationed at Kirton, and one of the acts was theirs.[7] They mimed to gramophone records and even cajoled

---

6   All RAF Cinema Corporation cinemas were named 'Astra'. The RAF motto 'Per Ardua Ad Astra' was often skittishly translated as 'From work to the cinema'.

7   They later became radio and television personalities.

an unpopular SP to come on stage, much to the amusement of the audience.[8]

The cinema also had daytime uses. One day our course was marched to it for 'Lecturettes'. I was astounded, even before we had all found seats, to hear my name called and being told to go up on the stage. Before I actually got there I was told to speak to the audience, for three minutes, on 'Gates'. I couldn't have been luckier. I knew the subject well. Others were less fortunate and mumbled and "erred" and stumbled through. We had two sessions of this, so that everyone had to speak on their allocated topic, gaining or losing course marks accordingly.

Our 'official' but personal diaries of events and attitudes during the course were handed in weekly for scrutiny. Marks were awarded for the standard of English and the accuracy of descriptions. There was an event which I considered worthy of more comment in my diary than usual; this was the administration, by the MO, of our 'jabs'. We were detailed to assemble in the partially underground decontamination block adjacent to Station Sick Quarters after lunch on an unusually warm afternoon.

In the crowded darkness and anticipation several of our number began to feel unwell and a couple of Cadets actually fainted while waiting. This delayed proceedings and it was some time before all of us received our injections. In my diary I recorded this event and likened it to being unnecessarily caged up in circumstances analogous to the 'Black Hole of Calcutta'. This, on being read, was regarded as a matter for further investigation and I was called for interview. Apparently, and surprisingly, no-one else had dared to mention the event. I was questioned at length and asked whether I had told anyone off-camp about it. I had not, and was asked not to. Procedures were altered for ensuing courses.

There was one incident which I did not record in my diary. I was attending a lecture and sitting in the back corner of the lecture room in one of the hangars, paying attention and minding my own business, when I got a tremendous blow on the top of my head. I momentarily blacked out. On coming round everyone was looking at me. There, on my desk, was a lump of concrete which had chosen to drop on me from the ceiling. I dusted myself down, and the lecture continued. I didn't

---

8   SP = Service Policeman, another loathed breed at that time.

record the incident because I didn't want to appear as though I was complaining and, thereby, possibly lose marks.

During the course we were taught field craft, the use of camouflage, rifle shooting and the cleaning of weapons, including Stens and Brens. The rifles were different to those we used for drill. The latter were regarded as being past their proper use and deemed to be worn and inaccurate. We were also taught how to protect ourselves from a gas attack. This extended to our being taken to Scampton, one of the local heavy bomber stations, to experience tear gas in a gas chamber. It was advised that a couple of glasses of gin were a good antidote for the after-effects of tear gas but our NAAFI didn't sell it, and none of us could have afforded it even if it did!

As I remember it we were given two 36 hour and one 48 hour pass during the course. The first weekend home I travelled by train from the local station (almost two miles from camp), via Retford, Sheffield, Manchester and Liverpool. It was neither an easy journey nor fast. For the next two breaks those of us living on the west side of the Pennines hired a bus to take us to Manchester – and back on the Sunday evening. This simplified matters enormously and didn't cost all that much.

One particular Church Parade sticks in my mind. After having marched to the church and been instructed to file into the building, the SNCO at the church door repeatedly shouted "Ats orf in the 'ars of Gawd", much to everyone's amusement.

As each course took its final exams there was much relief and singing in the NAAFI. (That is apart from those Cadets who had failed and had been quickly posted away elsewhere). It was time for them to relax until the results came through. To create an annoying 'distraction' that course would usually raid the barrack block of the following course and remove the light fuses. The chaos, ire, and retribution (threatened and actual) was more than one would imagine. Such added to the tensions in the student lives of aspiring 'Officers and Gentlemen'.

Passing Out Parades were conducted with the course passing out marching on as the first Squadron, followed by junior courses as supporting Squadrons. Guests and parents were always invited. Drill was impeccable on these occasions. We reckoned it was as good as anything the Pongos could put on – and we were probably right.[9]

---

9   The Army, a nickname we were later ordered not to use because certain brass hats in khaki took exception to it.

By a mischance, not of my making, I failed my course. I felt cheated. I knew that I had done better than I had been told so sought redress with my Flight Commander, and asked to have my exam papers rechecked. He agreed, but not before I found myself on my way (along with a handful of other failures) on the train to the Personnel Holding Unit at RAF Innsworth, Gloucester, while decisions were made as to my future.

Innsworth was an awful camp. Discipline was lax. And there were WRAFs, many of whom were after Airmen's bodies, and snogging was rife in the NAAFI and the cinema. Barrack huts were cold, and bedding was damp. Fortunately I was there for less than a week before I was summoned back to Kirton-in-Lindsey for an interview.

National Service Acting Pilot Officer.

I was greeted warmly and was told that a mistake had indeed been made. It was explained that there was someone else on the course with a similar surname to mine and our marks had been confused. By this time he had been passed and posted to Canada for flying training, and I had been chopped – on his marks. The sad sequel to this was that he was killed during later training.

I could not now be passed out on my own so was re-coursed to join the then Senior Course. I sat the exams again – and passed.[10] Some of us were fortunate at this time to have a half-day visit to RAF Binbrook to see, close-up, the new Canberra bombers and to talk to some of the aircrew. This was a big morale booster after our severe regimen.

Passing Out Parade rehearsals began in earnest and much time was spent in perfecting our drill. In case the weather was bad there was a plan to hold the parade in an empty hangar. To try to march to an RAF band and keep in step within the confines of an echoing empty building needed concentration almost beyond the call of duty. The more so because some floor area had to be kept free for spectators, the band, and the Saluting Base. In the confined space, too, drill manoeuvres had to be very tight and accurate.[11] Practising on the open parade ground was a far better proposition. By comparison it was enjoyable!

We were kitted out with our Officer's uniforms by representatives of approved military tailors, sang in the NAAFI, and breathed sighs of relief. Smiles returned to our faces once more. Inspections were over, and our barrack room became cluttered as each of us had our flying clothing and our new Officer's clothing. Only then was our Sidcot flying kit formally handed in. Just why we had to keep it on personal charge for so long was not explained to us, for it had been in store since our arrival.[12]

As a National Serviceman I was neither given a clothing grant nor expected to acquire a full 'Best Blue' uniform. I was issued with a basic Officer's uniform instead. Unlike me, the majority of this course had

---

10 They weren't the same question papers. The Central Examination Board set a different selection of questions for each course.

11 I well remember one Erk (nickname for Airman) whose sole job, it seemed, was permanently to sweep the hangar floor with a platform brush. Every time I was anywhere near the hangar he was there.

12 I had parted with my own flying kit before my previous departure to Innsworth.

'signed on' for short service commissions, so were expected to have full kit.

On the morning of the last day at Kirton we were woken by the Orderly Sergeant, his voice ringing out "Come on gentlemen, 'ands off cocks" well before Reveille so that we could get all our kit together and prepare ourselves for the final Passing Out Parade.

Instead of passing out in May as I should have done, my turn came on June 3rd, 1952, when, as Parade Right Marker, I was the first to march on to the parade ground before the assembled guests, including my parents. Lord de Lisle and Dudley took the salute as we marched past. I was now an Acting Pilot Officer and was given 6 days leave. My parents took me, and my kit, home by car. My name appeared in the 'London Gazette' two or three issues later.

On leave, between courses, with my grandmother in the newly laid out garden extension at our cottage in Shropshire.

6. Basic Flying Training

MESSRS REID & SIGRIST, wartime aircraft builders, owned Desford airfield where I was posted for ab initio flying training.[1] They were contracted by the Air Ministry to teach us how to fly Chipmunks. Staff, of course, were civilian. The airfield was grass. Peckleton was the nearest village, and Leicester the nearest town – to which there was a public bus service.

We were housed in the 6 room bungalows of what had been a peace-time residential flying school. Our individual rooms were small and basic yet adequately equipped, and we had our own wash-basins. Showers and toilets were located to one side of a central corridor. Female cleaners came in on weekdays, so 'bull nights' were a thing of the past. We had a reasonably comfortable Officers Mess, and food was served to us. Compared with what we had all just been through, life was luxurious indeed. In fact two of our bachelor civilian instructors, out of choice, lived permanently in the same accommodation.

The RAF aspect of the course was run by a Flight Lieutenant who was the Commanding Officer, and a Flying Officer who was in charge of us u/t pilots.[2] There was a small Orderly Room, bringing the permanent RAF staff to no more than 12. There were 33 of us on the course, and only one course was run at a time. We were officially designated as No.5 Basic Flying Training School, RAF Desford.

The course was divided into two Flights so that each day was split into morning ground school and afternoon flying (or vice versa), alternating between the two Flights. My flying instructors were Mr Hendry and, later, Mr Lewin. New modern flying clothing was issued to us all.

---

1   This firm built an experimental prone position fighter during the war. Its fuselage was still in one of the hangars and we were allowed informally to examine it later in our course.

2   u/t = under training.

In ground school we polished up our knowledge of rules of the air, aviation law, meteorology, and the internal workings, systems, and handling of the Chipmunk T10 aircraft. This was further enhanced with a good schooling in fieldcraft so that, if caught on the ground by an enemy, we could give a good account of ourselves, defensively, with whatever weapons were to hand. Officer training continued, as did instruction in other aspects of RAF administration and procedures, as well as the all-important art of navigation. We were issued with several Air Publications to study, and notes had to be taken. There were end of course examinations to pass.

The u/t pilots and Officers in charge of our flying course outside the ground school building at RAF Desford. Being the tallest, I am in the centre of the back row.

The flying aspect was the greatest attraction. Pre-flight documentation (Form 700 and the Authorisation Book) and inspections, cockpit checks, and R/T and emergency procedures all had to be mastered before we could fly.[3] These exercises were all 'hands on'. Only then were we taken for our first flights to familiarise ourselves with strapping on

---

3 R/T = Radio Telephone.

a parachute (and how to use it should we have to), settling into the cockpit, strapping ourselves in tight, starting up, and intercom formalities.[4] These were immediately followed by taxying and the sights, sounds and feel of being airborne, keeping a lookout, circuit procedure, landing, taxying back, shutting down, getting out, and debriefing.[5] There was a lot to do, much more than we had done on Tiger Moths at Digby. With further flights we learned to do all these things ourselves as well as learning the primary and secondary effects of controls, turns, climbing, maintaining straight and level flight (not as easy as one might imagine), use of the trim control, gliding, correcting the swing on takeoff, and coping with airborne emergencies. This was no sinecure, we were busy, and after two flights in an afternoon or morning, we were tired. There was so much to absorb which had quickly to become second nature to us.

Our knowledge and confidence grew with each successive flight. The actual flying, once airborne, was (comparatively) the easy bit. Taxying, take-offs, and landings demanded much more practice and skill. Much attention was paid to these and to circuit procedures and differing wind and weather conditions until, eventually, our instructors would start doing 'quickie' circuits so that we could concentrate on take-offs, landings, and overshoots. We were also taught the difference between a spin and a spiral dive, and how to recover from both. It is often said – and it is absolutely true – that one never forgets one's first spin. To deliberately create a spin the aircraft is brought, engine throttled back, to the point of stall and full rudder kicked on as the nose drops. Suddenly the world becomes chaotic. You think you are still but you know you are falling while the world rotates dizzily outside and the ground begins to get nearer very quickly. It was usual for us to initiate recovery action after three turns, pull out of the ensuing dive, and regain level flight or climb away if you were going to do the exercise again. Fairground roller coasters were very tame after that!

On the afternoon of June 25th, 3 days after my 19th birthday, I was adjudged fit after 7 hours 45 minutes 'dual', to make my first solo flight. It lasted all of 10 minutes. Everything went perfectly, almost as though I

---

4   My own first flight in a Chipmunk was on June 12th 1952 and lasted fifty minutes.

5   Although much of this had already been covered, in passing, at Digby the training now was more disciplined.

could still hear my instructor's voice guiding me through it. Many of us said the same as each of us soloed.

My next flights alternated between dual and solo as weaknesses were corrected and skills developed. We practised emergency landings, short landings and take-offs, low flying, and aerobatics. When thought to be competent we practised these solo.

We had an emergency landing field not far away for practice purposes. We would glide down and land, roll forward, open up, and take off again without stopping. During one such solo exercise I came in low over the trees at one end, landed and rolled to take off again. I had slowed too much and one of my wheels sank into a rut in the ground, bringing me to a rapid halt, fortunately without nosing in. I was stuck and couldn't move forward even with a fairly wide throttle opening. So as not to be caught in that predicament I disobeyed all rules, left the engine on tick-over, jumped out, and went to each wing tip in turn and slewed the aircraft forward, one side at a time, so as to free the wheel from the hollow, jumped back in, strapped up, and took off promptly.[6] I dreaded being spotted from the air and suffering a roasting back at base, but no-one found out.

There was a low flying area not far from Belvoir Castle which we used. Low flying is as dangerous as it is exciting. We were never authorised to go below 250 feet above ground level. Instructors, although it was illegal, habitually ignored this restriction. The ground was undulating and bracken-covered, making contours difficult to follow. More than once a Chipmunk landed back at Desford with bracken in its undercarriage, rapidly to be pulled off before the Chief Flying Instructor (CFI) saw it.

The flying examiner, Mr Hall, was a taciturn, morose, humourless, incommunicative individual whom none of the student pilots liked. (It was said that if he was married his wife probably didn't like him either). He took me for my interim flying test. That was on July 14th and I had completed 15 hours 15 minutes dual and 10 hours 15 minutes solo. I knew what I was doing but was discomfited by the examiner's presence in the rear cockpit. Hearing his gruff, cheerless, voice on the intercom

---

6   I did not dare stop the engine because it may have needed priming to restart it which I would probably have, in the circumstances, found impossible to do alone. I was also concerned that had I had to use the Koffman starter I would have been a cartridge short; a fact that would have been discovered by the ground staff before the next flight.

was no help at all. He grumpily said I had passed after we landed – a perfect three pointer – and taxied back to dispersal; as to what marks I was awarded I have no idea. Not everyone passed this test. Those who failed went up with the CFI, Mr Hester, for further assessment. As far as I can remember he failed none of our course.

The next phase of training now followed and included cross-country navigation and instrument flying, both real and simulated. Mr Lewin now became my instructor. My longest solo cross-country was Desford – Wellingborough – Peterborough – Desford and took almost an hour and a half. It was my last long distance flight on this course. I must admit that I found this sort of flying easy and, in those days, one was helped in finding large population areas because of the heavy pall of pollution (industrial haze) over each. There were more railways then and these greatly facilitated map reading above densely populated areas. We also practised short take-offs

Myself, Mr Lewin, and Neil Davidson who later became a well-known competitive glider pilot.

and landings. It was possible to set a Chipmunk on the ground and come to a halt in something like 50 yards.

On the 12th of August I had my first night flight, dual of course. On the 14th I flew my first night solo. Taking off and landing on a featureless (other than patches marked as bad ground which couldn't be seen in the dark) grass airfield tended initially to involve more good luck than flying skill. The 'runway' was a T-shaped pattern of goose-neck flares laid out according to the wind direction at the time; landing was on one side of the leg of the 'T' and take-offs on the other. Aldis lamp signals and, in dangerous situations, Verey lights, were the only visual means of control in addition to the R/T. The control tower couldn't see us properly in the dark and couldn't readily distinguish one aircraft from another. A sharp – particularly sharp – lookout was essential. There was a 'Chance Light' which, when switched on, usually caused one (instructors included) to tend to 'land' about six feet above the ground and thus hit the ground heavily for the real landing.[7] Airfields had 'Pundits' in those days. These were red beacons which repeatedly flashed an airfield's identity in Morse code. When it came to night navigation these were an enormous help. But I had a problem. I had a

In National Service Mess Kit outside my room window
before going to a Dining In Night.

---

7   Chance Light = The commercial name for a unidirectional floodlight which could be switched on to shine a beam along the landing side of the flare path.

complete block when it came to learning Morse code. To me it was like trying to sight read Chinese without previous knowledge. I got by in ground school at four words a minute provided the words were short. In the air I had a piece of paper carrying the code fastened to my right knee where I could always refer to it. Neither Morse code nor calculations came easily to me when airborne. To navigate by both day and night I relied heavily on my strong inbuilt sense of direction and have to say that I never got lost, even in or above cloud.

One day, quite unexpectedly, we were all gathered together by the CO and told that we would be taking part in an Escape and Evasion exercise as defenders of a make-believe country called Lestrutshire which was the combined area of the counties of Leicestershire and Rutland. As defenders we were to be on guard at what we were told would be critical locations past which escaped 'foreign' airmen were supposed to be making their way to a 'safe house'. The 'foreigners' were none other than trainee pilots from other airfields.

Defenders were made up of Police, Army, RAF, and Civil Defence personnel. Our stint found us, late one chilly summer night, being bussed to some strange location where there was a bridge on a main road in a housing estate which was regarded as 'important'. None of us saw anything at all suspicious, and the night was only memorable for our acute tiredness and the shivering cold in the hour immediately following sunrise. To us, it was a total waste of time and taught us nothing.

We had to keep up appearances and that, of course, meant haircuts. Most of us used to go into Leicester on the bus on a Saturday afternoon to do some shopping (we could afford that now) and to pop into Prentice's barbers' shop in Belvoir Street. The place stank of some foul-smelling chemicals used in the ladies' salon upstairs. We even smelt of it when we got back to camp. Our batwomen could smell it on our clothes and always knew when we'd been for a haircut.

One Saturday, two of us who had done some riding decided to go to the local riding school. After some questioning by the owner, we paid our dues and were given our mounts. Mine was a frisky beast and during the accompanied ride decided it wanted its own head and galloped off down a bridleway. I hung on like grim death, not wishing to be thrown. Eventually, after having had my face brushed with the branches of low bushes, I was able to rein the animal in. The riding school owner was not best pleased and accused me of all sorts. We returned to the stables at a sedate walk. After that episode I have never ridden again, neither am I particularly keen to do so!

We were encouraged to build model aircraft, the better to understand aerodynamics and control. I built a 3 foot wing span glider from a kit. Very good it looked, too. There was a snag. No matter what adjustments I made it would, after release from a towline, flip onto its back and glide merrily on – upside down. This caused some chin-scratching among our instructors who had been teaching us aerofoil shapes and efficiency, and the reason for aircraft staying in the air, yet here was my model literally inverting everything they said. Eventually it crashed and broke up. I think some people were quite relieved!

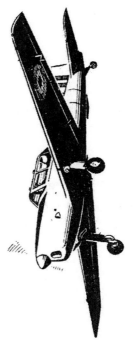

Mentioning inverted flying: we were taught inverted gliding as part of the aerobatics aspect of our training. During one solo flight I inadvertently took this to extreme and the engine stopped! The propeller was a dead piece of wood, doing nothing, while I continued to glide on upside down. Stick back (to dive), quickly gain speed, push forward and roll out, dive again, and the engine started – with plenty of height to spare. My sweat took a while to dry!

Performing a barrel roll.

Aerobatics were great fun. I particularly enjoyed stall turns and loops. The thrill of pulling the nose up, losing speed, kicking over the rudder to bring the nose facing downwards, and accelerating whilst diving away, is something I shall never forget. Likewise, the climb into a loop, looking up behind my head to see the ground coming up whilst keeping the wings level with the horizon, going over the top, diving out, and then, if there was enough height, repeating the process.[8] Slow rolls were never easy in a Chipmunk and took a good deal of practice,

---

8   Our minimum permitted height for commencing aerobatics was four thousand feet.

whereas any form of hesitation roll was difficult whether it was a four point or the nigh on impossible eight point variety. I was never good at barrel rolls; no matter how much I practised them, or was shown, I always seemed to swish out in a less than satisfactory manner. To do a roll off the top of a loop involved diving to gain almost the maximum permitted speed before pulling up and doing the manoeuvre.[9] To do a second one straight after the first so as to fly a vertical figure of eight took a deal of practice, and it was possible to grey or black myself out during the pull up. Any attempt at a vertical climbing roll or 'Upward Charlie' was doomed to failure owing to lack of power or skill, probably both.[10]

It was during the later part of the course that one Chipmunk landed on the top of another beginning its takeoff run. Nobody was injured but it was a close thing. The propeller of the landing aircraft, as it screwed through the air, cut a groove in the fuselage just behind the instructor's head in the rear cockpit of the aircraft on the ground. Its next half rotation cut a groove through the cockpit canopy between the pilots, and the first blade then cut away the top of the engine cowling. The one aircraft came to rest on top of the other. Nasty, but it could have been worse, for there was no fire.

Chipmunk instrument panel.

---

9   The official maximum permitted speed was 173 knots but anything more than 150 knots made it feel as though the wings would come off.

10   The tab on the first aid kit in the starboard wing root would move forward in the reversed airflow as stalling speed was approached. With this unofficial indication it was not necessary to look at the airspeed indicator. Usually the actual stall was presaged by slight buffeting and a tendency to drop a wing. If not corrected this would lead to an incipient or actual spin. The maximum number of turns I have done in a spin is eight, by which time the spin was beginning to flatten out. Later marks of Chipmunk had modifications to the rear fuselage to correct this tendency.

The Rover experimental jet-engined car had just been announced to the public and was under development at the motor industry research facility at the nearby old Nuneaton airfield. On overflying that facility I was dismayed to find that the car, when flat-out on the test track, would go considerably faster than a Chipmunk in straight and level flight!

In those days there was very little civil aviation. The RAF ruled the skies and, as long as we kept a sharp lookout, we could do very much as we liked, or were ordered to do. As an example: during a low flying exercise I was following a railway line and caught up with a passenger train travelling in the same direction. It was on an embankment, so I dropped down and throttled back to formate on it. I could clearly see the passengers looking at me and waving. I waved back. The train then shot into a tunnel, but I was still there when it came out of the other end, very much to the passengers' surprise.

Final examinations came along, and the final flying test – with that awful Mr Hall. He kept flicking the back of my helmet with a stiff piece of paper if he thought I might have done something a little better. I have never come across a quicker way to unnerve someone in the air than that. I think it must have been with great reluctance that he passed me out as 'Average'.

There were parties to celebrate the completion of each major phase of training. We usually went to a nearby hostelry and used a pre-booked room for such occasions. The end of course party was particularly riotous. Much drink was drunk – and we weren't used to it. As the evening wore on bawdy songs were sung as loud as possible – to both the disgust and curiosity of customers in other rooms. Some of them learned new words to old tunes; others wished they could have joined us. I have vague recollections of "Sweet Violets", something to do with "Kirriemuir", "The Good Ship Venus", "Mr Banglestein", "Foggy Dew", and others for which lewd impromptu verses were composed as the evening progressed. All put the words to "Colonel Bogey" in the shade. Most vociferous in these choral attempts were our instructors, the CFI, and our CO, all of whom taught us more that night than was on the curriculum.[11] With heads ringing we returned in slovenly fashion to our rooms. Some wag, as a practical joke, removed the light bulb from the

---

11 Later in my RAF career I realised that some of those 'songs' had even viler versions but, by that time, only a small proportion of aircrew would stoop so low as to sing them. However, they were commonplace and frequently aired during the war years.

ceiling fitting in the room of a chap who was the worse for drink and somewhat later in getting back. Drunk as he was, he knew what to do. On striking a match he spotted the bulb on his bed. Next, in the dark and swearing mightily, at the second attempt he succeeded in climbing on his bed and reached for the ceiling with the logical idea of sliding his fingers along until he found the light fitting, and so to replace the bulb. No such luck. His little plan didn't work out as expected. Instead of touching the ceiling his fingers went straight into the lamp socket and touched the live tits. His knees buckled and he collapsed onto his bed. Quickly recovering, and somewhat more sober than hitherto, he chased, caught, and debagged the culprit who by now had owned up. The bulb was eventually replaced. After some further minor skirmishes we settled down for the night.

One afternoon an Oxford flew in low and fast over the airfield, without warning, in the middle of normal flying, and beat the place up at less than 30 feet, only just managing to clear the chimneys of a nearby building. The pilot was a student from either RAF Welles-bourne Mountford or RAF Pershore. The aircraft number was taken and reported. The pilot, identified as a previous Desford trainee, was immediately admonished and chopped from his course. In wartime his spirited flying would have been admired and, after having the stupidity of his actions pointed out to him, he would have continued his flying career. In peace-time discipline was rigorously enforced.

With 30 hours dual and 28 hours 45 minutes solo, including totals of 3 hours 30 minutes night flying and 4 hours 15 minutes instrument flying (IF) entered in my Log Book, I left Desford on the 1st of September for a week's leave before my posting for the next stage of training.[12]

---

12 This was additional to the separately recorded previous 12 hours and 5 minutes dual in Tiger Moths during Grading at Digby, i.e. 70 hours and 50 minutes airborne in all.

7. Twins

HAVING LEARNED SOME VERY basic flying skills these had to be developed and progressed. We were therefore posted to RAF Wellesbourne Mountford in Warwickshire where I arrived on the 9th of September, 1952 for the start of a six month course. On successful completion of this course we would be awarded our flying badges, better known as our 'Wings'. We had heard before arrival that the chop rate was high, particularly for National Service trainees. Flying would be done in twin-engined Oxford Mk II aircraft.

Wellesbourne is roughly equidistant from both Leamington Spa and Stratford-upon-Avon. It was a full-blown RAF camp without any civilian mollycoddling. WRAFs were stationed there as part of the permanent staff. In addition to the 2 Squadrons (two courses) of u/t pilots and their instructors and support staffs of No.9 Advanced Flying Training School, there was also the school of Airfield Construction for those Officers with appropriate civilian qualifications who were to be in charge of building and maintaining Air Ministry sites throughout the world. It was a big hutted camp.

This was the first time any of us had lived in a 'proper' RAF Officers Mess albeit a wooden one although, in this case, we students had our own anteroom so that our instructors and permanent staff had after-hours privacy. By this time we all had appropriate calling cards and had to 'Warn In' and 'Warn Out' of the Mess, and Mess bills had to be paid by the 10th of each month.[1] We had bar books in which all drinks were recorded by the duty barman. We could not 'treat' a friend to a drink;

---

1 Officers' cards were always to a standard layout, wording (according to rank) and lettering style. Most stationers produced cards which were too fancy. Strange as it might seem, many officers bought their cards from a printer's stall at the back of the old St John's market in Liverpool.

the drink you would expect to pay for which was consumed by one's friend was automatically charged to his account. There were questions to be answered if drinks bills went above a certain amount in a month. Whenever the CO, Group Captain N. de W. Boult, walked in we all stood to attention. In response he would always (as was customary) say "Sit down gentlemen". Whilst this all sounds very formal it was not as strict as some Messes in which I later had occasion to stay.

We had individual rooms in prefabricated 'Seco' huts. There were about 8 of us to a hut, each room having a wash-basin, adequate furniture, and big enough for two beds if such were necessary. Floors were of polished 'compo' tiles. There were no mats other than an outside door mat. Ablutions were at the end of the hut and cleaned (as were our rooms) by the hut batman. We looked after our own uniforms but washing was sent out weekly to a commercial laundry.

Our course was split into two Flights so that when one was flying the other was at ground school. Surprisingly, in view of our experience at Kirton-in-Lindsey, there was no inter-course rivalry. The attitude of u/t pilots was, thankfully, now much more mature than hitherto. My flying instructor was Flt.Sgt. Ken Knott, a very experienced pilot and an excellent tutor.

Ground school covered the use of a Link Trainer for instrument flying practice, having to go to the Met Office to collect weather data and actually giving (in turn) the daily Met briefing to one's Flight, the study of engine systems, initially that of the Cheetah 10 which powered our Oxfords, and later of other engines both radial and in-line, including the Rolls Royce Merlin, which at that time was powering the still-operational 4-engined Lincoln bombers and other aircraft. These engineering aspects were taught by a very experienced Flight Sergeant of the 'old school' who was a wonderful artist when it came to blackboard and chalk drawings of engines, propeller hydraulics, and carburettors. He was a joy to watch and learn from.

Aviation medicine was further explained to us by the Station MO, Sqn.Ldr. Routh. I was to meet him again at the very end of my RAF career. There were sessions in the gym, Wednesday afternoon sports, and a range of other activities all designed to further our knowledge of flying and associated subjects.

One thing that particularly sticks in my mind about ground school was the lecture cinema. It had very comfortable club chairs, and if a film was shown immediately after lunch following a morning's flying it was not unusual for at least half the class to fall sound asleep and for the other half to have missed at least some of the film. Fortunately for us, most films were shown more than once during the 6 month course. The films themselves covered topics extending from medical matters, road safety in RAF vehicles, arctic, jungle, and desert survival, surviving crash landings and ditchings, technical topics directly related to aircraft management and, most interestingly, the latest in aircraft developments. We were grateful, owing to the 'sleep factor', that we were never tested on the subject matter of any film until it had been shown at least twice.

Unlike Desford there were parades each Saturday, and an AOC's inspection and parade to prepare for.[2] There were many rehearsals so that we would put on the best possible demonstration of parade ground discipline and not let ourselves or our Station down.

Before our flying began we had to report individually to the Parachute Section to collect a parachute and see it checked over before signing for it. The Section was run entirely by WRAFs. On approaching the open door the continuous string of expletives I heard as part of their normal conversation almost made me cringe. I had never heard women using such language before. If the bawdy song episode at Desford was rough, the way these women strung the most unmentionable words together was a lesson in the grammar of the obscene. The swearing stopped as I entered. I chose my parachute – No.13 – the one that no-one would ever take instead of their own, and took it back to my clothing locker in the Flight hut. Everyone flew with almost anyone else's parachute but mine stayed where it was, just as I thought would be the case. From then on, wherever I flew in the RAF I always chose the same parachute number. It never was borrowed and, thankfully, I never had to use it. We were, however, thoroughly trained in how to bail out, how to control a parachute, and in landing techniques. We had by this time spent many hours in the gym learning how to fall and roll over properly so as to minimise injury on landing.

Flying a stolid, slow, clapped out, twin-engined, non-aerobatic Oxford was entirely different to handling the light and agile Chipmunks

---

2   The annual visit and inspection by the Air Officer Commanding the Group in Flying Training Command of which our Station was a part. This was a very important occasion and things had to be absolutely right throughout all aspects of the Station and its work.

we had left behind. I think what worried us most at first was the retract-able undercarriage. We all dreaded forgetting to raise it or, worse, lower it before landing. Such basic operations were, of course, instilled into us when we learned, even before our first flights, all the necessary cockpit drills by heart and, indeed, as with all service pilots, to recite them at all appropriate stages of start-up, flight, in the circuit, after landing, and shut down.

Taxying was easier than in a Chipmunk for several reasons: the forward view was better, tarmac taxiways were used rather than grass, the wheels were set wider apart and differential braking was more effec-tive, and it was possible to increase speed with one engine to assist a turn.

Oxford Mk 2.

I soon found that I was very lucky indeed if the particular aircraft I was flying could maintain height on one engine. Single-engined flight usually meant that I was effectively in a power-assisted glide with one leg shaking with the effort of keeping the rudder hard over (in spite of full trim correction) to stop undue yawing. Such things were demon-strated to us very early before we flew solo on type so as to be ready for such an emergency situation. I was told that I was particularly fortunate because I had long legs. If keeping the rudder over was hard for me, heavens knows what agonies a shorter pilot had to suffer.

While on the subject of asymmetric flight (it was always included in flying proficiency tests) I opted, when doing a single-engine approach, to throttle back the live engine and do what was in effect a glide approach and landing.[3] I found this much easier than adjusting rudder pressure when throttling back the good engine to adjust or maintain approach speed. I felt more comfortable at the much steeper angle of approach and was never criticised for doing this.

It was important, although not essential, having taken off and throttled back into a normal climb, or level flight, to synchronise engines. That is, to eliminate the thrum thrum thrum of the combined noise of both engines going into and out of phase. On some aircraft the throttle positions were quite different for each engine in order to achieve this, even though the tachometers were reading approximately the same speeds. Once synchronised, should the engines then go out of synchrony, it was wise to check all engine instruments and settings to ensure nothing was going amiss like an impending engine failure or, more likely, one of the throttle levers moving because the tensioning screw hadn't been tightened enough.

I flew 6 hours dual before my first 15 minute solo flight. By the end of September I had flown over 11 hours dual and over 9 hours solo. Instead of aerobatics, instrument flying, formation flying, night flying, and cross-country navigation, were to become major components of our training.

It was widely held that should an Oxford go into a spin, and if recovery was not initiated and successful within the first two turns, the spin would flatten out and stabilise to the point that recovery was assumed to be unlikely and a crash inevitable. Just in case such a situation arose, there was a knotted rope down the fuselage from the pilots' seats to the door near the tail. With this, by 'climbing' along it, over the main spar, and against the centrifugal forces of the spin, we were supposed to be able to reach the door, jettison it, and hopefully bale out. I never heard of this actually happening to any course students but doubtless such things must have occurred during the 14 years or more that Oxfords had been in RAF service.

Usually my instructor was Ken Knott but occasionally Fg.Off. Len Higgens, a Volunteer Reserve pilot, would stand in for him. Len was a little more daring in his attitude to flying. There was also a Flt.Lt. Knight who I flew with from time to time. He didn't have regular students, instead he seemed to fly with almost all of us at random.

---

3   Asymmetric flight = Flying on one engine.

He was not liked for his habit of nearly always grabbing the controls during the final stages of approach and landing. Because of this he soon became known among us as 'Windy' Knight.

Progress checks were, of course, conducted by more senior instructors, usually Flight and Squadron Commanders. These were unnerving experiences, particularly in view of my recent encounters with Mr Hall at Desford. My 30 hour progress check on October 7th was carried out by our Squadron Commander, Sqn.Ldr. Irish, who had a reputation for having a 'downer' on National Service pilots. 45 minutes grilling in the air was as daunting in prospect as it was in reality. I considered myself fortunate to pass.

Most RAF airfields in the 1950s had at least one Open Day each year. Wellesbourne Mountford was no exception. We student pilots were, of course, detailed off to help with various activities. Those on the senior course, which we were not, took part in fly-pasts, while our instructors laid on the more humorous part of the aerial entertainment. The junior course – that was us – were given ground tasks to supervise along with other members of the permanent staff. My job was to liaise with the local riding school who were giving 'Equestrian Experience' (as the RAF put it) to the youngsters of the visiting public. This involved my supervising the layout of a suitably convenient walking track for the horses on a patch of grass which was nurtured and held dear by the Station Warrant Officer, Mr Williams, outside of whose office window it was located. Water had to be fetched for the horses, and their droppings disposed of under a nearby laurel thicket.[4] Fortunately for me I was relieved of these duties just in time to see the 'How to deal with unruly tribes' part of the display. This involved flour-bombing a group of suitably attired 'rebels' who had invaded the runway. Their incursion had been accompanied by much use of thunderflashes and smoke grenades.[5] The Station Flight Tiger Moth was duly scrambled to deal with the white-robed insurgents and landed alongside them, at which point an insurgent climbed into the rear cockpit before the pilot could take off, and so followed a sequence of crazy flying during which an 'armoured' car also went into action. It, too, was hijacked. The Tiger Moth landed

---

4   Said laurel thicket, as it turned out, had been the secret snogging ground (along with another nearby) of Airmen and Airwomen who had used it as a location for close intimate contact.

5   Thunderflashes = A form of pyrotechnic having an extremely loud bang.

nearby to go to its rescue and, after much cavorting on the ground its hijacker was evicted. The Tiger Moth then took off again, trailing coloured smoke, to chase the hijacked car which promptly dashed for cover into a hangar, leaving the aircraft to land quietly at the end of the sequence.

The same Tiger Moth was occasionally scrambled to deal with incursions of deer on to the airfield from the adjacent Charlecote estate.[6] The system used was to stop all flying activity when the deer arrived except for the Tiger Moth taking off from a remote corner of the airfield away from the animals. Then followed a sequence of diving at the herd to steer it back to the break in the fence, accompanied if necessary by the firing of Verey lights to hurry them along. I was to witness this performance several times during the six months I was stationed there.

There was a Station Sports Day in which all personnel and all ranks were expected to take part. I was entered in a boxing competition and matched against my Flight Commander, Flt.Lt. Howorth, a thick-set, muscular, ex-lorry driver. Fortunately for me the match was cancelled. He would have floored me at the first punch. There was an amusing side to the Sports Day notices. There were a series of events titled Intercourse Championships. On a mixed camp – Wow!

When it came to instrument flying training, unless there was enough cloud about at the time, we used what was called 'two stage amber'. When using this the aircraft windows were covered with removable amber shields through which the instructor could see. I, as student, wore blue tinted goggles. The combination of colours was such that I could not see out through the amber but I could clearly see the flying instruments. All was comparatively easy until I was being taught recovery from unusual attitudes. To make things difficult the instructor would take control and perform a manoeuvre to topple the instrument gyros which meant that they were wholly unusable until they self-corrected after maybe 15 minutes. This done, control would be handed back to me and I had to bring the aircraft into straight and level flight as soon as possible on those remaining. Easily said, but when my body was telling me that I was flying on my left ear when the instruments were telling me something else I had very quickly to learn to ignore my own feelings and, instead, implicitly trust the instrumentation. We were

---

6   Nowadays owned by the National Trust.

also taught how to make R/T controlled descents back to base through cloud.[7] The final IF test would involve flying a strict and timed pattern of climbs, climbing and steep descending turns, and some level flight.[8] The pattern had to be properly and competently flown before gaining a White Card Instrument Rating.[9] Throughout my flying career I, as did all pilots, had to take similar 'Standardisation' tests on an annual basis.

Oxford instrument panel.

One such instrument training flight involved an unscheduled cross-country flight with Ken Knott to RAF Cranfield with no greater purpose than to deliver a pair of a Senior Air Staff Officer's pyjamas! Said Senior Officer had been visiting Wellesbourne Mountford and had failed to take them back with him after an overnight stay. This return flight lasted an hour. It involved 30 minutes of simulated IF navigation. It was a very useful piece of training.

Shortly after this my first serious (pre-planned) cross-country was with Windy Knight. Careful pre-flight planning was done using a Dalton Computer, maps, and forecast winds.[10] The route took us from base to Swaffham, thence to Banbury, and back to base. A flight log had to be maintained of all course corrections, calculated changes of wind

---

7   Known as QGHs after the then out of date, but still lingering in use, RAF 'Q' code.

8   IF = Instrument Flying.

9   There were two standards, White Card and Green Card. Green cards were awarded according to competence and instrument hours flown.

10 A Dalton Computer was a simple, manually operated, hand-held mechanical device.

speed and direction, and predicted deviations from ETA.[11] The keeping of this log was my responsibility whilst flying the aircraft. Windy was there primarily in an advisory capacity. The trip took some two hours and ten minutes, the keeping of an accurate log whilst en route being the most stressful part of it.

My very next flight, on October 27th, was a solo navigation exercise from base to Wisbech, then to Chipping Norton, and back to base. The whole lot was down to me. Using (as was standard) a pencil sharpened at both ends in case of lead breakage, I was maintaining my log with some difficulty for figures never came easily to me in the air when, horror of horrors, I let go of my pencil and it rolled on the cockpit floor out of my reach. Rather than risk the inevitable bollocking (and potential course failure) for not carrying out my scheduled task I had no alternative but to take drastic action. Ensuring that the aircraft was on the right heading and trimmed as near as possible to climb slightly, I unstrapped myself but still couldn't reach that dratted pencil. There was no alternative other than to leave my seat, squat down, retrieve the object and settle down again; at least that was my plan. In the event, on leaving the seat I knocked the control column and put the plane into a steep turn nearly throwing me over into the co-pilot's seat which I promptly made use of. I regained level flight but the pencil rolled away. By now sweating profusely, occupied with correcting my course and searching the floor at the same time, I eventually retrieved the object of my near demise, regained my own seat, strapped myself back in, and carried out some frantic map reading to discover over which part of England I was now flying. Worried about my log which was now some minutes out of date (and position) I made the entry "Course alterations made to avoid several other aircraft". I was lucky to get away with it, and forever after always carried a spare pencil. My Flight Commander, Flt.Lt. Howorth took me up shortly afterwards for an unscheduled extended IF flight. I wondered at first if he was going to check my navigation skills, but all passed off quietly even though the log of my previous flight didn't exactly bear very close scrutiny.

During a dual flight I began to feel muzzy and generally unwell after being airborne for about half an hour. Reluctantly I had to tell Flt.Lt. Poyser, my instructor, whereupon he said he too had a headache and was

---

11 ETA = Estimated Time of Arrival.

finding it hard to concentrate. He told me to undo my oxygen mask.[12] On seeing that my lips were quite blue he at once told me to open my clear vision panel while he did the same on his side and also turned off the heating. We were suffering from carbon monoxide poisoning and returned to base for a medical check. Neither of us flew again that day. The cockpit air was heated by passing it through a muffler round an engine exhaust pipe and thence through a mixer into the cockpit. The exhaust pipe, on investigation, was found to have split inside the muffler and could have brought about our deaths.

Each of us tended to fly only one of a small group of aircraft whose vagaries and idiosyncrasies we got to know over a period of time. One day, however, I was selected (at random) to undergo what was called a Central Flying School Standardisation Check. This is better explained as a sort of ad hoc, but routine, check of the standard of teaching at flying training establishments throughout the RAF. It was as much a check of instructors' ability to teach as it was of the standards reached by students following a number of hours of training. The examiner was unknown to anyone. He selected a trainee (me) and an aircraft in which I was to fly. He decided to check my instrument flying capabilities. The aircraft was strange to me and was a bit of a pig. It took some time to synchronise the engines because, in that state, the throttles, instead of being more or less in the same side-by-side position were some two inches apart. Making small changes of power needed to carry out the actions demanded of me, and at the same time maintaining engine synchronisation, was a major distraction in itself. After 55 minutes under two stage amber of a one hour and ten minutes flight I climbed out with my examiner to be told that I was satisfactory but the aircraft was to be placed unserviceable! This particular flight was also recorded as 'Other Flying' and not regarded as a part of the course.

I had always suffered from hay fever and, since joining the RAF, had undergone several medical tests to try to establish the cause of my allergy. I have to say that it never bothered me in the air because most flying was done above the dust and pollen layer which usually clung fairly close to the ground. There was a Royal Air Force hospital at Cosford at which I was due to attend so, rather than take time off the course, I was scheduled to fly there with Flt.Lt. Len Higgens.

---

12 We were never on oxygen, but used masks because they were fitted with microphones for the intercom and R/T.

This return flight would not be a part of any particular exercise but obviously had a cross-country, land away from base, content. Len let me fly to Cosford and land there. Now Cosford has a railway line on a low embankment which might cause some turbulence just at a critical stage on the approach to the main runway. I was aware of this and came in a knot or two faster than normal to compensate. What took me by complete surprise was to suddenly find myself flying through 'cloud' at that crucial stage. I had not seen the train approaching and flew through the steam being let off by the locomotive's safety valves. All Len said was that it was always wise to be prepared for the unexpected!

With the medical tests carried out it was time for the return flight. Over lunch in the Mess we had discussed the possibility of flying over my grandmother's home in Shropshire, not far away. Len said he knew the area from his wartime days but I would do the navigation. That was OK by me so we set off for this minor diversion on our journey back to base. We found the house, but there was no sign of life after circling twice at as low a level as we dared. Sod's Law worked against us. Len then said, "I have control" and set off in the direction of Tilstock airfield, now derelict. He said he had flown from there and knew it well. At this stage I was only there for the ride. Len, mistaking the main A41 road for the old main runway, set up a straight-in approach for a roller landing and rapid take-off. So far so good. On the last stage of the approach, wheels down, he realised his error, opened up the engines, pushing the throttles 'through the gate' and raised the under-carriage to climb away smartly as a car was approaching along the road from the opposite direction.[13] Just before we were over the car the driver swerved off the road and bailed out to lie flat on the grass alongside. We must have missed him by about 25 feet. With engines nearly bursting we climbed away straight ahead as rapidly as the old kite could take us. Len's only comment to me when turning for base was "Ken, if ever you get into a situation like that make sure you climb away straight ahead because from that angle they can't see your number. Never ever bank to have a look at what you've done".

Formation flying is not easy for a beginner. The tendency to think that the other (leader's) aircraft is the one that is moving up and down

---

13 Through the gate: This was a wide open throttle position only to be used in emergency and for very short periods because of potential engine damage. It was not normal practice to do this.

in relationship to you is almost overwhelming to begin with. Slowly I learned to steady down and make constant variations of throttle settings to maintain position, then with added practice to tuck in tight and hold close formation. After this there were the different formation positions to practise, and then to fly in multi-aircraft formations, with changes of position during the flights. At first the strain of close formation flying for any length of time was such that the sweat soaked my clothes. An hour of that was like a day's work doing almost any other job. Eventually I grew more used to it but all of us found it very tiring. In fact we became sufficiently proficient, as was expected of us by that stage, to do a formation fly-past on the day the Senior Course (the one ahead of us) passed out.

Life was not all course work. Most weekends it was possible to take a trip into Stratford-upon-Avon or Leamington Spa for shopping or a stroll. We were also given several 48 hour passes which gave us chances to get home for a night. My usual route home from Wellesbourne was by bus to Leamington, train to Wolverhampton, and then train to either Shrewsbury, followed by a taxi to my grandmother's at Welshampton where my parents usually spent their weekends, or direct to Birkenhead, Woodside station, and by bus to Upton where my 'proper' home was. If I went to Upton and I had time I would occasionally make a trip to Liverpool, to Moss Brothers the military tailors, to top up my kit, for we had a clothing allowance supposed to be sufficient to cover the cost of all uniform items which we bought (along with other clothing) ourselves.

One of my fellow students, 'Ginger' Watson by name, wanted to visit his old school, Worcester College, which wasn't that far away from Wellesbourne.[14] He asked me to go along with him one Saturday afternoon. This I did. We were entertained by his old schoolmasters and shown round. Afterwards we went to a nearby Greek restaurant and treated ourselves to a meal of curried lobster and a glass of wine. Travel was by train and bus. The day out was memorable for me, if only for the meal.

About once a fortnight there was a Dining In Night in the Mess which we were expected to attend. This was a formal gathering for cocktails, dinner, the Loyal Toast, and afterwards there could be riotous

---

14 Ginger failed the course well before the end. It was said that he was one of Squadron Leader Irish's victims because he was a National Service Officer.

games. One had to have an extremely good reason (not excuse) for non-attendance, and one had to stay until the Senior Officer present (in most Messes this was the Commanding Officer) himself left. This could be very late. At Wellesbourne the students' Mess was less demanding; once dinner was over we were usually permitted to disperse. I attended Guest Nights later in the course. These were the same as Dining In Nights but with Officers' Ladies and local dignitaries present, both Messes combining for the occasion. They followed the same format and went on longer but had the advantage of us being able to meet and entertain a wider range of people. They were good for public relations.

I shall remember one event for ever. It was an escape and evasion exercise in which we, as aircrew, had to imagine that we had come down in enemy territory and had to evade capture. This time we were on the opposite side to that in the exercise held during the time I was at Desford. It only lasted 24 hours but let us into some dramatic situations; ones which we hoped would never have to be experienced in reality.[15]

We were granted a week's leave at Christmas, from the 20th until the 28th of December. Christmas, being a time of relaxation and celebration, gave us the excuse for holding a course party at a hostelry in Stratford-upon-Avon before going on leave.[16] Compared with the party at Desford this was a restrained affair and the more enjoyable for it. I well remember, however, following the example of the senior ground school instructor and eating the petals off several large chrysanthemum blooms, and both of us being threatened with eviction by the innkeeper!

Flying resumed on December 29th with a flight that included 30 minutes simulated and 20 minutes actual IF to settle me back into hard work and stark reality.

Early in the New Year Ken Knott and I were airborne when a "Sixpence Combine, General Recall" message was heard on the R/T.[17] This meant a rapid return to base to land as soon as possible and was only used when bad weather was known to be closing in. In this instance it was a severe snowstorm and we were lucky to get on the ground and clear the main runway before it hit us. We had just completed our after-landing

---

15   This exercise is covered, in some detail, in Appendix 1 (page 398).

16   Probably at the White Horse.

17   "Sixpence Combine" was our Station general call-sign at that time. My own call-sign then was "Sixpence 216".

checks when the weather closed in. The snow started very heavily and visibility dropped to the point when taxying became hazardous. We called Air Traffic Control and told them we couldn't see the edges of the taxiway and were, in response, told to proceed with extreme caution. We couldn't, without risking getting our aircraft bogged down. There was no alternative but to set the engines to 1000 rpm, the accepted idling speed, and wait for things to improve. We heard other aircraft telling the Tower that they, too, were staying where they were. Snow built up on the windscreen effectively blinding all forward vision. Any attempt to open the side clear vision panels resulted in snow falling in on us in large lumps, so that idea was temporarily abandoned. It was a full 20 minutes before the storm abated and we were still a long way from our Flight dispersal area. The airfield now appeared totally flat; taxiways, runways, French drains, and 'bad ground' boards had been replaced by a white featureless desert. There were five or six aircraft in the same predicament – engines running and no way to move. Those aircraft which hadn't made it back to base and had stood off away from the storm were now arriving overhead seeking permission to land. No chance. They were diverted to RAF Pershore which wasn't affected. Eventually, after what seemed like ages, vehicles began to appear and, their drivers being able to see features more clearly, lead us back to our dispersal areas. We taxied by sticking our heads out of the clear vision panels on each side of the cockpit and shouted directions to each other as we carefully weaved our way back at a snail's pace. It was the end of flying for that day. The Station Met Officer said later that over two inches of snow had fallen during that one vicious squall.

During routine training flights some extraordinary things happened. There was one sad occasion when flying dual that my instructor and I were keeping an eye on a Percival Prentice doing aerobatics in case it strayed into our flight path. To our horror we watched one of its wings break off as it pulled out of a loop. My instructor put out a Pan call to inform the emergency services of what we had seen.[18] I heard no more about it, but my instructor had to attend as a witness at the ensuing Board of Inquiry held at another airfield. There was an occasion when I could hardly believe what I was seeing. There, off to one side, was a

---

18 A Pan call was the second highest emergency call, used in this case on behalf of another aircraft. A Mayday call was inappropriate because we ourselves were not in an emergency situation.

four-engined bomber gaining altitude with all four engines feathered – about the least probable situation one could expect. On reporting this at the end of the sortie I discovered that it was an experimental airframe (probably an old Lincoln or Lancaster bomber) which was used as a flying test bed for a new type of jet engine which was fitted into its bomb bay, and this unseen (by me) engine was providing the power. Another oddity which I saw more than once was an aircraft fitted with a large cage built on to its fin and rudder. It was being used for icing tests and, in the right conditions, sprayed water mist in the hope that it would freeze on the fin and lessons could be learned from it.

There was an instance witnessed by several of us from just outside our Flight hut. We were watching a routine take-off, during the later part of which an engine was throttled right back to simulate engine failure so that the student could take necessary corrective action and institute forced landing procedures. A moment or two later there was a puff of smoke and a loud bang as the 'good' engine failed. It was a moment or two before the throttled-back engine powered up with the aircraft still heading steeply downwards. It came very close to the ground before control was regained and level flight resumed. As luck would have it that particular Oxford was one that could maintain height on one engine and make its way back for an emergency landing on the airfield. Flt.Lt. Oliver was the instructor and he told us afterwards that he came to within 200 feet of crashing into the nearby Ministry of Agriculture Research Station greenhouses. As was usual in such cases both instructor and student took to the air again almost immediately afterwards so that there would be no chance of them losing their nerve.

Again viewed from the Flight hut were two other occurrences, one humorous yet damaging, the other more serious. It was usual (downright necessary) to wear a greatcoat or other official protective clothing when outdoors during the winter. With the engines of several aircraft running at the same time on the dispersal hard-standing a good lookout had to be maintained if out there on foot. In these circumstances it was possible to be unaware of another aircraft approaching. This being so, we watched an Airman walking along the taxiway who, it was obvious, had not noticed an aircraft approaching from behind. He was off to one side of its path but not far enough. As a result, and by pure misfortune, the pitot head of the plane caught in his greatcoat collar and effectively dragged him along by the scruff of the neck for several yards before he disentangled himself. Too late, the damage was done and the pitot head was bent back out of position. Said Erk quickly found himself on a fizzer and was charged with damaging one of Her Majesty's aircraft. The other instance occurred in similar circumstances. An Airman, confused by the noise, actually walked through a rotating propeller and came out the other side unscathed. We wondered if he would ever know but an Airwoman also saw it happen, screamed, and fainted on the spot. This drew the Airman's attention to what he had just done, whereupon he too fainted and had to be carried off to Sick Quarters. We never heard what happened to either of them but neither was seen again.

As an adjunct to proper instrument flying we also had to do several hours simulated IF in Link Trainers. These machines were equipped with a small cockpit in which were full flying controls and a full instrument panel. They were mounted on a swivel so that banking, climbing, diving and, to a lesser extent, yawing could be emulated and felt by the 'pilot' inside. Sitting inside one of these machines with the lid closed was a fairly good, but very unsophisticated, representation of being at an aircraft's controls. There was a system whereby the instructor, who sat in the room alongside the machine, could inject turbulence and simulate emergencies so that trainees' responses and reactions could be monitored. We used Link Trainers to practise the flight patterns we were expected to fly in our instrument rating exams. These patterns were recorded by a mechanical crab which left a trace on a map on the instructor's table and showed the accuracy of our flying. None of us liked Link Trainers, we always preferred the real thing, but they certainly had their uses when the weather was clamped in. It was possible to feel quite disoriented on climbing out after an hour's session. I spent a total of 16 hours on Link Trainers in 22 sessions.

I don't think any of us particularly enjoyed night flying but, nonetheless, we had to learn and practise it. When doing circuits and bumps it was usual to taxi to the end of the runway (or at an intersection) and turn right to use the taxiway on the far side of the airfield to arrive back at the take-off point for another go. The taxiways were well marked with coloured lights and that part of the exercise wasn't difficult. The trouble was that if the runway in use was one of the shorter runways, as opposed to the main runway, there was a wooded hill ahead topped with a red hazard light. It was often said that many of us, in these circumstances, if we got things a bit wrong, were seen to fly past the side of the light, missing the tree tops by mere inches. Night cross-country flights could be very confusing but there were bonuses. At Rugby the GEC and British Thompson Houston factories both had very large illuminated signs clearly visible for quite some distance from the air. Our airfield pundit continuously flashed out WM in red, and waterways (rivers and canals) showed up well when looking towards the moon. These were very useful aids. At no time were we ever under radar control. In fact, the word radar was, in my recollection, never used during the course and we were told nothing about it.

During one of these night flying sessions I had landed and taxied back for another take-off. There were two more aircraft ahead of me which took off in turn. Then came an R/T call telling me to hold because an aircraft was in the circuit and was due to land. I sat there watching events, waiting my turn. The aircraft landing had failed to lower its undercarriage. I could hear the scraping and noise above that of my engines, and I've never before seen such a shower of sparks as it ground to a halt. It did not catch fire and no-one was injured. I'd better explain that an Oxford's main wheels protruded slightly below the engine nacelles when fully retracted. In that position, with landing wheels up, the propellers would bend but the wheels would allow the machine to roll forward for quite a distance. That was the end of flying for the night. While taxying back to dispersal I heard, over the R/T, the call to the two aircraft that had just taken off, instructing them to check their fuel states. This done, and there being sufficient, they were ordered to stooge around and stay airborne at endurance speed until first light, by which time the runway would be cleared and checked for them to land.[19] The alternative was for them to divert to Shawbury, the nearest Master Airfield. On going to bed I could hear these two planes crossing and re-crossing the airfield, doubtless keeping more people than me awake that night.

Later in the course our Officer training had reached the point when we were instructed to assist the Station Orderly Officer with his duties. These were more time consuming than onerous. My turn came and somehow, although I suppose I should have known better, I had a brush with Mr. Williams, the SWO.[20] Being still only an Acting Pilot Officer this was a matter for corrective action and I was reported to the

---

19 Endurance speed was 115 mph (not knots) IAS (Indicated Air Speed).

20 Station Warrant Officer. The most senior NCO on the camp. Usually a position held by a man of vast RAF experience who would command the respect of all personnel.

Station Adjutant, by whom I was duly disciplined and, as punishment, was given three more Orderly Officer Duties to carry out. Whilst this hurt me intensely at the time because people on such duties were not allowed to fly, it cannot have done me any real harm, but it worried me that I might have accumulated enough black marks on my record to prevent me passing the course.

The next time I flew I was determined to enjoy myself. It was a day with some quite heavy rain-bearing cumulus cloud about. It was fun flying round these cloud pillars, but then I spotted an arch of clear air below me under a large cloud and decided to dive through it. I misjudged the distance and my speed, and it took a seeming age to get to it by which time the arch had filled with heavy rain. I had committed myself and, with engines screaming, the lumbering old Oxford was reaching its maximum speed of 230 knots and juddering like mad; I just had to level off. Now in heavy rain, water started pouring in and running down the instrument panel. Then suddenly I found myself on instruments in dense cloud. Fortunately the cloud cleared almost as soon as I went into it. The rain stopped. I collected my wits after having frightened myself, steadied down, and made my way back to base.

It may have been with my recent series of Orderly Officer duties in mind, or it may have been because quite a percentage of students who had begun the course had had the chop, for there were markedly fewer of us than when we arrived, that I sought an interview with my Flight Commander and signed up for a Short Service (8 year) Commission, subject to my Acting Commission being confirmed on passing out. When I next chanced to meet Sqn.Ldr. Irish he told me that I had made a very wise choice and that he was pleased that I had done so. Well, as someone said, "He would be, wouldn't he!"

With the course drawing to a close our ground school training now included dinghy drills, the use of Lindholme rescue gear, and information as to the use of an airborne lifeboat should any of us ever have the misfortune to ditch in the sea. There was also much instrument practice on the Link Trainer with instruction and training in the use of SBA and other landing aids.[21] This latter proved of great value in preparation for

---

21 SBA = Standard Beam Approach, a system of radio beacons and transmitters creating an audio pattern of dots and dashes by which the pilot of an aircraft fitted only with R/T could find his way to the runway threshold of a suitably equipped airfield for landing in conditions of low visibility. Wellesbourne Mountford did not have this equipment.

my final Instrument Rating test, for which, on passing I became the proud holder of my 'White Card' Instrument Rating.

By this stage in the course the walls of my room had become adorned with reminders and lists of data critical to my passing exams. Compass bearings and reciprocals, quadrantal heights, the Morse code, Vital Actions and emergency procedures of use whilst flying, equivalent ranks in the Army, Navy and Air Force, the new NATO phonetic alphabet, meteorological symbols used in the station circles on weather charts, compass deviation and variation, navigation formulae, signals square signs, and much else.[22] All were read and re-read to the point when they became thoroughly ingrained in my memory. Other students did their swotting from books and couldn't always find the right pages. Everything I wasn't sure of got written down and pasted on my walls.

For some strange reason I took, and passed, the Final Navigation test before doing a solo cross-country, during which exercise I had to land away at a strange airfield. Landing away had always bothered me. Whilst I could find my way to a place in the air I was worried that I wouldn't be able to find my way around a maze of taxiways on a strange airfield. As it happened I was tasked with flying to RAF Feltwell in Norfolk via York and then back to base via Shepton Mallet in Somerset. The first leg took 2 hours and 55 minutes, one hour of which was instrument flying in thick cloud and heavy rain which poured in and trickled down the instrument panel to form a pool near my feet. On arriving near Feltwell and contacting the Tower for a VHF/DF bearing I was told that I had overflown the airfield, but I hadn't seen it.[23] I overflew it three more times, each time at a lower altitude, before I saw it. The reason why? – It was a grass airfield and half of it was covered with snow making it look like two medium sized farmers' fields; the camp site I took to be a small village. There were no taxiways to worry about and I was able to taxi to the area where I was marshalled into place. Another lesson learned, and I got a bit of ribbing when I checked in to Air Traffic Control prior to refuelling. As it so happened the ground crew who started the engines for me by kneeling on the wing, as was standard

---

22 Until now we had been using the old 'Able, Baker, Charlie, Dog' version and had quickly to change to the 'Alpha, Bravo, Charlie, Delta' version which most of us, at the outset, found difficult to get used to.

23 A bearing taken from my R/T transmission. This could be in the form of a track to be made good or a back bearing (the reciprocal of the former).

practice whilst winding the inertia starter handle, on being unready for the engine firing up, were blown off by the propeller wash and rolled holus-bolus across the hard-standing, narrowly missing damaging the tailplane on the way past. Not having learned the lesson the same thing happened when starting the second engine. The R/T from the Tower was not very complimentary following this even though it wasn't my fault. The homeward leg was in much better weather, taking 2 hours and 5 minutes, including 25 minutes IF.

As if to take the seriousness and worry off the impending end of course exams a number of Chipmunks were allocated to Wellesbourne Mountford during January. It was said that we needed a refresher on single-engined aircraft as we, on passing out, were due to be trained as fighter rather than bomber pilots. So it was that we were able to turn the tables on our instructors. Whilst our Log Books showed our instructors to be first pilot (Captain) on any dual flights they were in fact our pupils because, unlike us, none of them were qualified on the type! Ken Knott had his first Chipmunk flight with me on the 20th of January, it lasted 45 minutes and I think I answered all his questions. Two solo flights followed and, as with other students we soon learned not to land just past the runway threshold but either to approach and land further along or to fly a few feet above the ground for most of the runway's length and drop into a perfect three-pointer and draw up just short of the far end; it was great fun. Ken Knott flew with me once more, during which, after carrying out our allotted duties, we threw the aircraft around and had a wonderful time. That was the day before my Final Handling test on Oxfords.

My Final Handling Test was conducted by Sqn.Ldr. Forster, the CO of No.1 Squadron (our training course was No.2 Squadron). He was very fair and put me through my paces for an hour and ten minutes. I passed, and that was the final flight of the course and my last flight in an Oxford and, little did I know it at the time, it was the last time I would be officially at the controls of an RAF piston-engined aircraft.[24]

Not only were our flying skills put to the test, there were ground school exams to pass, too. These were all written papers and most of them were of the multiple choice answers variety. Even so, some of the choices were cleverly worded, and so nearly right, that they made me

24 On February 20th, 1953.

think quite hard. More students failed, even at this late stage, and the course ended with about 60% of the original intake going on to prepare ourselves for the Passing Out Parade.

There was an end of course party, again held at the same hostelry in Stratford-upon-Avon. This was a very relaxed affair. Sqn.Ldr. Irish, our course CO, informally congratulated us on our achievements and wished us well. Rather too much liquor was consumed but its effects were delayed if not mitigated by the consumption of quantities of ham rolls, sausage rolls, cheese sandwiches, and other 'blotting paper'. Our senior ground school instructor, having eaten chrysanthemums at Christmas, decided to help himself to the now seasonal tulip petals. I tried one petal but found it fleshy and not at all to my taste. Heavy hangovers were duly nursed the next day.

We passed out and were individually presented with our flying badges during a parade held on Wednesday the 25th of February, 1953. It was a great feeling to have passed the course and to be on parade, have the usual low level fly-past of a formation of Oxfords as soon as we were presented with our 'Wings', and then to be able to show our parents round the Station as well as the cockpits of both Oxfords and Chipmunks. There was a celebratory drink and buffet in the Officers Mess for all who attended. Three weeks leave then followed during which all of us were individually informed that we had lost our acting rank and were instead now substantive Pilot Officers. As was customary, our names, as newly Commissioned Officers, were published in the London Gazette.

Now that I was a 'regular' RAF Officer, and no longer a National Serviceman, I had to kit myself out with a full uniform. I did this as a matter of priority whilst on leave in readiness for my next posting. Much money was spent at Moss Bros as a result, and I opened an account with them which was to prove very convenient in the future.

8. Faster And Higher

I HAD AN ENJOYABLE leave, during which I was sent my next posting information together with an appropriate First Class Travel Warrant. On the 17th of March 1953, I set off for RAF Merryfield in Somerset where I arrived in the late afternoon.

'A' Flight, 29 Course. From an official photograph.

Merryfield is situated next to the small hamlet of Ilton, between Taunton and Ilminster. Ilton station was a wooden unmanned halt on the now defunct single track railway linking those towns. At Ilton there was an alehouse, a tiny shop, some very pretty thatched cottages, and little else. The village of Wellesbourne Mountford was a metropolis by comparison.

I Warned In at the Mess and was allocated a double room in one of a group of Seco huts on low ground some distance away from both the Mess and the Flight huts. The latter also doubled as our class-rooms and were on the edge of the airfield. The Mess and the airfield were uphill from our accommodation. I shared a room with John James Smith who had just married during the last leave. He was an ex-apprentice of Jones & Shipman, machine tool makers, of Melton Mowbray, and answered to either 'JJ' or 'Smithie'. We were to get on well together. There was a civilian batman who also lived in a room in the hut and looked after its 8 occupants.

The camp buildings, comprising some new Seco huts, some old Nissen huts, and some newly rendered brick buildings, were all painted in NATO colours. The Astra Cinema, Station Sick Quarters, and our Mess were all Nissen huts.

Our hut batman asked me if I knew anyone who wanted a bicycle in exchange for a Pound Note. I had a look at the machine and it was fully serviceable and even the height of the saddle, surprisingly, suited me. I parted with the money and the bike was mine. It proved invaluable and saved me a lot of leg work travelling between camp facilities.

Across the airfield from our Flight huts was a group of buildings and a hangar occupied by Westland Aircraft Ltd., who shared the use of the airfield for test flying.

Our designation was 208 Advanced Flying School, and I was there to learn to fly jets. The aircraft we had were two-seater Meteor T7s for dual training, and Vampires, Marks 5 and 9, for solo flights. There were also some Vampire T11s for further dual flying. Parked on hard-standings were a number of earlier Mk 1 Vampires which were no longer in regular use.[1] My flying instructor was Fg.Off. Bennett, with whom I initially had a compatibility problem. Flt.Lt. Greenfield was i/c 'A' Flight, to which I was assigned.

There were two Iraqi pilots on our course. One had the nickname Abu Avtag after the aviation fuel we used.[2] They were sent by the Iraqi Air Force on the understanding that if they failed the course they would

---

1 These aircraft had been used until the previous November and were eventually flown out later during my stay.

2 His Iraqi name was unpronounceable by us. Two types of jet fuel were in use at the time: AVTAG and AVTUR. We used AVTAG for our aircraft.

have to pay for it themselves. One did fail and, I heard later, committed suicide as a result.

At Merryfield the accent was on flying. Ground school lessons dealt primarily with meteorology and navigation at high altitude, aircraft systems, and aircraft recognition. Personal qualities and general abilities were still being assessed but were not, at this stage of training, regarded as such a critical part of the course.

Before flying we were given a once-over by the MOs, Flt.Lt. Markham and Fg.Off. Frame. This done, we were taken by bus to RAF Weston Zoyland to have further tests in a decompression chamber, just to make sure we were all OK, and to experience anoxia under controlled conditions.

The decompression chamber looked like a horizontal boiler with thick glass windows. There were seats and an oxygen supply inside, and there was an air lock for use in emergency. We were put in the chamber, four at a time. We put on our oxygen masks, and were taken up, in stages, to the equivalent of about 40,000 feet. In turn, we had to take off our masks and, at the same time, write on a piece of paper the numbers One, Two, Three, Four, etc., in sequence. As anoxia set in (and none of us could recognise its onset) our writings failed to a scrawl and then stopped. Our heads then fell forward as we became unconscious. Oxygen was then blown across our faces from an open-ended pipe and, on regaining consciousness each of us started writing again at speed and with increasing clarity as we recovered. By the time we had recovered fully our speed of writing had slowed to normal pace. We then came down to 'ground level'. Anoxia is as insidious as it is dangerous.

Before starting flying we had to be taught the use of Mae Wests and dinghies as this was the first time we came anywhere near flying over open water. We were given wet practice in the necessary drills in the public baths in Taunton. Trying to right an inverted one-man dinghy and then climb into it while wearing flying clothing is an art at which we had quickly to become proficient. It was difficult enough in the smooth water of a swimming pool. We all hoped we would never find ourselves having to do it in a cold rough sea.

My first jet flight, in a Meteor T7, impressed me because of the shove I got in my back and lack of tendency to yaw on take-off, also the lack of engine noise as we climbed to over 20 thousand feet – much more than twice the height I had ever been before. It sounded, from within the cockpit, more like being on an electric train than being in any aircraft which I had flown previously. Fg.Off. Bennett shut down one engine and did some minor aerobatics before pointing out various useful features visible on the ground from that height. He re-lit the engine and handed control over to me. I was too timid for his liking and he told me so. This was the beginning of our incompatibility. He said I was not decisive enough at the controls and should be throwing the aircraft about. I thought his judgement unfair on what was my first jet flight, and told him so after we landed. It was not exactly the best way to start a flying course.

There was a lot to learn before going solo. Emergency procedures and cockpit drills and checks are essential knowledge before flying any type of aircraft new to a pilot. I was flying dual on Meteors and had to swot up everything there was to know about them, and the same for Vampires, because the first solo jet flights for any of us on the course were to be on these single-seaters.

I had nine dual flights on Meteors, five of which were with Fg.Off. Bennett, the rest were with two other instructors, probably because Fg.Off. Bennett didn't get on with me. I had no problems with the other instructors. I was checked out, on the last of these flights, by Flt.Lt. Greenfield as fit for my first solo. I had completed 5 hours 55 minutes. The longest flight was 45 minutes and the shortest just 25 minutes.

I had been trained on tail-wheel aircraft. Now I was flying tricycle undercarriage types, and found them much easier to taxi and land.

I had sat in a Vampire cockpit many times already so as to familiarise myself with the location of all controls and equipment which would be of use to me in flight. I rehearsed the drills and procedures until I could recite them parrot-fashion. However, there's nothing quite like sitting in your first single-seat jet aircraft knowing that you are actually going to start it up, taxi it, fly it, land it, return to dispersal, and shut it down – all on your own. On April 13th, 1953, I did just that.

Engine start-up in a Vampire could be tricky until you got the hang of it. The fuel cocks had to be set just right and the start-up sequence demanded accurate timing; it was not automatic. I fluffed my first engine start. I got jet pipe resonance which indicated a wet start and at once shut down. The ground crew came over and climbed onto the tail to weigh it down, tipping the rear downwards so as to drain out the unburned fuel from the jet pipe. An instructor came across and the only thing he said to me was that a wet start was more dignified than a wet fart, and left me to try again. Knowing the probable state of students' stomachs when about to fly a first solo on a single-seat aircraft for the first time in their lives, this was neither as vulgar nor as irrelevant as it might seem, and especially in view of our having recently been instructed as to the expected effects from wind expanding in the gut when quickly ascending to high altitude.[3]

A Vampire FB5. This aircraft was originally used by De Havilland when compiling the Pilots' Notes. Although I never flew it at Merryfield, I flew it later at both Pembrey and Jever.

Start-up was successful at the second attempt. With cockpit checks done again, and with adequate brake pressure, I moved forward slowly and steering by differential braking came to a halt just clear of dispersal, as I had been told to do. I called the Tower for clearance to taxi, adding, as instructed, that it was a first solo. They replied with the runway in use and the QNH.[4] I acknowledged, and rolled forward. I was very close to the ground and felt as though I was looking up at everything.[5] After a little hesitance and uncertainty I soon got the hang of taxying. I quickly found that I had to anticipate my power requirements because a jet engine is far slower to respond to a change of throttle setting than a piston engine. I approached some corners on the perimeter track too slowly and at others I had to brake hard. Before I approached the runway the Tower gave me clearance to take off in my own time. There were no engine run-ups to do, no mag-drop checks, I had done most of my pre

---

3   Gut gases expanded and one had to let go. We used oxygen so there was no anti-social aspect. This was nowhere near as dramatic as the 'sixpence, half a crown, dustbin lid' syndrome said to be experienced on becoming really frightened.

4   QNH is another 'Q' code, still called Queenie Nan How in spite of the introduction of the NATO phonetic alphabet. It is the airfield barometric pressure at the time of take-off, to which pilots set their altimeters.

5   You were more than twice that height when taxying a Meteor.

take-off vital actions, the rest were done in moments.[6] I swung on to the runway, lined up on the centreline, held the brakes on and opened up the engine, keeping an eye on the jet pipe temperature and engine revs. In seconds all was right. I released the brakes and accelerated down the runway, but not as quickly as in a Meteor, and, at the right speed eased back the stick and was airborne. I squeezed the brake handle to stop the wheels spinning and selected undercarriage up. With wheels retracted I climbed away and began to experiment with the responsiveness of the controls. It was a clear day and I could easily pick out the landmarks I had learned during previous flights. I had been briefed to try a mock approach and landing drill at altitude. I did this and was reasonably satisfied. I tried a gentle stall. That was OK, so I did a few steep turns. The Tower called and reminded me I had been airborne 35 minutes; it seemed like five. I made my way back to base, called the Tower, joined the circuit, and called "Downwind". With wheels down, air brakes and flaps in the correct position, and checks done, I called "Finals", and was cleared to land. In moments I had greased the Vampire on to the ground without really feeling anything. As I slowed I raised the flaps and closed the air brakes, opened the canopy, and taxied back to dispersal, shut down, and climbed out. I was walking tall on legs of jelly. I had done it! What a blessed relief.

On entering the Flight hut I signed the Form 700 to say the aircraft was OK, and entered 'DCO' and 40 minutes flying time in the Authorisation Book.[7] There was a short debriefing, at the end of which the blackboard was pointed out to me. I was booked to fly solo again in half an hour's time!

Everything went well on the second solo. Taxying was better. I was more confident in the air, repeated the exercises of the previous flight and had a better look round the countryside. Although I was airborne 10 minutes less on that sortie I seemed to pack more into it. My first flight had been in a Vampire 9. This latest one was in a Vampire 5. There was no difference as far as handling. The Mk 9 had air conditioning (of a sort); the Mk 5 did not.

---

6 A mag-drop check is done only on piston engines and is carried out to ensure that both parts of the duplicated ignition system function were within prescribed limits. Mag = magneto.

7 A Form 700 is a blue serviceability log book. Each aircraft has one. DCO stands for 'Duty Carried Out'. The Authorisation Book records all flights, duties, and flight times. It is signed prior to boarding an aircraft and after landing.

Three days later I had another solo flight lasting 30 minutes. The break between flights was a little unsettling but any nervousness disappeared as soon as I had strapped myself in the cockpit.

Meteors were known to be a bit tricky, and we were aware that quite a few had been falling out of the sky in an undignified manner.[8] I lost several friends from previous courses who were killed when flying them. We were thankful that we were being trained on Vampires.

The next flight was booked 'dual' with Fg.Off. Bennett. On taxying out to the runway a fire warning light came on for the starboard engine. I spotted it and was already taking action before he spotted a flare of flame coming from its jet pipe. Both engines were shut down immediately and the on-board fire extinguisher system doused the fire. Fg.Off. Bennett had the canopy hinged back in an instant while I was doing all this. I took all the actions while he was slow to react, even though, as first pilot, he was technically in charge, but I was in control at the time. He called the Tower, told them what had happened, and a tow vehicle came and pulled us back to dispersal while we sat out on the edge of the cockpit ready to jump down if anything started to fry up again. We were greeted by the usual crowd that gathers when something serious, or potentially serious, goes wrong. Friend Bennett modified his attitude towards me after that.

I have to say that I was never quite happy in a Meteor. I disliked the heavy tilting cockpit canopy, I found the sliding throttles very awkward, and I always felt that the aircraft was fighting its way through the air rather than sliding through it. Later in the course, when I flew Vampire T11s I found the side-by-side seating extremely uncomfortable. I hated sitting with my shoulders pressed close to someone else's. I never ever enjoyed flying dual on these types but I had to do it.

The first part of the course dealt with enhancing our knowledge of jet flying, high altitude handling, and speed runs during which we experienced the effects of compressibility leading to eventual loss of control.[9] During the middle part of the course there was more solo than dual flying. At this stage we were practising aerobatics (spinning was

---

8   Many years later it was acknowledged that the pilot training in Meteors was very substandard. As a result many accidents, aircraft losses, and deaths, were due to consequential pilot error. Reliability was lacking too.

9   A Vampire would 'break' at about Mach .81. That is, it became totally uncontrollable. Control was quickly regained on slowing down a few knots.

forbidden because of the risk of flame-outs) and formation flying. Aerobatics were effortless compared with doing them in a piston-engined aircraft; there was so much more power available. Upward Charlies, hesitation rolls, and Derry turns were a piece of cake. The drawback was that we rapidly found that we could easily black out in a steep turn or when pulling out of a dive. I must have greyed out or blacked out dozens of times through pulling too much 'G'. Later in my career there was hardly a flight when that didn't happen. The required skill was to be able to pull as much 'G' as possible without blacking out.

As the course progressed there was an amount of concentration on low flying. If it was fun at slow speeds it was downright hairy in a jet. Everything came up so fast and navigation at that height became more difficult as a result. During the third week of May I did one low-level cross-country with Fg.Off. Bennett in a Meteor and then two Vampire solo runs. These lasted 40 and 45 minutes, each over Exmoor. Exhilarating as they were, they were also very tiring. Flocks of birds were the biggest danger.

I have already mentioned going to Cosford for hay fever tests when I was at Wellesbourne. The outcome of these was that I was to have regular desensitisation injections of increasing strength over a period of some weeks. These injections were still taking place while I was at Merryfield. I had just started the final series of the highest strength. I had been to Sick Quarters on a Saturday afternoon, so as to avoid interference with my flying training, for this jab. I was advised, because of its strength, to go back to my room and lie down for an hour, so that any adverse effects it might have could wear off. I didn't get as far as my room, probably only about half way there, when my chest began to tighten and breathing became difficult. I turned around and made my way back to Sick Quarters because I felt so ill. On arrival I was gasping for breath and gurgling at the same time. The MO was summoned and, on taking one look at me put me on oxygen, at the same time lying me (now semi-conscious) face down on a bed with my head out over the end. An Orderly fetched a bowl and put it on the floor under my face, the oxygen mask was removed and a jet of oxygen played on to my face instead while I coughed up quantities of green frothy stuff. My lungs had filled with fluid and I was on the point of drowning in my own juices. I was given an antidote injection and, after about half an hour things began to improve. The MO, Fg.Off. Frame, didn't leave me the whole time. I lay there for another hour or more before I had recovered enough for him to let me sit up. By now it was time for afternoon tea in the Mess, so he took me there and had me sit alongside him at the Permanent Staff table and wouldn't let me go back to my room until he was absolutely satisfied that I was OK. Next morning, Sunday, when I went to see him for a check he told me that, if I hadn't been given oxygen I would have very soon died. I had no more hay fever injections.

When we went shopping it was usually to Taunton. Ilminster didn't have the same attraction. Depending on the weather we went either by bus if it was wet, or by train if it was a nice day. It was a pleasant walk to Ilton Halt in fine weather, but the bus stop was nearer the Guardroom. The train was a one-engine, single-carriage affair, one of the old Great Western Railway 'rail motor' trains. It was the prettiest branch line I have ever been on. The sides of the track were covered in blossom and the countryside some of the prettiest in the land. We were not interested in pubs; in any case they were all shut on Saturday afternoons. It was usual for us to do whatever shopping was needed, or have a haircut, and then go into Thornton's café for afternoon tea and cakes before making our way to the bus or train for our journey back to camp. None of us ever went into the Ilton alehouse. We regarded that as strictly for the locals and they respected us for it. Life, off-camp, was very civilised.

I was at Merryfield at the time of the Officers Mess Annual Summer Ball. We students had all heard of such events, but none of us had ever been to one. I found myself involved in the preparations and decoration of the Mess. There was at least a week's spare time hard work involved. I found myself helping with creating a thatched roof over an extra bar in the anteroom and then, on canvas flats, painting a large representation of a castle to adorn the end of the dining-room which, on the night, became the ballroom. On the morning of the ball almost all the walls in the Mess were decorated with trellis interwoven with creepers and fresh flowers. It was a sight to see.

As members of the Mess we were all expected to attend and, quite properly, had the right to invite guests. I invited my parents and booked a room for them at the Shrubbery Hotel in Ilminster. Dignitaries from Taunton and Ilminster, local landowners and farmers, Senior Officers from Flying Training Command, and executives of Westland Aircraft were all invited with their ladies. Officers' ladies, of course, were expected to attend. Unaccompanied Officers were asked to greet guests on arrival and to escort them during the evening.

All guests were received by the Commanding Officer and his lady. Welcome drinks were served but thenafter all drinks had to be paid for. It was an excellent event held on a warm evening. The Mess was full to capacity. Other members of my course met my parents and all went well. There was plenty of excellent food at the buffet. The band was good. Not being a dancer I sort of led my Mother while she more or less shoved me round the floor – just once – to say that I had done it. It was after midnight when the event drew to a close but not before some wag had poured detergent in the ornamental fish fountain and waterfall that had been rigged up in the entrance hall. There was froth all over the place and the poor goldfish must have choked to death on the bubbles. It was a good night.

Flying at high altitude over the West Country in clear weather was a remarkable experience. On one such flight when I was briefed to climb to height and do a Mach run from 42,000 feet, I could see, just by turning my head, well beyond the South Wales coast and along Cardigan Bay to the north, Lands End with the Scilly Islands in the distance to the west, some light cloud which must have been over the French coastline to the south, and the industrial haze over London to the east. I never had such good visibility at any other time over the British Isles. The triangle of runways at base were below me as I started the Mach run, aiming for it as I dived. As the Vampire 'broke' I was amazed to see a Westland Wyvern turboprop aircraft pass me. It turned out that it was flown by Harold Penrose, the Westland test pilot, who sometimes flew from that company's facility at Merryfield. He had been stalking me since I took off. He told me so over a drink in the Mess bar the next Saturday lunch time. The Wyvern would 'break' at about Mach .83, Mach .02 faster than a Vampire. I realised from that same flight that I had to keep a far better look out in the air.

Toward the end of the course many hours were spent on instrument flying. I was in an all-weather air force, in an all-weather aircraft and had to fly competently in all weathers. Dual and solo exercises were carried out and QGHs practised in both aircraft types.

I had four flights only in a Vampire T11 at Merryfield. These were more for familiarisation purposes than anything else. I have already said that I didn't like the cramped side-by-side seating, and I found the type comparatively clumsy to handle. Because of their shape they were nick-named either 'bananas' or 'wheel barrows' because of their generally up-curved side view when sitting on the tarmac.

A Vampire T11.

Our satellite airfield was Dunkeswell. It was inhabited by civilians but there was a small contingent of RAF personnel who manned the fire tenders which are necessary on any RAF airfield. Dunkeswell sits atop an escarpment at the edge of a deep valley. The approach to the main runway was over this valley, and the escarpment was subject to down-draughts. The first time I went there I was flying dual. I approached to land in what I thought was a normal manner after having completed the downwind leg of the circuit at 1000 feet above airfield level, as was routine. Caught in a down-draught, I realised that the runway thresh-old was level with me, and then above me; red Very lights rose from the runway controller's caravan. It was not the best way to try to land. With air brakes in, throttle open wide, undercart up, and flaps up, I climbed out of the situation. I went round again, had another go and fared much better, but I reckoned I was still too low. At the third attempt, having started my 'finals' descent much later, I was satisfied and completed the landing. My instructor, during all this, never uttered a word until I had rolled to a stop. He then said that I had to watch out in the future because, like this one, not all airfields are as pilot friendly as Merryfield. He hadn't needed to say anything. I had just found out!

I must mention that by this time we were no longer flying rectangular circuits. There was no cross-wind leg to finals; the approach was done on a continuous descending 180° turn from the end of the downwind leg. In this way we were in the circuit less time and the circuit itself was much tighter. At this stage of training we reckoned only bombers had to fly long angular circuits. We were fighter boys now, and were expected to behave as such.

June 9th saw me make my first long distance dual cross-country at altitude, with Fg.Off. Bennett. The flight plan was to RAF Driffield via Penrith. The amount of pre-flight navigation was considerable and had to take account of wind changes with increased altitude on the climb, work out each change of heading to maintain track as we passed through each 5,000 ft height band, and then add them vectorially for an average course to steer throughout the climb. The descent, being faster, was less complicated, but the high altitude winds, sometimes up to 150 knots, had very much to be taken into consideration. The calculations took a long time so flight planning started over an hour before ETD.[10] The flight itself was unremarkable. Where there was cloud we were well above it. Just for the exercise, rather than out of necessity, we called for radio fixes to confirm our position en-route. At no time were we in touch with any radar station.

We landed at Driffield in glorious sunshine, taxied to the visiting aircraft dispersal, and checked in at the Tower. While we were being refuelled we took a walk over to a group of pilots sitting on the grass outside a dispersal hut. I was instantly recognised by some of them. They had been with me on the course at Kirton-in-Lindsey from which I was chopped. None of them had expected to see me again, least of all in a flying role. It was then that I was told of the death, at an air base near Winnipeg in Canada, of the person with whom my exam marks had been confused at Kirton-in-Lindsey. I was able to explain what had happened from my point of view. They also told me of fatal Meteor flying accidents. We bade farewell and I never met any of them again.

The flight back to base was via Morecambe. We did no serious pre-flight planning beforehand, save to estimate a climbing course from an average of the forecast winds. We asked for more fixes but these, again, were for practice rather than necessity. It took us 55 minutes to get to Driffield, and exactly an hour to get back. Annoyingly, when

---

10 ETD = Estimated Time of Departure.

flying over the Wirral peninsula, my home area, there was full cloud cover and I saw nothing of it.

Three days later we went on a map-reading cross-country, without the use of radio aids, as one might have to do over enemy territory. Things come up very quickly even when flying at medium altitude. Railway lines, water features, prominent hills and large conurbations were the most useful landmarks.

During the final two weeks of the course we were taken to see a radar station at Exminster. We were told almost nothing about the use of radar other than it being an aircraft detection system used during the war to locate suspected enemy planes. We had no formal radar instruction at all and had little idea what to expect.

We arrived on a bleak site close to the river Exe and the Exeter canal. We first saw that there was a security fence and a small Guardroom. Inside the fence stood what looked like a group of derelict buildings. There was a mist blowing across from the river and I don't think any of us saw any aerials; they were certainly not pointed out to us but they must have been there somewhere. There were a few old huts and an obvious latrine block which must still have been in use. Near these stood a brick building surrounded by a brick and earth revetment. Inside this building there was little light, and a smell of damp and of ozone generated by electrical apparatus, such as one expects at some of London's underground tube stations.

I recollect there was a main room with racks of electrical apparatus towards one side, a small plotting table, a switchboard, and several of what looked like oscilloscopes. I saw no more than six personnel. One was wearing a head and breast set and was apparently connected to a headquarters by telephone line. Another sat at an oscilloscope, another was by a plotting table and the other three didn't seem to be doing anything in particular. During the hour we were there we were told practically nothing other than that this Station was used for detecting aircraft approaching from over the sea, and had been built at the outbreak of war. No-one explained to us how the aircraft were detected or what happened next. We didn't find out whether the personnel lived at the site or came to work from another, larger, RAF Station. As far as we were concerned the entire trip was of little interest or value to us. We thought someone had lost the point of the visit and should have told us more. No one ever did. The one thing we agreed among ourselves was that if anyone wanted to catch tuberculosis it seemed the right sort of place to be posted to. This was the only time radar was mentioned during my entire flying training.

During the third week of June I took my Instrument Rating Test. Flt. Lt. McMahon, Officer Commanding No.1 Squadron at Merryfield was my examiner. The flight lasted an hour, of which 35 minutes was under two stage amber, with ten minutes 'actual' flying in cloud. I passed and therefore retained my White Card rating. Two flights later I had my Final Handling Test taken, surprisingly, by Fg.Off Bennett, my usual instructor. It lasted 50 minutes and I passed that too.

My last but one flight from Merryfield, which I had to complete in order to pass the course was my solo, landing away, cross-country. The weather had clamped down and most airfields which were used as destinations for this exercise were closed. As there were no diversion fields open near them my flight was delayed almost until the last minute. In desperation, with the flying part of the course drawing to a close, I was instructed to fly to RAF Shawbury and, if it was open, to land there and then return to base. I took off, climbed north, and soon found myself above cloud and then flew into a wall of cloud. Flying on instruments, I suspected that something was wrong. My airspeed seemed to be dropping, I was in level flight, the engine was behaving, and my altitude was as it should be. It took a few minutes diagnostic thought to gather that for some reason my Air Speed Indicator (ASI) had decided to malfunction. I became busy. Without indication of speed I had no means of accurate navigation. Not to be outdone I called for a series of VHF/DF fixes at regular intervals and plotted these on the map strapped to my right knee with my log pad. I called Shawbury but they were clamped down, so a landing was impossible, as was a QGH without an ASI at any airfield. My one hope was that base was still open and the visibility there was still good enough for a visual approach and landing. The weather was still thick when I turned early for base. With the ASI still obviously unserviceable I headed home, checking my position all the while with more VHF/DF fixes. The weather cleared over the Bristol Channel giving me a visual fix and I altered course slightly towards base. I contacted the Tower and told them my position and my lack of an ASI, which, by this time, had decided to rest on the pin at zero. They cleared the circuit for me in advance so that I had priority to take whatever action I needed if I thought my approach speed warranted drastic correction. On joining the circuit, and judging speed by experience alone, I did my pre-landing vital actions, lowered the wheels and, as there was no undue noise to indicate that I was going too fast, lowered the flaps, but left the air brakes in. My aim was to land a little fast rather than stall on finals. Ahead of me, by the runway threshold was a fire engine and ambulance – waiting for me – a lovely thought. I did land fast, but without any bother.

That hour-long experience was better than any instrument rating or final handling test. I had proved something to myself if not to anyone else.

From a flying point of view I was now regarded as a capable jet pilot and was qualified also to carry out a daily inspection on Vampires Marks 5 and 9. Such would be necessary if ever I had to land away and stay overnight.

The next few days involved waiting for ground school exam results. No-one, of those of us who had started the course and who had got to this stage, failed. There had, however, been several students chopped earlier on, either through being unable to cope with high altitude or having failed a progress test.

During this slack period, while we were waiting for our next postings, we happened to be sitting outside our Flight hut enjoying the sunshine when word came on the grapevine that a Vampire was in trouble. The pilot had joined the circuit to land but only two undercarriage legs had come down; one of the main legs stayed up. He flew past the Tower for visual inspections and advice two or three times. He then went away to pull some high 'G' to see if that would work. It didn't. Then, with fuel getting low, he elected to retract the two legs that were down and flew past the Tower again to make sure they were actually up. Going round again, this time to land, on finals he cut his engine and landed gently on his belly on the grass and slithered to a halt. Surprisingly little damage was done to the aircraft, save from some scuffing on the underside. The wings had stayed level and the flaps weren't damaged. It was said that it would be flying again within a week. Had a landing been attempted with only two wheels down it would almost certainly have ground looped, maybe several times and even broken up and been a write-off, and the pilot would probably have been injured, or worse.

I should add that, to bail out of a single-seat Vampire, one was supposed to roll it inverted, jettison the canopy, undo one's seat straps, and drop out. It was said that to attempt to climb out of the cockpit with the aircraft upright, the chances of being cut in two by the tail plane were far too high to be acceptable. Fortunately I never had to do either, although it came close once or twice. I fitted into the 22" wide cockpit very snugly, as if wearing the aircraft on my back, and I intended to keep it that way.

On July 9th I flew in a Vampire T11 with Master Pilot Culverwell specifically on an aircraft familiarisation exercise. We all had such flights. They were designed properly to familiarise us with the type as it was unlikely that we would fly Meteors again and future dual flying would almost certainly be in T11s. It was my last flight from Merryfield.

The instrument panel of a Vampire FB5.

Our posting notices came through and we discovered, much to our dismay, that there would be no end of course leave. My room-mate, John Smith, was particularly disappointed as he had been looking forward to sharing a few days with his new wife. In fact, we were posted en-bloc to the Operational Conversion Unit at RAF Pembrey in South Wales. A group Travel Warrant was issued and those of us who had successfully passed the course left Merryfield to travel by train to South Wales on the morning of Sunday July 12th. We took bottles of beer with us for sustenance.

9. Learning To Fight

WE DIDN'T CONSUME OUR bottles of beer until late on the journey to Pembrey. We had changed trains at Bristol and had to change again at Llanelli. By this time the bottles were an embarrassment because the whole of Wales was 'dry' on Sundays. For uniformed Officers to be seen with beer was not acceptable. At Llanelli station, while we were waiting for a local train to Burry Port where RAF transport would meet us, we got chatting to a Welsh postman who was waiting in his van for mails to arrive. One of us offered him a beer and he asked if we each had bottles, which we had. He opened the back of his GPO van and bundled us in. We drank up. When we had finished and he unlocked the doors there were some raised eyebrows from bystanders watching as we all piled out into the station concourse. The kindly postman disposed of the empties for us.

RAF Pembrey had been closed down since the war. Not long before we arrived it had been re-opened as No.233 Operational Conversion Unit. The aircraft were Vampire 5s, with some T11s. The purpose of the course was to teach us aerial tactics and the use of armaments. The Station CO was Group Captain Beresford.

On arrival we joined some of the ex Kirton-in-Lindsey students who had been posted to Canada, the USA, and Rhodesia for pilot training and who were now joining the same course. Those who had been trained in Canada and the USA had picked up American accents and terminology. On the first day of the course they were told that aircraft weren't 'ships' and, in no uncertain manner, that they were expected to use the Queen's English henceforth. These same people soon found difficulty navigating in the UK because there was too much ground detail for them when compared with the vast open spaces over which they had been flying. They had been used to almost continuous blue skies, so the weather over the UK was to cause them trouble too.

Our accommodation was sub-standard. The buildings were wooden huts and only just habitable. We had individual rooms but there was a tendency for the roofs to leak in rainy weather. I, for one, had to leave my mackintosh over my bed to keep it dry, rather than to wear it in wet weather. There were communal latrine blocks in a very poor state. Not all the wash-basins had taps or plugs and many of the toilet seats were loose or needed repair. We also seemed to be living among personnel of ill-defined rank who dwelt in scruffy caravans. There was a shortage of water and bathing was forbidden. There were no showers that I can remember so we had to have strip-down washes in those windowless latrines or swim in the sea to keep clean. Food in the Mess was poor and often amounted to mince as a main course, and Sunday lunches, if we were lucky, were nothing more than scotch eggs. Discipline was lax, as befitted the run-down ambience of the place. The end of the course couldn't come soon enough for any of us. We weren't sorry it was to be of just less than 8 weeks duration.

The hangars were as shabby as the crew rooms; the training class-rooms were little better, but at least they didn't leak.

My first flight, on July 16th, was dual in a T11 and Lt. Rouse, RN, was my instructor. He showed me the area, the airfield features, gunnery ranges, and danger areas. There were two artillery ranges to keep clear of, one by Pendine sands, and the other at Watchet on the Somerset coast of the Bristol Channel.

We started ground school. Our instructors explained aerial tactics, gunnery, tail chases, the types and purposes of battle formations (as opposed to close formation), keeping a good look-out (we would be liable to be 'bounced' at any time).[1] The use of the sun and cloud, tech-niques for low flying and tactical approaches to targets, aircraft and army vehicle recognition, the use of camouflage, and much else which we needed to know to be able to use our machines both aggressively and defensively. This was all to be put into practice in the air.

Major Mercer was the ALO and was responsible for the military aspect of our training.[2] He had a lazy, evil-smelling, pet spaniel which accompanied him everywhere. It was a most objectionable creature

---

1   Bounced: To be the target of a mock (or real) attack by another aircraft.
2   ALO = Army Liaison Officer.

when it was wet. It spent much of its time lying down and its master was wont to slide it across the floor out of the way with his foot.

My second flight, five days after the first, was solo and was primarily a Sector Recce lasting 55 minutes.[3] The same day I flew twice more: solo aerobatics for 40 minutes, all the while keeping an eye open for any other aircraft which might 'attack' me. The third flight was to be a first, loose, battle formation practice but was aborted after just 15 minutes in the air. This day was the first of many on which I was to suffer neck-ache with having to swivel my head round so much and so often in order to keep a vigilant look-out.

Low flying, in the Exmoor low flying area, was practised both alone and in line astern battle formation. It was usual to do a formation take-off and drop into line astern low level battle formation before we had even climbed to 500 feet. Our leader, always an instructor, would typically turn south and drop to sea-level when we would wave-hop towards the Somerset coast. The leader's down-wash was often visible as ripples as we flew over the water. On approaching the coastal cliffs we would climb over them to continue our exercise. We made use of surface features as cover on approaching for mock attacks on 'chance' targets announced by our leader over the R/T. The order "Not below 250 feet" was, frankly, not ignored but forgotten. These flights were darned hard work and showed us what to expect if ever we were to become involved in enemy interdiction work.[4]

One such flight nearly ended in disaster. We crossed the Bristol Channel very low and, as a formation, left it late to pull up over the Somerset cliffs. There was a down-draught which caught the four of us. The leader shouted, "Pull up" over the R/T. Two of our number flew through the bracken but didn't hit anything solid. The R/T was definitely non-standard for a moment or two. The sortie was tempo-rarily abandoned while we composed ourselves before carrying on. At debriefing we were told never to try flying lower than that!

I usually flew two or three sorties on each flying day on the course.[5] Most flights had an element of battle formation flying and tactics at various altitudes from low level to over 40,000 feet. In this way we

---

3   A reconnaissance flight over the immediate area around base.

4   Interdiction = taking out bridges, interfering with enemy supply columns and trains, tank-busting, etc.

5   None of us flew every day.

could discover for ourselves and adjust to the change of handling characteristics with altitude.

There was the usual IF check for each of us and then we moved on to tail chases. I had two IF flights 'under the amber' in a T11. Why I had two, and the others mostly only one, I have no idea, especially when I told of my IF flight without an ASI at Merryfield. Maybe no-one believed me!

It was usual to fly as a pair for a tail chase, with an instructor leading while I, as a student, would try to stay on his tail during which time he would be doing anything in the book (and often not in it) to shake me off. On one such flight I caught his slipstream when close astern and flicked over on to my back to start an incipient inverted spin. I don't know how I recovered, but recover I did. There was no let-up because of this. The instructor was on my tail now and I had to try and shake him off. That was another neck-ache day!

During a similar sortie two Vampires touched in mid-air, damaging each, but not sufficiently to prevent them landing safely, if a little fast, because of wing damage. Both pilots were clearly shaken. Both had to fly again within the hour so as not to lose their nerve.

Wednesday and weekend afternoons saw most of us walk across the airfield, through the coastal sand dunes and down on to the beach. There we would strip off and do our best to bath ourselves in the very shallow water. Unless we waded a long way out swimming was impossible. We soon learned that trying to use domestic soap in salt water was a total failure. Many of us used PT shorts instead of swimming trunks. These were almost as bad a failure. When wet they were heavy and the elastic wasn't strong enough to keep them up. Skinny-dipping, provided there were no females about, became almost normal. Thus we kept ourselves reasonably clean, even if we did have sand in our socks.

One of the Flight Commanders who lived with us in the Mess was so appalled at the food that he decided to augment the rations by fishing. We all realised that when in the water we would sometimes put our feet on flatfish lying on the bottom. Without seeking permission he, and one or two others, appropriated some tennis nets and some staves from we knew not where. They made good fishing nets with the staves threaded through and tied to them at intervals. The technique was, with a man to each stave, to walk 25 yards at right angles to the shore keeping the bottom of the net hard against the sea bed, and then to swing round to form a bag and drag any fish towards the beach where we could catch and dispatch them. It worked well. Most fish were small (we called them dabs because we didn't know what they were) but they augmented our dinner menus.

On one Saturday during the course we became aware that the Orderly Officer, an aircrew member of the permanent staff, had been drinking heavily in the bar, something no Orderly Officer should ever do. Stupidly, someone challenged him to the effect that he wasn't very good at aerobatics. An argument followed and, without further ado, the said Orderly Officer, full of alcoholic ambition, walked to Station Flight and ordered them to prepare a Vampire for take-off.[6] Orders are orders, so he was obeyed, but with some reservation. A parachute was placed in the cockpit. In the meantime the word had spread around as to what was happening and a few spectators gathered on the edge of the hard-standing. Without helmet, any flying clothing, or Mae West, this Officer climbed aboard, started the engine, taxied to the nearest runway, and took-off. None of us who were watching had ever witnessed so impressive a display of flying and aerobatics at low level before – and I dare say, since. After about 15 minutes the plane landed perfectly and taxied back to Station Flight, shut down, and that was all. The pilot did not open the canopy and could be seen slumped over the controls. The ground crew ran out and got him out of the cockpit whereupon he collapsed, dead-drunk, on the concrete apron. The Duty Officer, who had by now been summoned, placed him under close arrest and, with an escort, he was taken to Sick Quarters. Nothing more was heard by us as to the outcome of this escapade but some very serious charges would have been laid against that weekend 'Orderly Officer'. None of us saw him again and the matter was never officially discussed.

There was an AOC's inspection during our stay. There were no special preparations made in advance because, it was said, Group Captain Beresford wanted his Station to be seen as a working Station doing a job rather than all bulled-up for a special inspection. From what we heard the AOC was less than pleased and even told our Station Commander that he needed a haircut! Another inspection was scheduled at a later date when it was expected that RAF Pembrey would be 'up to standard'.

---

6   Station Flight is usually on standby at most duty flying Stations in readiness to receive airctaft in distress or possible visiting aircraft. It is independent of the flying Squadrons.

The middle part of the course was devoted to the use of our gyro gun-sights and the ranging and tracking of target aircraft with them. The technique of making quarter attacks on aircraft was much practised and, at the same time, we started taking ciné film through our camera guns for later analysis. Initially these sorties were Vampire on Vampire but they soon became Vampire on a towed target drogue.

The ciné films were closely analysed and faults were obvious when they were screened. This way we developed our methods and were advised how to make improvements. It was effectively target practice without firing a shot. None of us found this aspect of our training easy but it was essential if we were to become competent fighter pilots. This, after all, was what all our flying training was for.

We were shown real wartime ciné films and these were analysed for us.[7] It was valuable to be able to make comparisons. Some attacks had been fly-throughs where an enemy aircraft had flown across the path of a fighter. When these were analysed it was shown that, taking into account the rate of fire of the fighter's guns, the speed of crossing, range, and attitude of the crossing aircraft, it was possible to fly through a stream of bullets without being hit. Such bursts of fire, although understandable in the heat of battle, were largely a waste of ammunition.

The ciné film we took of our attacks on the flag (as we called a towed target drogue) were checked very carefully lest any of us tended to come in from too far astern or kept 'firing' long enough to endanger the towing aircraft. When adjudged safe we were taken up in a T11 for a dual check to make sure that we were doing all the right things. Then, and only then, were we allowed to fire live ammunition.

The method of scoring when live-firing was to have the nose of the ammunition of one's aircraft dipped in a sticky dye thus facilitating the identification of which aircraft had hit the flag. The colours used were usually red, green, blue, and plain. As a bullet passed through the material of the drogue some dye was wiped off round the bullet hole, thus the number of hits of a particular aircraft could quickly be counted by the crew retrieving the flag in the drop zone. There were thus four live-firing sorties to each drogue-towing sortie. We were allocated a specific 'time on flag' in which to make our attacks. The pilot of the towing aircraft controlled who was firing and for how long. Scoring

---

7   Many of these same films are nowadays seen in war documentaries on television.

was measured as the number of hits expressed as a percentage of the number of rounds fired.

Having been briefed yet again as to the safety aspects of flying an armed aircraft I found myself sitting in the cockpit of Vampire 'N' November waiting to taxi out to take-off for my first live-firing sortie. As was normal for such sorties only two of my four 20mm cannon were loaded. I climbed to my briefed height and stood off from the firing range until called in by the tug pilot. I made my first attack and, as many times before, pressed the firing tit, but this time was greeted not with silence but with the thug – thug – thug – thug as both cannon discharged their rounds towards the flag. It was a sound I didn't expect. The sound of guns firing from one's aircraft was entirely different to the noise one heard from the ground. Momentarily distracted by this I narrowly missed flying into the flag and pulled round for another attack. I forget how many attacks I made that sortie but my score was 4.34%, a low average.

During one flight, after firing at the flag, I became aware of some resistance when pushing on the stick to descend whilst setting up another attack. It had a crunchy feel and then freed off. On glancing between my knees I found that a multi-pin plug on the armaments panel below the main instrument panel had come adrift (probably with vibration) and, having caused the resistance to movement, had broken. There was smoke and a tongue of yellow flame rising from it. I simultaneously aborted the attack and sorted the matter out with my gloved hands. Satisfied with the situation, I continued with my sortie. I was told, afterwards, that I should have landed at once.

My scores on live-firing flights varied between missing the flag altogether, although I disputed that, and a reasonably high 13.2%. I flew eight live-firing sorties on the course. The average score for all of us was something like 5 or 6%.

If these scores seem low it must be remembered that we were only firing with half our armament on a target much smaller than any aircraft and could not close in to line astern for a 'kill'.

By now instances of neckache had disappeared. I had become able, with no difficulty, while strapped firmly in the cockpit, to see either tail fin – and just beyond – of my own aircraft. That is: with shoulders firmly facing forwards, I could see directly behind me – essential for the survival of any pilot in a dogfight.

We received instruction on the firing of rockets and on bombing, but we had neither simulated nor live practice with these munitions, neither did we receive any training or information to do with radar controlled interceptions.

I passed the course and by now had, in all, a total of 55 hours, 40 minutes on Vampires Mks 5 & 9, and 7 hours 5 minutes dual on Meteor T7s and Vampire T11s. Total flying hours on all types at this stage of my career, which was effectively the end of formal flying training, amounted to 297 hours and 30 minutes, plus a small amount of passenger flying.

During the last days of the course we were told that we would all be posted somewhere within the European theatre. Had we been posted farther afield we may have needed to buy tropical kit and would have been told. We were, however, not given our precise postings; they would be notified to us at home during the (hopefully) three weeks embarkation leave we were now about to enjoy. I say hopefully because I was warned that, as a qualified (but obviously inexperienced) fighter pilot, I could be called earlier to any posting and so had to be ready to leave home at virtually any time.

I was not sorry to leave Pembrey and its hardships but, as I was soon to learn, my training was far from over.

Part 2

AD ARMA PARATI
(ET CETERA)

10. In Transit, Not So Gloria

D URING MY END OF training leave which, in effect, also turned out to be embarkation leave, I received notice that I was to report to No.93 Squadron based at RAF Jever in Germany. I was sent a First Class Travel Warrant and instructions to report to the Rail Traffic Officer (RTO) at London's Liverpool Street station early in the evening of Saturday the 19th of September, 1953.[1] Some very rapid geographical research work followed to discover where Jever was. I eventually found it north of Oldenburg and close to Wilhelmshaven, not far from the North German coast.

At Liverpool Street station I met a few others of the Pembrey course and compared notes as to where we were being posted. Only two of us were going to Jever, 'Danny' Daniels and myself, but Danny was going to No.4 Squadron. I saw John Smith and found he was going to RAF Fassberg. There were only two or three more and they were going to other 2nd Allied Tactical Air Force Squadrons in Germany. None of us knew about anyone else from our course.

Danny and I were told to take our seats in a specific carriage on a troop-train already standing at one of the platforms and, thereafter, to show our posting notices to whomsoever in authority asked to see them. We were assured that that way we would arrive at Jever next day.

I was carrying a kit bag full of flying clothing and whatever else I could cram into it, as well as two suitcases and a greatcoat. Danny was similarly loaded. We were hot, not helped by our sense of uncertainty and physical effort, yet found the best way to carry our heavy coats was to wear them. The platform was full of RAF and Army personnel, some wandering on their own, others being marched about in Flights

---

1   My official arrival at Jever is recorded as being on September 21st, a Monday. The journey there from home was spread across two days.

or Platoons, and all appeared to be carrying heavy kit. Some carried weapons. Danny and I, being Officers, sought and found the assistance of a porter with a trolley and thus were helped to our allotted seats.

From our carriage window we could see the platform slowly clearing as all boarded the train. We found, by asking rather shyly, that we were bound for Harwich where we would board a troop-ship for the overnight journey to the Hook of Holland. There we would board troop-trains to take us close to our destinations. We were advised unofficially to 'follow the crowd' and keep our eyes open for anything saying Jever. Sound advice, as it turned out.

On arrival at Harwich, Parkeston Quay, we Officers tumbled out with our kit and made our way to the Officers Transit Mess. No one gave us any directions, we just followed the crowd. The Transit Mess was nothing more than a comfortably furnished waiting-room with a small bar-cum-canteen for snacks, and a large illuminated aquarium full of idle-looking fish. Those fish knew more about what they had to do than did we at that stage. The Mess was full of Officers of up to Field Rank, and some had their nervous wives and fractious children with them.[2] It was not a restful place.

Suddenly the Tannoy announced that we were being called forward to board the ship. I caught a glimpse of the name 'Empire Parkeston' just visible on its grey bow. I also noticed that it had two dissimilar funnels and looked old and battered.

Struggling with our luggage we were directed down alleys and companionways to our bunks in a large area filled with berths, three high and with little space for kit, undressing, or much else. Not only were there Junior Officers in there but what appeared to be some other ranks as well. The shipboard Tannoy kept blurting out instructions of one sort or another just to add a certain piquancy to the already existing hubbub. Emergency actions were relayed to us but I don't think much notice was taken of them.

Having organised myself and my belongings, and taking a careful note of where I had to find my way back to, I decided to explore my surroundings, find the latrines and, if possible, get myself a warm drink. I seemed to be greeted with "No Sir, you can't go that way" more often than not. In the latrines were rows of wash-basins, urinal bowls and

---

2 Field Rank: RAF Squadron Leader or Army Major and above.

cubicles with half doors on them. I was going to have to be hyper-organised in the morning so as to get washed and shaved, etc. I found a small NAAFI canteen and bought a drink and a sandwich. After the struggle with my baggage I was ready for a snack even though I had eaten earlier before arriving at Liverpool Street station.

The ship's engines started at about the same time that personnel in my 'cabin' were readying themselves for bed. The Tannoy told us what time Reveille would be and then remained silent for the night. But there was no silence: just about everything that could rattle rattled in synchrony with the throb of the engines, doors, pieces of kit, bunk frames, the lot. It was not a peaceful night, made worse by the odd character who made a dash to the latrines to be seasick. I slept with my uniform and underclothes spread across my blanket. It was the best place for them and I was warmer that way because there was a punkah-louvre blowing cold air in my direction. I also sorted out the minimum of 'small kit' in readiness for the inevitable scrimmage in the morning.

My father had given me a wrist watch for my 18th birthday. It had a luminous dial. I seldom took it off except to wash or bathe and that night it proved invaluable. On checking it I was able to rise and perform my ablutions before Reveille was sounded and a stern voice blurted out the order "Get up. Get washed. Get shaved. Get dressed," – an announcement that was greeted with much cursing.

In due turn we were called ashore at the Hook of Holland, a short distance along the quay from where the civilian steamers arrived, and close to a station full of waiting trains. Danny Daniels and I were directed to the 'Blue' train which would take us near to Jever. All the trains were colour-coded according to their ultimate destinations. Our 'Blue' train was making for Oldenburg and beyond.

Continental carriages are wider and more comfortable than those in the UK. Danny and I found our seats and stowed our kit as best we could. We were then called forward to the dining-car for breakfast. Our knowledge of equivalent ranks was put to the test because some of the names of ranks we had been taught were different from those we heard being used. We had to watch our 'Ps and Qs'. Our train moved off as we were returning to our seats.

Our journey took us through Rotterdam and Arnheim. I was surprised how neat and clean the Dutch towns and houses looked. The countryside was flat all the way across Holland, save for some very low sandy hills near Arnheim. We crossed the German border near Arsbeck. Once in Germany we could see the remains of wartime devastation everywhere, particularly along the railway line where sidings and marshalling yards had been bombed and not repaired. München-Gladbach heralded the beginning of the dismal and dirty, partly derelict, Ruhr district. We passed through Düsseldorf and Wuppertal where the old Schwebebahn (overhead suspended monorail train) dangled in its precarious way over and along the river. Hamm marshalling yards, or what was left of them, followed. Then we struck north across the flat lands again to stop at Münster and Osnabrück after which we found ourselves on single track. Another stop was made at Ahlhorn where we saw RAF Meteor NFIIs flying overhead. Late in the afternoon we drew in to Oldenburg where we alighted. The train left us behind, almost alone on the platform, to continue its journey.

Danny and I found a German porter (Gepäckträger) who took us to the RTO's office. There we checked in and were told to catch the next train to Wilhelmshaven and to get off at a place called Sande where RAF transport would meet us and take us to Jever. In the meantime we lost our porter. Danny found another but couldn't speak German and started shouting at him until I came along and, using schoolboy German, made myself understood. Our baggage was duly taken to the appropriate track (Gleis) where we settled to wait.[3] The station was quiet but there were obvious signs of aerial activity about even though it was Sunday afternoon. Vampires in low level battle formation kept sweeping low over the town at frequent intervals. Our future Squadron friends were so near yet so far away!

The short, very old-fashioned, train to Wilhelmshaven drew in and we climbed aboard. The journey to Sande didn't take all that long. We had to keep our eyes open for the station signs because we didn't know how far it was or how many stops to expect. The concourse of Sande Bahnhof (station) reeked of stale cigar smoke. There was an inviting looking Imbiss-Stube (station buffet-restaurant) but we had no local currency so couldn't buy a drink while we were waiting. We had been served a good lunch on the train but now it was well past teatime and we were thirsty.

---

3   The tracks are numbered in Germany, not the platforms.

A Thorneycroft 3-ton truck fitted with seats in the back under its canvas tilt drew up and we climbed aboard. The roads to Jever were rough and mostly laid in brick, so our journey was unpleasant. We checked in at the Jever Guardroom and then were driven to the Officers Mess. It was a large building, ex-Luftwaffe, but with recent extensions. We entered and were greeted by tall, blonde Hildegard, the Mess receptionist. We Warned In, were allocated our rooms and checked the meal times.

We had arrived, and the journey had taken the better part of 30 hours. Curiously, there was hardly anyone about, although that matter was shortly to be explained.

The gate and Guardroom (left) at RAF Jever on an afternoon in the depths of winter. One passed along the main road by the married quarters on the right before arriving at this gate. Ahead, in the far distance across the airfield, can just be seen the corner of No.4 Squadron's hangar.

On entering the gate and turning left one came to the Officers Mess. On turning right just inside the gate were the Malcolm Club, Church of England Chapel, PSI shop, the MT Section, MTSS, and Station Fire Section. This road then became the ring road past the GSO barracks and ended just after the aforementioned hangar at the firing harmonisation butts and pig farm.

Ahead from this gate, on the left before getting to the airfield, were Station Headquarters, the Education Section building and, lastly, just across the railway siding, the Equipment Section building. Technical Wing buildings lay to the right, but other facilities and barrack blocks lay mostly to the left of this road.

The Pekol bus service into Jever town had its terminus behind the camera position.

11. "Get Settled In"

M Y ROOM WAS ON the first floor of a recently built, two storey, ochre-rendered block, No.163, situated a short walk away beyond the tennis courts and lawns from the back of the main Mess building.

On entering I set down my cases and kit bag, stripped off my greatcoat, and took stock. I couldn't see any other buildings from my window because of the dense pine forest in which almost the entire Jever domestic site was built.

My 11' x 15' room, one of 12 on each floor, was at the rear of the block and looked out on to the pine trees about 5 yards away at most. There was a bed, bedside cabinet, a patterned bedside mat, bookcase, writing-table, chest of drawers, and a wardrobe. There was also a wash-basin, with hot and cold taps and a mirror above, on the left just inside the door. The walls were painted an off-white shade but were otherwise bare. Pretty curtains and a similar valance dressed the double framed, double-glazed, window. The outer frame opened outwards and the inner, inwards; a feature which foretold of hard winters. It was inviting enough, and was to be my home for the next two and a half years. Toilets and bathrooms were in the centre-rear of the block on each floor, adjacent to the batwomen's ironing rooms. All the floors were highly polished and brown in colour.[1]

The duty batwoman that evening was Frau Pinnau who, as it happened, was to be my own batwoman and who also tended to the needs of three or four other Officers. She spoke only broken English and was of helpful disposition.

---

1   I must add that my room was big enough for a second bed and, on occasion, during major NATO exercises another bed was moved in so as to accommodate another Officer for the period of his stay. This happened infrequently.

My first priority was to wash and freshen myself up ready for dinner. Serious unpacking would follow later in the evening in preparation for whatever would befall me the next day, Monday.

One of the rooms very similar to mine in Block 163.

Having undone my cases and hung up my uniforms, suits, and trousers, I made my way back to the Mess, taking my time. There was still no-one about outside which I thought strange although there was obvious activity from the airfield. As I walked past the old Luftwaffe Officers' accommodation blocks each side of the Mess gardens I could see that they had pergolas hung with wisteria and other vines. They were fine elegant buildings in red brick and with a raised brick patio along each garden frontage. They looked well against the backdrop of dark green pine trees. The rear of the Mess building also had a wide terrace overlooking the garden, lawn, and tennis courts. I had never seen anything of this standard at any UK camp. Everything was neat and tidy, well kept, and comfortable to the eye. There were five Officers blocks in all. Only the two ex-Luftwaffe blocks and the Mess were in sight of each other.

On going round to the front of the Mess I was greeted by Hildegard who pointed out the dining-room, anteroom and bar. She gave me my bar book number via which all purchases would be booked to my account, and be paid for by the 10th of each month as was usual in Officers Messes throughout the RAF.

I entered the anteroom, a cavernous room with two large chandeliers hanging from its lofty ceiling, a minstrel gallery at one end, and paintings hung on the walls which were, themselves, decorated with relief plasterwork panels with features in an almost baroque style. The comfortable furniture, easy chairs and settees, had chintz covers which echoed the pattern on the curtains. That part of the room, separated from the main space by several columns, overlooked the rear garden and had a carpet on the floor. This apparently empty room, as far as I then knew, was the home of the pilots of two flying Squadrons, and the Officers of the Station Administration and Technical Wings.

As I was standing, taking all this in, a brother Officer entered and asked my name. I told him and he introduced himself as Johnny MacKnish, a Pilot Officer of 93 Squadron, the Squadron I was about to join. He quickly explained to me that there was a huge 2ATAF and BAOR exercise in progress and that was the reason no-one was about.[2] Everyone was in tents dispersed in the forest, and the Station for the time being was on a war footing. Johnny himself had been detailed to look out for me and other newcomers to the Squadron, and to welcome us and show us round and help us settle in. I was the first of the newcomers.

Johnny took me to the wood-block floored dining-room and showed me which table was normally used by 93 Squadron, and to avoid that used entirely by members of 4 Squadron. Although those from 93 didn't necessarily stick to the one table, those from No.4 almost always kept to theirs. There were more tables laid, each for from four to twelve persons, with seating in comfortable dining chairs. Windows were down each of two opposite sides of the room, making its lofty volume light and airy. A third wall was hung with long dark-blue curtains as a dressing. I was

---

2 2ATAF = 2nd Allied Tactical Air Force. BAOR: British Army of the Rhine. I think the exercise was code-named 'Grand Repulse'.

too late for tea, usually taken in the anteroom, but dinner would be served soon.

We went back into the anteroom and I met some other Officers who had just entered. On talking to them I discovered that the Station, since the end of the war, had been used as a displaced persons accommodation centre but some two years ago had been refurbished and extended before being taken over by the Royal Air Force. I also found that both Squadrons were flying Vampires so, to my relief, I didn't have to convert on to a different aircraft type. Other 'shop' talk was avoided as was the convention when off-duty in the Mess.

I went to dinner and was served by German waiters and waitresses. The food was to a high standard, better than most I had enjoyed in the UK. Afterwards I made my way to the bar which was accessed either directly from the hall or through folding doors under the minstrel gallery in the anteroom. Wolfgang and Herbert were the bar stewards. While stood chatting over glasses of Coca-Cola the Station Commander, Group Captain Powel-Sheddon, wartime Battle of Britain fighter ace, came in. He saw that I was a stranger and walked across to me and asked who I was. When I said my name was Senar he chuckled and stammered out "Well, from now on I'll call you 'Pod'." From then on it was by that soubriquet that I was to be known for the rest of my RAF career![3]

After a polite pause I withdrew from the bar and returned to my room to finish unpacking, set my alarm clock, and retire for the night.

I slept only fitfully at first, in spite of being tired after my travels, because of the almost continuous night flying activity. At one stage I looked out of my window to see, in what little visible sky there was, searchlight beams scanning the cloud base. There was also the noise of other occupants coming into the block at various times in the night.

Next morning, ongoing to breakfast, I met Johnny MacKnish again. He introduced me briefly to some other members of the Squadron whose names I had difficulty remembering. Then it was down to work. As when one is posted to any new Station I had to go through the

---

3   Group Captain Powel-Sheddon had a very bad stammer and, as a result was known to many (behind his back) as 'Fo-Fo'. Another possible reason for this was that his full names were George ffolliot Powel-Sheddon and his unusual middle name may have been the prompt. He was also known conversationally as either 'The Groupie' or 'The CO'. He died in November 1994. Squadron COs were usually known as Squadron 'Bosses'.

'Arrival' procedure. This involved my being given a small Arrival Card which had to be signed by all the departments with which I would be expected routinely to come into contact during my stay. 'Arriving' meant much walking: Equipment Section, Personnel, and Accounts were the main ones, but with the addition of maybe a dozen more, and the various offices being so far apart on a Station as big as Jever, it took me well over half a day to nearly complete. It was one way of finding my way around and learning the shortest route on foot along the brick paved roads and paths through the trees between buildings. I still had to gain signatures from my Squadron which was based in a hangar on the opposite side of the airfield to the domestic site. As well as personnel in RAF uniform there were others in Wehrmacht style bottle-green uniforms. These were GSO members. The GSO, or German Service Organisation, was made up entirely of German personnel employed by the RAF on maintenance, driving, cleaning, vehicle maintenance, gardening, and other support duties. They lived in a barracks in a remote corner of the camp. Most of these men had become totally separated from, or lost, their families owing to the ravages of war and were glad of this sort of employment.

Getting from one side of the airfield to the other involved a journey of about a mile and a half to go clear round the end of the 2000 yard 29-11 runway. It was usual to either hitch a lift on a service vehicle or to use the hourly 3-ton truck bus service run by the Duty Squadron's MT Section.[4]

I hitched a lift and, instead of being taken to the Squadron hangar, was driven into the forest where the Squadron was occupying a tented camp for the duration of the exercise. I was introduced to 93 Squadron Boss, Sqn.Ldr. 'Bob' Allen, who asked me questions about my RAF and civilian background, allocated me to 'B' Flight, introduced me to Flt. Lt. Keith Pearch, 'B' Flight Commander, and signed my arrival card. I also found that my new nickname 'Pod' had preceded me! I stayed for a while chatting to other Squadron pilots, including Sgt. 'Dickie' Night, Flt.Sgt. 'Shrubby' Shrubsole, Flt.Sgt. Telfer and his Alsatian dog, Plt. Off. 'Bernie' Revnell (nephew of Ethel Revnell the stage comedienne), 'Al' Ramsay, 'Sandy' Sanderson (son of a Padre in Bulawayo, Rhodesia),

---

4   MT = Mechanical Transport. In a Tactical Air Force each squadron had its own MT Section so as to be capable of packing up its equipment and moving it to another operational site with maximum efficiency in the least time.

'Black' Hannah, 'Tommy' Balfour, and others. I was to meet the Crew Chiefs, Flt.Sgts. Blair and O'Neil and their maintenance teams later.

I was excused duty until the exercise was over and was told to find my way around, hand in my Arrival Card, and familiarise myself with the layout of the Station and its facilities, get to know as many people as possible and "Get settled in".

It was not long before I discovered that in addition to the two flying Squadrons there were also an RAF Regiment 'rock ape' Wing comprising LAA and searchlight Squadron and an armoured car Squadron, also stationed at Jever.[5] It was the first time I had come across any such personnel. Clearly I was part of a very large RAF Unit with a total, all ranks head count, of well over a thousand.

Although not immediately working with my Squadron, I had arrived, was available, and had been accepted.

Officers block 163. My home. My room was at the back, opposite the next to end upstairs window on the right. The road led to the third modern, but then little used, Officers block at the back of the Mess.

---

5   LAA = Light Ack-Ack. Armed with 50mm Bofors anti-aircraft guns and searchlights.

12. Starting Work

93 SQUADRON'S MOTTO WAS "Ad Arma Parati" which, when translated, means 'Prepared for War'. How true. As a new sprog pilot with the Squadron I was aware that I could have to put my training into practice – for real.

It is often said that when one thinks one has finished training that's when the real learning begins. And so it was for me. I was in a new environment, in a strange country, and with professionals in a potential war situation. Russia and its Eastern Bloc were a recognised and serious threat to the Western world. Each was always testing the other's defences and looking for weaknesses. We knew we were not going to attack them, but we were always unsure of Communist intentions and therefore had to be ready immediately to counter any aggression or border incursions from the other side.

The task of 93 Squadron in its primary Ground Attack role was to counter the advance of any potential enemy's ground forces by the use of 20mm cannon fire, rockets, or bombs. Close low level reconnaissance was also a possibility. This, in the jargon of the day, was termed 'interdiction'. The Squadron's secondary role was that of day, high level, interception. In other words, to do as much damage to an attacking air force as possible by intercepting any enemy aircraft and destroying them. The Vampire was ideally suited to the first role but far from adequate for the second. The rate of climb was too slow to be of much use, and the rate of turn at altitude was not tight enough. Nonetheless we had to practise both roles and, strangely, the one practised most often was that of interceptor, for the Squadron's duty was, in its turn with other Squadrons, to maintain a four aircraft Battle Flight at readiness, fully armed up, for virtually immediate scramble when ordered to do so by 2 Group, our higher authority. This was real and serious stuff, and one never knew whether any scramble was for practice or something else. Our job was front line defence. We were supposed to be all-weather capable, but that was very much open to question. To attack a target at night or in extreme meteorological conditions was simply 'not on' and could not be practised.

Settling in took a long time. In addition to obvious things like drawing a parachute from the Parachute Section and maps from the Map Section there was a great deal to familiarise myself with, not only with regard to Station domestic routines, Station Routine Orders, Flying Wing Detail, and Squadron Orders, but also with unfamiliar Squadron routines and methods which I could no way have been taught about or experienced before.

It was seven days after my arrival that I had my first chance to fly. It was a dual, 35 minute, flight in a Meteor Mk 7 with Flt.Lt. Keith Pearch, 'B' Flight Commander (my Flight) as captain to check me out and show me what the local area looked like from the air. The terrain was flat, so flat that it was often said that you had no need to climb above 100 feet to get from the Lincolnshire Wolds to the Urals in Russia. The only hazards would be wireless masts and tall buildings.

That same day, and the next day, the 28th and 29th of September, I took a Vampire up for two more 35 minute flights to further familiarise myself with the area. Obvious landmarks, apart from the coastline and off-shore islands, were the Jade and Ems basins, the Ems-Jade Kanal which links them, the Zwischenaner See, Oldenburg, Emden, and Wilhelmshaven. Further east lay Cuxhaven, the river Weser, Bremerhaven, Bremen, and Hamburg, but that was not our usual area of operation. Railway lines and water features were the most important visual aids to navigation, with the shapes of forests and villages coming a poor second. Diversion airfields were Oldenburg, Ahlhorn, and Gütersloh. There were disused ex-Luftwaffe airfields, the nearest being Wittmundhafen, each of which was dotted with bomb craters and the obvious marks of runway sabotage by the Allied forces. These airfields were of curiosity only and totally unusable.

It was almost a week before I flew again. The weather had clamped in and lectures and training films filled our time, as did sport and time in the gym. More of that later. Battle Flight was on standby only. As I was not yet classed as 'operational' I wasn't involved with that and, as with other new pilots, wouldn't be for some weeks. I next had three flights in one day; a further 50 minute sector recce, then I was tail end Charlie in a low level battle formation and, late in the afternoon, some practice ciné ranging and tracking on other 'target' aircraft. The low flying was of note because, although we were authorised only to fly above, and not to go below, 250 feet above the ground. The order was generally ignored. The formation leader took us at tree-top height and would call and identify a target, at which point we would climb briefly to descend and 'attack' it, then continue this sort of routine throughout the sortie. It was on this, the first of many such sorties, that we swept in low, literally at roof-top height, over an old farmhouse. The jet blast from the lead aircraft damaged the roof. More damage was done by numbers 2 and 3, and, on looking back after I had also passed too close over it, I could see that many roof tiles had been displaced. The cloud base was so low that the sortie involved 10 minutes of low level formation IF. On return to base I mentioned the farm to the leader who snarled "Well, who won the bloody war?" I wasn't sure what to think. It brought home to me the point that, in reality, we were on active service as an occupying power.

The next day there was a similar low level sortie with me at number 4 again. This time we were really low and I had to make a snap decision as to whether to fly over or under some power cables. I went under rather than mushing into them on attempting a rapid pull up.[1] My other sortie of the day was spent more sedately doing ciné work at a more comfortable altitude.

During the next days the Squadron was doing live air-to-ground firing at Meppen Range near the Dutch border. My own flights were more of a training nature, aerobatics, sorties involving getting radio fixes, and practice QGHs.[2]

The weather was generally awful and little flying took place before the end of October. There was none for me. There were other things afoot, instead.

As a Squadron we were due to attend and witness live-firing, bombing, napalm, and rocket attacks at Sennelager Range just north

---

1 A Vampire, with gear up, was less than six feet high and easily slithered through such gaps. The trick was to aim to just miss the ground. The rest took care of itself. I hasten to add that it was not regular practice to do such things. The biggest hazard on such sorties were flocks of birds. A bird strike at almost zero feet could be fatal to the pilot as well as the bird.

2 Radio (not radar) controlled descents.

of Paderborn, over half a day's bus ride away.[3] After rising early in readiness the weather at the range clamped in and the trip was off. Next day, at 06.30, we set off again and got to Sennelager only to find the show was off again. The bus broke down on the way back not far from 2 Group HQ at Sundern near Gütersloh. At Sundern we were able to visit the Operations room and to see the general Group set-up before returning very late to Jever. What amazed me (and I should have known better) was that all facilities were in vehicles which could be disconnected and moved to a new location at short notice. Yes, I was a member of a highly mobile Tactical Air Force. This was further brought home to me on realising that all main routes were given code names clearly marked at frequent intervals by army signage. Ace, Spades, and similar designations were used. They would have been clearly visible to convoy commanders and others in black-out conditions.[4]

The mobility aspect was also brought home to me when the Squadron Boss, Sqn.Ldr. Allen, appointed me as Squadron MTO in addition to my normal duties.[5] I could fly an aircraft but I couldn't drive – legally at any rate – as I had no driving licence. I almost panicked, not knowing what was involved, or what my responsibilities were. A quick word with Johnny MacKnish, now Squadron Adjutant, revealed that there were files in his office which dealt with MT matters. I borrowed them (they were Unclassified) and took them to my room in the Mess where I burned midnight oil trying to educate myself. After the initial shock I chatted around and found that Flight Sergeant 'Chiefy' Blair was able to fill me in a great deal. A trip to the Station MT Section and a meeting with Flt.Lt. Wright, Station MTO, revealed that there were two Land Rovers and a dozen or so Thorneycroft 3-ton trucks on Squadron charge but in store in his garages. He rapidly apprised me of my responsibilities and in no time at all I had signed for a whole convoy of vehicles and their tool kits. Joy of joys – I was responsible for my first Inventory and had a lot more to learn about how to look after it, as well as my own Squadron MT Section and its drivers.

---

3   Sennelager Range on Sennelager Heide (heath) was an old German weapons training area and now used for similar purposes by the NATO occupying forces.

4   Such signs were used during the war at home. These in Germany had a similar familiar significance.

5   MTO = Mechanical Transport Officer.

We did eventually get to Sennelager and witness nearly all that was planned for us. If it did nothing else the events of the day demonstrated to us the firepower we could muster, and its effectiveness, should we be called into action.

Thus ended the foggy, and increasingly cloudy and cold month of October, but there was more: there was sport, a vital part of aircrew fitness routines. I shall tell of that next.

13. Sport And Associated Matters

SUPER-FITNESS CAN BE DETRIMENTAL to the airborne performance of a fighter pilot. Good average fitness is desirable, indeed necessary, for the human body to withstand the stresses, strains, and 'G' forces experienced when doing tight manoeuvres in the air. Another aspect is the need to be fit enough to be able to survive, and hopefully to escape, in the event of coming down in enemy territory.

I never was a lover of participatory sport. I loathed it at school where I was frequently verbally chastised by the PT instructor for what he reckoned was my underperformance. I did, however, manage to wield a good stick at hockey and I quickly discovered that I could exploit this to my personal advantage at Jever.

I found that during my early days with the Squadron there were sessions in the gym for all of us, basketball was played competitively, as were soccer and rugger. Aircrew were not encouraged to participate in boxing contests.

I well remember my first session in the gym. I arrived a little late to find the pilots knocking about with a basketball. As I entered the door the ball came in my direction. On picking it up I aimed for the net and it went cleanly through the hoop. I had never done that before and was quickly nominated for the Squadron team. I have to say that I never did it again and was just as rapidly dropped!

Soccer and rugger were of absolutely no interest to me, but there was hockey. I had to do something, and hockey it would be.

The Station Hockey Team, under the supervision of Flt.Lt. 'Kim' Lee, Station Intelligence Officer, was short of players. I soon found myself having an all-ranks practice game. After several more such games I was picked for the Station Team representing RAF Jever. It was generally accepted, provided one was good enough to stay in the team, that it was a 'good skive' to be able to travel off camp to play away matches.

Events happened quickly. Within two days of being appointed squadron MTO – that's just 31 days after arriving at Jever – I was on my way with the team to play hockey against various Units located as far apart as Holland and Fassberg.[1]

We were officially detached from the Squadron for over a week for our excursion with the hockey team. Johnny MacKnish and I, with George Hickman, Don Exley, Frank Price, all from 93 (no-one was from 4 Squadron or the Regiment) and Kim Lee were the Officers. The rest of the team was made up with other ranks. Our first match was against the Royal Netherlands Air Force at the RNAF Station at Volkel, near Eindhoven. We were guests of the RNAF and stayed two nights in their Officers Mess. We had earlier been warned to expect things to be different to the standard of living in the RAF. On arrival we went to the Mess and were shown our rooms by a solitary Junior Officer who spoke good English in a disinterested sort of way. In each of our small rooms there was a fold-up bed, a wash-basin, a cupboard, and a single chair. Toilet facilities were down a long passage and of a different design to those to which we were accustomed. On looking for the bar, so as to socialise, we found no-one about. Eventually, after a search, we found someone to ask what was going on. It turned out that at weekends almost everyone went home. We were provided with an evening meal of a plate of ham sandwiches and black coffee. That was all. Next morning, for breakfast, we were served dry white bread and apple sauce, with a piece of fruit loaf and more coffee. Lunch was marginally better – we had a boiled egg with dry black bread!

The match itself was unremarkable and played on a wide open sports field with almost no spectators. We lost 2-0.

Now hungry, after going back to the Mess to shower and change, three of us decided to get a taxi to take us into Eindhoven where we went to a café for a snack as it was still too early for a proper evening meal. We spotted a cinema showing, in English, 'The House of Wax'. In we trotted, bought tickets, and joined a queue moving forward into the auditorium down a long passage. It was quite crowded and, on seeing a gap in the crowd, I moved to go into it and promptly hit my nose hard

---

1 RAF Fassberg was the most easterly RAF airfield in the British Zone of Germany.

on what I hadn't realised was a wall of mirrors! I had tears in my eyes when the usherette handed me my 3D specs. It was the first 3D film any of us had seen and, as with most other people, we ducked when objects apparently came out of the screen to hit us.

Following the show we made our way to a cosy little café called the Spinning Wheel. It was run by three delightful ladies who looked after us very well. After a grilled gammon steak followed by dessert and coffee, and after having paid the bill, we stood up from our table to leave when, in so doing, I hit my head on the big bronze ball at the base of a mostly crystal chandelier hanging over our table. The ball was attached to a central rod on which there was a hook from which the whole thing hung. On hitting my head, quite hard, the whole contraption unhooked and crashed to the floor around me, fusing most of the lights in the room at the same time. In spite of the damage and inevitable kerfuffle, the ladies were more concerned as to my well-being than anything else. There were profuse apologies on all sides, and much concern for me from other diners. A taxi was hailed and we returned to Volkel.

Our hockey tour was far from over, for we next went to RAF Wahn for another match. I was blamed for something I didn't do in the Mess at Wahn. It was a mixed Mess. In the evening after dinner I was innocently sitting in the fairly crowded anteroom, minding my own business trying to read a paper when, suddenly, a junior WRAF Officer let out a scream. On looking up, as one does, I saw a blue, wind-up, clockwork mouse making its way towards her from my side of the room. As it got close to her, up went her legs to reveal a pair of yellow and dark-green hooped passion killers! As one can imagine this caused great amusement among the men and a lot of tutting from the females, one of whom, of Senior Rank, accused me of setting the mouse off. It took a while trying to convince her of my innocence and I was rescued from her verbal onslaught only after at least three of the menfolk interrupted and spoke up in my defence. Whoever perpetrated the trick got away with it but lost his mouse.

Whilst whom we played next, or where, is no longer recollected, but records state that we lost 6-0 to RAF Fassberg. I think our final match of this trip was against a Unit in or near Hamburg. My stay there was memorable for different reasons.

We travelled by train through the endlessly flat countryside, with evidence of the recent war all around. At centres of population there was reconstruction work, hard work, being done wherever one looked. On approaching these one first saw forests of tower cranes at building sites, something we did not have back home. Shortly after passing through Harburg and before crossing the Elbe Bridge, which had somehow survived, there, at the trackside, by a group of sidings, were gangs of women cleaning bricks from bomb sites for re-use. It was being done on an industrial scale with great piles of bricks and rubble all around. On entering Hamburg itself signs of the ravages of war were still obvious all the way until we eventually arrived at the Hauptbahnhof where we alighted.

The Officers in the team spent their nights in the Streits Hotel (the Officers Hotel) overlooking the Binnen Alster close to the centre of the city. It was German-run and the beds were notable because one slept on a sheet on a mattress, had a pillow on an uncomfortable firmly-padded wedge at the top of the bed and, for cover, two half-length, feather-filled, thick eiderdowns. Being tall I had the most damnably uncomfortable nights. At my every move the eiderdowns kept moving about and leaving a chilly strip somewhere across my middle.

Looking across the Binnen Alster in 1953. The Streits Hotel is one of the buildings on the right.

The centre of Hamburg had suffered horrendous fire storms in the war but little evidence of that was to be seen. Most buildings had either been rebuilt or replaced and, within obvious constraints, the city was thriving. The trams were running, the S-Bahn and the U-Bahn were fully operational, and the population was reasonably affable towards us.[2]

On one of our evenings Johnny MacKnish and I took the S-Bahn to the St Pauli district to walk along the infamous Reeperbahn and see the sights. The others had a different agenda. It was sleazier than Soho in London. Just about every form of 'entertainment' was there, from brothels (in the Herbert Strasse), night clubs, strip joints, to pavement touts selling (genuinely) filthy post cards. All these, and other outwardly more respectable establishments lined the thoroughfare. We walked round in the crowds, took in the sights, and after a couple of hours we had seen enough, so went back to our hotel. On our return to Jever on the last Saturday in October, our Squadron Archivist, Flt.Lt. Brian Iles, recorded our tour as a 'social success'. I am prepared to let him have the last word.[3]

The following Friday, after the Squadron trip to Sennelager Range, I was off with the hockey team again. We left Jever in the afternoon by train for Hannover where, after a snack in the Salvation Army 'Red Shield' canteen on the platform, we joined the overnight troop-train to travel through the Russian Zone to Berlin.

On the troop-train we were ordered to keep all blinds drawn and to show as few lights as possible. We had couchette accommodation and were able to undress for the night. It seemed strange that we were in our pyjamas in potentially enemy territory. My feeling of personal vulnerability was difficult to suppress. The train stopped several times in the night but we arrived on time in the cold light of the following morning. Transport took us to RAF Gatow where we were to stay for that night (Saturday) before arriving back at Jever late on Monday.

Our match was against the Kings Own Yorkshire Light Infantry at a pitch close by the old Olympic Stadium. The result was a 1-1 draw.

---

2   S-Bahn = Stadtbahn or metro surface railway. The U-Bahn was the underground equivalent.

3   Brian Iles owned his own Miles M18 private aeroplane. It was understood to be the only one of its type. More of that later.

On returning to Gatow we had a meal and then went into 'town' to see what Berlin looked like. There was more obvious war damage than in Hamburg and, on finding little to do, we went into a theatre bar for a relaxed Pils or two. We had to be careful to avoid the East Zone border so did not stray far before returning to Gatow.

Next morning we booked a trip with the Salvation Army for an afternoon bus tour around West Berlin and into the Russian Zone.[4] But before lunch two of us decided to have a walk round the airfield perimeter. Well wrapped up against the distinctly cold weather, we set off. On the far side of the airfield we realised that the perimeter fence, in effect, marked the East-West frontier, on the other side of which was a Russian training area. We heard a tank (a T33) draw up not far away and, being curious, stopped to look at it, watching as its turret swivelled round until its main armament was pointing directly at us. After a pause and some muttered comments between us, we continued our walk as nonchalantly as possible, yet always aware that for quite a distance we were still being tracked. Back in the Officers Mess, we were told "Oh, they usually do that, it keeps them amused!"

Our afternoon bus trip lasted a couple of hours and we had a very good German guide who explained a lot. She had been a nurse during the war and had seen and experienced the horrors of the Russian invasion of her city first hand. Her graphic descriptions of what it was like were reinforced as she pointed out significant landmarks and places of particular activity.

We travelled through the Brandenburg Gate into the Russian Zone, picking up a Russian Commissar on the way. He kept shouting communist slogans at us in broken English in an attempt to disrupt our guide's explanations. We were shown the site of the old Reichs Chancellery and that of Hitler's bunker, both in a wasteland of dereliction. Unter Den Linden had been renamed Stalin Allee and was lined with gaunt, severely four-square, blocks of flats. We could see down the side streets that behind the new buildings was dereliction and shells of buildings in the same state as on the day the city was occupied. Red flags and communist slogans adorned all buildings of significance, and many that were not. We passed what had been a railway station and could see

---

4   The Salvation Army had somehow negotiated the facility to run a sightseeing bus for British servicemen in uniform into the Russian Zone, but only on a Sunday afternoon. We were lucky.

inside its shattered shell the remains of a train that had been caught in an air raid and never touched since.

The supposed highlight of the afternoon was to visit a cemetery dedicated to the fallen of Mother Russia.

There was a long avenue of low, rectangular, engraved monuments. At its end stood representations of the Red Flag made out of (so we were told) red marble stripped from the Reichs Chancellery. At the other end of this avenue was a conical mound surmounted by a circular mausoleum on top of which was a statue of a Russian soldier, child in one arm, and a sword in the other, striking a broken Swastika at his feet. We climbed steps up the mound and into the mausoleum. The mound, it was said, contained a multitude of Russian dead. On entering the building we were shown a representation of the Order of Victory in the ceiling.

In the cemetery were several flights of steps which we climbed. In doing so I noticed some iron grills in the risers at one part and became curious. I whispered to Kim Lee what I had seen. On making our way down, at the significant part, I dropped a handkerchief which we both turned round to pick up and there, behind us, a grill had been slid back to reveal the business end of a sub-machine gun pointing at us. Pretending not to notice, we continued our walk back to the bus, passing several extremely scruffy and visibly dirty Russian soldiers on the way. We said nothing about what we had seen until we were safely in West Germany on our way back to Jever.

The Commissar alighted back at the Brandenburg Gate, but before he did so, I bought a set of post cards as a memento of the afternoon. Some of these photos have survived and are reproduced in Appendix 2.

Back at Gatow, Kim nearly went berserk when he spotted, from the bus, the camp GSO Superintendent. Kim recognised him as Chief Ferret from when he had been a prisoner of war in Stalagluft 3 at Sagan in Poland; we had a job to simmer Kim down. I have no idea what would have happened had the two met face to face.

Our journey to Jever was uneventful. We arrived back as planned on Monday, ready for work the next day.

I must point out at this juncture that all this had taken place, and I had done all these things, before the 9th of December, and before I had completed 10 weeks Squadron service.

I have to add that, as with all RAF Stations, there is an ever-changing population and it wasn't long before better players took our places in the Station Hockey team. I didn't stop playing, but my future matches were of a more local nature involving far less travel.

It was after my return from Berlin that I read on SROs that I had been appointed Officer i/c Tug of War.[5] A brief mention of this to the PFO elicited the information that there was little interest in the sport, and no equipment.[6] I decided to lie low for as long as I could get away with it.

More to my liking was the recent innovation of indoor hockey. It was played in an otherwise empty hangar on the domestic site side of the airfield. The pitch was roughly the size of that for Ice Hockey and with similar goals and board surround. We played using standard (not Indian) hockey sticks and a hard ball instead of a puck. From memory, we played 20 minutes each way, with a team of seven a side. Play was fast and downright bloody dangerous if the ball picked up above knee height. I played with the Squadron Officers' Team on many occasions. There was much inter-Section, inter-Wing, and Squadron rivalry. It was a popular sport and was usually played well, with scores as high as 12 for any one side not being unusual. Most matches were in the evenings, sometimes with two or three being played in one session. When the ball flew the spectators had to take care of themselves and this added excitement to watching the matches.

During my two and a half year tour at Jever I maintained my general fitness by participating in Squadron visits to the gym, playing hockey, and, in the summer season, swimming, and by a great deal of walking. The Station pool was really only a large EWS tank with shelving sides and no shallow end.[7] It was good to have a swim after tea and before dinner on a hot summer's evening.

As for the walking, the Station was so big, and I had no private transport, that walking was an inevitable necessity. Even the Astra Cinema was outside the camp at the outer extremity of the approach road on the fringe of the married quarters, getting on for half a mile from my room.

---

5 SROs = Station Routine Orders.
6 PFO = Physical Fitness Officer.
7 EWS = Emergency Water Supply. Used by the Fire Section in cases of emergency.

As mentioned, other pilots involved themselves with soccer, rugger, basketball, volley ball, tennis (in season), and squash. I tried my hand at squash but, although my reach was good, couldn't control my gangling frame with sufficient finesse to do justice to the game; tried twice and that was enough. Tennis was a no-go area for me because of my tendency to hay fever. Whenever I attempted to play I had to give up because of streaming eyes and sneezing. I think the dust from the hard courts at the back of the Mess had something to do with it.

Having mentioned physical fitness, sport, and my associated experiences, I shall henceforth refer to them again only in passing and in due course. It is time to go back to work.

14. To The End Of 1953

FOLLOWING MY TRIP WITH the Station Hockey Team to Holland and Fassberg, I arrived back at Jever to fly three times on Sunday, November 1st, totalling 2 hours and 10 minutes, including 15 minutes IF. The weather was clamping down with the onset of winter but the usual ranging and tracking exercises were carried out, as was a tail chase following battle formation practice. In increasing cloud, the final sortie of the day involved battle and close formation work.

I did not fly the next day, but the day after, following 40 minutes aerobatics, I was detailed to fly to Gütersloh with some letters from our Station Commander and, for the second time in my life, to deliver a Senior Air Staff Officer's pyjamas back to him after he had forgotten to pack them during a recent visit. There was no problem with the 25 minute flight there, but before the ground part of my mission was accomplished the weather closed in and Gütersloh airfield closed down. Fortunately I had my beret with me, but that was all. Using borrowed items from other Officers I spent the night in the Orderly Officer's room in the Mess. Next day the weather lifted a little and I was allowed to return, taking half an hour, with 10 minutes instrument flying in dense cloud on the way. The aircraft I used for this sortie, a Mk 5, was VV221 which I had previously flown at Pembrey and, in its earlier days, was used when the original Pilot's Notes were written up at Hullavington in 1948.

I flew 3 battle formation sorties on the day I set off for Berlin with the Hockey Team. On return I flew dual in a Meteor with my Flight Commander who showed me the Meppen air-to-ground firing range, close to the Dutch border. Other Squadron pilots had flown many live-firing sorties there since my arrival. It would soon be my turn. That evening I flew my first night flight from Jever, primarily to see what could be seen in the area after dark.

Winter weather prevented almost all flying for the next fortnight during which, had I not signed on for a Short Service Commission, I would have completed my National Service and been demobbed. I was very happy with what I was doing.

The bad weather didn't stop us using the parade ground, nearly wearing our legs down to stumps on it. We were practising as a Supporting Squadron for the parade to be held at the time of the presentation of their Standard to 4 Squadron by Marshal of the Royal Air Force, Sir John Slessor.

On the day of the parade, Friday, 20th November the weather was kind, and I found myself not on parade but assisting with showing invited VIPs and guests to their places as spectators. I then became a spectator as well.

With the parade over, the Standard was marched to the Officers Mess for display. An excellent and very relaxed formal luncheon then took place, with guests and all Jever Officers and their wives present. One of the RAF Regional Bands played at the parade and then serenaded us from the wide passageway outside the dining-room during lunch. As is often the case after such and similar occasions in the RAF the celebrations continued, and continued well into the early hours of the next day, taking in their stride, as it were, an informal dance and a general thrash. Fortunately the Station was stood down for 48 hours as it was anticipated that such would take place. The Sergeants Mess celebrated in their own way, as did the Airmen – in the NAAFI – and elsewhere. The official historian recorded that the 'situation became fluid'. It certainly did, and not a little riotous as well. The next day, Saturday, was spent nursing hangovers. Those who decided on 'hair of the dog' treatment did just that. By Monday we were just about ready for work again.

The embroidered silk 4 Squadron Standard on display in the Officers Mess dining-room.

Waiting for the rest of the guests to arrive.

*Celebrations are well under way. Some of the Mess and Squadron
silver can be seen on the table. You can only see the top of my head
in the front of the picture.*

The rest of the month was notable primarily for poor weather. We
attended lectures, attended to extraneous duties, and spent time in the
gym. I did manage to fly three sorties: one of ciné quarter attacks, one
of routine practice ranging and tracking, and one, after a journey by
road to Oldenburg, when I flew a Vampire Mk 9 back to Jever to go on
Squadron strength. That flight lasted 15 minutes.

My duties as MTO occupied any spare time I had. I had been able to draw from the Air Publications Section several APs dealing with MT, its use, and operation, including convoy rules and regulations. These were of value to me for I had heard that the Squadron would be going on detachment to the island of Sylt for air-to-air live gunnery practice. I would have to take a convoy there, so I needed to have some idea of what was expected of me.

At about this time, too, the Squadron had been allocated a brand new 88" wheelbase Land Rover. Its registration number was AA 00 01, which told everyone that it was the first of its type in 2ATAF, if not the RAF. Sqn.Ldr. Allen made sure he had priority use of it as his personal vehicle, and I had to make sure it was kept clean!

Our Met Officer was Arthur Hull.[1] He and his team had the unenviable task of trying to forecast local weather. These were the days when weather satellites were just a science fiction writer's dream. Every four hours a synoptic chart was produced using information collated from other weather stations and sent in by teleprinter. Local weather at Jever could be very unpredictable as it was close to the coast. Damp from the North Sea could produce days of haze and poor horizontal visibility, and fog could roll in without warning. When flying, as pilots, it was our duty, and for our own protection, to radio in any changes to the forecast weather. Occasionally we flew special Met sorties. To date there had been much haze and drizzle and some fog but little yet in the way of frost. Arthur Hull was responsible for presenting weather information at each morning's flying briefing in Flying Wing Headquarters which all we pilots had to attend before going to our Squadrons.

As the month changed to December so did the weather improve, but only for a short time. Three sorties were flown on the first day, the usual ciné quarter attacks ending with a QGH, then a dusk flight, taking off in the evening and landing after dark. After this I flew a night cross-country over to Schleswig Holstein and back. All sorties were of 40 minutes duration. I was never keen on night flying unless there was a bright moon. Night IF seemed particularly onerous and stressful.

---

1   He was senior meteorological officer and wore uniform only when formality demanded. He usually wore an old brown tweed jacket with leather patches on the elbows. He was employed by the Met Office but attached to the RAF and could be posted anywhere like the rest of us.

For a considerable part of this cross-country I was out of sight of the ground and had to get several R/T fixes.

Next day the weather was marginal and my morning sortie involved a mock combat mission in very poor visibility. So bad was it that I, and the other pilot, became separated and decided to make our individual ways back to base. I stooged about while the other aircraft started its QGH and landed, then it was my turn. I got as low as 1,000 feet and couldn't see the ground so broke off the QGH to climb up and have another go. This time I risked going down to 750 feet but still didn't see the runway although Air Traffic said they could just see me. Too late. My fuel state was getting low and I was at once diverted to Ahlhorn, the nearest open airfield because Oldenburg was clamped in. I landed there in clear weather, reported to Air Traffic as usual, and waited for instructions. On arrival I found that the Squadron Battle Flight had been diverted there as well. By early afternoon the weather at Jever had cleared enough for me to return. On going to my aircraft I was told that when I had shut down there were only 7 gallons left in my tanks. The engine would have cut out after another two minutes. The five of us, that's the Battle Flight four and me, taxied out together, did a stream take-off, formed up in line astern formation and were back over base in 10 minutes to fly down the runway, do a formation break into downwind, and a stream landing without further ado.

Although I had not yet been assessed as 'operational', on the 4th of December I was detailed off to fly as No.4 on Battle Flight in the morning. This meant taxying my armed aircraft out to the readiness pans close to the end of the runway where there was a dispersal hut for the pilots and necessary ground crew. The routine was, once in flying kit, to sign the Duty Book, see Chiefy and sign the Form 700 of one's allocated aircraft, and walk out to it, carry out a thorough pre-flight inspection, get in, and taxi to the dispersal at the end of the runway in use.[2] Once facing in the right direction and parked up, one shut down the engine and climbed out, being careful to leave the parachute and seat straps tidy and immediately accessible for strapping in in the minimum of time in the event of a scramble. We left our helmets, with

2   The Form 700 was that particular aircraft's serviceability log. It was signed by the pilot as accepting the aircraft, then, on landing, the pilot would record any malfunctions and sign the entry. The ground crew would rectify the fault (if any) and/or carry out any scheduled servicing, and record what had been done, whereupon the aircraft would be ready for flying again.

goggles and oxygen mask attached, beside the gun-sight on the cockpit coaming. We did not remove our Mae Wests during the duty period. The ground crew connected up the trolley-acc in readiness and made sure that the wheel chock chains were laid out so that chocks could be pulled away smartly. In the dispersal hut we spent away our time reading, chatting, dozing, or maybe playing cards while we waited for something to happen. Sometimes nothing did, so, at the end of our stint we just taxied our aircraft back to dispersal, duty done, signed the Form 700 and the Duty Book, and that was it.

On this particular morning we were airborne three times. The phone rang and we were given the order to scramble and make for a given height on a given heading and, when airborne to change radio channels to a given frequency and call a given call-sign. Running out to our aircraft the ground crew helped us to strap in and, sometimes even before we had our helmets fastened, we started our engines and taxied out and did a stream take-off, calling each other to check our radios. Rapidly forming up into battle formation we climbed on our given heading. The leader then told us to change channels, then another brief radio check, and the leader then called the given call-sign to see what 'trade' there was.

On those three scrambles we intercepted, under radar control, several 'bogies'. Each intercept unfortunately ended up as a tail chase, either through controller error, or our inability to see the target aircraft soon enough to carry out good quarter attacks. After each attack the controller gave us 'Pigeons to base' (the course to steer to, and distance from, base). When on potential combat missions such as these the last thing we needed to be concerned with was map reading and worrying about where we were. After landing and returning to the readiness pans our leader would debrief us and we would discuss what, if anything, went wrong, and how to improve our performance. In the meantime our aircraft would be refuelled and tended by the ground crew in readiness for the next scramble. Each of our sorties that morning lasted 45 minutes.

This was the very first time that I had personal experience of being in contact with, and controlled by, radar. The subject was still a mystery to me as I had had no training in its use whatsoever.

This, too, was the first time I was doing the job I had been trained over a period of two years to do. And I was still only a beginner.

There was another aspect to this, for I was still a novice regarding the way a Tactical Air Force was run. I had seen the mobile Group set-up at Sundern where it was brought home to me that 'Tactical' also meant 'Mobile', in as far as having to move from base to temporary base in a short time according to the demands of a changing war situation. At Jever there was no control tower; all Air Traffic Control functions were carried out from caravans in a yard at the rear of Flying Wing HQ. The controllers operated 'blind' and could work from any concealed position adjacent to an airstrip. The only person at Jever in visual contact with aircraft movements was a Senior NCO in the black and white chequered caravan to one side of the runway threshold. Among the caravans at the back of FWHQ was one for the Duty Pilot. It was his task to maintain contact with Group regarding the scrambling of Battle Flight and other matters relating to tactical (as opposed to training) aircraft movements. When it was my turn for such duty there was no briefing as to what was expected of me. On the telephone line to Group was a person of, to me, unknown rank or status who was called the 'Ops B'. He was the person who gave orders to Jever. There was an almost indecipherable instruction manual for the Duty Pilot to read, and to sign as having read and understood, when coming on duty. Everyone I spoke to, without exception, said they didn't understand it either but signed it regardless, it was so appallingly written. Nobody could tell me who 'Ops B' was, and all I asked were in awe of his voice when the phone rang. All chosen for this solitary duty in this cheerless caravan were, like me, in a mixed state of near panic and boredom, entirely through lack of proper briefing. As with the absence of any instruction about radar, this was a serious gap in our training which so easily could have been corrected.

Also on the 4th, the same day that I had been on my first Battle Flight duty, the Squadron celebrated its second birthday in the evening and held an all ranks party in the loft over the 93 Squadron Airmen's barrack block. Ex-Luftwaffe barrack blocks such as this were substantial structures with reinforced concrete floors at all levels. The loft floor was no different, and the loft spacious and high enough to accommodate everyone. Access was via a built-in let-down ladder.

Following my Battle Flight stint in the morning I, and some other pilots and Airmen were detailed off to go and set things up. 'Tables fold flat' were found and taken up, sheets were laid as tablecloths, and some greenery and Christmas-style decorations were hung to take some of the bareness off the roof space. The cases of beer and other drink were fetched from the NAAFI. Glasses were borrowed from I know not where, and just before teatime some substantial sandwiches, ham rolls, and the like (to serve as blotting paper and soak up the drink) were fetched from the Malcolm Club. With everything ready, all ranks were placed on their honour not to enter the loft until party time. Nobody did.

It goes without saying that the party was a success, so successful that I can remember little of it except having to leave early. The Erks had their own band, a precursor of the soon to be popular skiffle groups. I dimly recollect the Boss saying appropriate words and 'Al' Paterson telling some tale or other before the party descended into a dirty song session at about the time I made my way, super carefully, down the ladder and back to my room. No work was done after all, or nearly all of us, were on Station Commander's Parade the next morning.

Such parades were held at intervals from almost weekly to no less frequently than once a month. They were generally loathed by most participants but, on the other hand, recognised as good for discipline and personal pride. One of the larger hard-standings was used as the parade ground, and with two Flying Squadrons comprising the Flying Wing, two Regiment Squadrons comprising the Regiment Wing, the Admin Wing and Tech Wing, they were massive affairs with several hundred men for the Parade Adjutant to shout at. I paraded as a Super-numerary Officer with the Squadron. As such, I had no orders to give. I just had to obey them!

I got used to parades and, knowing that I had to do them, I decided to learn as much as I could by carefully watching, listening hard to the orders, and memorising as much as I could. I found them to be similar to a slow motion dance routine. The fact that I couldn't dance was irrelevant.

I did not fly again until Sunday, December 20th. The weather had been awful and our time was filled with lectures and talks. Aircraft systems, aircraft recognition, ciné ranging and tracking analyses, tank recognition lectures and sessions, as well as the inevitable periods in the gym, filled almost all our time.

I flew two sorties that Sunday. One was 40 minutes unofficial circuits in a Tiger Moth with Flt.Lt. Eric Hughes who was i/c Station Flight at the time. The second sortie was to air test a Vampire which was fitted with under-wing drop tanks in readiness for the flight to Sylt. It was my first air test so I casually enquired what might be expected and was told, quite curtly, "Start the bloody thing up, take-off, fly around, make sure everything works, and bring it back in one piece!" I couldn't argue with that and should have known better than to ask. I was airborne for 55 minutes in cloudy conditions, my longest flight on the Squadron so far. It involved 10 minutes instrument flying and a QGH. The next time I flew was at Sylt.

We had been given notice a while back that the Squadron was to be detached to Sylt for live-firing practice. Plans had been moving forward with this in mind for some time. A Movement Order had been written and promulgated. It listed the duties of those involved; that was all of us. As MTO, I was to take a convoy of wagons laden with spares, office equipment, and much other materiel. I had warned those who were to be drivers of what would be expected of them, and that we would be overnighting and refuelling at RAF Ütersen, north of Hamburg. Chiefy Blair was allocated to me and would drive one of the trucks containing a small amount of ammunition. His advice proved invaluable. It was my job to check the route, plan stops, and generally ensure that convoy regulations were obeyed. Johnny MacKnish, who was Squadron Adjutant at this time, would be my 2 i/c. I was well occupied, as one might guess. My inability to drive, officially, was no help to me at all. This, clearly, was a matter in need of rectification, but not yet awhile, at least until winter road conditions improved.

Preparations for the journey had to be made for the departure of my convoy on the 27th, the day after Boxing Day. Chiefy Blair supervised the loading of the vehicles and the drivers were given a full briefing. The rest of the Squadron was preparing equipment for loading on a special train due to depart the day after.[3]

The Mess was decorated so well to the extent that parts of it almost looked like a Department Store Christmas Grotto. This created a very relaxed and festive atmosphere. The NAAFI was decorated, as was the Malcolm Club, and the Sergeants Mess and Corporals Club, too. On Christmas Eve, with the assistance of some of our Officers, a bar was set

---

3 The train was to depart from the camp siding by the Equipment Section. The use of such special trains was not unusual. Each RAF Station had its branch line, connected to the Deutsche Bundesbahn, and a diesel shunting locomotive in its own siding. Aviation fuel was brought by rail tankers, so the use of the railway was a permanent and operational feature in the running of an RAF Station.

up in the Squadron Airmen's block, so that they could entertain themselves in their own way.

We Officers were in our Mess bar at opening time and, after dinner, some of us went to Wing Commander Russell-Bell's house for drinks.[4] Following this we went back to the bar for the Christmas raffle.

On Christmas Day, in uniform, we followed the usual RAF ritual of inviting all members of the Sergeants Mess for drinks. Then we changed places and walked over for drinks in their Mess. Some, of course, opted to do neither and attended Morning Service in the Station Chapel. At one o'clock we all, from both Messes, entered the Airmen's Mess to serve lunch, as was traditional throughout the Royal Air Force. Hilarity began as we entered the building. There were cheers and not a few good humoured cat-calls. Some Erks were in fancy dress and one character, in drag and wearing make-up, stood out from the rest. We served an excellent roast turkey dinner, with soup to start, and Christmas pud to follow, all amid much banter and jollity. Then came the CO's address. As he stood up, the character in drag went up to him and stood by him throughout, showing a gartered leg and making lewd gestures at the Groupie during his light-hearted speech. That part of the festivities over, we were cheered, took a bow, and departed for our own dinners.

To say that the Christmas dinner served to us in our own Mess was more than adequate was an understatement in itself. I had soup followed by the main course served on a large plate laden with a full turkey leg and some breast, sausages, stuffing, and a range of vegetables, with gravy and sauces served from jugs on the table. Afterwards Christmas pudding and cheese and biscuits were available. All was accompanied by appropriate wines. Neither I nor anybody else that day could eat everything put before us, but many of us tried. Some, regrettably made themselves almost ill in the attempt. Uniforms were loosened to make room, but to little effect. Sated, almost to a man, we staggered away back to our rooms to sleep it off.

Almost no-one turned up for afternoon tea, but most managed a light dinner. Soon afterwards, Fred Maycock, an able pianist from 4 Squadron, was thumping out popular song tunes on the minstrel gallery piano. It was an admirable performance peppered with one or two risqué ditties. Drink was flowing again, and Officers and their wives

---

4   He was the Officer in charge of the Admin Wing.

from the married patch came and joined us for an extremely convivial evening to Fred's accompaniment.

Saturday, Boxing Day, was quiet indeed. The traditional Officers v Sergeants football match was a non-starter owing to a lack of players. Everyone took it easy, for the next day was a full working day on which there was much preparation to be done.

I was up early in the morning and, with bags packed, had an early breakfast before making my way to the Squadron hangar to check everything was in order for the 07.30 start of our journey to Sylt. Official records state that I had a Land Rover and only two Thorneycrofts in the convoy but that is wide of the truth. I recollect there being about six vehicles, maybe one or two more. There was a delay because one of the wagons wouldn't start, no matter how hard the driver swung the starting handle. On my approaching the scene he was heard to mutter "It's like walking a dead frigging cow" (or similar). He was sweating profusely, so I told him to take a break. After a brief conversation with Chiefy Blair and Corporal Hudson, my driver, I went over and swung the handle myself. Just one turn, and it started. After more expletives, and a grin from me, the driver climbed aboard and we started on our way. After calling at the Airmen's Mess for hayboxes containing victuals, and a large, insulated, full, tea urn, which we placed in the Land Rover, we set off through the gate and out on to the open road. Our vehicle, as lead vehicle, carried a blue flag, the wagon with the ammunition on board carried a red flag, and the final vehicle carrying emergency tool-kits carried a green one.

I sat in the front for a while, Corporal Hudson drove, and Johnny MacKnish and another Corporal sat in the back. Progress was good. After an hour or so we stopped for 5 minutes break and a mug of tea for everyone. It was decided to press on as fast as possible to try to get through Hamburg as early as we could, but there was a long way to go yet. We moved off again and, after passing through Bremen, joined the Autobahn. Traffic was quiet so, as discussed earlier as a possibility, and at my behest, we waved our vehicles past us and, now at the back, caught up with each in turn, formated on it, and handed up sandwiches to the crew and filled their mugs. Whilst strictly outside official procedures the ploy worked a charm. Everyone was happy as we carried on driving. Then came a problem. A driver of a German lorry was trying to throw his weight about, ducking and diving amongst us. My drivers, who had experienced this sort of thing before when an anti-occupation zealot started messing about, knew what to do. Corporal Hudson prompted me to watch their reaction. My drivers bunched up round, and boxed in, the truck and kept it tied in until just before the next pull-in when they slowed down almost to a stop, forcing him off the road into the rest area. That done, everything returned to normal, with smiles of satisfaction and 'thumbs up' all round.

Hamburg's Elbe Bridge in 1953. Not far from here we picked up our convoy escort.

The Bremen – Hamburg Autobahn had two lanes in each direction with a grass area separating them. On the outer side of each carriageway was a rumble strip of two lines of stone setts before the grass verge. The concrete surface was laid in jointed sections. On a long trip such as this the constant b-dum, b-dum, b-dum, of our wheels over the joints could become very wearing. That, coupled with the notorious constant scream of the Thorneycroft gearboxes, could lead to fatigue. Another break was called for. We were already near Hamburg, close to a scheduled stopping place. This was also where we picked up our Police motorcycle escort. After stretching our legs we reboarded and moved off. Our escort, a member of the local Polizei, led us through the city, stopping traffic, and clearing our way through. He didn't bother about speed restrictions, and some of our drivers struggled to maintain the pace through twisting streets and over what should have been, but for our escort, very busy junctions. It was exciting stuff. We stopped at the fringe of the northern suburbs, bade our escort farewell after thanking him, and had another break.

The drive to Ütersen was uneventful. On arrival we took the vehicles to the MT Section, had them refuelled, and parked up for the night. Chiefy and the Corporals saw to it that the Airmen were accommodated, and Johnny MacKnish and I made for the Officers Mess.

Johnny MacKnish (left) and myself in the Keller Bar at Ütersen.

Ütersen was still stood down for Christmas and there was almost no-one about. The only person present in the Mess was the Duty Officer, so Johnny and I were left largely to our own devices. We had dinner, went for a drink in the Keller Bar, and played a couple of games of skittles in the bowling alley before going to our rooms to retire for the night.

The bowling alley at Ütersen.

15. Sylt, January 1954

MY OVERNIGHT STAY IN Ütersen was without event and our convoy set off early for the island of Sylt, off the north-west corner of Schleswig Holstein, adjacent to the Danish frontier. Our route took us north through Itzehoe, Rendsburg, Schleswig, and Flensburg. There were one or two interesting moments for the drivers, for this was rolling countryside and that meant hills. Some drivers had only driven on the absolutely flat North German Plain and had never had to change gear to go up a hill, either for a very long time, or never in their driving careers. With much graunching and double-declutching our progress was slowed but continuous at each rise in the ground. We had one of our stops at Rendsburg. All of us were amazed to see cows drinking the sea water, for we had stopped by an inlet of the Baltic Sea which is almost fresh water. There were reeds growing in it, too.

From Flensburg we turned west, on a road parallel to the frontier with Denmark, to make for Niebüll, our next destination.

We arrived at Niebüll in good time to meet the train which was to take us across the Hindenburg Damm, the causeway to Sylt. There is no road connection with the island. I checked in with the RTOs Office and was told what to do to load the vehicles and that there would be no need to lash them down on to the flat trucks. Chiefy Blair and I saw to the loading, each driver taking his vehicle up the ramp at the end of the train and driving along it from truck to truck to fill up from the front, and be properly spaced out. I loaded a Thorneycroft first and it sat behind a black Opel Kapitän saloon car, the first vehicle on the train. My Land Rover was at the rear. The weather was cold but not

Opposite: A 1953 German map of Sylt with the airfield superimposed.

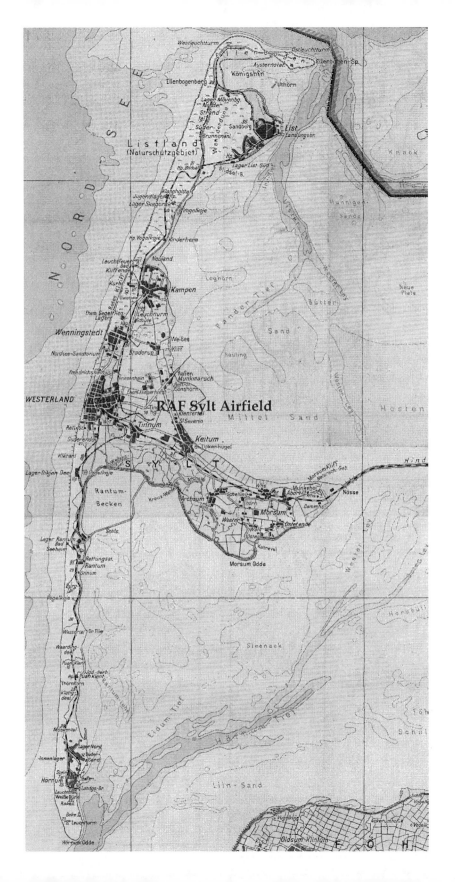

bitterly so, and there was a fresh breeze. A locomotive backed on to the train, coupled up, and we moved off. We were allowed to dismount from our vehicles because the motion of the train, transferred through the springing of the vehicles, could have the effect of making the occupants travel-sick. Many of the drivers dismounted but soon found the breeze, added to the wind created by the forward movement of the train, was far too chilly for comfort so, to a man, they opted to travel in the comparative warmth of their cabs.

By this time the train had left the mainland and was crossing the Hindenburg Dam when, suddenly, there was what seemed to be an emergency application of brakes. Five of my wagons slid forward on the greasy, wet, wooden surface of the trucks and cannoned into each other. The train didn't actually stop but accelerated again to its original speed and continued until it reached the unloading siding at Westerland, Sylt. In doing so, those wagons which were in contact with each other scraped together with the train's motion and turned what would originally have been slight damage into something more significant but, fortunately, not disabling.

That was not all. The lead Thorneycroft was pushed from behind into the back of the Opel Kapitän which, itself had been forced across the buffers into the back of the locomotive's tender – and looked a sorry sight. Its driver, so we quickly discovered, was no less than the Senior British Officer, a civilian responsible for liaison between the Occupying Forces and the civilian population of that part of Germany. A VIP if ever there was one. I have to say that he was very understanding and was concerned that none of us should be blamed for what had happened as the whole incident was totally beyond our control. Johnny MacKnish, Chiefy Blair, and I, set our drivers to the task of getting the Opel out of its predicament and on to terra firma. It was driveable, just. The Bahnhofmeister was fetched and informed of what had happened. That done we drove to RAF Sylt. Journey over.

We had arrived in mid-afternoon, some hours before the main party drew in on their special train. During that time Johnny MacKnish and I were the only 93 Squadron Officers present.

The purpose of RAF Sylt was to accommodate Squadrons on detachment for live gunnery practice over the sea. Their personnel were well rehearsed in allocating accommodation and directing newcomers to their various destinations, so there was no problem with our settling in.

I had to inform both the Station Adjutant and the MTO of our railway 'adventure'. In proper RAF fashion, forms had to be filled in for each damaged vehicle. Had they been only 'paint jobs' we would have said nothing, but some metal had been bent, and there was the matter of the Opel Kapitän.

The Boss, Sqn.Ldr. Allen, arrived with the other pilots and aircraft next day. He had to be informed but wasn't too bothered. I had to fill in five Forms FMT3, in triplicate. These are multi-page documents and each had to be accompanied by an appropriate memo. There was a snag. Johnny MacKnish, as Squadron Adjutant and therefore responsible for providing the Orderly Room and Admin facilities, had omitted to ensure that a typewriter had been brought from Jever – and there was no carbon paper. Rather than for the Squadron to lose face by admitting this omission to others, the Boss told me to complete all these forms by hand; a job which took several days (between other activities) whilst sitting at the end of the Crew Room table, and amid the inevitable distractions.

Whilst not wishing to give a detailed flight-by-flight account of my activities I shall mention, primarily, the significant sorties and events on the ground.

Winter had set in and frost was generally widespread. Added to this the island was subject to poor visibility and unforecastable banks of low cloud and fog drifting in from over the North Sea. It could also be very windy. Towing aircraft (Tempest) serviceability also had its effect on the flying programme. My first flight, on the last day of 1953, was a case in point. Once airborne, I made contact with the tug pilot, only to be told that he was returning to base owing to a snag with his aircraft. I flew a Sector Recce instead and was airborne for 35 minutes.[1]

In the evening there was a dance in the Mess but a few of us opted to go into Westerland, the main town on the island, instead. Some of us had been to Sylt before and knew of a restaurant where we could get a good meal. There, I can remember having, among other things, Känguruhschwanzsuppe (kangaroo tail soup) for the first time in my life.[2] On the way back to camp the youth of the area were letting off fireworks,

---

1   This was to familiarise myself with the lie of the land, location of firing ranges, etc.

2   I was surprised at the availability of such 'exotic' food. There were also bananas and sweets available in the shops, off ration, and all this in a 'defeated' nation. Back in the UK such items were scarce to non-existent and rationing was still in force.

mostly bangers, to celebrate the New Year, and took the opportunity to drop or throw many of such close to us to test our reactions.[3] Our British stiff upper lips held sway and no satisfaction was allowed these revellers.

The very next day, with many pilots nursing hangovers, mercifully there was low cloud and no flying in the morning. However, Bernie Revnell and I went to Hamburg to represent the Squadron at the funeral of Plt.Off. Stacey of 4 Squadron who had been killed in a flying accident at Jever on December 28th. His funeral, a cremation, was with full military honours. It was a particularly sombre occasion in the freezing weather. The deceased's family had been flown in by the RAF and it was up to us all to help comfort them as much as we could. One of the bearers, a brother Officer from 4 Squadron, had to go 'behind the scenes' at the crematorium to witness the destruction of Plt.Off. Stacey's body. This was done without his family knowing and was apparently to comply with regulations in force at the time. Bernie and I stayed overnight at the Streits Hotel and returned to Sylt by train the next day. What a way to start off a new year.

I didn't fly for a week, and then only for 35 minutes ciné on the flag. All our ciné film was quickly processed after landing, and each day was analysed and criticised by the Pilot Attack Instructor in front of all Squadron pilots. It was the 9th of January before it was my turn to fly again. This time dual with the PAI in a Vampire T11 for live-firing. I followed this with another ciné sortie in heavy salt spray which, on drying on the windscreen, obscured forward vision somewhat. A further flight for the same purpose the next day lasted less than 10 minutes and was aborted because my aircraft became unserviceable soon after becoming airborne.

Conditions were icy and bitterly cold, and flying was minimal. My highest score was 9% of rounds fired. That was on the 12th. Then there was a week during which I didn't fly at all, nor did hardly anyone else owing to the extremely cold and filthy weather.

The highlight of this period, between the incessant lectures, gym sessions, demonstrations, training films, and general boredom, was when Plt.Off. Doug Fewell and I contrived to go on a 'swan' one

---

3   This was the first time I had heard of fireworks being used in the New Year celebrations. It certainly didn't happen at home. I knew the Chinese used firecrackers at their New Year but that was all.

day for a trip on the RAF Air Sea Rescue Launch based at List, the old Luftwaffe seaplane base at the northern tip of Sylt. With skipper Fg.Off. Saunders at the helm, and well wrapped up in the bitter cold, we set off for the northern range area, being careful not to stray into Danish territorial waters as we rounded the northernmost tip of the island. Our duty was to warn off shipping which looked like straying into the danger area, and to be there in the event of an aircraft and/or pilot coming down in the sea. There was very little flying, and no shipping near enough to warn off. We drifted, engines off, on a choppy sea, in the duty area, for seeming hours. The novelty wore thin, so we went below for a brew. The paraffin heater in the cabin gave off noxious fumes to the point when, after having had a hot drink, and suffered the erratic movement of the vessel in that reeking atmosphere, both Doug and I moved back on deck so as to counter a growing sensation of queasiness. No-one on board was ill, but it was a near thing. With our stint nearly up, the skipper started the engines and gave us a maximum speed demonstration, warning us first of all to hang on tight. We bounced from wave top to wave top and crashed into the sides of some. With spray coming over the top, and seeing the wake, and hearing the roar of the twin diesels on full power, it was an exhilarating, if bitterly cold, wetting, experience. That done, we made our way back to harbour in a gentler fashion. We were told that, next day, there was ice floating on the sea off List. Our experience whetted the appetite of a group of other pilots in the Squadron to organise a similar trip some days later when the ice had moved away. To a man, their queasiness turned out to be completely uncontrollable!

Whilst mentioning the cold: it was our habit, regardless of conditions, to go for walks and explore the area near the camp. On one of these ventures three of us decided to go down to the coast on the mainland side of the island to the south of the Hindenburg Dam as we had heard that the sea had frozen in that sheltered area. Frozen it was, and thick too. We ventured on to the ice, thinking that maybe we could walk across to the mainland a couple of miles away and return by train. We innocents soon discovered the folly of our intentions and retreated with some difficulty back to whence we had come. What we had found, and should have known, was that the ice, with the action of the tides, had fractured and each heavy piece (ice floe) had collided with the next, often riding on top. This caused an extremely broken, often steep, and very slippery uneven surface on which to make any sort of progress. In places there was open water thus creating extremely dangerous conditions. We were lucky to get back to dry land safely.

Later in the month the weather improved sufficiently for flying to recommence once ice had been cleared from the runway. My next flight involved 50 minutes of local flying and aerobatics. The day after I scored just 3% on the flag, with a second sortie aborted after 15 minutes because the tug pilot didn't show up on the range. That same evening I flew a night cross-country back to Jever and followed it with another sortie from Jever involving local flying and a QGH. Jever seemed lonely as there were few 93 Squadron pilots there.

The next day with Squadron mail on board, I flew back to Sylt, initially in formation. As the flight proceeded I found that I was progressively losing aileron control and had to break formation and continue separately. There was increasing resistance to stick movement when applying port aileron. Everything was free when banking right, but not to the left. With minimum stick movements I approached Sylt, told the Tower of my problem and requested a priority landing. I could not turn port on to the runway heading and had to do a gentle right circle to line myself up, kicking the rudders to yaw the aircraft on to the runway heading so as to have minimum stick movement during a straight-in approach. The landing was entirely successful, and I taxied back to dispersal. I shut down, unstrapped myself, and went to retrieve my beret from the stowage hole which we all used at the right side of the cockpit. My hat had to be pulled out quite forcibly. Curious, I looked into the hole and found fluff on the control cable where it travelled round a pulley. On moving the stick to port, I found it was free, as it should be, and the same cable moved in the direction of the pulley. My hat had jammed the controls. Had the airborne situation worsened I could have descended to earth in a totally different fashion.

The matter had properly to be reported and I was given a dressing-down for my carelessness. I was quick to point out, though, that I knew that other pilots also used that self-same hole for stowing their own berets. This was accepted, and a verbal warning was given to all aircrew flying Vampires from Sylt. I was detailed, as a sort of punishment, to write an article about my mishap for the RAF internal periodical "Accense" which was distributed to all flying units throughout the RAF. This I duly did, in longhand in the absence of a typewriter, and submitted it to the appropriate authority. I never did see it in print, and doubt that it was ever published.

Almost immediately after this incident I was airborne again doing a 10 minute air test on a different aircraft. It was common for pilots who had just had a potentially dangerous flight to be sent aloft again very soon afterwards. This was such an example.

On landing, I was told to report to the Station Adjutant's Office immediately. Thinking that this would be something to do with the train episode I was surprised, and caught totally off balance, when he accused me of failing, that morning, to report for Orderly Officer duties. The fact that I was in Jever at the time cut no ice with him. Also, I was absolutely certain that the relevant SROs weren't posted on notice boards before I left Sylt the previous day. (I always, of habit, checked the notice boards daily, and usually twice a day). This also cut no ice, and I was, totally unfairly in my view, given a severe dressing-down. I protested and was accused of being insubordinate, for which I had to apologise at once to this ill-tempered Adjutant who was a Flight Lieutenant New Zealander on detachment from the RNZAF. I had to do the rest of the duties for that day and, for my troubles, told that I was to be Orderly Officer for the following three days as well. I have to admit that his manner, probably grossly unfairly, has coloured my attitude to Kiwis ever since.

The Squadron overall score was rising and it was thought possible that it might become high enough for it to be in contention for the Duncan Trophy, awarded to the Squadron with the highest air-to-air gunnery score in a given period. With this in mind the higher scoring pilots were favoured with more flag sorties; this to the detriment of newer pilots who, like myself, would have benefited from as much live-firing practice as we could get so as to improve our techniques. To have a few high scorers on a Squadron while the rest of its pilots were out of favour in the light of competitive shooting is, when translated into a real battle situation, to have two or three aces and a number of other pilots who, through biased training (e.g. like this situation at Sylt) are not to the standard required of them. I was aware of this, didn't like it, but could do nothing about it in the prevailing circumstances. I wanted more tuition and practice but was denied it.

I flew again twice on the 24th. The first sortie was aborted because the tug pilot didn't show up on the range, and on the second I scored a miserable 3%. This, though, should be put into context. When doing gunnery practice such as this only two of the available four 20mm cannon are being fired. One can assume therefore that with four guns firing there would logically be twice the number of hits. I, for one, would not be at all keen to be flying an aircraft which was receiving even a small number of hits from explosive 20mm cannon shells. Add to this that all our flag attacks were quarter (i.e.: curving) attacks which had to be broken off early for fear of shooting down the tug aircraft, when many combat attacks are made during tail chases wherein the target presents a more relatively stable aiming point. Many of our sorties were practice tail chases with this objective in mind (as well as that of learning to evade potential stern attacks on oneself). The flag, too, presents a smaller target than almost all potential target aircraft. Logically therefore, even a low score on the flag can be translated into an extremely damaging attack on an enemy aircraft.

It is opportune also to mention at this juncture that, with constant practice in keeping alert and a good lookout, both in tail chases, and when flying non-flag sorties, I could, with shoulders held back firmly by my seat straps, swivel my head right round so as to be able to see, from either direction, not only the tail fin on the side I was looking but, with peripheral vision, just see the other one as well. I thus had all round horizontal vision. Vertical vision was only restricted by the distance I could tilt my head back until movement was limited by the armour plate at the rear of my seat.

Back to flying: the following day I scored 4% and 11% on two live-firing sorties. These were separated by cross-countries to Jever and back to pick up the Squadron mail. My total time airborne that day amounted to just 1 hour 50 minutes.

My next flight, the following day, was a 40 minutes aerobatic mission followed by a QGH. I was airborne only three times more before the end of the detachment, each time I was briefed to fire on the flag which I did twice only because the tug aircraft didn't show up for the other sortie. My average score was a miserable 4.67%. The Squadron average score was 13.9% which made us a clear winner of the Duncan Trophy for that year. My score, as a non-operational pilot, was not included in the calculations.

Scoring, for those who have never fired the guns of an aircraft, was done by calculating the number of hits on the target as a percentage of the number of rounds actually fired. As it was usual for four aircraft to fire on the same flag a means of identifying which aircraft made how many hits was necessary. This was done by the use of sticky dyes, as at Pembrey during training. It was then a simple expedient for the Flag Recovery Team in the dropping zone to recover the flag and count the number of holes of whatever colour, the dye having wiped off the rounds as they passed through. This count was then signalled back to the Squadron where the scores were correlated, calculated, recorded, and posted on the duty board for all to see.

It was the end of the month and the end of the detachment. This was also the time when I was officially recognised as being an operational pilot. My assessment at air-to-air gunnery was, unsurprisingly in the circumstances, described as 'Below Average'.

All that was left to do was the repacking and reloading in preparation for the journey home to Jever.

I, with the road convoy, left Sylt for Jever on Monday, February 1st, and, after overnighting at Ütersen, arrived the next day, on schedule, following an uneventful journey.

16. Back To Jever

BY THE TIME I and my convoy arrived back at Jever the Squadron flying programme was in full swing.

Almost before I had unpacked my personal kit and given my laundry to Frau Pinnau to attend to, I was detailed, for the first time, for an air-to-ground rocket-firing sortie at Meppen Range. By now the weather had turned snowy. It was not without some difficulty therefore that I found the range in its camouflage of patchy snow. I have no scores for any rocket sorties, but I never did badly.

Practice rocket firing, using 60 lbs concrete head (i.e. non-explosive) rockets, meant a dive angle of 30 degrees, a given start height, and a stated minimum break off altitude (safety height). To fly lower after firing rockets could mean that bits of rocket could (sometimes, but rarely) ricochet off the ground and strike the aircraft that had just fired them. When practice-firing, the rockets would streak ahead of you, without recoil of course, their (sometimes erratic) smoke trails visible, until you actually caught them up and overflew them, almost never seeing whether they hit the white 10 feet square canvas target. The Range Controller radioed the accuracy of your aim back to you. It was usual to use the range in pairs, the Range Controller detailing which one of the row of targets you were to aim at when called in to fire.

I flew two such sorties in quick succession that day, the second being aborted after very few minutes as my aircraft proved unserviceable after take-off. The next day I flew two further air-to-ground sorties using cannon. The first of these was aborted because of unserviceability, but the second, of 45 minutes duration, was successful in spite of cloud and frequent snow showers.

Later that same day I was detailed to fly a night cross-country which could have turned into disaster. My briefed turning point was a town (name now forgotten) in northern Schleswig Holstein which meant flying across the Heligoland Bight and back. There was patchy cloud and no moon; what one might call a 'dark' night but reasonably clear. Climbing on a north-easterly course from Jever I reached altitude and continued across the sea, but I did not pick up the lights on the islands or the coast to the west of my turning point. I have always had a good sense of direction, even above cloud, and was seldom far from knowing whereabouts I was. Right now I sensed something was wrong. There was little cloud and only the blackness of the sea below. I checked round the cockpit and, as usual, went to reset the reading on the DI to coincide with that of the compass and, instead of it having precessed only a few degrees out (as was not unusual) I discovered it to be wide of the mark.[1] Something was clearly wrong. I could have been heading anywhere. A call to base revealed that my signal was weak indicating that I was some distance away. I called for, and transmitted for, a fix.[2] I was given a low grade fix some distance to the north-west of Heligoland, way off course and well out to sea. Although I had never been taught astro-navigation, common-sense told me that if I could pick out the Pole Star through the high cirrus, I would know which way to head south, hopefully to pick up the coast. It was some anxious minutes later that the cirrus cleared enough for me to pick out the Plough and Polaris, and I was heading north. Throttling back for maximum economic cruising conditions I did a 180° turn as judged from the star and my DI. I called base again and reported my predicament. Then followed a series of calls for radio fixes from which I was able to deduce a more accurate heading and set my DI accordingly. It seemed ages before lights on the North German coastal islands came into view through the bits of cloud below. Another fix, coupled with my sighting of the coastline, told me which way, visually, to head for base. The distinctive lights of Wilhelmshaven

---

1   DI = Direction Indicator.

2   We were trained in what was called DI orientation but, in this case, the radio fixes were initially inaccurate because of distance and location of fixer stations. In those days to obtain a fix involved changing radio frequency to request the fix, then transmitting for thirty seconds so that the fixer station operators could tune into, and read off, the bearing of the radio signal and then report it by land-line. This bearing was then matched to the bearings taken from the same transmission by other stations (at least two, preferably more) to be able to plot the location of the transmitting aircraft. This information was then relayed to its pilot. It was a lengthy process and, in the instance related above, I spent much time transmitting for fixes once I had realised my predicament.

soon showed up – a blessed relief. I called base again, stated my position, descended, and came in to land. I had only been airborne for 30 minutes but it had seemed like an age. A check of the aircraft revealed that the compass was u/s and the DI suspect. Both instruments were changed, the compass swung, deviation card updated, and the aircraft declared serviceable again.

With the incident of the night behind me I was, next day, detailed for Battle Flight duty.[3] We were scrambled three times. On the first sortie I flew the spare aircraft and scrambled as ordered but then broke away at 10,000 feet for a 25 minute solo aerobatic sortie.

It was during this sortie that there was a very strong westerly jet stream at altitude. Realising this, and knowing that the briefed wind speed was greatly in excess of a Vampire's stalling speed, I carried out an experiment. I found that if I reduced speed to just above the stall, with lowered undercarriage and flaps, I actually flew backwards over Wilhemshaven. Slowly, certainly, but I actually flew with a negative ground speed. This must have been done many times before in early stick and string aircraft, but to have done it in a jet gave me a degree of personal satisfaction.[4]

The next sorties, of 40 minutes duration each, involved practice attacks on 'Bogies' picked out for us by the GCI Radar Controller.[5]

That same day we were told officially that we had won the Duncan Trophy. Squadron Leader Allen threw a celebratory party at his house that night, at which, as a member of 'B' Flight, the lowest scoring Flight, we had to pay for the drinks during the first part of the evening. The Boss's house was the first on the left just outside the Guardroom on the married patch. It was larger than average, one of its rooms having been, in Lufwaffe days, some sort of control room. As such it was big enough for the Boss to be able to entertain all his Squadron pilots without too much disruption to the domestic scene.

---

3   Battle Flight aircraft were always fully armed. They were used as the first response in the event of a hostile attack.

4   I have to be careful here. This may not have been the actual date, but I certainly achieved this at this time of year, and this appears, from my Log Book, to have been the only opportunity when it could have taken place.

5   GCI = Ground Controlled Interception. GCI Stations were radar sites monitoring the skies for potential enemy aircraft and at which the Intercept Controllers were based. It was from these sites that battle flights received their instructions after being scrambled by Group.

With the award of the Duncan Trophy it was standard ritual that a Presentation Parade was called for. The first rehearsal (of many) for this followed the Station Commander's Parade next (Saturday) morning. With flurries of snow about, and a stiff breeze which swept the unprotected parade ground clear, it was essential to dress to protect oneself from the conditions. Parades meant a lot of standing still, either 'At Ease' or 'To Attention', with comparatively little marching. Harsh winter weather, in these circumstances, would soon penetrate through a greatcoat and other clothing. On very bad days – and there would be quite a few – when we were either rehearsing for a parade or actually on parade (virtually the same thing) further protection was necessary for one's personal comfort. Layers of underclothing could be used to good effect but I always chose another method. That was to cut out a waistcoat from thick brown paper and put it on over my vest and under my shirt and pullover. This was very effective in keeping the wind out and the warmth in, with the added advantage that it was not bulky. I heard that some folk, unable to find a big enough piece of brown paper would resort to using newspaper. This not only tended to tear easily, it also left ink marks all over underclothing – to the annoyance of our batwomen who had to try and wash it out.

With snow around and unacceptable flying conditions, the next few days were spent on lectures, extraneous duties, parade rehearsals and, because we had been told that we would shortly be losing our Vampires, studying F86 'Sabre' Pilots Notes. Indoor hockey was also played, not only during this immediate period, but regularly throughout the winter season. Sometimes I was picked for the team, sometimes I wasn't, but I enjoyed a game when I could get one. Another event also took place. That was the 'Dining Out' in the Mess of Wg.Cdr. Coulson, our Wing Commander Flying, who was leaving us. It was to be a formal Guest Night rather than a routine Dinner Night (for living-in Officers only) or a monthly Dining In Night. Wing Commander 'Hammer' West had only recently been posted in to take over as our new Wing Commander Flying.

Such events demanded formal dress, mandatory attendance, and the pleasant task of welcoming invited guests from other Units, both RAF and Army, and occasionally civilian, for pre-dinner cocktails.[6] The

---

6 Formal dress meant Mess Undress (also called Mess Kit with its tight trousers, cummerbund, and bum-starver jacket) or, if one didn't have that, Interim Mess Dress.

Loyal Toast was drunk and formal after-dinner speeches were made. Then matters would become less formal. Under-table pranks would occur, like tying someone's shoe laces together, or even, after having done that, setting fire to a serviette that was also attached to the victim's laces. Wiser people always sat back a distance from the table at this stage of proceedings. On wilder nights, but not usually when ladies were present, the occasional thunderflash would be thrown. After dinner, and on 'retiring' to the anteroom and bar, more high jinks would usually take place. Maybe a victim's bare feet would be covered in soot and he be hoisted bodily to the ceiling for him to leave his footprints for all to see for almost ever after, or at least until the room was redecorated. Bare arse prints were not unknown, but were usually cleaned off before many days elapsed. At Jever it was common for 'parachute' jumps (with no parachute) to be made from the minstrel gallery on to a pile of settees and arm-chairs arranged below. It was not unknown for limbs to be broken when things got out of hand. The game 'High Cockalorum' was banned for this very reason, but almost as injurious, 'Are you there Moriaty?' was played viciously at times.[7] Inter-squadron Mess rugby was a favourite. Using a cushion as a ball, and with furniture judiciously placed as obstacles, each side would attempt to get the 'ball' to the opposing end of the anteroom. It was free for all as just about anyone could join in, and did, from the Admin and Tech Wings – and they changed sides, too! The losers bought the drinks for the winners. It was an Air Force tradition, indeed etiquette that no one should leave the Mess until the CO departed. Sometimes Fo-Fo would be enjoying himself enormously and that could mean a very late night indeed.

While on this subject, I well remember one evening when, for some drink-inspired reason, everyone was expected to take their trousers off, or be debagged if they didn't. It was a riot. 'Wilbur' Wright (Station Signals) and Jim Yates (Personnel) were enjoying a game of darts at the time and, not wishing to be disturbed or be conspicuous in their trousers, quietly took them off, placed them safely to one side, and carried

---

7   'High Cockalorum' was a human pyramid game. It was banned throughout the RAF after several injuries. 'Are you there Moriaty?' was a game with two blindfolded combatants, each lying on the floor and armed with long, hard, rolls of newspaper (or similar), the object of which was, using sound location, to wallop one's opponent over the head, hard. The one scoring the first three hits was declared the winner. Headaches were not unusual afterwards.

on playing. The same Jim Yates also had a party trick up his sleeve. I only ever saw it performed once. After some coercion he was dared to perform it by RAF Regiment Sqn.Ldr. Dougie Bliss. The trick, as stated, was to boil an egg using two razor blades, and then to eat it at once. "Impossible", we all said. After a due pause while the requisite egg and razor blades were fetched, and a piece of electric flex found, the demonstration began. The ends of the twin flex were separated and bared. At one end a razor blade was attached to each wire. A glass tankard of Pils was sent for. With part of it drunk, the egg was popped into the half full glass. The other ends of the flex were pushed into a live power socket and held in place with match sticks. The separated razor blades were pushed into the Pils, one each side of the egg. No, there was no flash, but the Pils started to boil, thus cooking the egg. After the necessary, seemingly endless, five minutes had passed, with all onlookers silent and spellbound, Jim pulled the flex out of the socket, tipped the egg into an empty glass then, fishing it out and holding it in his handkerchief, peeled the shell off, at the same time ordering another Pils. Once shelled, he popped the still almost boiling egg, whole, into his mouth and swallowed it in one action, hastily following it with the glass of Pils to cool his innards down. The astounded look on Dougie Bliss's face was a picture to behold.

It was over half way through February, and after more parade rehearsals, that the weather cleared enough for us to be able to fly again. 50 minutes battle formation was followed by my being leader in a four-ship tail chase. This sortie was followed by an hour of flying in the No.3 position in a six-ship formation involving a snake climb to altitude, form up, fly around involving 10 minutes of close (very close) formation in cloud, then a snake descent back to base. I flew again the next day, firing rockets on Meppen Range.

Practice for the Presentation Parade had reached the point when full dress rehearsals were called for, both outdoors and indoors, for the actual Presentation the following day.

On the day itself the parade went ahead in light snow. The band's instruments froze it was so cold, yet, regardless, the parade continued to the beat of drums, and was entirely successful. The Presentation was made by Air Marshal Sir Harry Broadhurst, C-in-C 2ATAF. The outdoor business over, a formal luncheon followed in the Mess. The C-in-C visited the Squadron hangar later, so restrained drinking was called for during lunch. Indoor hockey followed, with the C-in-C among the spectators.

My next sortie in February was 45 minutes of close formation. With all the practice we had by now, our formation flying was very tight, and always with one's wing tip tucked in close behind one's leader's trailing edge. Such flying could be very tiring due to the concentration involved. We took pride in our formation work and reckoned that we were at least as good as anyone else.

Three days later I flew again, this time in a sixteen-ship formation in low visibility and below a 1200 feet cloud base. There wasn't much room to manoeuvre in a tight turn. Depending on which way the turn was, a wing man could find himself not only formatting on his next aircraft but, with the most fleeting of glances the other way, on a factory chimney not far away below, or be in the cloud.

On the same day I was sent off on a search for a crashed Anson. After patrolling my allotted area for some time I was told over the R/T to call the search off as the Anson had been found and the pilot was safe. Later in the morning I flew a 1 hour sortie involving battle formation and a QGH, with 15 minutes IF through thick cloud with some icing.

On the evening of the first day of March we Dined Out Flt.Lt. Al Paterson, our 'A' Flight commander. There were the usual speeches and high jinks. It was the norm on being dined out, to present a piece of silver to the Squadron, and for the Squadron to present an engraved silver tankard to the person leaving. This was usually filled with beer, spirits, and liqueurs, in random quantities. The recipient was expected to down this lethal mixture in the minimum of time, if possible without taking a breath. The effects could be disastrous and involve a hasty departure from the scene, not to be seen again until very late next morning, and then only under duress.

That same week I had two sorties of close formation aerobatics. These were strenuous and the trick was to stick close to your leader regardless of attitude because, to put it simply, if he was flying, so were you! Your relationship with, or attitude to, the ground was totally immaterial. Flying upside down in formation at the top of a loop or barrel roll demanded exactly the same concentration and expertise as when flying straight and level. To even glimpse at the ground could be very distracting.

PARADE ON THE OCCASION OF THE
PRESENTATION OF THE DUNCAN TROPHY (1953)
TO NO. 93 (F) SQUADRON

by Air Marshal

Sir Harry Broadhurst K.B.E., C.B., D.S.O., D.F.C., A.F.C.

R. A. F. Jever, 19th February, 1954

FORM OF PARADE

March on of the two supporting Squadrons.
March on of No. 93 Squadron.
Arrival of the Inspecting Officer.
General Salute.
Inspection of No. 93 Squadron.

PRESENTATION OF THE TROPHY.

Advance in Review Order.
General Salute.
March Past by Squadrons in Column of Route.

Music by No. 3 Regional Band Royal Air Force

Order of Parade for the Duncan Trophy presentation.

Following these sorties, several of us went by bus to Oldenburg for dinghy drill practice in the municipal baths. We practised righting inverted dinghies and climbing into them. It was awkward enough, with inflated Mae West, to struggle aboard a one-man water-filled dinghy in a calm swimming pool and warm water. Heaven help anyone having to do it in a freezing cold rough sea. The thought of that was in all our minds and made us practise all the harder. I was never a strong swimmer but coped with the best of them in spite of my size. It was during this practice that our instructor emphasised to us the need to carry a dagger or other sharp instrument with us when flying. The recommended place for carrying it was to sew the scabbard on the left, upper, sleeve of one's flying suit. This was the easiest place to access it in the event of either a Mae West or dinghy accidentally inflating in the cockpit. The dagger would be used to shred the inflated item in order to deflate it as quickly as possible for, should this ever happen, the stick could be forced forwards and control lost, not a desirable situation, and one which had to be remedied with utmost speed. We were warned, too, to try not to touch the dinghy CO_2 cylinder when inflation was taking, or had just taken, place. As the gas expanded from within, the temperature of the cylinder dropped to below freezing point, as witnessed by the formation of ice on cylinders during the practices. In the cockpit we sat on our dinghy packs which fitted in the seat trays and acted as cushions. It was always, we had been told earlier in our training, important to make sure the CO_2 bottle was placed properly, as otherwise, it could be most uncomfortable, especially when pulling high 'G'. Whilst it was our habit always to do that, when in the water, it was brought home to us to make sure that the webbing tie from the dinghy pack was always attached to one's Mae West. If this wasn't done the dinghy would sink away from one on immersion or, if inflated, float away in a breeze and leave one stranded. It was hard enough to catch a loose dinghy and board it in the swimming pool. In other circumstances it would be a matter of life and death.

Still the weather was bad. Some of us even joked about the fact that we were supposed to be an all-weather Air Force! Nevertheless, below a 1000 feet cloud base (that's normal circuit height) I flew two low level sorties. One was in battle formation, generally beating up anything we saw and, frankly, having a whale of a time. My second low level sortie was a solo navigation exercise which included flying along the Küsten Kanal. I couldn't resist beating up the barges and watching the bargees duck, or even lie flat, as I approached. I applied the rule taught to me in training: "Don't go back or they'll get your number!" In the afternoon four of us practised high level battle formation at 20,000 feet in brilliant sunlight above the solid cloud mass.

That evening I flew, in slightly improving conditions, a night cross-country via Stade, Verdun, Wesemünde, and back to Jever. At one part of this sortie I was aware of a glow at my wing tips. Normally at night I would expect to see some sort of slight glow from my navigation lights, especially in or near cloud, but this was very different. The whole of each wing tip was glowing a pale lilac colour. When I flew into rain, as the droplets hit and tracked back over my cockpit canopy, they too were glowing. It was my first, and only, experience of electrical brush discharge, better known to ancient mariners as Saint Elmo's fire. It was uncanny while it lasted, but soon passed off as my 45 minute flight progressed, otherwise uneventfully.

My final sortie in March was on the 9th and was to Meppen Range, firing rockets. Little did I realise it then, but this was to be my penultimate flight in a single-seat Vampire. My final solo Vampire flight would not be until mid-April. In the intervening period I was due to go on a course, to Ehrwald, in Austria, to learn about and practise Arctic survival techniques.

As this was, to all intents and purposes, the end of my Vampire flying, it is time for me to mention several incidents which I am unable to relate to specific dates or sorties but which are worthy of mention.

There were joys when flying, two of which spring to mind. One of these was, after climbing for seeming ages through dense cloud, to come out into brilliant sunlight, then, when flying over the cloud top, to look down and see myself, or rather the image of my aircraft with me in it, surrounded by an ice-crystal halo against the cloud. With the sun shining through the canopy, and with a bit of height adjustment, it was possible to wave to myself in the centre of this perfectly circular rainbow. Another similar spectacle was, after climbing to height on a dusk sortie, to see the ground darkening below while I was still in bright but reddening sunlight, and for this red light to illuminate the cloud columns in a pink glow, the columns themselves being white at the top and then pink as one looked down them, until they turned grey below sunset level, and, nearer the earth, turn darker, almost to black, at their bases.[8] Most of us would occasionally mention these things.

A little different, but still on the subject of cloud, was the day when I was briefed to climb to altitude for a solo cross-country. The cloud base was low and dark although the forecast was excellent. Climbing, I was soon in dense cloud and was quickly having trouble with the climb

---

8   These phenomena can be seen, given the right conditions (very common), by passengers in the window seats of modern jet passenger aircraft. Sadly, most passengers are too engrossed with in-flight entertainment to be bothered even to notice these beauties of nature.

because I was being tossed about. At one moment my VSI showed almost no climb at a given attitude, air speed, and throttle setting, and the next I was climbing at an almost alarming rate.[9] I was in extreme turbulence and suffering the effects of severe up and down draughts. Staying on my chosen heading, I eventually broke out into clear air. Looking around I realised that I had just flown up through a burgeoning cu-nim, and it was the only one anywhere over the North German Plain![10]

Most of 93 Squadron's pilots. This photo was taken during the January 1954 detachment to Sylt, before Al Paterson left. As always in such photos, I am at the centre at the back.

An entirely different event occurred during the time that some extension work was being done to the apron (hard-standing) outside the Squadron hangar. A trench had been cut a short distance away outside the hangar threshold and parallel to it. The Erks had the unenviable task of pushing all aircraft over this trench by using three wide, suitably placed planks. It so happened, one day, when I was the last to land and taxi in, rather than, as per orders, stopping the aircraft and climbing out on the outer hard-standing I decided to help the lads. With plenty of forward speed and more than adequate brake pressure, I stopped the engine and carried on rolling forward, lining myself up with the planks. With still enough speed in hand, and perfectly lined up, I let my aircraft

---

9   VSI = Vertical Speed Indicator.

10   Cu-nim = abbreviation for cumulonimbus, a cloud of marked vertical development. In this case a developing thunder cloud.

roll across the planks, then stopped immediately afterwards, much to everyone's satisfaction. With my cockpit canopy back I could hear a cheer from the lads as I had saved them work, and speeded things up so they could get away for an earlier tea than expected. I was immediately popular, but for one thing. Hearing the cheer from his office, the Boss looked out of his window and saw what had happened. I was sent for and received a stern, yet mild, ticking off for my troubles. The consequences of my actions, had anything gone wrong, were well and truly made clear.

Another incident, of which I am ashamed, was the time when I did not do my pre-flight checks thoroughly enough. I taxied and took off with my pitot head cover still on. Nobody noticed that I had been careless. I found myself climbing away at zero airspeed! It took me a moment to check round the cockpit and found that both my VSI and altimeter appeared to be behaving strangely. Everything else was OK. Fortunately I was in clear air. It was only when I looked aft that I noticed the warning streamer still flying from the pitot head cover. By this time in my flying career I knew well how an aircraft felt at different speeds so, with no-one about to see what I was doing I slowed and switched the pitot head heater on, hoping it might burn its way through the cover. It didn't, and I didn't want to lose face. I had a landing to make and certainly didn't want to call any emergency. Next, I climbed to what I judged to be high enough for a Mach run. The streamer tore off in the air flow and, in so doing, must have put enough stress on the fabric cover to peel it back away from the end of the head. Suddenly I had altitude, speed, and a working VSI! I nominally completed my sortie, landed, and taxied back to dispersal. The aircraft marshal didn't notice anything amiss, but as I climbed out of the cockpit one of the ground crew saw the pitot head cover ruckled back against the fin. He was alone so I swore him to secrecy and walked aft and pocketed the offending item. Nothing was said.

In preparation for the Squadron's conversion to Sabres we were issued with new flying kit. Our flying suits remained the same and we retained our Mae Wests, gloves, and aircrew watches, but we handed in our leather helmets, goggles, and oxygen masks. In their place we were issued new oxygen masks, soft inner helmets incorporating slim headphones, and an outer hard helmet (bone dome) to which was attached a dark visor for high altitude work. We were also issued with string vests, soft collar-attached shirts, a 'G' suit, 'Sabre boots', and a very comfort-able anorak.

Before converting to Sabres I had to cut a slit in the side seam of my uniform trousers so that the pipe from the 'G' suit (worn over our underclothes) could protrude. String vests were initially popular but were soon not used because, to put it in the vernacular of the time "They rubbed our tits off". The new helmets took some getting used to, and later proved themselves essential. The new 'Sabre' boots were like shoes, but with a boot extension above. This was said to make them waterproof and, in an evasion situation, could be cut away to resemble shoes. They replaced our then habit of wearing crêpe-soled shoes for flying. These were silent when marching and became dangerously slip-pery on spilled aviation fuel.

17. Extraneous Duties And Jever Life

S O FAR I HAVE concentrated mainly on Squadron life and flying duties, but there is another side to being an Officer in the General Duties (Flying) Branch of the RAF. It is timely now to look at these changing aspects as they had a bearing on my activities throughout the rest of my service career.

My embarrassing situation of being a Squadron MTO, and officially being unable to drive, had to be rectified. On seeking the advice of the Station MTO I found that the only qualified driving instructor with authority to 'pass me out' was a Flt.Lt. Higgins. Due contact was made, and during a chat, he discovered that I been driving agricultural tractors, towing all sorts of loads and implements, since age 13! He then decided that a bit of practical wagon driving was called for. After no more than three hour-long sessions in a Thorneycroft 3-tonner he was satisfied that I was competent to be given the necessary authority to drive RAF vehicles in Germany.[1] A licence was issued. After a couple of further, unofficial, sessions with friend Higgins, I was, most unusually for an Officer, given authority to tow aircraft should the need arise.

When Sqn.Ldr. Bob Allen, the Boss, heard this he told me to start teaching a dozen or more Airmen how to drive and get them checked out as Class 'B' drivers. So, in very quick time, I became a driving instructor!

I had better explain that the Duty Squadron maintained an hourly bus service from the domestic site to the 4 and 93 Squadron hangars on the opposite side of the airfield. 4 and 93 alternated, week in, week out. A Thorneycroft fitted with seats under its canvas tilt was used. I had two drivers for this who were mis-employed from their proper trades

---

1   I practised hill starts using the MT vehicle drive-up servicing ramp as there were no hills within many tens of miles of Jever.

for the purpose. This was unfair on them and it was time to release them and use others whom I now had to train. That is not to say that these were the only drivers on the Squadron, for enough had been found for our convoy to Sylt. A Tactical Squadron which had to be able to move at short notice to a new operating base had to have drivers and, through postings and personnel changes, 93 was now short. Hence my task. I used Wednesday afternoons for training. Volunteers were forthcoming, mostly from those who wanted an excuse to skive off organised sport. During ensuing sessions I familiarised each learner in turn with the controls and how they worked. I personally drove them round a large hard-standing out of harms way and showed them how to start up and engage first gear and stop. I then sent them solo. In this vast area they learned how to steer, start and stop, at slow speed. I had several learners doing this at the same time. Next, I showed them how to change gear, and they drove faster as a result. This they did until they could go through the box, double-declutching and without too much graunching of gears. Thus the lessons advanced. I sat with each learner in turn, as necessary, to check them out, then I tried a brief convoy of maybe half a mile or so along the perimeter track. Reversing was more difficult. Using sand bags as markers, each learner had to reverse into a 'bay'. As they grew more competent the bay was made narrower. Finally

Two of my Thorneycroft 3-tonners on convoy practice north of Jever. Whenever we stopped, as in this case, we almost always attracted a crowd of youthful spectators.

I sat with each driver to test them out. Tuition in road signs was interspersed with practical lessons and it was only a matter of a few weeks before I had drivers competent enough for duty. The whole operation became known as 'Pod's Circus'. In the summer we held convoy practices of four or five vehicles to as far as the north coast for a spot of swimming or messing about on the beach. These sessions proved very popular and the Squadron was never again short of drivers in my time.

The other Squadron pilots had their duties. Bernie Revnell looked after the accounts of the Squadron Fund, from which purchases were made for the Coca-Cola bar, Squadron ties, and other odds and ends. Brian Iles and George Hickman, in their turn, kept the Squadron Diary (Form 540). One or other of us would take a turn for a few months as Squadron Adjutant.

Brian Sanderson, Geoff Couch, and 'Al' Ramsay recorded the Squadron month-end statistics, filling in charts in a prescribed manner, using 'Uno' stencils. Others held barrack inventories or were responsible for overseeing sports and diverse activities across the Station. On a camp as big as Jever there were enough Officers to share these duties fairly evenly without too much doubling-up. This was unlike the situation

Filling a jerrycan from a drainage ditch to quench the thirst of a Thorneycroft. Gerry Busby on left, myself in the middle, with SAC Rose filling the can.

later in my career when I was at a small Unit where to have at least four onerous and demanding extraneous duties was the norm. These, of course, were in addition to one's prime duty and purpose for being there.

In addition to being Squadron MTO and i/c Station Tug-of-War (which I was still able to dodge because of continuing lack of interest) I was allocated two other tasks: that of being i/c Visits by Air Squadrons and Summer Camps, and being overseer of the PSI Gardens. In neither instance was there any hand-over from the previous incumbent. Each is worthy of further explanation.

The Visits by Air Squadrons and Summer Camps job was an infrequent responsibility. Indeed there was only one such visit, by a University Air Squadron, during my time. It was my duty to co-ordinate accommodation for, and the activities of, the visitors. On this occasion the whole Station was involved to some extent so much of the work was done for me. All I had to do was to liaise with the visitors and make sure everything ran smoothly for them. It is of passing interest that among the group was an old school pal of mine who had been in the CCF with me. We were each surprised to meet. But it was not the last time that we would meet in the RAF.

The PSI gardens were a thoroughgoing business staffed by a number of GSO men under the supervision of head gardener Herr Goldbaum. Officially, the prime duty of the gardens was to produce flowering plants for the ornamental gardens at the Guardroom, Station Headquarters, Officers Mess, and other significant locations on the Station. The secondary task was to produce plants and flowers for sale in the PSI Shop to the married patch and, added to this, the production of fresh vegetables, both for use in the Messes to supplement basic rations, and for sale in the PSI Shop.[2] The shop itself was run by volunteer ladies from the married patch.[3]

---

2   PSI = President of the Station Institute. This was an 'On Station' organisation run by a committee and concerned itself with the sales of plants, crops, etc., grown on the Station land, the NAAFI, Malcolm Club, SSAFA, and other welfare facilities which may be present. On small Stations this hardly existed, but on a large Station like Jever it had a significant influence on the running of matters of welfare.

3   The shop was built on, or close to, the site of what had been the families' hostel building. This building, one of the few wooden ones at Jever (the cinema was another), had burned down just before my arrival. Those families lodging there lost all their possessions, but there was no injury or loss of life. Flt.Sgt. Telfer of 93 Squadron was one of the unfortunates.

The market garden, for that is what it was, was about two acres in extent and had three large greenhouses. One was a 'stove' or hothouse, the other a 'moderate' house, and the third was only heated enough to keep the frost out. The garden was situated in a clearing in the forest on the far side of the airfield, behind some concealed hard-standings not far from 93 Squadron hangar. Add to this the area of land either side of the ring road at the end of the airfield (nearly four acres in extent) which was used for growing potatoes and other crops, and the 'parish' for which I was responsible became significant.

It is relevant here to mention that there was a pig farm near 4 Squadron hangar. This was the responsibility of Danny Daniels. He had over 100 pigs, a boar and several breeding sows under his command. GSO staff were employed to look after it. My connection with the pig farm stems only from the time when I looked after things for Danny when he went on leave (he did the same for me), and the fact that quantities of pig manure were used by my gardeners and on the farm to augment supplies from the stables of the equitation facility.[4]

Profits from the gardens and farm went into PSI funds. It was my responsibility to make sure that, after all official garden expenses and messing supplies were covered, the sale of products via the shop turned in a profit. With the skill of the gardeners, and the fertility of the soil, this was no trouble. Few on the Station knew of the 'behind the scenes' activities of my gardeners. I was officially responsible for the gardens to Wg.Cdr. Russell-Bell, Wing Commander Admin., with whom I had to liaise, especially when it came to harvest time on the open farm. I left it to him to arrange for the necessary Wednesday sports afternoons to be used for the grossly unpopular task of potato picking, and, in the following year, to arrange for a local farmer to sow, and later harvest, a crop of barley which was sold for PSI funds.

The gardens, as with all Station facilities, were subject to periodic inspections, usually after Saturday morning parade. As soon as the parade was over I would hasten to the gardens and warn Herr Gold-baum what was afoot. He then made sure the gardeners looked busy, and together we would wait for the inspecting Officer, usually the

---

4 This facility and stables were run by a GSO man who was an ex-cavalryman. It was overseen by Brian Watson of 4 Squadron and was located to the rear of Flying Wing Headquarters. It was used primarily by families, although anybody could use the facility and take riding lessons for a modest fee.

Station Commander. On one such morning Wg.Cdr. Russell-Bell came instead and promptly criticised the rows of vegetables for not being straight! As if in retribution, one of the Squadrons, seconds later, and just as Wg.Cdr. Russell-Bell had entered a greenhouse, made a sonic attack on the airfield.[5] Some glass shattered and fell on 'himself', much to the concealed amusement of the German staff and me. At this instant he declared the inspection complete.

Herr Goldbaum spoke next to no English. My knowledge of German was still elementary but expanding, and dictionaries sometimes had to be referred to, but we managed surprisingly well and with good humour. The names of plants were a problem until we realised that Latin was a common language; that was helpful. Later, towards the time when I was due to leave Jever, I could even understand him when he called me on the phone, even if I did have a job to put together my reply in simple German.

Not exactly market gardening, and certainly nothing to do with the RAF, was the occasion when, walking back to camp one Saturday afternoon, I saw in a field adjacent to the road a heifer giving birth to her calf. One or two people were watching not realising that she was having great difficulty delivering her offspring. Having had experience of this sort of thing before, I decided to help. Climbing the fence, then stripping off my jacket and rolling up my sleeves, I did what was necessary to ease the birth of a healthy calf, right under the eyes of the German onlookers. After wiping as much slime as I could from my hands and arms on the grass, I picked up my coat, slung it over my shoulder, and continued my walk back to camp for a good wash.

Now for a change of subject:

As soon as I had any contact with the wives of married Officers ('Officers' Ladies', to be precise), usually on weekend evenings when they were always welcome to visit the Mess bar or upstairs Ladies room, I found a high proportion of them to be extremely rank conscious, almost more so than their husbands, many carrying it to the point of downright snobbishness. This caused friction on the married patch, in the Families' NAAFI Shop, and on tennis courts. Wise were they who were bold enough to stand aside, for it was extremely difficult to ignore. It sometimes went so far as to disrupt family life, even to cause

---

5   By this time we had converted to Sabres.

separation and lead to divorce. In reality, although some would only very grudgingly accept it, no wife had any rank. They were civilians whose husbands had joined the Royal Air Force, and that was all.

Marriage itself was frowned upon until the Officer was well into his 20s, preferably over 24, and then, when planned, had officially to be approved by the Station Commander, not that he could do anything to prevent it. He could, however, in cases where he had very good reason to disapprove, arrange for an immediate overseas posting so that matters could sort themselves out on the basis of absence making the heart grow fonder – or otherwise.

Social contact between Officers' families and those of other ranks was difficult without incurring adverse comment, yet in no way was it forbidden. Many facilities were shared, the aforementioned NAAFI Shop, the PSI Shop, Chapels, married patch sports facilities, Astra Cinema, BFES School, and the bus into town, were all places of contact and necessarily used by all wives, yet this rank consciousness still persisted.[6] Separation was generally the norm but never the rule. It must have been very difficult for young wives setting up home for the first time in this artificial environment.

There is another aspect: if an Officer found that a relative or close friend from civilian life, maybe an old school chum, was posted to the same Station, and was not of commissioned rank, Confidential Orders dictated that the two should only meet privately, off camp, and not to be seen conversing in friendly fashion while at work. Whilst seeming at first sight to be harsh, this was necessary for the prevention of favouritism and for the maintenance of good discipline.

As a living-in Officer I was occasionally invited into the married quarters (homes) of friends. This could be awkward, for it was traditional to take some small gift for one's hostess on such occasions. The usual thing was to go to the Mess Shop and buy a box of 'Black Magic' or similar confectionery and take that, but the choice was limited.[7] Having always been handy with my hands, during my first leave I bought several

---

6 BFES = British Forces Education Service. This organisation ran the schools on Stations where there were families. Teachers had officer status and, at Jever, lived in the Mess but usually kept themselves to themselves, retiring to the Ladies room for certain occasions.

7 The Mess shop was upstairs, across the landing from the Ladies room, and stocked a range of necessities including cigarettes, confectionery, and toiletries.

marquetry kits and a small box of necessary tools. The pictures I made up during spare time in my room became suitable alternative gifts.

My main hobby was 8mm movie photography. Initially I had a simple camera given to me by my father, but it wasn't long before I went to Staschen Optik (a photography shop in Jever from where I had previously bought a radio) and traded it in for a better model. I took many hundreds of feet of colour film but I couldn't see the results without a projector. On another leave I bought the necessary machine as well as a kit of basic editing equipment. I was then able to edit my creations, learning at the same time how I could improve my techniques, and, after cutting out much waste, I turned the resulting product into one of acceptable quality. Ron Gray, from 4 Squadron, had a similar hobby and between us we produced some amateurish records of events at Jever. It was not unusual, after a filming and editing session, for there to be a film show, using the wall as a screen, in either Ron's or my room.[8]

Travel, off camp, was either by RAF transport when on official business, or by the use of the local Pekol bus. Pekol ran a frequent service between the camp gates and the centre of Jever and was regularly used by all Jever personnel. It was cheap and convenient. Some, however, had their own cars but they were in the minority. 'Jock' Jack from 4 Squadron had a motorbike. Brian Watson and Pete Smith, also both of 4 Squadron, owned cars, the former a Ford 'Popular'. Al Colvin and George Hickman of 93 both owned old Opel Kapitäns. There was talk at one time of John Culver and myself buying NSU 'Quickly' mopeds but those much discussed plans came to nothing. Brian Iles owned not only his yellow Miles M18 private plane but an ancient Riley 'Nine' as well. There were few private cars about in those days.

My rare visits to Wilhelmshaven were by train or in someone's car. My abiding memory of it as I approached was of a distant landscape dotted with building-site tower cranes. Getting much closer, I saw new buildings rising out of old rubble fields. Most of these were blocks of flats and small industrial units. A large typewriter factory was very prominent. On nearing the centre of the town I saw toppled circular, cone-topped, or bullet shaped, reinforced concrete air raid shelters. Any

---

8   The surviving results of my film making at Jever are lodged in the Royal Air Force Museum at Hendon and can usually be viewed, subject to prior appointment. They have since been video-taped. Disappointingly, apart from one sequence, there are almost no shots of aircraft in action on account of security considerations at the time.

houses were very small by UK pre-war standards. Private houses were not as common as at home because most town-dwelling Germans lived in flats. There were shops, but not that many. Annoyingly, there was no rationing and bananas were on sale.[9] The old Kriegsmarine dock-yard and nearly all dock buildings had either been flattened during the war or dismantled by the Allied Powers afterwards. What had been the dockyard was wired off and notices saying 'Eintritt Verboten' and 'Gefahr Sprengstoff' were every few yards along the boundary.[10] Within the fence there was hardly anything to be seen. One of the few town buildings which appeared to have survived the war largely undamaged was the brick and reinforced concrete, slab-sided, Teutonic-looking, Rathaus. It was tall, and it was possible to climb flights of bare concrete steps to a flat viewing area on the roof. The stairwell, as in other German public buildings, absolutely reeked of stale cigar smoke, making it a pleasure to get out into the fresh air. From the top, on a good day, I saw right across the Jade Busen and, to the north, the coast and the nearer low-lying off-shore islands, and the Heligoland Bight beyond. The forest of Jever, and Jever Schloss, were also clearly visible in the flat landscape, but not the airfield. Nearer to, Prince Rupert boarding school for the children of British servicemen was also plainly visible and was one of the larger buildings in the area.

My free time on camp was taken up with my photographic interests, letter writing, reading, marquetry, listening to my radio, or going for walks. There were a goodly number of drinking sessions, or 'thrashes' as we called them. They were a part of air force life. Some of us, and I was one, tended not to indulge in the alcoholic excesses in the way that others did. As a result, I was able to save money rather than waste it buying a filthy hangover. Many was the time when there was a thrash after which some of us would go for a walk in the cool of the pine forest on a fine summer's (or any) evening. Even if there was gale it was quiet on the forest floor, walking on the springy pine needles. This was a favourite thing to do especially after a Dining In Night. We knew our

---

9 There was still rationing when I left the UK, and I hadn't seen a banana since before the war.

10 Eintritt Verboten = Entry Forbidden (keep out). Gefahr Sprengstoff = Danger Explosives. The latter notice could be seen almost anywhere in Germany in places where live ammunition was suspected. Much that was still around was usually in a dangerous, unstable, state.

way along the forest tracks even in the dark, and we didn't have to go off camp to do it, so big was the site.

Off camp there were plenty of walks. A popular one was to go across the airfield and out through a crash gate to the Forsthaus pub for a glass or two of Jever Pils. This was a fairly strong lager, somewhat more powerful than a similar quantity of bitter beer at home. I never did like bitter and, at my age, I much preferred the Pils and indeed, still do – when I can get it. On one of these Forsthaus excursions someone locked the crash gate while we were out. I can say from experience that climbing over a high chain-link fence with strands of barbed wire at the top to get into an RAF site is no easy task, even using the bars of a crash gate. But we did it.

Another favourite walk was to go off camp and approximately follow the perimeter fence for a distance through the countryside and back. It was when doing this that we found the Wolf Gibbet where, it was said, the last wolf to be found in that part of Germany was ceremoniously hanged. Not far from there was Heidmühle where there was a working windmill. It was an almost medieval sight watching the sails turning, hearing the machinery inside, and seeing a farmer with his horse and cart unloading sacks of wheat for them to be hoisted aloft into one of the high doors near the top of the mill. Meanwhile, another man with his horse and cart was loading sacks of flour from the bottom door. A memorable sight indeed, one that few will have seen in recent times.

Fg.Off. Fred Maycock of 4 Squadron lived in the top, right-hand, front room of our Officers block, on the corner and diagonally oppo-site to my room.[11] He was a good pianist and also keen on sound and radio receiving equipment. He made and modified his own circuits and adapted older tackle to suit his requirements. His room was like a radio workshop. It was his hobby and mostly we left him to it. However he annoyed us somewhat when, late one evening, he turned his gear up to max volume (several tens of watts power) and deafened us, actually shaking the building with the sound. After remonstrations he reluc-tantly promised not to do it again and, give him credit, he never did, at least when anyone else was around. One Saturday afternoon I helped him to string up an aerial from the corner of the block near to his room to a tall tree across the road. I climbed the tree, to quite a height,

11 Looking at the photo on page 108, Fred's room was at top, right.

with a line tied round my waist when, to our horror, the CO drove slowly underneath in his car. I froze. Fred tried to look innocent, and the Station Commander didn't stop. We strung up the aerial and Fred's gear worked the better for it. On returning to our rooms after tea the following Monday we found that the aerial had disappeared. Nothing was ever said! Fred later wired his sound equipment output to the newly installed Station Tannoy system but was disappointed that, in spite of using maximum power, no noise came out of any of the speakers, not even the nearest ones.

Most of us had radios in our rooms. Our favourite stations were Radio Luxembourg, BFN, and AFN.[12] The news on the latter, which was always proudly announced as coming from "The wires of AP, UP, and INS", was very naive and introspectively American, with little world information, almost as if items outside the American Zone or the USA had been censored out.[13] BFN relayed the news from the BBC and was more reliable, of greater interest, and had a wider coverage of subjects. We nearly always listened in to the request programmes on BFN. Some of us were lucky enough to hear our names announced by Barry Aldiss, a popular DJ at the time. Some of us tried tuning into the BBC's International News Service but reception wasn't good on short wave. We were thus able to keep up with all the popular songs of the day on the medium wave in this pre-skiffle period. German radio, typically the Nordwestdeutscherundfunk, had just as sloppy love songs. It was of interest to those of us casually trying to increase our knowledge of German. We were able to compare our Met briefings with their Wetterbericht, and so improve our knowledge of their weather terms.

I had two years of German language lessons at school but did not take any serious exams. I was surprised at Jever that the general level of knowledge of German was slight to almost non-existent. I had hoped that I would have been able to improve my fluency. There was even an element of mockery of those wanting to learn. Indeed, we all spoke English (in various dialects) on camp, so the need was not great. I spent some time attending German lessons in the Education Section but these were so elementary that I gave up. Flt.Lt. 'Phil' Phillips, the Senior Education Officer, did the teaching, not a local German as I had

---

12 BFN = British Forces Network. AFN = American Forces Network.

13 AP = Associated Press. UP = United Press. INS = International News Service.

hoped.[14] I had to content myself with learning as many nouns as I could and coupling them together with my sparse knowledge of grammar. This seemed to get me by in most situations. The Education Section did however have its uses when it came to swotting up for Promotion Exams. At this critical period all of us who were candidates were able to attend lectures, both during the day, and in our own time in the evenings, to acquaint ourselves with the types of questions we could expect to be asked, and to receive further tuition in any areas of special difficulty.

Just occasionally someone in our block would have his radio turned up far too loud and too late at night. If our rooms were close enough to the culprit we could counter this by tuning in to the same station and, with our volume turned right down, by very careful manipulation of the tuning knob create an interference howl which, with practice, we could vary in pitch and intensity, thus jamming the culprit's reception. The message was quickly understood and peace would be restored.

There was a kerfuffle in our block one Saturday night after a drinking session. There was horse-play in the room opposite Fred's and next to mine (occupant's name now forgotten) when the wash-basin was torn from the wall, severing the hot and cold supply pipes flush with the plaster. Said occupant found himself with a finger up each pipe in an attempt to stop two powerful jets of water, one cold, the other uncomfortably hot, from flooding not only the room but the whole block while yelling his drunken head off for someone to turn off the supplies at some unknown master valves. This went on for about an hour until, somehow, with assistance, the flow was staunched, I think with whittled sticks torn from a nearby tree and rammed into the pipes. And they called us Officers and Gentlemen!

One of our less responsible sports was bicycle polo. This took place on the Mess lawn, usually between the two flying Squadrons, after someone had made the challenge during a Saturday lunchtime session in the bar. Weapons used were hockey sticks, a hard ball, and bikes purloined from just about anywhere, including those on loan from the Station Warrant Officer's Bicycle Store. There were almost no rules. Thwacks on ankles were not unknown and could be as frequent as hits on the ball. The 'game' stopped after sufficient players had fallen off,

---

14   Phil was promoted to Squadron Leader and, on promotion, instead of being posted away as was usual, he remained at Jever for the rest of his tour in Germany.

bicycles damaged, or players hurt! A stop was put to this 'sport' after Warrant Officer Dale, the SWO, found his bikes were getting damaged and reported the matter to the CO.[15]

Flt.Lt. 'Wilbur' Wright, Station Signals Officer, had recently moved into the Mess following a break-up of his marriage. His room was in one of the old Luftwaffe Officers blocks overlooking the Mess lawn. There were upstairs dormer rooms in these blocks which were not usually occupied. Wilbur, though, being keen on model railways, had taken over one of these for his hobby. Over time he built up a layout of considerable size and complexity, so much so that he needed a hand with its construction and operation. As a result of chance conversations both Tommy Balfour (of 93) and I became closely involved with 'Wilbur's trains'. The three of us spent many long and happy hours up there. The amount of wiring involved was considerable, with lengths of large multi-core telephone cable linking complex sections to the relevant control panels. It became well known in the Mess and there were frequent visitors to this Märklin HO gauge layout. It even became a subject of inspection, more out of curiosity and genuine interest than officialdom, by the CO after Saturday morning parades. Almost everyone was disappointed when Wilbur was posted back to the UK, and watched him drive off with huge chunks of layout strapped to the roof rack on his car.

Pay, of course, was of considerable importance to everyone. The Airmen had Pay Parades fortnightly. These irksome occasions meant standing, sometimes for an hour or more, waiting for everyone's name to be called out in alphabetical order. It was usual for there to be a Paying Officer and two Witnessing Officers. I dreaded being nominated as a Paying Officer because of the amount of notes which had to be counted out, something at which I was absolutely no use. It never happened, but I was a Witnessing Officer more than once and each time there was neither a surplus nor a deficiency, something which would have given rise to an enquiry, with any deficiency being made up from one's personal funds.

Our own pay, or 'Emoluments' as they were called, was paid directly by Government nominated bankers directly into our private bank accounts each month. In Germany, however, there were strict currency

---

15 A filmed sequence of this is held at the Royal Air Force Museum, Hendon.

controls and we could elect, through the Station Accounts Office, to draw a portion of our pay in either Deutschmarks or BAFSVs.[16] The German currency was for use off camp, whereas all on-camp transactions were done in BAFSVs, with only penny and halfpenny coins being used for small change. Large amounts such as Mess bills were settled by personal cheque. It could be difficult when going on leave because BAFSVs were not accepted in the UK, so it was always advisable to keep some Sterling back from the previous leave for these occasions until it was possible to call at a Bank. The official, and fixed, exchange rate was 12DM for £1-0-6d. Pounds Sterling, whether in BAFSVs or not, had the same value.

A threepenny note.

The reverse face of a threepenny note. 3d would buy a tot of Three Star Desroche brandy in the Mess bar.

---

16 BAFSVs = British Armed Forces Special Vouchers. We all called them 'Baffs'. The lowest denomination was a 3d note and the highest, I heard, was a £5 note although I never saw one.

18. Ehrwald

JUST AFTER LUNCH ON Saturday, March 13th, 1954, Fg.Off. 'Dinger' Bell and I were driven in an open Land Rover to Sande station. In civilian clothes and carrying light hand luggage we were on our way to Austria for a fortnight's Arctic Survival Course. We caught the Wilhelmshaven to München (Munich) overnight train and arrived at Munich Hauptbahnhof the following morning. After a short wait, and after breakfast in the station buffet, we caught a train to Garmisch-Partenkirchen, arriving there shortly before lunch. An unmarked RAF bus met us, and took us to our course headquarters in Erhwald across the Austrian border.

No.6 Arctic Survival Course, Ehrwald. I am 8th from the left, back. John Lovell is 1st from right, back. Sqn.Ldr. Daniels is 7th from the left, back. Dinger Bell is 6th from right, back. The CO, Sqn.Ldr. Uprichard is centre, front.

Austria by then had become an independent nation following the withdrawal of the Forces of Occupation. Ehrwald, and Lermoos, the village across the valley, had jointly been a British Forces Leave Centre during the occupation. It was because of this that the locals agreed for the RAF, but without any identification, to hold the course in that area.[1]

Ehrwald from the slopes on which we learned to ski.

Our HQ was the Gasthaus Thörle on the road from Ehrwald to the Zugspitzbahn, the cable railway to the top of the Zugspitze (the highest mountain in Germany but with the greater part of its massif in Austria). Our accommodation was sparse, the sun room on the south side of the Gasthaus was our dormitory equipped with three-tier bunks. We had blankets but no sheets. Food was cooked for us by the innkeeper's wife and was plain and mostly varieties of stew or goulash with bread rolls. There was one toilet and only one bath. The effluent from both poured out on to the sloping forest floor not five yards from the veranda but didn't stink as it was quickly frozen into a disgusting and increasing mass. Washing and shaving, using tin wash-basins, was done outside in the cold, but was a more pleasant procedure when the sun was shining. We used our reflections in the windows as shaving mirrors. Ablution

---

1   The Austrians probably had their eye to business, for several of us were to return there on holiday in later years. I went back three times, the last was in 1973 when the Gasthaus Thörle was in process of being demolished and rebuilt.

times saw shivering naked and semi-naked men out in the snow, cleaning themselves as best they could and as quickly as possible. There was often a queue for the toilet. We usually urinated in the nearby forest, even in the middle of the night when wearing pyjamas. Speed was of the essence.

Looking towards Ehrwald in the bottom of the valley, with the Zugspitze behind.

We were regarded as civilians and it was only by chance that any of us found out another's rank. It turned out that we varied in status from Wing Commander to Pilot Officer. First names were the norm. The CO was Sqn.Ldr. Uprichard (in civvies, of course). He lived in the village with his wife during the time he was in Austria. The permanent staff numbered no more than six or seven and lived in what were normally the guest rooms which had their own sparse facilities.

We were issued with ski boots, ski clothing, and skis, and for most of the first week we were taught to ski on the nursery slopes at the back of Ehrwald. I had a personal difficulty in that there were no boots that would fit me. Fortunately, after nearly crippling my feet by wearing a pair that were too small, for a whole day, one of our Austrian Instructors told me where to go in the village to hire some boots of the right size. But damage had been done and my feet hurt, so, as a result, for most of the time I lagged behind the others in proficiency. Even so, we had great fun helplessly colliding with each other and falling over until we found our feet (or our skis) and attempted to regain an upright posture. Even though the spring thaw was setting in and there was much grass to be seen where there had been snow, we were able to use the drag lift and ski back down to the village as many times as necessary. Later, in view of the decreasing snow cover, we transferred to the shadier slopes at the other side of the valley behind Lermoos. Our last ski run was down-hill for over a mile and was completed successfully, and without mishap, by all. What a thrill it was to glide down this long steady slope on my own feet at thirty miles an hour!

The evenings were filled with survival instruction from both our own instructors and invited Austrian specialists. We were even visited by someone from the Secret Service who advised us on methods to use to evade capture in potentially enemy territory. We never knew his name, and he disappeared off, on foot, into the night when he had finished his talk.

The first week over, there was a party on the Saturday night. Beer was fetched from the village by a group of students, one of whom didn't return. The party went well, and late. Three American Officers joined us, one a female. When the singing got going, 'The Happy Wanderer', as sung by the Obenkirchen childrens' choir, being the favourite at the time, we became, after suitable lubrication of the vocal chords, quite good at the falsetto bits. Yodelling was attempted with much hilarity, but was judged to be a failure. The American female did her bit but her absolutely flat and tuneless voice was described by someone as being that of a constipated duck – out of her hearing, of course.

The missing student walked sheepishly and slowly back from the village on the Sunday morning. He had found a willing Fraülein and had spent a randy night with her.

The emphasis during the second week was on evasion and survival. We had been taught how to make traps, set snares, build an igloo, build a fire on deep snow, build a shelter to protect ourselves from the elements, how to keep warm, make snow shoes – all from what we could find – and minor first aid. Now it was our turn to put these skills into practice. On the Sunday evening one of the village elders came to brief us on what to do if things went wrong, such as a broken limb, or similar. Accordingly, we were issued with whistles and told the whistle codes to use to summon help; codes which everyone in the area would recognise as coming from someone in distress. Search parties would then be sent out. We were then told to pair up with someone we hadn't known before coming on the course. Flt.Lt. John Lovell and I teamed up, were given a local map and were told where to make for across country from the place where we would be dropped next morning. There would be people looking for us, and we had to avoid them.

As expected, the following day, with pieces of aluminium, an empty can each, a block of chocolate, a small amount of hard-tack rations, two tins of food for use only in an absolute emergency, and some parachute panels and cord – all to simulate what we might rescue from a downed aircraft – together with our dinghy knives, a small machete and a sleeping bag each (the only 'home' comfort allowed), we lined up to board the bus. We were ordered not to team up with another pair until we reached our briefed final destination area, at which place we would be contacted at the end of the exercise and told to return to the Gasthaus.

John and I were dropped a good four miles from our final rendezvous point and were told to start making our way to it from within the edge of the forest up a long and steep grassy slope. Our route would take us across several ravines, then down to cross a main road and railway line, before climbing again over a bluff to the finish. We had three days and nights in which to do this.

We climbed up the open, partly snow-covered, alpine pasture and on into the forest for our start. At this height there was lot of patchy snow, some of it very deep, but in the trees there were clear areas as well. Because of the nature of the terrain we decided it was too dangerous to move far after dark so, from our starting point we made our way along, within the edge of the trees, as far as we could before deciding to stop for the night.

We made camp on a dry patch of deep pine needles. After gathering some stones to make a hearth we lit a fire of pine twigs, melted considerable quantities of snow in the tin cans to get enough water to drink, nibbled on a bit of chocolate and settled down for the evening by our fire so as to be ready for an early start next day. Before settling into our sleeping bags we melted more snow for a morning drink and checked out our kit and supplies so as to make best use of what we had. As instructed, we took off our boots and put them in our sleeping bags with us to stop them from freezing, then settled down under a clear, starry, frosty sky.

The firebed was still hot next morning and we soon were able to melt the ice in our tins for a hot drink, this time with some chocolate peelings in it for flavour and a little nourishment. After dowsing the fire with snow, and clearing up after ourselves, we started on our way but soon found our route blocked by an impassable tree-lined, deep, rocky, ravine. Having no alternative but to find a way round this obstacle we headed downhill into low cover, cautiously crossed some open ground and started back up towards the cover of the forest.

We hadn't been careful enough and had been seen. A shout "Halt, wer ist da?" came from a lane in the valley below. We were going to dive for cover when the voice shouted "Halt oder ich schiesse". Standing by some rocks, but in poor cover, we had no alternative but to reply "Ja, wir warten hier, wo sind Sie?"[2] Panting up the steep slope came a rotund Austrian Policeman brandishing a gun rather too purposefully for our liking. We moved into the open so that he could see us. Again he shouted breathlessly "Halt, oder ich schiesse". So we stood still. Just then, and by now less than fifty yards from us, he tripped, fell on his face, and dropped his hand gun. It was too much for us and we both burst out laughing. Picking himself up, and now very red faced, he stumbled on towards us, and we moved down to meet him in friendly fashion. With our hands now raised because of his gun, we explained who we were, what we were doing, and where we were from. We showed our identification to prove what we had said. Satisfied, he put his gun away, shook hands with us and made his way back down the side of the valley. We made for the trees again and moved on as fast as we could.[3]

We made very good, surprisingly good, progress and, instead of taking two days to get to our rendezvous we did it by nightfall that same day. Now we could relax and set up a proper camp. There was just light enough for us to set up a hearth on some bare ground in the forest and light a fire. By the light of this we cut enough wood to construct a lean-to in the manner we had been taught, and did a very rough thatching job. That night after opening some of our hard-tack, for by now we were getting very hungry after not stopping at lunch time, we boiled

---

2   Translations: Halt, who is there. Halt or I'll shoot. Yes we're waiting here, where are you?

3   It turned out afterwards at debriefing that this Polizist had mistaken us for German smugglers crossing the border with illicit goods (our packs) and which was only a mile or so away from where we had been seen.

up some sort of stew with melted snow. Very tired, we settled into our sleeping bags.

It had rained in the night but our rough thatch had kept us reasonably dry. We at once set about improving our shelter so as to cover in part of the front. With spruce fronds we made a mattress some four or five inches thick across the floor. We moved the hearth to nearer what had now become the doorway to our snug little nest. As the day wore on we decided to apply some camouflage and covered much of the roof with loose leaves and detritus from under some deciduous trees. By now the snow had melted considerably and only lay in patches. We ate and drank what we could, even mixing dissolved chocolate with edible lichen scraped from trees, just to find what it tasted like – awful! Knowing that the exercise would be over next day, and we had completed our journey early, put us into a more relaxed mood.

Early that evening we made ourselves a reasonable meal of what we could of the hard-tack and generally lounged about by our fire. Then we heard voices – English voices. Listening harder we could hear the CO and that dreadful American woman. Evasion now came to the forefront of our minds in the growing darkness. We saw a torch flashing about in the trees. It wouldn't be long before they saw our fire. We had to move, and move quickly and silently. Fortunately they were making more noise than us. We crept over to some glacial boulders not far away in the gloom under some particularly dense pine trees. They spotted our fire. Now they were looking for us. Rather than run, John and I curled up together among these boulders and quickly scraped together pine needles to scatter over us as camouflage. Our trackers wandered around for a bit and, finding no footprints in the snow patches, split up to search the clearer areas. It was all of half an hour that they searched, even coming as close as five yards from us and shining their torches at the boulders. Our camouflage worked and we were not found. Eventually the voices became more distant and we cautiously made our way back to our bivouac thinking they may have destroyed it. We were lucky; everything was still there. By now it was late so we settled down for a very comfortable night on our new mattress. It rained again but our roof held and we stayed dry and warm.

During the night we heard other students arriving and setting up shelters in the dark and rain not far away. They had a miserable night. We met up in the morning as more stragglers arrived. One chap had a call of nature when he was on deep snow. During his bowel movement he found himself sinking deeper. Already preoccupied, there was nothing he could do about it. By now blue and shivering in his predicament, it was all he could do to clean himself up with more snow. Not a happy experience, but one which he graphically described in unnecessary detail as a warning to us all. Pine needles, he said, were not an option.

With the exercise over we returned to the Gasthaus for shaves and thorough strip-down washes out in the drizzle. Debriefing followed and advice was given. John and I told of how close we were to being found and were given credit for our initiative, but were criticised for not having dowsed our fire before we hid from the search party.

There was an end of course party and, next morning, we packed and prepared for our journeys back to our respective camps.

En route back to Jever 'Dinger' Bell and I had time to spare in Munich, so we visited the Hofbraühaus to see this enormous drinking hall, hear the singing, and watch the barmaids in Bavarian costume serving countless steins of beer. The atmosphere was convivial, with no obvious drunkenness. Everyone was seated at long tables, up to ten or so down each side. Snacks and Schnapps were available to order. A traditional Bavarian band provided music and when there was singing it was usual for participants to sway from side to side in time to the music while holding their steins aloft. We were reluctant to leave and had to catch a taxi to the station as we had left it a little late to risk walking.

Our train left the Hauptbahnhof not long before midnight for our overnight journey. We had breakfast on the train and duly arrived at Sande. Transport met us and took us back to Jever in time for a late lunch.

No sooner had we arrived than I was told to get myself ready for an early departure the following (Sunday) morning as I was to go to Wildenrath with other Squadron pilots to learn to fly F86 Sabre aircraft.

It was only with the utmost co-operation of Frau Pinnau, my shared batwoman, that my kit was ready for this immediate change of occupation.

Although it hadn't affected us at all, while we were away the Squadron had been detached to RAF Ahlhorn while the Jever runway was resurfaced.

19. Sabres!

AT WILDENRATH WE WERE allocated rooms in the Officers transit accommodation which was little used and felt damp. Regardless, we were ready for our first day's instruction on the Monday morning. To my surprise, the course CO was Sqn.Ldr. Daniels, the very man I had been with at Ehrwald during the previous fortnight. We had a few quiet words about Ehrwald, otherwise it was down to business.

We had, previously, been able to read 'Sabre Pilot's Notes', back at Jever, but there is nothing like reading them when actually sitting in the cockpit of an aircraft. Vampires, size for size, were like kiddie-cars when compared with the huge bulk of a Sabre. I could stand by, and look down into, the cockpit of a Vampire whereas I had to stretch up and could only just get my fingertips on to the coaming of a Sabre cockpit – and I was the tallest pilot on the Squadron. The top of the tail fin was about 15 feet above the ground. To us, it was a massive aircraft. The cockpit was roomy too; each side of a Vampire's cockpit touched my arms when I was flying, but there was space in the Sabre to turn right round in it with straps undone. We even joked that the 'Yanks' had provided space for a Coke bottle, and that British designers put the pilot in as an afterthought, but the Americans built the aircraft round the pilot. On the other hand, in a Vampire there were a mere couple of dozen controls and switches of interest to a pilot in flight. A Sabre had about 180. You could waggle the stick in a dead Vampire, yet in a dead Sabre the stick was rigid because the controls were hydraulically actuated and wouldn't move without power. Clearly there was a lot of learning to be done in less than two weeks.

The first week of the course was devoted almost entirely to ground school work. This consisted of lectures and physical familiarisation with the aircraft. New Vital Actions had to be learned: emergency proce-dures, speeds for take-off, climb, stall, and landing, had to become second nature and reeled off verbally, and instantly, when asked. We spent much time sitting in cockpits learning the new layout, for this was entirely different to the British 'standard' layout with the six flying instruments panel always grouped in the same way. In a Sabre they were 'all over the place' and instrument flying was going to be difficult initially until the eye was trained to locate the relevant instruments as second nature. Fuel was measured in pounds, not gallons, and engine handling was going to be different. The Sabre had the Allison J47GE13 axial flow engine as opposed to the centrifugal compressor fan of the Vampire's De Havilland Goblin 2 engine.

Sitting in a cockpit in a hangar had its uses. Most of us learned quickly to be able to touch (blindfold) all the major instruments and to recite, at the same time, the routine and emergency procedures neces-sary for any pilot to know. As the learning progressed we were able to sit in the cockpit of an aircraft 'powered up' from a Struver diesel-en-gined starting generator (Vampires used Trolley Accs). With the power on, the electric and hydraulic systems became 'live', relevant warning lights and instruments began to mean something, and real-time cockpit checks could be practised. Our Course Instructors checked us out and tested us for competence in all the aspects possible while still on the ground, from simple but different things like strapping-in, to a full range of emergency procedures.

With the week's ground school formally over, we spent a nervous weekend, all of us with our Pilot's Notes in our rooms to continue our familiarisation. In the coming week we were to actually fly the brutes. There were no two-seater Sabres so each first flight had to be a solo affair.

My first flight came on Monday morning, April the 5th. Nerves were on edge in the crew room as we sat there all kitted up. Smokers smoked harder than ever, some of us couldn't sit still, and tensions ran high while we waited for our names to appear on the Detail Board. Three or four of us flew that morning. I was the third to go. I remember it as a clear day with little wind and being helped by an instructor with strapping-in and watched as I went through the engine start procedure for the first time. He reminded me of the Station and my personal call-signs, then he descended the ladder and he and the ground crew cleared the area. The past week's training took over. I called the Tower for taxi clearance, waved the chocks away, gingerly opened the throttle until I crept forward, engaged the nose-wheel steering by pressing on the button on the front of the stick with my little finger, and rolled out from the hard-standing on to the peri-track, checking the feel of the brakes as I did so.

Putting the fleeting thought that I was in charge of a quarter of a million quid's worth of Royal Air Force kit out of my mind I tried various throttle settings as I taxied my way to the runway threshold for take-off. Given clearance, I lined up on the centre-line, held the brakes hard on as I opened up to full power then, satisfied that all instruments were 'in the green', released the brakes and rolled forward with increasing rapidity, keeping straight with the rudder until I was airborne, leaving the usual thick trail of black smoke behind me.

Thus far I had learned how to start and taxi the thing, now I had the flying bit to do.

After a moment's hesitation to put my hand on the control I raised the gear. It clunked up and indicated up. I can't say that I climbed away steadily, but climb I did – with a slight porpoising action. The hydraulic controls were so sensitive that the merest movement of the stick resulted in a response from the aircraft. By the time I radioed that I was clear of the circuit I realised that I was still accelerating on the climb and that some rapid map reading was called for so that I could find where I was above this unfamiliar bit of Europe. Everything was happening so fast and, not wanting to stray too far from base, I throttled back to 85% power, levelled off at what looked like a sensible height (it was 15,000 feet when I checked) and shoved the stick over to port to do a 180 back towards base. Wham! My head hit the side of the canopy, so fast was the rate of roll, and I was nearly inverted, my 'G' suit inflated and took me by surprise, squeezing my legs and gut as it did so. That was off-putting in this first-time situation. This brute was vicious. With gentler control movements I taught it manners, but it took a while to stop over-correcting on the stick and reduce the consequential wing-waggling and porpoising. I have to admit that I was busy and keeping a good look out became a secondary occupation for a while. Shortly I became more comfortable and reached the point when the machine had stopped taking me for a ride and I was more or less making it do what I wanted. Gaining in confidence, I tamed the creature by trying out the usual raft of manoeuvres that one would do on an air test. I didn't stray far from Wildenrath, probably within a 40 nautical miles radius or so. A call came from the Tower to check my fuel state and to tell me that I should be thinking of landing.

Returning to Wildenrath I called for permission to join the circuit and, that given, I set up a wide circuit pattern to give time to carry out and check the slightly different vital actions for landing. Sweeping round at the end of the down-wind leg I called 'Finals' and lined up for my approach, aware that touch-down would look different as I was going to be much higher from the ground than in a Vampire when landing. OK, I landed a good 10 knots fast, at just under 130 knots, and have to admit that I used almost all of the near mile and a half long runway to stop. After that, taxying back was a doddle. I had done it, all 30 minutes of it!

I was a little late returning to the crew room after lunch and found that several pilots were really edgy, kicking chairs, being sullen, being fidgety, and generally creating an atmosphere of tension while waiting for their turns to solo. Having done it myself there was a degree of jealousy, the more so when my name appeared on the board for a second flight early that same afternoon.

Whilst my first flight was designated as 'familiarisation on type and sector recce' which had turned out to be more 'famil' than 'recce', this second one was 'familiarisation and general handling'.

Getting into the cockpit this time and starting up unsupervised was a step forward. I felt more assured but not yet very relaxed as I taxied out and took off.

It was a clear day with only a very few tufts of cloud as I climbed to something over 20,000 feet to start throwing the aircraft about, very much in charge of it, rather than it of me, this time. Then I had a peculiar feeling of being watched. It was as uncanny and unnatural as it was unexpected, but it was strong. I was flying more or less east at the time, with the sun on my starboard side. On scanning the sky for another aircraft in case someone was about to 'bounce' me there was nothing to see, only the sun, and emptiness. Still looking around, and still having this feeling, I noticed a patch of light to starboard which I at first thought was an internal reflection from something within the still strange cockpit. Turning a little to starboard, I proved it was no reflection and the patch of light stayed in the same spatial position. It was circular, white to bluish-white in colour, and almost looked as though it was liquid. It was smaller than the sun and not near it, being at the same apparent height as me. Not knowing its size I had no concept of its range. It fascinated me and held my attention. It started to move forward of me without my changing from straight and level flight. I then turned towards it and it disappeared momentarily as the windscreen strut passed over it and then it reappeared ahead. That proved conclusively that it was no reflection. I felt it was looking at me, and I didn't like it. Opening up to 100% power I headed and aimed for it. Within seconds, and with no increase in its apparent size or change of other characteristics, it accelerated vertically at enormous speed and disappeared. The feeling of being watched ceased at the same time. That gone, I had to put the matter out of my mind. I got on with my familiarisation sortie and now really gained in confidence at the controls, experimenting still further with the handling characteristics and getting bolder all the time. With a phenomenal roll rate (with stick hard over) you could almost emulate the flight of a shell shot out of a rifled barrel. Straight line 'slow' (bloody fast) rolls were a cinch. Pulling tight turns was simple, initially up to 7 'G' was easy with the 'G' suit squeezing my torso. Only after 7 'G' did I have to use standard techniques to delay grey out and black out. We were told we could not over-stress the airframe because our bodies would give up first. The rate of climb was good, and far exceeded that of a Vampire. Strangely, though, it was virtually impossible to move the rudder pedals in flight because of the aerodynamic loading on the rudder. Their only real use was when taxying, keeping straight on take-off, and towards the end of a landing run.

The 35 minute flight went well, in spite of the encounter, and this time I landed at the right speed.

As to the patch of light: I had never seen anything like it before – or since. I didn't report it on landing for fear of being ridiculed as it was widely held that such things were seen only by people who believed in fairies.[1]

I flew again the next day, but in cloudier conditions, this time climbing to 35,000 feet to get the feel of the aircraft in thinner air. Being

---

1   It was many months later before I spoke of this phenomenon. This is reported in a later chapter.

at greater altitude and with consequent reduction in fuel consumption this sortie lasted 45 minutes.

It was two days later when I flew again. By this time everyone on the course had gone solo and, as a result, there was much comparison of experiences in a more relaxed atmosphere. My first flight of the two on that day included general handling again and a practice QGH so as to get used, in clear air, to flying on instruments and controlling the aircraft under necessarily precise conditions.

The second flight involved the use of the Radio Compass – to us a new navigation facility not installed on Vampires – a Mach run, and finishing off with another QGH. I climbed to over 45,000 feet, rolled over on my back, and pulled through into a vertical dive with 100% power. As I accelerated towards the ground the Machmeter crept up, then there were the effects of compressibility, some juddering, and then it showed more than Mach 1 for a few seconds. Still diving vertically, with the details on the ground growing ever larger in my windscreen, I began to slow down because of the denser atmosphere, and slowed quickly below Mach 1 when, at below 20,000 feet, it was time to pull out of the dive without doing a high speed stall. I had flown faster than sound – that was something to tell the folks at home! Now in level flight I began to sweat and realised that the friction of the air had heated the airframe to the point when the canopy felt quite warm to a bared wrist. What the local population thought of the constant sonic booms they must have been hearing, and the damage done to their windows, I never knew. Later in the year we were ordered not to do any more Mach runs over land.

Using the Radio Compass gave us a chance to listen in to BFN or some other radio programme that appealed, (seldom) using its transmitter as a point of reference for navigation purposes. Seriously though, fixes could quickly be obtained by getting the bearings of two known radio transmitters and, without having to transmit, would not give away our location or identity to a potential enemy.

On the morning of Friday the 9th of April, the day our course ended, I was briefed for a sortie involving range and endurance flying at 40,000 feet. This sortie lasted 1 hour and 25 minutes, longer than I had been airborne in any one flight since my days of flying Oxfords.

Some of us were able to hitch a lift back to Jever in a Communications Flight Anson that afternoon. Lumbering along as a passenger in a clapped out old Annie in worsening weather bore no comparison to the exhilaration experienced at high speed in the past few days. Worse, the further north we proceeded the worse the weather became, to the point when Jever was clamped in and closed down. We had to divert to Oldenburg and continue our journey by road.

The Sabre Conversion Course at Wildenrath.

Five days elapsed before I flew again. This was for two reasons: the first was the generally poor weather, and the second was a scarcity of aircraft during the Sabre re-equipment phase and hand-over of Vampires. What turned out to be my last flight in a single-seater Vampire was in a Vampire 5, WA344. This aircraft, like all the others leaving the Squadron, had to be checked before it was ferried away. The sortie, therefore, was an air test and QGH. It was of 50 minutes duration, including 15 minutes Instrument Flying.

To get back in a cosy little, ground hugging, kiddie-car after flying the comparatively massive Sabre was like a step back into the past and I had, temporarily, to unlearn my recent retraining. This flight brought home to me the advantages of the RAF standard instrument layout over that of the more random Sabre instrument panel, as well as the lack of power of the Vampire which now seemed to scratch and crawl its way up to any altitude. Even in this slower aircraft the shortness of the Jever runway, compared with that at Wildenrath, was now all too apparent. Landing a Sabre at Jever had much potential for proving 'interesting'.

Unfortunately, as it happened, I would not have the chance to fly a Sabre again for some weeks as I was due to go on leave immediately after the imminent Easter break. It is appropriate to digress:

We were allowed two periods of three weeks UK leave and ten days 'Continental' leave at this time. Few single Officers bothered taking the local leave; it was more use to those who wanted time off with their families living in married quarters.

To get to the UK involved the issue of Travel Warrants for the European and UK rail journeys, and the use of the 'Blue Train' from Oldenburg to the Hook of Holland, overnight on either the 'Empire Parkestone' or 'Empire Wansbeck', and the troop-train to London's Liverpool Street station. From there on each of us made our own way home. The reverse was true for the return journey to Jever. Just occasionally, but this was very rare, it was possible to hitch a lift on a visiting transport aircraft back to the UK. Although one could end up landing almost anywhere, and paying for one's rail journey home, it usually meant an extra day's leave, and that was an over-riding advantage. Before leaving Jever it was essential to visit Flt.Lt. Wright, the Accounts Officer in SHQ, to change BAFSVs into Sterling coinage and notes for use at home. To forget this could prove embarrassing.

My own journey home was either to the Wirral or to Shropshire. My family had houses in Upton, near Birkenhead, and Welshampton, near Ellesmere. I favoured the Shropshire destination as the journey was shorter. The same train (from Paddington) stopped at both Shrewsbury and Birkenhead, Woodside, but after Shrewsbury began to call at all stations, a very frustrating situation which added a considerable time to the journey.

At home, my priority was always to arrange for any new uniforms or clothing, as such had to be ordered and fitted at a tailor's before the end of my leave. I used Moss Brothers in Liverpool and had an account with them. It was usual for the first week of the leave to be spent unwinding and forgetting about the RAF. The second week was relaxation, and, it was generally accepted by all, the third week was spent preparing for the return journey and re-attuning oneself to the forthcoming months away again in Germany.

It was on this first leave that my father gave me an 8mm movie camera to take back with me.[2] I well remember using it to film the German countryside from the Blue train on the way back to Jever, and someone pointing out to me that I still had the lens cap on!

---

2   The use of this camera has already been discussed in Chapter 17, page 166.

20. Back To Work Again

I ARRIVED BACK AT Jever on Sunday the 16th of May, unpacked, caught up with the latest news, and prepared myself for work the next morning.

I was scheduled to fly early, and I have to admit that I was nervous, very nervous, for over five weeks had passed since I last sat in a Sabre. Trying hard not to show my concerns, I duly kitted up and walked out to my allotted aircraft. With the pre-flight examination done, I climbed into the cockpit and at once began to feel slightly better. It was not until I had started the engine and begun to taxi for take-off that my confidence returned. The sortie was to allow me further familiarisation on type in not very good weather. It involved 5 minutes IF, ended with a QGH, and lasted an hour and five minutes, far longer than any normal Vampire sortie had done. I had to judge the landing on the 2,000 yard runway very carefully so as to touch down at optimum speed, bang on the threshold, use maximum aerodynamic braking, and then make pretty hard use of the wheel brakes to ensure that I stopped without going into the overshoot. I had been warned to be careful because some of the experienced Sabre delivery pilots hadn't always got it right and new aircraft had had to be towed out by tractor. Fortunately I did get it right and taxied back, much relieved that the sortie was over.

I flew again the same day and climbed through cloud to over 40,000 feet to practise, only for the second time, high altitude handling. It was a sortie of an hour and ten minutes duration.

Two more sorties followed the next day, each of an hour and ten minutes, and each involved the use of the Radio Compass, IF, and ended with QGHs. Then the weather clamped in for several days.

On the 24th of May the weather was still not good. I was briefed for a low flying sortie. This was my first in a Sabre and, Oh Boy, could you cover the ground fast! There was no thinking of dodging under power wires with that high tail fin behind, so ground hugging was no longer an option. I did however spend a few minutes wave hopping over the sea. The skin friction warmed the aircraft to an uncomfortable level and cockpit air-conditioning had to be adjusted accordingly. In spite of the increased fuel consumption near the ground, I still managed a sortie of an hour and five minutes.

My first close formation sortie took place in the afternoon when I flew as No.2. With swept wings, positioning was different to that in a Vampire and a new set of criteria had to be used to line up on the leader. This took a bit of experimentation at first. Engine handling was more delicate than in a Vampire, and with the very sensitive flying controls an extremely light touch was needed. After an hour and a quarter's concentration I was soaked in sweat when I landed.

Next morning gave me the chance to practise medium level battle formation when I flew as No.4 for an hour and 20 minutes. This was much easier than I had thought it would be.

On May 27th I flew two more sorties in very good weather. One was high level aerobatics lasting an hour and a half. The second lasted 45 minutes at low level.

During the aerobatic sortie I flew east to over the Kiel Kanal and, towards its Baltic Sea end, spotted a high railway bridge. Temptation was too great. I dived with 100% power on and flew under it, climbing away nearly vertically into sun to continue with the aerobatics. There is nothing about this in my Log Book! It has remained my secret until now.

21. Meppen

F OLLOWING THE PREVIOUS REASONABLY intensive
flying session I was, with some misgivings, on Sunday May 30th,
temporarily posted for a week to Meppen Range as Range Safety
Officer and i/c the Unit based there. RAF Oldenburg was its parent
Station, but as long as things went well there was no need to bother
them, except for the occasional phone call to the Flying Wing Adjutant
to let him know we were still alive and well.

One of the Jever MT Section drivers took me to Meppen with
enough kit for a week's stay in a small hotel in the town. There was no
Officer accommodation on site. My expenses would be refunded on my
return.

It was a lonely posting with virtually nothing to do in the evenings
except go for a walk, have a Pils in the bar, or go to my room to read.
Day times turned out to be little better. The entire establishment was
of no more than 20 personnel including a Sergeant and two Corporals.
The other personnel were made up of a cook, drivers, Medical Order-
lies, and range crew. Fortunately it was a friendly site which had been
set up as recently as 1952 and most of the lads were capable of doing at
least part of each other's duties.

There was a garage separate from the main building and on to this
was built the CO's office, my office for the duration of my stay. We had
an ambulance, a Land Rover, and a couple of trucks. The single storey
main building included all accommodation, rest room, kitchen, and
Mess. The Sergeant saw to it that all was kept in order and maintained
discipline, not that that was ever a problem.

When there was no flying (during the time I was there, flying and
firing on the range only took place on two days) the Airmen occupied
themselves with keeping the place tidy and routine maintenance. They

had dug a vegetable garden both for their own amusement and for the fresh produce. There was also, of course the standard RAF 'garden' comprising a bed of sand on which the words RAF Meppen were spelled out in whitewashed bricks. There was no perimeter fence and no Guardroom. This, the domestic site, was too isolated from any habitation to attract even passing interest.

Nearby were demolished buildings, blown up by the Army, which had housed the generators and offices of what had been the wartime Krupp munitions testing ground. In this heathland setting were huge quantities of unexploded munitions, shells, mines, bombs, and other nasties scattered in the scrub and heather. It was extremely unwise to stray from marked paths. On my arrival all ranks were quick to advise me of the hazards of exploring, which I didn't do; the dangers were too obvious anywhere more than 50 yards from the RAF buildings and cleared area. Not far away was a huge shell. It was empty and must have been all of 16 inches in diameter and stood some 5 feet high. It had never been fired for it was obvious that the inset copper rings which would have gripped the rifled barrel of a gun were unmarked. Some of us thought it might have been either a naval shell or one designed for a huge railway-mounted gun.

There were a couple of Germans who 'worked' the area, picking up and defusing some of the ammo, then burning out the explosive before selling the metal for scrap. Dangerous work, but they eked out a living from it.

One afternoon there was an enormous bang, and a few minutes later one of these chaps came staggering up streaming blood, with torn clothing, and clearly about to pass out. The Sergeant and I saw him coming towards our buildings. One look told us all. We immediately started up our ambulance, loaded him onto a stretcher, and with our Medical Orderly tending him, took him, warning bell ringing, to the local hospital in Meppen. The Krankenhaus was run by Nuns, with one doctor present who fortunately spoke a little English. The patient was stretchered indoors and I was bidden to follow. There, without anaesthetic, Herr Doktor pulled out a huge piece of shrapnel from the man's thigh. I nearly passed out, and quickly moved away. I explained to the doctor what had happened and the Polizei were informed. We reclaimed our stretcher and blanket, and our job was finished.

The large vegetable allotment was close to our buildings and received almost constant attention. Someone would be weeding, removing Colorado beetles from the potato plants, or doing some other seasonal task. One Airman was digging and struck metal. He called me and I went to investigate. It was apparent that he had found some Bazooka (or similar) bombs. They were dangerously close to the buildings. Action had to be taken. Foolishly, rather than inform Oldenburg, and call out a Bomb Disposal Unit (which would have meant our temporary evacuation), I took the matter into my own hands. After ensuring that all personnel were a distance away, I carefully dug round the offending objects and was able to hook a garden fork through the fins of the three of them at the same time. Even more carefully, I raised them out of the shallow hole and carried them to what I judged to be a safe distance away into some trees, and carefully lowered them into a hollow in the ground. Problem solved. I had got away with it.

Near that spot were trenches; in them were Wehrmacht helmets and water bottles with bullet holes through them, and several heavily rusted small arms – clearly the scene of a wartime firefight.

One of the afternoons turned out to be very hot. There was no flying scheduled for the range site, so there was no point in going there. In the distance across the scrubland were several minor tornadoes or dust devils sucking the dust up to several hundred feet. They were worth a minute or two to watch. Then one came close, and came closer. Suddenly I found myself clinging hard to a roof column of the porch of the main building to prevent being taken up in the air to join a couple of dust bins already high in the column of swirling dust and debris. I felt as though my uniform was being torn from me. Grit was in my eyes, and I was hanging on for dear life. Then it was all over. No damage was done to the buildings, only to my pride. The Airmen had dashed for cover and I was the only one caught out. The dust bins were retrieved, empty. My cap, torn off by the wind, was later found a couple of hundred yards away, deposited and filthy, in the centre of the entrance lane.

The actual firing range was several kilometres north of the domestic site and on part of the same extensive heath. To get to it took about 20 minutes' drive and one passed through the hamlet of Lathen, and crossed over the dry and abandoned workings of what would later become a new Dortmund-Ems canal before seeing first the Range

Safety Tower and then the targets. Apart from the wooden Tower there were only a small toilet block, a store building for target materials, and a vehicle hard-standing on the site. It was a desolate place. On firing days we took the ambulance, a truck and the Land Rover. Firing schedules were notified to us at the domestic site in advance. It was my duty to man the R/T and to make sure that the range was safe before, during, and after each firing practice. This included the raising and lowering of red flags and posting a guard on the approach lane.

The two firing sessions, one on the Monday and the other on the Thursday, each lasted no more than half a day and both were with Sabre aircraft. No rockets hit any of the 10 feet square targets although there were some pretty good near misses. I called the aircraft down to fire and then reported the results from the radio in the Tower. A log was kept of the call-signs, number of rockets fired, and the results of each firing. These results, in addition to being radioed to the pilots, were telephoned to their Squadron as soon as each session was complete.

I have to say that I was surprised at the way the vortices from the aircraft rippled the grass and by the strange noises that they made. I was surprised, too, at the erratic flight of some of the rockets. Well aimed they probably were,

The Tower at Meppen Range.

but some would, after leaving the aircraft, veer off or spiral from their intended path. This was probably because of damaged fins which should have been checked by the armourers when fitting them to the aircraft. The pilots, clearly, could not be blamed for this and the matter was the subject of a talk I gave to the Squadron after my return. On the Tuesday afternoon a firing session was cancelled after we had set up the range. Reluctant to return quickly after the journey, I telephoned my Squadron to see if anyone would be able to pay the range a non-firing visit. Tom Balfour was due to do an air test and, that done, he duly arrived. With my radioed consent (and no entries in the range log book) he did several low passes close to our tower, at least one of which was below the top of the Tower. It was as thrilling for him as it was for all of us up there watching. I had my movie camera with me and recorded some of the runs. The film, later shown back at Jever, came out well and was most impressive.[3] Probably more important was the effect on the morale of the range crew who had never seen such a performance by a Sabre before.

Rockets spat out unburned cordite from their ventures as they flew. Some quite long lengths, of similar cross-section to that of a car fan belt, could easily be found under the rocket flight paths. It could be ignited at one end and would burn quietly until the length became too short to be held and had to be dropped from the fingers. The range Sergeant and I, quite irresponsibly, decided to fill a spent rocket with this loose cordite, leaving a long tail of the stuff to ignite after having propped up the weapon, pointing it in the down-range position. We set fire to the tail, retired smartly, and waited. We expected the rocket to spit a bit of fire or, at worst, explode. It did neither but took off and disappeared, straight as a die, into the distance to land we know not where. With both of us now somewhat chastened we left the range, he dropped me off at my hotel while he returned to the domestic site, each of us to wonder what might happen. On the way, though, we hastily concocted a cover story which, fortunately, never had to be put to the test.

Apart from these happenings and one evening in the hotel when, in the bar I was getting more than a little lip from an unrepentant Nazi and knocked him out cold with a single punch to the jaw, the rest of my Meppen stay was extremely dull. For much of the time I sat in my office reading the Manual of Air Force Law or Queen's Regulations & Air Council Instructions for want of something better to do.[4] In all other respects it was the most boring week of my RAF career. I suppose it did some good because when I later came to take my Promotion Exams I found the questions in the law paper reasonably easy to answer.

---

3   These film sequences comprised part of a longer film covering activities at Jever and is now held by the RAF Museum at Hendon.

4   Better known as MAFL and QRs & ACIs.

22. Summer 1954

WHIT WEEKEND STAND-DOWN BEGAN the day after I returned from Meppen. On catching up with the latest events at Jever I found that the Queen's Birthday Parade was being rehearsed regularly and that there had been a collision between two Squadron aircraft on the runway, fortunately without injury to the pilots. I was also told that we would be going on another detachment to RAF Sylt in September and that our runway was due for extending at the same time. After catching up with the recent notices and SROs, and deciding that there was nothing urgent in need of my attention, I settled to a relaxed weekend and viewed a batch of developed films returned to me from Kodak which were waiting for me in the letter rack.

It turned out that in June I did very little flying compared with the amount I did in May. I flew first as soon as Whitsuntide was over. It was a 1 hour and 5 minutes sortie involving no less than 30 minutes instrument flying done climbing and descending through a thick turbulent mass of cloud to find clear air above for my briefed aerobatics exercise. In these circumstances the much-practised radio let-down and QGH was a necessity. The IF was useful practice as I was soon to have to take an Instrument Rating Test to renew my White Card rating.

Next day, the 9th of June, there was another parade practice. The day after was the Queen's Official Birthday, the day of the actual Parade. The large number of spectators watching that day included visiting dignitaries and a good turnout of wives and families from the married patch.

I flew again on the Saturday morning on a very similar sortie to that earlier in the week. On the following Tuesday, and the Friday afterwards I flew again. All five flights were dual in the Meteor T7, with Plt.Off.

Don Exley as 1st pilot while I polished up my instrument flying, mostly under two stage amber, in preparation for my forthcoming examination. My dislike of the Meteor, its sliding throttles, greenhouse canopy, and lack of pressurisation did not help my performance. I found it difficult, too, to recite all vital actions out loud as was required whenever flying any dual aircraft. It wasn't that I didn't know them, of course I did – and used them – it was the actual saying of them after having flown so many solo flights that I found difficult. This became as big a point of practice as the instrument flying itself. In all, those five flights lasted a total of 4 hours and 35 minutes with 4 hours 15 minutes IF, 1 hour of which was 'actual' rather than under the amber with the blue goggles on. As it turned out, through no fault of mine, it would not be until the end of July before I could take the actual test.

If June was a famine as far as flying hours were concerned, other events made up for it. The two highlights were, the Queen's Birthday Parade apart, firstly, my promotion to Flying Officer on Friday the 18th and, secondly, my 21st birthday on the 22nd which was duly celebrated in the Mess on the evening of Saturday the 26th. Of the two I rated my 21st to be the more important because my promotion was automatic, based on time served as a Pilot Officer, and my having a clean record. At least I wasn't a 'sprog' pilot any more, and I got a pay increase.

Plt.Off. Gerry Busby and I shared our party as his 21st was within a day or two of mine. We asked for permission for our Mess bills to be allowed to exceed the maximum allowed for our rank – and got it. That done, we arranged for special snacks to be available in the bar that evening. An open invitation was given to all Mess members and wives to our 'drinks on us' party. About three quarters of them actually turned up for at least part of the evening. As can be imagined much liquor was consumed and some had very sore heads afterwards. When the bill was added up and shared between us, each of us paid less than £5 for drinks, and that included the cost of our own drinks consumed throughout the whole month.

It was during June that several changes were made within the Squadron hangar. Coincident with this, a decision was made to adorn our aircraft with our recently designed and approved Squadron markings. It was decided that all would be ready for the Station Commander's Inspection of our facilities on the morning of the 26th, our 21st party day.

The crew room was moved to the previously little used other side of the hangar. The room chosen was the one in which I had all my MT vehicle tool kits laid out. These had to be moved to a new, smaller, location. This task side-tracked me from the main effort of shifting furniture, flying-kit lockers, parachutes, and other gear from an upstairs room on one side of the hangar to another on the other side. In the meantime other offices had to be cleared and moved, as well as the aircraft painted with the new insignia. Not to be left out, I made sure that, during the intervals when the stencil for the escarbuncle on the tail fins was not in use, it was 'snatched' by one of my drivers so that the same could be painted on all our vehicle doors. This caused a minor altercation because Flt.Sgt. Chiefy Blair had curved the stencil to match the curve on the fins, whereas my lads flattened it to use on their doors. There was some 'heat of the moment' protestings but all was sorted out, done, and ready in time for the inspection. Group Captain Powel-Sheddon was pleased with our performance and said so.

That was not all for me. After the hangar inspection the CO was scheduled to visit my PSI gardens. From standing to attention in the hangar, in the next moment, as soon as I dared, I ran about three hundred yards through the forest to the greenhouses to line up Herr Goldbaum and his gardeners before the CO's driver could get him there in his car. The CO, not realising he was going to meet me again, in a different capacity, so soon, was quite surprised at seeing me again and asked me how I got there in time! That inspection went well too. Afterwards, though, one of the new gardeners asked Herr Goldbaum who the CO was, never having seen him before. The conversation went – "Herr Goldbaum, wer was das?" to which the reply came "Mein Freund, das war Gott!"[1] The CO was very amused at what had been said when I told him about it at my party that evening.

Not only had we recently had the Queen's Birthday Parade and the CO's Parade and inspection, we were due for the annual AOC's Parade and Inspection on the first day of July. There was more square-bashing and polishing up of drill for almost all Station personnel, namely 2 flying Squadrons, 2 RAF Regiment Squadrons, and 2 more Squadrons of personnel from the Technical and Admin Wings who made up the parade. Added to this was a Squadron fly-past and a vehicle drive-past.

---

[1]   Translated: "Herr Goldbaum, who was that?" Answer: "My friend that was God".

The RAF Regiment Armoured Car Squadron practised formation driving almost endlessly. They had to, for there was little enough vision for the drivers through the tiny grid-like windscreen.[2] Our Squadron wasn't going to be upstaged by this so I hastily organised a six-vehicle line abreast drive-past of our cleanest Thorneycroft 3-tonners resplendent in new Squadron markings. Some of my drivers weren't quite up to such precision driving so they were replaced by the more experienced NCOs. So as not to give the game away by displaying driver's ranks, all drivers wore plain clean denims.

The AOC's Parade, Fly-past (almost in low cloud), Drive-past, and Inspection passed off uneventfully and with a satisfactory outcome. The AOC was pleased enough with our performance to award us a one-day stand-down. Praise indeed! He did not inspect the PSI gardens. I afterwards wondered how Herr Goldbaum would have described someone more important than God, had he done so.

Monday, July 5th, was perfect weather. I flew two sorties, each of an hour's duration. The first was solo handling practice at all altitudes, with aerobatics, followed by authorised low flying. The second was, in effect, a low flying, map reading, cross-country. It was a necessary exercise, little practised in the past, and certainly not in a Sabre. I had to be very quick and accurate reading the map when flying at over 500 knots at only 300 feet above the ground. Such is necessary when doing intruder work, the Squadron's secondary role. Flying a constant height above ground, looking out for flocks of birds, masts and tall buildings, while following an accurate track checked against the map, kept me extremely busy and demanded a high level of concentration. It was possibly more demanding, and certainly more hazardous, than close formation flying in rough air. Anyone on the ground would not have heard my approach. The first intimation of my presence would have been a sudden horrendous overhead noise when, on looking up they would see the classic Sabre low-level trail of black smoke disappearing, from their point of view, at tree-top height. None of us could have been very popular on such exercises.

My Log Book tells me that on the following Thursday I flew as No.2 in a four-ship formation at dusk in a tail chase. The Squadron record

---

2   Some of us had, on a previous occasion, been given the opportunity to drive a Daimler armoured car. It was a claustrophobic experience with forward visibility limited to what could be seen through the narrow slatted visor.

is at variance with this but I well remember this tail chase in increasing darkness. It grew dark to the point when I was following the light from the leader's jet pipe before we switched on our navigation lights. We landed in total darkness. The sortie was recorded as night flying of one hour's duration.

The next two days marked the occasion when Jever hosted the 2nd TAF sports event. WRAF competitors were housed in the upper floor of Flying Wing Headquarters which was specially partitioned off for their benefit. There was no formal Squadron activity, with most personnel enjoying their time as spectators. It was at this time that I shared my room with one of the visiting RAF competitors. Jever came 7th, with Headquarters Unit, 2nd Allied Tactical Air Force being the winners. Some of us wondered whether HQ had 'pulled rank' and temporarily posted in, on their strength, some keen sportsmen for the event. Being HQ they would never have admitted it if they had. Never before had I seen the Station so busy with so many personnel present than on those two days.

Whilst these sports and the preceding parades and other distractions do nothing to enhance flying hours, my recording of them here explains why so little flying was done when compared with that in the month of May. It must be remembered that Squadron pilots were all mustered as part of the General Duties (Flying) Branch of the RAF, and, as such, there were times even when flying on Active Service (as we were at that time), that the General Duties aspect took precedence. In an active war, as opposed to the Cold War which we were then prosecuting, things would perforce be very different.

Another week elapsed before I flew again, firstly as No.2 in low level battle formation. That was until my aircraft flying controls decided to malfunction and I made a hasty return to base, burning off fuel as I went so as to reduce my aircraft to below its maximum landing weight. After some nifty work by the ground crew the aircraft was declared fit to fly by afternoon. I was detailed to carry out the air test, quickly found everything satisfactory and spent the rest of the 50 minute flight cavorting around, but not in, the multitude of cu-nims created by strong thermals rising from the North German plain.

The entire week commencing Saturday July 17th was devoted to Exercise Dividend, a NATO exercise in which UK defence systems were tested. We were to emulate Eastern Bloc 'enemy' raiders, simulating waves of bombers. Squadron participation was limited owing to mostly poor weather at Jever. My personal involvement was just two sorties, one of which proved very eventful. My other sorties during that week were purely local and involved ranging and tracking exercises using the new (to us) radar ranging gun-sight in preparation for our forthcoming detachment to Sylt.[3] The second of these sorties was a routine loose formation (neither close formation nor battle formation but somewhere in between) cross-country from Jever across the North Sea to supposedly 'bomb' a target in Norfolk and, yes, we were bounced by Fighter Command at least twice before we reached the coast, but otherwise it was uneventful. The first however had a different outcome.

It was a gloriously sunny Sunday afternoon following a morning of bad weather, the 18th of July to be precise, when we were in the crew room waiting for anticipated orders to do our bomber formation stint. This sort of waiting time usually made us edgy. We had already done our pre-flight checks on our designated aircraft, so there was little else to do until we were ordered off. Some of us sat around and smoked or drank Coke from our Coca-Cola bar in the crew room. I was one of the latter. Others aimlessly wandered about the hangar just killing time. Then orders came that we were to take off in 15 minutes. After last minute dashes to the toilet we made our way out to our aircraft, climbed in, and sat there waiting for the order from Sqn.Ldr. Allen, our formation leader, to "Press Tits".[4] We taxied out for a stream take-off, quickly formed up, with me as a No.4 in the 8-ship (two fours) formation, set course for Blighty, and climbed to 37,000 feet. Visibility was superb following a morning of dense cloud. As we crossed the island of Texel off the Dutch coast we could already make out the evidence of land ahead in the form of haze and rare tufts of cloud over the East Anglian coast. It was a relaxed, well disciplined, pleasant flight early on a summer Sunday afternoon. It was one of those days when it was an absolute pleasure to be in the air. We had just crossed the point of no return over the North Sea when 'Bang' and my cockpit misted up and, simultaneously my gut swelled up and my ears nearly burst. I was in severe pain owing to cockpit explosive decompression. It was usually,

3   One of these sorties was in Sabre Mk 4, XB 812, which is now preserved and displayed in the RAF Museum at Cosford, Shropshire. Until early 2006 it was displayed at the RAF Museum's Hendon establishment.

4   The vernacular for initiating engine start procedures.

in equivalent circumstances, my immediate reaction to swear volubly but I couldn't speak. Neither could I see out because the inside of the canopy had misted up and was freezing over. It was a moment before I did the safe thing and veered off to port so as to avoid a collision with the formation which by now I couldn't see. My next reaction was to turn up the oxygen flow. By this time someone was calling me over the RT to tell me to get back in formation. Somehow, in considerable pain, and with the shortage of breath due to high altitude, I gasped out a Pan call, and at the same time commenced a westward descent into denser air. Our leader ordered George Hickman to accompany me for an emergency landing in 'enemy' territory in the UK. George realised that I was having difficulty speaking and made all the RT calls on my behalf, at the same time telling me what heading to steer. In less pain as I descended I was able to scrape away some of the ice from inside my canopy to see outside and signal to George. Realising by this time that my cabin seal had probably ruptured and that I had not been hit by an unseen defending aircraft (my first initial thought), also that there was no other apparent malfunction, I began to feel more confident. My stomach hurt beyond belief. It was full of wind from the Coke I had drunk before take-off. I couldn't belch it out, neither could I fart. I would gladly have messed my trousers in an effort to release the gas and the pain. By now at under 5,000 feet, the pain began to become more bearable and my canopy and windscreen began to clear so that I could see out without having constantly to scrape away ice from the condensation of my breath. I was now over Norfolk and George was calling West Raynham, the exercise diversion airfield, to apprise them of the situation and request an immediate emergency landing. I could now speak more easily and explained to the Tower that I needed a doctor but was in full control of the aircraft and could, as far as I knew, land perfectly normally.

I landed first and George followed me as I taxied to the visiting aircraft hard-standing by the Tower and shut down. An ambulance was waiting for me and I went to Sick Quarters for an examination. The MO told me that had I not been wearing a 'G' suit and had both my parachute and seat straps not been done up as tight as they were, my stomach would probably have ruptured and that could have been the end of me. Some hearing tests followed and my ears were examined. Then I had a prolonged visit to the toilet, but to little effect. The possibility of

George and me having to stay at West Raynham was briefly discussed, but it was decided that without our caps, and without UK money, and considering the fact that both our aircraft were serviceable (apart from my cabin seal which was confirmed by ground crew as having split) a decision was made to return to Jever at no higher than 2,000 feet, provided I was OK when I got airborne. Air Traffic contacted Jever and told them of the situation. By now it was late Sunday afternoon and Jever wanted to close. In the circumstances they decided to stay open for our return.

George and I agreed that he would take-off first and I would formate loosely on him. We lined up for take-off and he went. I was on full power ready to go and, on releasing my brakes to roll I suddenly ground-looped left – on full power! Spontaneously I controlled the situation with my brakes, re-engaged nosewheel steering, lined up again and took off all within a few seconds. The Tower called me and said sarcastically "When you're sure you are quite ready you're still clear for take-off!" What had happened was that on lining up I had suffered little finger fatigue when holding in the nose-wheel steering button. Unaware of this, my nosewheel was cocked to port when I applied full power, thus causing the described event. The return flight, otherwise, was uneventful. It had taken me 1 hour and 10 minutes to get to West Raynham, with 10 minutes IF because I couldn't see out of the cockpit. The low level return flight took an hour, including 20 minutes IF in deteriorating weather. Sqn.Ldr. Hughes, the Senior MO at Jever, gave me a medical the following morning.[5] I was clear to fly again two days later.

My last flight of the month was my Instrument Rating examination. My examiner was Flt.Lt. Hughes, i/c Station Flight. I passed and therefore retained my White Card rating.

It would be wrong of me to omit mention of the epic flight of Flt.Lt. Brian Iles and Fg.Off. Sandy Sanderson's in Brian's Miles M18, yellow, open cockpit, privately owned aircraft to Bulawayo, Rhodesia. Sandy came from Rhodesia where his father was a clergyman. He hadn't been home on leave for some considerable time. When this came up in discussion with Brian the idea of flying there in Brian's aircraft was born. Initially the idea seemed impossible but, after further consideration and

---

5   Flt.Lt. McBride was the junior Medical Officer.

much discussion, not only between themselves, but also with Sqn.Ldr. Allen, our CO, the possibility of making such a round trip began to seem more feasible.

In due course serious planning was done and RAF hierarchy approved the flight, in principle at least. In the event the aircraft was modified to the extent of having an additional fuel tank fitted above the pilot's knees in the rear cockpit, as near as possible to the centre of gravity. To this were affixed an altimeter, compass, and ASI (air speed indicator). Several air tests followed to make sure that all was workable and safe. Maps were provided by the RAF, flight planning was done, and as far as was possible, flight plans filed. They had no radio. After some discussion with me, Brian bought an 8mm movie camera to record their trip. I gave him some brief advice as to how best to use it.

The safe range of the MI8 was little over 300 miles, so they had to resort to island hopping when crossing the Mediterranean. Then in Africa their route was determined by the availability of airstrips which had refuelling facilities, some of them very primitive indeed.

Brian and Sandy set off on Tuesday July the 20th, taking off from the perimeter track at Jever. Within a day or two a telegram arrived in the Mess from 'Brandy' very briefly reporting their progress. These telegrams arrived every few days and were eagerly anticipated and read by all Officers. It became almost a ritual to look in the letter rack for their latest news. Suffice it to say, their flights out and back were entirely without mishap. They, and their aircraft, returned unscathed to Jever some six weeks later. I was on leave at the time.

I did not fly during the whole of August. There was mostly poor weather following the August Bank Holiday stand down. It was during this time that I was involved with my extraneous duties and was attending lectures from Flt.Lt. Phillips in the Education Section preparatory to my taking my Promotion Exams later in the year. That did not mean, though, that I was never at the Squadron. On a day when there was flying I happened to be on the Squadron hard-standing watching the activity when a Sabre started up, waved 'chocks away', and the chain of one of the main wheel chocks caught and wrapped round the wheel. The Marshal signalled the pilot to stop immediately but didn't then know what to do, so looked to me. Using hand signals in the noise, I conveyed a message to both Marshal and pilot to hold still. I then crawled forward under the wing and released the chain, but before I could crawl away the aircraft moved off, turning as it did so. I had to lie flat to the ground, hands over head, while the jet blast passed over me. I came to no harm although there was some concern as to my well-being. Some months later I repeated this action, again without hurt to myself.

During the early part of August, Group Captain Powel-Sheddon left Jever and was replaced as Station Commander by Group Captain Tom Prickett. On Sunday the 8th we presented, at our hangar, an inscribed silver tankard to our departing 'Groupie'. It was a light-hearted affair and I filmed part of the event with my movie camera. To get back to the Mess afterwards no less than 12 of us, and Flt.Sgt. Telfer's pet Alsatian, piled into a single Land Rover and drove across the airfield. One of us had his feet on the pedals while another steered and yet another changed gear. It was a closely co-ordinated, if somewhat inebriated effort. With much shouting and discomfort we all arrived at our destination safely and without mishap. The remainder walked.

On Sunday, August 15th, I went on UK leave for three weeks. I bought new uniforms with my Flying Officer braid properly tailored into place. Until now I had done a sewing job myself, something at which I was less than confident, in order to put up my new rank.

The day after my return from leave on September 10th I was catapulted into a Saturday morning Battle of Britain Parade rehearsal. I also learned that the next Squadron detachment to Sylt would take place on September 17th, less than a week away.

This was a busy time, not only did I have to catch up with my extraneous duties and prepare for the convoy to Sylt, I had flying to do as well.

On Monday the 13th I flew a 30 minute refamiliarisation sortie, and on the 14th it was just my luck to be selected, at random, for a check of my general flying ability.

I was not the only one to have to do this, but very few were selected. My 30 minute flight in the Vampire T11 was with a Flt.Lt. Bountiff, an instructor from the RAF Central Flying School at Little Rissington. My Log Book records the event as 'Satisfactory'. Later the same day I flew an hour-long formation dusk sortie.

The next morning the Battle of Britain Parade took place in very windy conditions. I, like so many others in the RAF, was no lover of parades. I decided over a period that if I was going to have to go on parade it would be better for me to be a master of the situation than a slave to it. So, unlike others in my position, I borrowed a copy of the Drill Manual and thoroughly familiarised myself with parade routines. I even learned, by heart, the commands likely to be given by such as me should the situation arise. This gave me confidence and parades ceased to have any dread factor thenafter, even if some were conducted in inclement weather. Although I didn't know it at the time, this was to stand me in good stead in the future.

The 93 Squadron Sabre XB812 in the RAF Museum at Hendon. The Squadron markings either side of the fuselage roundel were often maliciously interpreted by pilots of other Squadrons as being arrows showing drunken 93 Squadron pilots which end of the aircraft to look for the cockpit! The escarbuncle insignia can clearly be seen high on the tail fin.

23. Sylt Again

THE DAY AFTER THE Battle of Britain Parade found me supervising the loading of my convoy for the imminent detachment to Sylt. I was involved in paperwork also, and ensuring that the necessary number of drivers and vehicles were available, and properly documented, in accordance with the Movement Order. Fg.Off. Doug Fewell was my deputy this time.

This was a 122 Wing detachment as the Jever runway was to be extended to 2,700 yards in our absence. Not only that, we would not be going back to Jever after our detachment, but moving straight on to a further detachment at Wunstorf until the work at Jever was complete.

We left Jever early the next morning for the first leg of the journey to Ütersen and the usual overnight stop. All went well, our Polizei escort took us through Hamburg at breakneck speed and we arrived reasonably early.

Instead of mooching around killing time in the Mess at Ütersen, Doug and I decided to stay at the Streits Hotel in Hamburg as he had not seen the city, apart from the brief run through earlier that afternoon. We arranged for a Land Rover to drop us off and pick us up early next morning in good time for our convoy departure to Sylt.

To our surprise, at the Streits, we met two other 122 Wing pilots who we didn't expect to be there. After a meal we all set off on the U-Bahn for St Pauli Bahnhof and the Reeperbahn. On turning right out of the station we made our way along the broad street, later described in song as the street of the hundred thousand lights. Youthful curiosity took us to the end of the streets designated as 'Out of Bounds' to British personnel and, yes, two of us dared to enter through the screens and quickly walk along the short and infamous Herbert Strasse and out of the other end. Whores exposing themselves in brilliantly lit shop windows were about the mildest of sights. There were even queues of men outside some brothels because some female inside had been designated the attraction of the night. The whole was sordid and degrading. It was with absolute disgust that we left the locality.

Back on the main road we came across a film company filming a sequence for the feature film 'Auf der Reeperbahn' which later, dubbed in English, reached the cinemas back in the UK. We watched the film crew for some minutes. I was able to draw comparisons between their professional and my rank amateur cinematic techniques. Moving on, the four of us decided to drop in at a night club called the 'Tabu' to have a drink and watch the floor show.[1] We bought a Pils each at over 6 DM a glass, a horrendously expensive price to pay in those days, and took our places at an empty table towards the back of the dimly lit room. There was a catwalk down its centre, a small band, and a diminutive railed-off dance floor. Other tables were occupied by young couples, popsies and sugar daddies, bosses and secretaries, and some foursomes of good-time girls. Ours was the only table occupied by four men and we were determined to keep it that way.

Dance music played for a while and then the lights dimmed further. The music continued and ultra-violet lights came on to reveal a group of performers on the catwalk, their white clothing glowing iridescent in the light. Announcements were made and then there was a fashion parade of scantily clad females, of good figure, strolling, in turn, down the catwalk and back as per a mannequin parade. It appeared to us that the show was sponsored by a lingerie company that specialised in virtually invisible single layer fabrics, for almost nothing of the feminine form was left to the imagination.

During an interval, when the lights were a little less dim, we spotted a couple of our older Airmen sitting at the end of the catwalk and made sure that they didn't see us. At the same time we were pestered by waiters who wanted us to buy more drink but we steadfastly refused at the price and made our single glasses of Pils last the evening. The show resumed and another fashion parade started. This time the dresses, if one could call them that, were much longer but equally transparent. Then one female swept along the catwalk and paused longer at the end than usual because of some comment from the clientele. In this very

---

1   I was told during a return visit to Hamburg in 2004 that the 'Tabu' was still a thriving establishment.

instant one of the Airmen rapidly pushed what looked like drawing pins through the tail of the dress, securing it to the catwalk. Said female went to continue her routine, the dress ripped away, she bent down, unadorned, revealing all, and gave the culprit an open-handed resounding slap across the face. The audience roared. It made their evening. We exercised discretion and decided it was time to depart.

Our stay at Sylt was noteworthy for most of the wrong reasons. The weather was mostly foul and there were severe storms with strong crosswinds on the main runway. The radar gunsights could only seldom lock on to the drogues, and the drogues themselves were frequently unstable in flight, thus causing sorties to be aborted. I had been at Sylt for two days before the first aircraft arrived and it was the 21st before all aircraft of both Squadrons had landed. There had been recent runway extensions at Sylt and the undershoot/overshoot areas were extremely muddy and wet. We were cautioned about this during our arrival briefing. The Officers Mess was undergoing considerable building changes while we were there, and there were extensive works to other buildings within the airfield perimeter.

Only two days after the flying programme commenced our old Boss, Sqn.Ldr. Bob Allen left us. He had been promoted to Wing Commander and was posted to lead the Flying Wing at Fassberg. The day before, newly promoted Sqn.Ldr. 'Des' Browne joined us. (He was often later referred to as Bwown with an 'e', due to a slight speech impediment preventing him from pronouncing the letter 'r' properly). He had been a Flight Commander with 20 Squadron at Oldenburg where, for various reasons, he had taken some ribbing.

Our new boss, far from being the butt of humour at Oldenburg, turned out to be a waspish and determined, sometimes inconsiderate, individual. Some of us did not take to him readily, but he was our new leader and orders had to be obeyed, like the man or not.

There is no record of my gunnery scores during the detachment, and no clues in my Log Book. My first flight, after the usual introductory briefings, was a 30 minutes ciné sortie on the flag. My second was the next day, dual with Flt.Lt. Goodwin, the Wing Pilot Attack Instructor, in a Vampire T11, live-firing on the flag. Conditions were not good owing to turbulence and thunderstorms in the area.

The weather remained the same during my next four sorties following the weekend, all of which were of 40 minutes or less, and all briefed for live-firing, although one was aborted due to weather. Two involved 10 minutes IF, so bad were the conditions. On taxying back to the hangar apron and shutting down after one of these sorties I noticed one of the ground crew whose hair was standing on end. On jumping down from my aircraft and removing my helmet I said so to him, whereupon he told me that mine was standing vertically as well. There was also a crackling of electricity in the air. Realising immediately what might happen, I shouted to everyone to get into the hangar. No sooner done, the hangar was struck by lightning, with the simultaneous crack of thunder nearly deafening us all in the corrugated iron building. No one was hurt and no damage was discovered, although Electrical Section personnel claimed that they had seen a flash come from one of the radiators in their workshop. As someone said afterwards, "The 'Sparks' would say something like that, wouldn't they?"

My fifth firing sortie, the second of the day on Wednesday the 29th, was also aborted owing to the flag proving unserviceable in flight. It lasted just 30 minutes, long enough to burn off sufficient fuel to allow an early landing which didn't turn out to be what I expected. Coming in to land, through heavy rain, I touched down spot on the threshold at the correct speed and throttled back as usual, preparatory to using aerodynamic braking in the normal way. Several hundred yards down the runway I realised that I still had power on and wasn't slowing down even though my throttle was hard back. The briefest of glances showed 60% power on the dial. With insufficient power for flight and a u/s throttle control, I had no alternative but to commit to the landing, so cut the fuel cocks to the engine. Still at some ridiculous speed I called the Tower, briefly saying that my throttle was stuck and I would be going into the overshoot. By this time I had only half a runway left, so gave up any attempt at aerodynamic braking, dropped the nose wheel, and commenced heavy use of the wheel brakes which were less than effective on the wet surface. If it hadn't been for the nose wheel steering I don't know where I would have gone as each main wheel randomly gripped or slid in the wet. Now out of runway, I only began seriously to slow down in the deep mud of the overshoot area and stopped dead just short of the first tall row of landing lights. Not liking my predicament, somewhat hastily, and without fitting the safety pins in my ejector seat, I opened the canopy and leapt to the ground, sinking up to my calves in thick glutinous mud. I was stuck where I had landed.

Fortunately, though, the rain had stopped. Looking back towards the runway a stream of vehicles was heading towards me. The Fire Crew Land Rover was first and on leaving the runway, continued a few yards and then bogged down, stuck in the mud. A Fire Engine did exactly the same. I saw the funny side of this and started laughing, especially when the crews got out of their vehicles and were stuck like me. The Sylt Wing Commander Flying came steaming up in his Volkswagen and also stuck. An ambulance followed, but wisely the driver parked on the hard surface. There was much shouting, and my laughing at this entirely bizarre episode did nothing to please anyone, especially the WingCo, who thought it was all my fault. He did not have the same humorous point of view as did I, cursing me whilst he too was stuck in the mud, and at the same time yelling at the others to help get him out.

Order eventually prevailed. Ladders from the fire trucks were unshipped and laid on the mud. The WingCo was rescued, although his car wasn't. He disappeared in one of several other vehicles which by now had turned up. One by one the rest of us were released. I was the last. Realising that the safety pins were not in the seat, I had to climb up and replace them. Then I sodged my way back to drier land, briefing the Crash Crew SNCO not to approach without crawling boards. I was taken back to the hangar and cleaned myself up as best I could. My Sabre boots had saved me from wet feet and had just been tall enough to stop the mud from getting into them. The aircraft was rescued, I was told, by laying boards on the mud and, using press-ganged Erks from anywhere, was lifted bodily by them and slowly dragged back on to the firm runway from where it was towed back to the hard-standing. It was filthy, as can be imagined. At this point I was considered to blame for going into the overshoot. It was, in everyone's view except mine, a classic case of pilot error. The first personal order I was given by my new Boss was "Pod, you did it, you dirtied it. Go and get a bucket and go and bloody clean it up – yourself!" "Sir", I said, as one does in these circumstances. "Thank you, Mr bloody Browne" (or words to that effect), I muttered under my breath, and then went and busied myself with the two hour task of stooping to clean the underbelly and under-carriage of XB802. There was neither apology, nor sympathy, when it was discovered and made known that the reason for my having over-shot the end of the runway was through no fault of mine but because of a failed fuel regulator.

I only flew four more sorties during the detachment. Three involved live-firing and one was an air test which was curtailed to a minimum because of unserviceable controls. During one of the live-firing sorties, that on the afternoon of Friday October the 8th, to be exact, I was waiting to be called in by the Mosquito TT, Mk 35, tug aircraft to fire on the south range parallel to the Hörnum limb of the island when, in clear air, a Sabre flew past me vertically down at high speed and dived into the sea. It was only a matter of a few hundred yards from me when it flashed past. I had witnessed the demise of Ken Richardson of No.4 Squadron. Within a second of seeing this I was called to fire on the flag and left the area at once so could not change frequency to report the incident on the emergency VHF 116.1 channel.[2] The following day, when conducting the repeat air test, I saw an Air Sea Rescue launch moored close to the clearly visible hole in the shallow sea bed where Ken had met his end. There was a small slick of fuel creating a rainbow effect in the sunlight on the water nearby.

As to the weather at Sylt I distinctly remember that there was an horrendous storm lasting for a period of over 24 hours.[3] George Hickman (with whom I shared a room in the Mess) and I were kept awake for part of the night with the noise of wind and lashing rain. It was as severe a storm as I can remember, so much so, that next morning at breakfast many of us wondered what damage had been done. It seems that there was little or no damage to RAF property, but there were rumours that the island defences to the north of Westerland may have been breached and sand dunes washed away. This turned out to be partly true as, in fact, the bed of the light railway line at Kampen which ran north to List had prevented the waves from cutting the island in two. I cannot date this event precisely but I distinctly remember being told to fly to the south, over the lesser islands in that area to look for damage. I must have combined this with a firing sortie for my Log Book has no specific record of the event. Anyway, on flying over these islands I could clearly see that at least one dyke had been breached and the sea had swamped the island farmsteads. People, their belongings, and some animals, were on the roofs of their properties. I flew low and

---

2   Ken Richardson had originally been involved in a tail chase with another 4 Squadron pilot who made the appropriate R/T calls.

3   In trying to date this event I contacted the Meteorological Office archive in Exeter. Tantalisingly they only have records of storms in the area at times when I was not there.

sensibly slowly over these poor souls and waved to them and waggled my wings to let them know they had been seen. They waved back. As briefed, I reported the situation on landing.

There were some fine days but there was little activity this late in the year on what was known in the RAF as 'bare arse beach', where overweight German nudists cavorted and displayed their obese, fat hung, bodies. There was a kiosk (beach café) at the south end of the northern beach which displayed a notice, in several languages, to the effect that 'clothing has to be worn in this establishment'. So it was. In there were, sitting at tables, bare bodies clothed in maybe a headscarf, or a towel over the shoulders, and nothing else. They were obeying the wishes of the management, just, and in so doing did not present a pretty sight. None of us in our fully clothed group had any desire to go inside.

On one of the weekends Tommy Balfour, myself, and some others, went for a stroll in fair weather to Keitum, a small picturesque hamlet

Tommy Balfour (right) and the author standing under the sign pointing to the Café Kliffsruh. The weaver's thatched house is to the left.

about half a mile away to the east of the airfield. After a cup of coffee in the local café and a stroll round we visited a weaver's house wherein several hand looms were in use. The actions of the weavers were fascinating to see and we stayed a while watching, almost hypnotised by their movements. I bought a fine woollen table cloth whilst there and kept it for many years.

To the south, and east of Keitum, was the hamlet of Morsum. It was a distance from the airfield and it was there on some marshy meadows where the target drogues were dropped by the towing aircraft. I was sent there for an afternoon's stint to supervise the scoring and phone the results back to the squadrons. The Mosquito and Tempest pilots came in low and were very accurate with their drops. Mosquitos carried a drogue operator. I regret to this day the time when, for some unimportant reason, I turned down the opportunity to fly in this role. I would, with hindsight, have loved to have had the fact that I had flown in a wooden wonder entered in my Log Book.

After a detachment marked by the loss of Ken Richardson, bad weather, and remembered by my going into the overshoot, and that tinned blackcurrants were on the Mess menu as a sweet after every meal except breakfast, it was time to prepare for our departure and the drive to Wunstorf.

24. Wunstorf

I ARRIVED AT WUNSTORF with my convoy late on the afternoon of Friday, October the 15th. Few of us had been there before. I never had. As with most RAF Stations in Germany, with the exceptions of newly built Wildenrath, Laarbruch, Geilenkirchen, and Brüggen which were new Stations and collectively known as the 'Clutch', Wunstorf was an ex-Luftwaffe base. With the arrival of 122 Wing added to its existing establishment it was overcrowded. Our Officer accommodation was in the roof space of some old Luftwaffe buildings and was both smelly and primitive, with tin lockers and airmen's beds. The smell was of drains as the toilet vent pipes terminated in our roof area. The Officers Mess was unremarkable and typical of many in Germany. The roads in the Station were noteworthy for the number of semi-derelict and derelict cars at their kerb sides, something I had not witnessed since Pembrey and which would certainly have never been allowed at Jever. The airfield hard-standings and aprons were vast, having been extended and heavily used during the Berlin Air Lift. We were allocated a hangar belonging to one of the home Squadrons, itself now on detachment. The nearest important town was Hannover and, from a flying point of view the local landmark was the Steinhuder Meer, a huge, almost circular, lake which I had overflown many times before.

It was at Wunstorf that I began to develop severe vomiting headaches. I had had them occasionally before, but now they were worse and more frequent. I saw the MO when I was suffering with one and he promptly ordered me to be sick in the wash-basin in his surgery. An order which I couldn't obey as I had emptied my stomach down a toilet not 15 minutes before. He didn't listen to what I had to say and told me in no short order that I had gone to him only because I wanted to skive off flying. Untrue. Thank you, Doctor.

As to flying: my first flight was a half hour sector recce and my second, on the same day, was as No.2 in a formation and involved a QGH and 3 practice GCA landings.[1] This was my first experience of GCA, something we didn't have at Jever.

Two flights followed on the 25th. Firstly I flew as No.4 in a battle formation and tail chase, then I flew alone and, for a reason not now remembered or recorded, I was diverted to Fassberg. I spent the night in the Orderly Officer's room which, tradition had it, was haunted as it had been used by Reichsmarschall Göring whenever he visited. I slept well.

After flying back to Wunstorf next morning, two more sorties followed. The first was as No.4 in a high level battle formation, and for the second I was detailed to go to a specific village and sketch a map of it from the air, adding as many salient features as possible. I flew round that little village on the North German Plain so many times that, by the time I left the vicinity, nearly all the population was outside watching me and pointing at me! Nobody bothered to look at my artistic efforts when I landed.

The 27th saw me airborne twice. In the morning I flew as No.2 in practice close and battle formations. Later, again I was No.2 in a close formation. We did a formation Vic take-off, climbed, and broke for a tail chase, then reformed in worsening weather and did a Vic QGH, clocking up 35 minutes IF in a sortie of 45 minutes duration. The same day I was checked out as being capable of, and qualified for, carrying out First Line servicing of Sabre aircraft. A Certificate is pasted in my Log Book to that effect.

Next morning, Saturday October 28th, will not easily be forgotten. After using an amount of subterfuge, which initially involved me recording, from Fassberg SROs when I was diverted there, when the next CO's Parade would be (this Saturday), and some accurate planning and co-ordination, I found myself flying as No.4 in a four-ship

---

1 GCA = Ground Controlled Approach. It was also known as 'talk down'. A radar controller at the end of the runway could, and did, guide pilots to the runway threshold in conditions of very poor visibility. This facility was a vast improvement on the usual QGH procedures to which we were accustomed and which only brought the pilot over the airfield at circuit height or just below.

formation. The official briefing was for us to practise battle formation and a tail chase. Whilst that was done for a time, the real (unofficial) purpose was to impress our old Boss, Bob Allen, who would be on parade with the entire Station. To do so, the first pair broke off from our official exercise and went low level while Sandy Sanderson and I went high level. We commenced our dive as the low level pair were approaching Fassberg. Timing it to a nicety, the low pair did a single pass beat-up of the parade ground just as our sonic booms hit the same area. Satisfied that we had done a good job, we formed up again and returned to base. On landing we were at once summoned to Wg.Cdr. West's office. The Station Commander, as I recollect, was there as well. We were told, in no uncertain terms, that we had overflown Fassberg airfield at low altitude without permission, and generally disrupted the parade. And we had broken some windows. We were each fined £5, to be put into the CO's charity fund, and given a thorough dressing-down. It was not the outcome we had expected. On saluting and leaving the room, but before we were out of earshot, we were called back in and informally praised for our planning and efforts and reminded, quietly, and with a smile this time, not to try that sort of thing again.

Fg.Off. Al Ramsay and I, on the last weekend of October when the Station was stood down for two days, were granted permission to leave early on the Friday for a weekend away. A British Forces Leave Centre was still open at Bad Harzburg and that was our destination, where we booked in to the Officers Hotel for two nights. The picturesque town had not suffered any war damage; being one of the last to be occupied it was never fought over. The Harz Mountains scenery was beautiful, although the highest mountain, Brocken, of Walpurgisnacht fame, was clearly visible bristling with antennae across the border in the Russian Zone. The weather was kind and still reasonably warm. We enjoyed walking in the town and surrounding woodland in the relaxed off-duty atmosphere. The shops were good and well stocked. On the Saturday afternoon we hired a taxi to take us to a building site! This was no ordinary building site, it was to see the new Okertalsperre (Oker valley dam) being built.[2] The enormity of the project spanning the river gorge was quite something to behold, to the point that we must have stayed

---

2   I visited the completed dam during a visit to Germany in the early 1970s. I have to say it was a disappointment because, by then, the dam had mellowed into the countryside and was nowhere near as spectacular, big as it was, as when it was under construction.

for well over an hour watching the activity. I shall never forget the dinner we had in the hotel that evening. I had the most luscious, tenderest, Porterhouse Steak I could ever have wished for. Sunday was a lazy morning, necessarily so, because I awoke with a violent headache

for no attributable reason. I walked it off after a late breakfast, had lunch in a café and, later in the afternoon, we caught a train to make our way back to Wunstorf.

It so happened that we did go on a low level strafing run again, to Jever, but with proper authority. This was to give those left behind, while the runway work was being done, a morale boost and to let them know we hadn't forgotten them. The main purpose, though, was to act as potential targets for the RAF Regiment Light Ack Ack Squadron for practice and to test their gun crews.

There was the usual run of flying training and GCA practices during the rest of our stay.

Al Ramsay (left) and I met a tame bear whilst walking in the Harz Mountains.

We also did air-to-ground firing, using Ströhen Range. It was a fiendishly difficult place to find, situated as it was, in open marshy countryside with no obvious nearby landmarks. I flew on Battle Flight duty just once, for a miserable 15 minutes.

On the final Tuesday night of the detachment we threw an all-ranks party in the NAAFI Club on the shores of the Steinhuder Meer. None of us was sorry that this was marking the end of our stay.

I flew a total of 13 hours and 15 minutes, including 1 hour 50 minutes IF, whilst at Wunstorf. Not a good total. I did not return to Jever by road as expected, but flew back, returning 'home' to our usual much better living conditions on November 15th.

25. The End Of 1954

I WAS PLEASED TO unpack and settle down again in my own room in Block 163. I brought back with me from my wanderings a further selection of village pennants to add to the string of them already adorning my window pelmet. I had better explain that, whereas it was popular to collect beer glasses or beer mats of the different German breweries, and there were many, I, as did some others, decided to collect village and district pennants. These would be far easier to pack when time for a posting came. These pennants were usually triangular and bore the name of the place and, if any, its badge or coat of arms. Some collected as many as they could find, and swapped them as would stamp collectors. For my part I only collected those of places which I had personally visited on my travels.[1]

The work on the runway, when we arrived back, was far from finished but a goodly length was available and safe to use as an overshoot area. Many trees had been felled and that end of the airfield looked vastly different compared with how it was when we left. There was some concern as to whether all the work would be completed before the winter frosts set in.

Squadron life settled down very quickly. The familiar cry of "Else's" was heard in the crew room again. This indicated that someone had thoughtlessly left a packet of fags around while they were flying or elsewhere, whereupon these would be handed round among all smokers present. It paid to be careful. It is probably true to say that more care appeared to be taken of cigarettes than of safety equipment (parachutes and Mae Wests), for these were often left lying around rather than tidied away.

---

1   The collection continued to grow until I eventually left the RAF. They existed for many years afterwards and are now in the possession of a relative.

There was one noticeable difference: a cupola had been built on the front of Flying Wing Headquarters. This formed an extension to Hammer West's office. From it he could now see all flying activity without having to go outside as previously. Similar extensions were built for the Met Office and for Air Traffic Control. Our Air Traffic Controllers, Flt.Lt. Love, and Flying Officers John Grice and 'Bunny' Warren, now had a Tower to work from, rather than, as previously, working 'blind' from the caravans at the back of the building. This was, in the opinion of all concerned with flying, an overdue improvement. The caravans, though, were still available for use should the situation, or an exercise, so demand.

The onset of winter weather affected our flying schedules for the rest of November. I flew two high level battle formation and tail chase sorties on the 16th and then the weather clamped in. Ground training was resorted to, and both training and historical films were watched. In one of these, dealing with the period a few weeks after the 'D' Day landings, there was a sequence showing a convoy of wagons moving forward. In that convoy were two of 'my' Thorneycroft 3-tonners. Their number plates were clearly legible. That sequence was wound back and re-shown several times to make sure I was right.

On November the 22nd, the last day of the month on which I was airborne, I flew with others from the Squadron in an old Anson Mk 12 on a liaison visit to Wildenrath. The flight, with me seated, without parachute, on the main spar and Warrant Officer Powell at the controls, took almost an hour and a half of grinding deafeningly through the atmosphere. In a Sabre it would have taken 20 minutes at the very most. At Wildenrath we visited the Sabre Technical Training Unit. It was a cram course. Fascinatingly interesting as it was, there was far too much technical detail to absorb in the time available. We snatched a quick lunch and were crammed with even more technical information before boarding the Anson for a late flight back to Jever. With a good tail wind the old 'Annie' did the trip in an hour and ten minutes.

I did not fly again until the 9th of December. Why I didn't fly for so long is not now remembered, especially when, in spite of variable weather, the Squadron was airborne most days. It is possible that I was doing inventory checks, a stint as Orderly Officer, duties as MTO and/ or work in connection with the PSI gardens. All these duties could add up to, and take, a considerable amount of time, especially after my absence at Sylt and Wunstorf.

It was during this period that Brian Iles took the opportunity to come to my room to use my film editing equipment and projector so as to cut and edit the film of his and Sandy Sanderson's flight to and from Bulawayo. The finished version, which I was privileged to see first, was shown many times on the Station. With their commentary and anecdotes it made extremely interesting and entertaining viewing.

Someone decided that living-in Officers should attend a weekly 'Dinner Night' in the Mess. This was additional to the usual monthly Dining In Nights and occasional other formal gatherings. Dress for these evenings was to be Dinner Jacket. We suffered these evenings for some weeks before we protested. On such evenings we could not go off-camp because there wasn't time, neither could any of us pursue our hobbies, sport, or other interests. To us, they were an imposition, especially when married Officers could go home and do what they liked. Some opinionated married senior individual thought that these weekly evenings would be 'good for us'! "Do as I say, but don't do as I do" was the maxim that applied in this instance. It took several bold young Officers to voice an opinion, and tactfully and carefully protest, at a Mess Meeting. There was much mumbling among senior married Officers before it was conceded that we had more than a little justification for complaint. Station Commander's Confidential Orders were amended accordingly. We signed as having read them (as we had to do regularly), and our lives returned to normal following the removal of this imposition.

When I did fly in December, which was rarely because of bad weather, the Christmas Grant and other distractions, the sorties came thick and fast.[2] On the 9th I flew twice. The trips were a half hour weather recce and low flying beneath an almost impossibly low cloud base. Next day, the 10th, I was aloft four times, all of them formation sorties in good weather, with me as No.2. It was during the first of these sorties that I was able to prove conclusively that I had better than average long distance sight at altitude. I had the ability to 'range' my eyes when searching for other aircraft, and to pick them out well before

---

2   Grant = time off.

anyone else in the same formation.[3] This annoyed my leader but he had to concede that I was right in every case. This attribute of mine was of immense use when flying on Battle Flight and when practising pair on pair interceptions and during quarter attacks under ground radar control.

An F86E 'Sabre'.

I flew four more times the following day. Sorties varied between low level battle formation, low level cross-country flying and target attacks, and high level tail chases, including formation take-offs and landings, with some preliminary formation aerobatics thrown in. Flights so far this month varied in duration of between 30 and 45 minutes.

Tuesday, December the 14th, proved to be an eventful day. I flew again four times. In my first sortie I flew as No.4 in a high level battle formation, followed by an 'each man for himself' dog fight at over 40,000 feet. There were times when I was pulling almost 9 'G' in some of the turns and pull-outs. Being tall, I was at a disadvantage when it came to pulling 'G'; shorter individuals had a higher threshold than did I, but I had a reasonably short body and prided myself on being able to wear anyone's parachute without adjusting the straps – even that of the shortest pilot, little Roy Garthwaite, on the Squadron. This I was clearly able to turn to my advantage. But I digress. During this hectic dog fight I had to throttle back quickly to avoid running into the tail of the man in front who had put his air brakes out when I was only feet behind. That was OK and part of the game, but on opening the

---

3   Usually, if there is nothing to focus on, one's eyes automatically come to rest on a point only a matter of a few feet ahead. It takes a conscious effort to overcome this normality. I had the ability to do this.

throttle again (slowly as one had to on jet engines) I had severe engine resonance and vibration. Throttle adjustment did not clear it, even on throttling back prior to throttling up again. The engine didn't respond, continued making rude noises, and flamed out.

All main services stopped with the engine. Cabin pressurisation was lost, as was demisting. Hydraulic pressure for flying controls became minimal and the 24 volt battery powering the 28 volt system wasn't going to last long. Fortunately I was in clear air and I knew that I was in the vicinity of Oldenburg. This was important because I couldn't see a thing as the whole inside of the canopy had at once misted and iced up. With no pressurisation I turned the oxygen full on and wheezed out a Mayday call stating that I would attempt a dead stick landing at Oldenburg. Frantically scraping ice away from the inside of the canopy while gliding like a pair of pliers, I was able to make gentle stick movements (to conserve hydraulic power and prevent my controls from locking solid) to position myself for a possible landing. Fortunately my engine was wind-milling and provided a necessary minimum of hydraulic power, thus saving my battery from having to drive the auxiliary hydraulic pump. I had control and a few moments to consider my options. There were three. I could use the bang seat and call it a day, but with thin clothing, a slipstream of 200 knots, and a temperature of something very low and nasty, my instinct was to stick with it, at least for a while.[4] The second and best option was to attempt a relight while setting up a landing at Oldenburg. Oldenburg called me and gave me clearance for an emergency landing. "Roger" was my brief reply to save my battery. Still scraping frantically at the ice I realised that another Sabre was formatting loosely on me but didn't know who.[5] Height was now the main factor. I couldn't relight above 15,000 feet because of lack of oxygen in the air. If I was to do a dead stick landing, to stand any chance of success, training told me that I had to be at the start of the downwind leg (or equivalent distance from the runway threshold) at no less than 10,000 feet, because the rate of descent would acceler-ate phenomenally as soon as I attempted to lower the undercart. If I couldn't do this, joining the Caterpillar Club was the only option. We had had it drilled into us never to attempt a wheels-up landing in open countryside because of the high number of drainage ditches which

---

4 Bang seat = ejection seat. This was an American type, not of British Martin Baker design.
5 I never did find out who it was.

would cause an aircraft to break up. At 16,000 feet, a smidgeon high, and possibly a little fast, I attempted a relight. No dice. Using my speed I pulled the nose up to drain out the surplus fuel from the jet pipe and immediately made another attempt. No dice again. Height was getting critical. At the third attempt, now at nearly 9,000 feet, as I set up my approach for Oldenburg, I had success. It fired up. Levelling off from my glide, and with careful throttle movements to nurse a sick engine, I called Oldenburg, thanked them, and told them that, having re-lit, and now with sufficient power, I would return to Jever. This I did.

With my engine making grumpy and unusual noises I called for a straight-in approach, landed satisfactorily, taxied back to the hangar, and shut down. 50 minutes of the unexpected was behind me, or so I thought. Immediate inspection revealed turbine blade damage, but all was not over. Sqn.Ldr. Des Browne called me to his office and debriefed me and questioned why I hadn't landed at Oldenburg rather than risk coming back to Jever. My spontaneous answer was to the effect that I didn't have my beret with me. There's no doubt about it at all that I got a rigid bollocking off him for further endangering one of the Queen's aircraft, and that in spite of my having taken a risk to save money and inconvenience by bringing XB913 back to Jever. I wondered afterwards what he would have said had I landed at Oldenburg!

I flew three more times that day, including another dog fight, high level formation practice, and finished off with a formation low level strike – on Oldenburg – of all places!

Next morning, at Met Briefing in Flying Wing HQ, I had to stand up and tell the other pilots what had happened, and the relight procedure I used. Two other pilots, Neil Hampton, and 'Podge' Page, both of 93, had recently had flame-outs and had had to do the same. In this way everyone was reminded of the procedures by those with first-hand experience.

Four more formation sorties, with me flying as No.2 or No.4, on the last day of the month, and all of a similar nature, rounded off 1954 as far as flying was concerned.

The usual Christmas rituals and festivities took place. The Sergeants visited our Mess and we visited theirs, then all of us served the Airmen their Christmas lunch as per standard RAF procedures.

During the Christmas and New Year period there was a fancy-dress party in the Mess. This primarily involved 'A' and 'B' Flights of 4 and

93 Squadrons in competition. An ad hoc group of suitably lubricated Officers from other departments were the judges. There was much prior planning and preparation for the event. Al Colvin, 'B' Flight Commander, gathered us for a discussion and council of war. It was decided that he would go suitably attired as an Eastern potentate and the rest of us as his harem. Those of us living in the Mess were at an immediate disadvantage with regard to supplies of materials and 'clothing', but we made do with what we had. Out of the curtains in my room I sewed up a dress and made a yashmak out of a white handkerchief. For those occasions when the yashmak had to be removed, as when drinking and eating, I decided I'd better shave off my moustache so as to, as 'Princess Pod', maintain the illusion of femininity. Others shaved their chests and wore bras borrowed from our batwomen and stuffed them with socks. 'LuLu' Leigh-Lancaster was one of these (with a nickname like that he didn't have much option). Lipstick and rouge were used and eyebrows were altered with boot polish. Sandals (desert wellies) and gym shoes were worn. Bernie Revnell found some ear-rings and wore those. We looked like a right pack of oddities when we arrived in the Mess, lifting our skirts and flaunting our 'feminine' virtues as we paraded behind our 'Master'. The evening was a riot and many questionable invitations were made – and declined! We, 'B' Flight, won the prize – drinks bought for us by the rest of those present.

Christmas 1954 in the Officers Club in Jever town. L-R: John Culver, the author, LuLu Leigh-Lancaster, Ron Gray, and Jean Balfour.

26. Early 1955

THE HEADACHES I MENTIONED earlier were still very troublesome to me but I managed to conceal them as much as possible in case I was taken off flying. They seemed to occur at weekends and usually a day or two after a Dining In Night. I found that, if I was suffering and due to fly, I could markedly reduce the symptoms by using the oxygen test rig in the crew room. This was available for us to use to check our oxygen masks. A few minutes, sometimes as few as two, on pure oxygen would do the trick. I discovered this as a result of being detailed to fly and, on feeling like death while sitting in the cockpit, as soon as I connected the oxygen supply I began to feel very much better. As a result, these violent headaches seldom affected me when in the air. Christmas, with no oxygen available because I had no excuse for going near a hangar, was a particularly bad time for me. Some thought I couldn't hold my drink, but this was far from the truth.

As soon as the New Year break was over, on the 3rd of January I was in the air again. The first two sorties were at high altitude, the first involved a snake climb, battle formation practice, and a snake QGH. The second was solo and included cloud flying and ended with another QGH. My third sortie of the day was at low level, beating up anything which took my fancy.

Winter weather was beginning to take its toll of flying hours. There was much thick cloud, and on the 4th, although I flew four times, all sorties were above cloud and at medium level practising ciné quarter attacks, with a tail chase and formation flying as extras.

Over the next two days I flew four times, three of them at low level. I flew two sorties on the first day to Meppen Range. Each of them was live target practice, air-to-ground firing, on the 10 feet square targets using only two of the Sabre's six half-inch Brownings on each sortie.

We never fired rockets from Sabres. The first sortie on the next day was similar, but that in the afternoon was at high level. Very high level.

There had been some discussion as to how high a Sabre could fly. Briefed for an aerobatic sortie ending with a practice flame-out landing, my additional and unofficial part of the mission was an altitude trial. Steadily climbing from base I reached 45,000 feet without difficulty. Thereafter the rate of climb slowed markedly. With oxygen full on, and using pressure breathing, I slowly reached 50,000 feet. Then things became very difficult. With 100% power, flying speed almost equalled stalling speed and at that altitude some very delicate control movements were called for. Any twitch, even the slightest twitch, of the stick would cause a stall and the height lost would slowly have to be regained. I could not improve upon 53,750 feet, indicated. At that height I was flying on a knife edge to stay there. The sky looked dark with the most part of the light reflected up from cloud far below and, of course, that penetrating point source of light, the sun. The horizon was visibly curved, the first time I could genuinely say I'd seen the earth's curvature. The top half of my body was frying from the direct rays of unfiltered sunlight, whereas the lower half of me was freezing cold in the shadow. I momentarily lifted my tinted visor and the blinding light was almost painful to the eyes. I was only at that height for maybe a minute. Descending steeply, I aerobatted my way to lower levels to comply with my briefing, and commenced a simulated flame-out descent from 35,000 feet. It didn't work out properly as a useful exercise because, with the engine still on, although throttled back, it was producing thrust and therefore reduced the dead-engine angle of descent. This, in turn, affected distances from which to set up a supposedly dead-stick landing. It was not like the real thing I had experienced. It was a poor, distorted, simulation which could be misleading, and I said so on landing.

I next flew on January 11th. The first sortie was a weather recce and then I joined up with others for battle formation practice. The next sortie was further high level battle formation practice and the third was to practise ciné quarter attacks on a towed target.[1] 122 Wing had by now set up a non-firing drogue towing range over the sea to the north of the islands of Spiekerooge and Wangerooge and parallel to the coast. There had been difficulties in doing this, particularly with the towing

---

1   This was the last time I flew XB812, the preserved aircraft now in the RAF Museum at Cosford.

aircraft. Sabres were unsatisfactory as tugs for a variety of reasons, so the Station Flight Meteor was used. There were also difficulties when it came to the radar gun-sights detecting and locking-on to the drogue. Much on-going experimentation was being done to try to solve this problem. Until it was solved – eventually by tying aluminium reflectors to the drogues – the gunnery results for Sabre Squadrons at the next live-firing detachment to Sylt would again be abysmal.

January proved bitter. There was snow and freezing rain. With strong winds and driving snow it was no longer practicable to walk across the airfield to our hangar after Met Briefing. On one occasion some of us piled into the back of Des Browne's Land Rover to drive there round the peri-track. It wasn't long before, in freezing rain, he calmly announced "Gentlemen, I am no longer in control of this vehicle!" With some difficulty thereafter we slithered and skidded our way, even sideways and backwards, for the last half mile. On getting out, several of us fell over on the dangerously slippery hard-standing. As Squadron MTO I had to set an example for ice driving and with practice born of necessity, became quite good at it, even on roads with a steep camber, but sometimes with my front wheels on the crown of the road and my right side rear wheels dragging close to the kerb.[2] At least I always got to my destination safely and without damaging anything. Al Colvin, as I remember, could never master this art, and many were the times when he would recruit us to help him extricate his own private car from the roadside drainage ditches. If we were summoned to do this in the evening, many of us suspected that there was not just ice but an alcoholic factor in some of his predicaments.

While mentioning winter weather I remember being on parade when it started to snow and, before the parade was over, every man had a pile of snow on his right shoulder up to the level of his ear. Another occasion, during freezing rain when things always seemed to go quiet, the only significant noise was that of the creaking of the trees giving way under the weight of accumulated ice, and the crash as whole branches broke off and fell to the ground.

Flying was impossible in these conditions and after significant snow falls. On several occasions the whole of the Station was mustered to help clear snow off the runway so that flying could take place. I have to

---

2   In Germany we drove on the right-hand side of the road.

admit that when this happened I would disappear to the PSI gardens and the warmth of the greenhouses where no-one would think of looking for me.

Ground training continued until flying could recommence. Tank recognition, aircraft recognition, ciné film analysis, lectures, war films of all sorts, work-outs in the gym, and a bit of bull here and there, kept us fully occupied. Occasionally one of us would be summoned to taxi an aircraft across to the Tech Wing hangar for servicing. This was usually on a Saturday morning when there was no flying or flying had ceased for the day. The routine was for the pilot so detailed (and it was often me) to phone Air Traffic and tell them what was afoot, and phone the Tech Wing to expect me. I would then, usually in normal uniform and often wearing a mackintosh and beret, climb aboard the aircraft, wave frantically to Air Traffic who probably couldn't see anything and weren't watching anyway, start up, and taxi the mile and a half to the Tech Wing hangar, being very careful to keep a good look out when crossing the runway in case an unexpected aircraft was landing. It was a good way to go for an early Saturday lunch.

Winter evenings could be tedious and there was always the temptation to go to the bar. An alternative was to play skittles in the Bowling Alley on the road to the Mess. It was here also that the camp barber had his room. A new innovation was the conversion of the Bowling Alley also to act as a .22" target shooting rifle range. We held competitions, either bowling or shooting, in there on many evenings. Sometimes it was too cold and cheerless to venture from our rooms where we would sit and listen to the radio, write letters, or indulge in our hobbies. Some of us, instead, would occasionally foregather and play cards. Gambling, however, was absolutely forbidden.

We did fly, when ground conditions permitted, during some beautiful but brief clear periods later in the month. The emphasis, again, was on battle formation work, ciné quarter attacks on the flag, tail chases and high level interceptions at which I was able to further demonstrate my abilities at high altitude long range vision. Although I had to admit to myself that my headaches were beginning to affect me in the air.

As pilots we had to be capable of servicing our aircraft and had to 'keep our hand in'. It was while standing on a wing helping the ground crew refuel a Sabre that I had inserted the filler nozzle into the wing tank and the fuel was flowing when the bowser pressure refuelling hose split and soaked me from head to foot in AVTAG. Fortunately there was no fire or I would have been fried alive. Stinking of aviation fuel, and my skin stinging all over from its effect, I was promptly taken back to my room to strip off, throw my flying suit and other clothing out of the window, and go and have a bath – with several changes of water. I took the rest of the day off. My clothes, left outside on some bushes at the back of the block overnight, soon lost the smell and, after Frau Pinnau had washed them, were none the worse. My flying suit likewise survived but was much cleaner after its soaking in fuel. It was fit for use again 24 hours later and had almost no residual smell.

I was only to fly a Sabre six more times. Four of these sorties were the now routine ciné quarter attacks and tail chases, each ending with a QGH. I flew an air-to-ground firing sortie at Meppen and my final flight, although I didn't know it at the time, was a 30 minute weather recce followed by a join-up and some close formation flying. That was on Friday, February the 4th.

What had happened to stop me flying was that, towards the end of January Sqn.Ldr. Des Browne caught me using the crew room emergency oxygen rig when there wasn't any flying. I had been vomiting and had a belting headache and must have looked pretty grim. On seeing me he straight away told me to get in his Land Rover, whereupon he personally drove me to Sick Quarters. I was seen by 'Doc' Hughes who questioned me closely about my condition. He wasn't very happy about me. The upshot of this was that he arranged for me to be interviewed and examined by a Medical Board. In the meantime, provided I didn't have a headache I could still fly.

Fg.Off. Gerry Busby flew me in the Station Flight Vampire T11 to Wildenrath on February 9th so that I could attend the Medical Board at the nearby RAF Hospital at Wegburg the same day. I had a small overnight bag with me.

I sat before the Board and was interviewed, medically examined, and interviewed again. Then I had to wait outside the room for a while. On being called back in, and now standing in front of four doctors, I was told that they had medically downgraded me to A3 G1, co-pilot only. My career as a fighter pilot was over. I phoned Jever to tell the Boss, and I was ferried back from Wildenrath next morning in the T11 by Fg.Off. John Sutton of Station Flight. This was my last flight, all 25 minutes of it, in an RAF jet.

During January and February promotion exam candidates were allowed time to study in the Education Section adjacent to Station Headquarters. We were given extra personal tuition and attended appropriate lectures. This was in addition to similar studies which I had done some months previously, but this time I was eligible, with having enough seniority as a Flying Officer, to actually sit the exams. My knowledge of Air Force Law, which we were not taught, was derived from my having, some months previously, bought my own copies of the Manual of Air Force Law and Queen's Regulations & Air Council Instructions, together with a subscription so as to receive all amendments as they were issued. With these books there was already a whole wodge of amendments to be cut and inserted. I reckoned that I knew my way around these books better than most by the time I had finished.

Just five days after being grounded I went to Oldenburg to sit the examinations. Staying in the Mess until the end of that week, the four of us from 93 spent our time either sitting the various papers or studying for the next ones. We were far from alone and, as can be imagined, the atmosphere was tense, with not only pay increases and promotions at stake, but whole careers depending on the results. The Oldenburg Mess was crowded with candidates from all over 2 Group. I felt reasonably confident with my answers to most of the questions, but less so with the Law and some of the Aviation papers, particularly the questions dealing with variable pitch propellers which I had never come across. I had done my best. There were no distractions and no headaches. Now all I had to do was wait.

Although still officially on the strength of 93 Squadron my days there were obviously numbered. I stayed with them until the end of February and was with them on a Ground Combat Course run for our benefit by the RAF Regiment. Our knowledge of field craft was updated. We were given the latest news on chemical warfare and its effects. The highlight of the week, which I enjoyed immensely, was the firing of rifles and Sten and Bren automatic weapons in the harmonisation butts close to 4 Squadron hangar. It was generally agreed that my shooting was 'pretty good'.

At this point I had no idea what I was going to do next. I still had five months of my two and a half year tour to complete in Germany. The only thing that was certain was that I would be posted away from the Squadron. Knowing this I set about handing over a Barrack Inventory to some unsuspecting junior pilot. My MT inventory and my duties as MTO were handed over to George Hickman. My parachute, aircrew wrist watch, Mae West, and other gear were returned to Stores. I was allowed to keep my flying clothing. Strange as it might seem, having handed over both my duties and most of my equipment, and officially 'cleared' from all departments associated with flying duties and, effectively, the Squadron, I felt as though a great weight had been lifted from me in readiness for some, still unknown, new beginning. For the time being I was still responsible for the PSI Gardens and Tug of War (which I had shirked so far), and responsibilities for potential visits by Air Squadrons and Summer Camps.

My final assessment on leaving the Squadron? Below average. In view of my personal condition and its inevitable effect on my performance I had no argument with that.[3]

On hearing this, some of my friends expressed the view that they thought Des Browne had a 'downer' on me. I was in no position to comment.

---

3   The reasons for the headaches are explained in the final chapter.

27. Down To Earth

EVEN BEFORE I HAD officially left the Squadron I was summoned by Fg.Off. Brian Watson, the Flying Wing Adjutant, to come and see the Wing Commander Flying, Wg.Cdr. Hammer West.[1]

I entered Brian's office and saluted, as was etiquette. Before my right arm had descended to my side Hammer West's voice said, almost all in one word, "Pod come in here and sit down." I entered, saluted, and sat on a chair in front of his desk. He then said "Pod, you won't salute me in here anymore because from now on you're going to be my Adjutant and we are going to have to work together – got it?" He then went on to explain that I had a week to take over the job from Brian and that he would be released to join 4 Squadron. "Stick with it", he said, "and don't take any notice of posting instructions you might get because I'm going to see to it that you stay with me for the rest of your tour."

All in the space of ten minutes I had changed jobs and was at once out of my depth. As a Squadron pilot the Wing Commander Flying was someone to respect and be wary of. He was your Boss's Boss. Now I was to work not only for him, but with him – as his Adjutant. That took some swallowing.

---

1 His initials were C.S. West. His first name was Cyril (which he kept secret), but he was called John by everyone on first name terms with him. His wife was Nancy and they had two children. They lived in Senior Officers married quarters within the Station perimeter fence fairly close to the Officers Mess. The SOMQs consisted of only four bungalows, occupied by the Station Commander, Gp.Capt. Tom Prickett, and his wife, the aforementioned West family, Wg.Cdr. Russell-Bell, Wing Commander commanding the Admin Wing, and family, and Sqn. Ldr. Peter Gilpin, OC 4 Squadron, with his wife and family. Wing commander Way, OC Technical Wing, was a bachelor and lived in the Mess. 'Shandy' was his pet Alsatian. Wg.Cdr. Alton, OC the RAF Regiment Wing, lived in the Officers married quarters outside the main gate, as did Sqn.Ldr. Des Browne, OC 93 Squadron (my old Boss), and his Australian wife.

All credit must go to Brian for showing me, and explaining to me, what to do, and when and how to do it. He took me through the Orderly Room routine (I had a Corporal and two Leading Aircraftman Clerks), the filing system (I was responsible for Secret and Confidential files as well as those classified as Restricted), how to handle visitors, arrange for disciplinary charges to be heard, tea brews, Met Briefings, minute taking, and even taking the Wing Commander's pet bull terrier 'Pinto' for walkies. Swotting for promotion exams was a mere doddle compared with this! Brian also introduced me to the nuances and vagaries of AP 3184, the Manual of Service Writing, the contents of which I had to adhere to. I had to draft, sign, and disseminate weekly Flying Wing Routine Orders and keep a log of all telephone calls. Not only did I have to be welcoming to visitors, but also something of a disciplinarian. As with all Adjutants, I would be my Boss's sounding board – there to be sworn at when he 'blew his top' after something had gone wrong.

I remember the first time Des Browne, my ex-Boss came into my office and asked me if it was OK to see the WingCo. That was quite a surprise, if not actually a role reversal! I have to say that, whilst I made mistakes to begin with, I quickly settled to my new job and was accepted by all who had reason to come to, or through, my office, Group Captain Tom Prickett our Station Commander included.

In this new position I had dealings with Officers and personnel from other departments with whom I had had little or no previous contact. Flt.Lt. Les Knell, Station Adjutant, and I had to liaise with regard to parades, disciplinary, and organisational matters. Flt.Lt. Les Tweed was i/c personnel. Then there was Sqn.Ldr. Gilpin, the CO of 4 Squadron, Wg.Cdr. Alton the Regiment Wing CO, and Wg.Cdr. David Way who ran the Tech Wing. The one Senior Officer with whom I had little contact, other than in my role as i/c PSI Gardens, was Wg.Cdr. Russell-Bell the Admin Wing CO. Strangely, Fg.Off. John Sutton of Station Flight, Flt.Lt. Love the Senior Air Traffic Control Officer, Flt.Lt. 'Al' Fairfax the Intelligence Officer, and Fg.Off. Dennis Tann the Gunnery Instructor, although all directly responsible to Hammer West, seldom came to see him.

I flew only once more at Jever on a base-to-base sortie after being grounded. This time I was a passenger in the back seat of a Percival Prentice. It was a joy-ride on what was officially a CRDF calibration run.[2] Fg.Off. Doug Bridson from 4 Squadron was at the controls and I had my movie camera with me. We were airborne for an hour and forty minutes in freezing weather. Only the runway and major taxiways were clear of snow. My film came out reasonably well and was later spliced into my RAF Jever movie.

Shortly after I had taken over from Brian and was 'going solo', so to speak, a posting notice arrived for me. I was to take over as the permanent Range Safety Officer of Meppen Range. The very thought of being posted to that God-forsaken place, and to have to live alone in a German hotel for the next five months, filled me with horror. I showed it to my Boss the WingCo. He said "Ignore it. Don't do anything. I'll fix it", and went on "Ignore it completely. That's an order. Blame me if anyone gets awkward". True to his word, he had the posting cancelled and it was replaced about a fortnight later by another, posting me as his Adjutant. That was a relief!

Now that I was officially off 93 Squadron strength it was time for the Squadron to 'Dine me out'. This event coincided with, and was tacked on to, a normal monthly Mess Dining In Night. After the formal part of the evening was concluded, all members of 93 foregathered in the bar. Due speeches were made by Des Browne and Al Colvin, my old 'B' Flight Commander and, of course, I had to reply. All parts of the proceedings were accompanied by a mixture of well lubricated cheering and jeering. Then came the serious bit. As was the norm on such occasions – and I can't remember which came first – I presented the Squadron with an engraved silver tankard and, immediately afterwards, I was presented with an almost identical (apart from the wording) engraved tankard. But there was another difference: I presented an empty tankard, as was usual, but the one presented to me was full of a cocktail of liqueurs and spirits, diluted slightly with Pils. It was my duty at once to down the lot in one breath. This I did, to great cheering all round. It tasted very strange, but not too bad and, much to the disappointment of the assembled throng, it had very little effect on me. They, and I, had seen other departing pilots in similar circumstances collapse, legless, within five minutes, or make a dash for the toilet to commune with

---

2   CRDF = Cathode Ray Direction Finding. This new equipment had just been installed and was a vast improvement on the old system which involved long R/T transmissions. With CRDF an instantaneous bearing from (or course to steer to) base could be read off and transmitted to the pilot.

nature down the big white microphone. I actually survived the rest of the evening without ill effect. Mind you, I did take two precautionary Alka-Seltzers before going to bed.

I was to remain an 'honorary' member of 93 Squadron throughout the remainder of my stay at Jever. Not to be outdone, 4 Squadron awarded me the same informal honour. I was still among friends.

The building in which I now worked, and for which I was soon to hold the barrack inventory, had been a wartime Luftwaffe hospital. In spite of this it was ideally suited for its use as Flying Wing Headquarters. It was almost cruciform in shape, rather like a church, but with one side arm of the cross foreshortened into a mere gable on the airfield side. This was the side on which my office was situated and from where I had a reasonable view through my double-framed, double-glazed, window of the flying activity. Outside the window were a number of juniper bushes which produced a fresh, tangy, pine-like, smell in the hot sun during the summer months. Indoors, the end office next to mine, with an interconnecting door, was the Flying Wing Orderly Room. It, as did my office, and all the other offices in the building, opened on to the long wide central corridor. This thoroughfare had a red coconut fibre runner along its length. The uncarpeted sides of the floor were highly polished and of a darkish chocolate brown colour. The walls were a pale cream. Each office or room had a protruding sign above its door stating its use or the title of its occupant.

Sitting at my desk, with my back to the window, the Orderly Room was on my right. On my left was the Boss's office with its own interconnecting door. Beyond that was the 'Stats' Room; a dark narrow room in which there was, at stand-up desk height, a sloping table running the length of the room on which were displayed the most recently available Flying Statistics from the Squadrons and Station Flight. It was my task to keep everything in there up to date. Usually, apart from my Boss, the only people to go into this room were the Station Commander and Squadron Commanders. Beyond, and further down the corridor to my left was the Aircrew Briefing Room with its map of Northern Europe on the end wall. It was my task always to attend morning Met and flying briefings in case any matters arising needed my attention. Near this long room was the Met Office itself, run by Arthur Hull and his two staff. Further along, at the end of the front of the building were other smaller rooms, one of which later had in it a demonstration

Martin Baker ejection seat. There was an outside door at that end of the corridor.

The Flying Wing Headquarters building. On the ground floor under the centre of the gable is the Wing Commander Flying's office with its bay window. To the right was his Adjutant's (my) office, and to the right of that the end window was that of the Flying Wing Orderly Room. The blanked out window to the left of the WingCo's bay was the Stats Room. The two storey bay housed, upstairs, Air Traffic Control and downstairs, the Met Office. To the left, the next three windows were of the Pilots Briefing Room. The white Stevenson's Screen in the 'Met garden' is to the right of the picture and barely visible in front of it, the Signals Square.

Returning along the opposite side of the corridor were cleaners' rooms, toilets, the teleprinter room, stairs to the upper floor, and access to the rear door, the junction with the cross-passageway, and then a blank wall before the end window outside the Orderly Room. The short cross-passage led to Flt.Lt. Alan Fairfax's Intelligence Office and display room. The latter had been the old operating theatre and had a tiled floor with a drain grid in it. Alan used to keep the drain covered with an old book because, if he didn't, the foetid smell emanating from it would permeate the whole building. Across the passage from Alan's room were the rooms occupied by the army Air Formation Signals Unit under the command of 2nd.Lt. 'Rod' Ping; he had a far back Oxford accent.

Upstairs were the quarters of the Flying Wing HQ Corporals and Airmen. That is, apart from the Air Traffic Control Tower and its associated offices. These lads had superb accommodation with small rooms rather than those in the large, shared, barrack blocks of everyone else.

On one of the walls of the Boss's office was an organisational chart of the Flying Wing, including the HQ, Air Traffic, Station Flight, and the Squadrons. It was my job to keep this up to date and to ensure that photographs of all Officers were displayed in their appropriate place. This meant sending newcomers to the Photographic Section so that they could bring me their own 'mug shot'. That bit was easy, except for one thing. The Boss had his name at the top of the tree, as was proper, but no photo. He had an aversion to having his photograph taken. Try as I might, I couldn't get a snap of him, official or otherwise. Quite unexpectedly one day while he was flying I noticed Pinto his pet bull terrier had taken a liking to sitting in his master's chair when he was airborne. I seized my chance and asked LAC Roseblade, one of my Clerks, who I knew had a camera, to go up to his room and fetch it and take a photo of the enthroned Pinto.[3] This done I, taking a risk, was later able to cut out the dog's head and fix it in the space for the Boss's photo at the top of the chart. This went unnoticed for some days, that is, until the Station Commander spotted it during a visit. I could hear laughter, almost to the point of giggling, before I heard the shout "Pod, come in here". The Group Captain spoke first and, smiling, congratulated me on both my initiative and my sense of humour. Hammer West couldn't criticise me after that but I did get a sort of old-fashioned grin from him. I then left his office, but Pinto's photo stayed in place for the rest of my time at Jever.

'Top Dog'.

---

3   I paid Roseblade for the film in his camera, and the processing. It would have been wrong of me to have done otherwise in the circumstances.

By chance the tables were turned on me not long afterwards. A bat had flown into the FWHQ building and become trapped. Where did it roost in the daytime? – hanging upside down from an electric conduit immediately above the centre of my office door! Thus, I became the centre of amusement for a few days until the creature was removed.

The Boss had a Volkswagen Beetle allocated to him for his use. It was the only one on the Station with chromed hub caps instead of the standard dark olive-green. It was his habit, each morning before Met briefing, to do a runway surface skid test in this vehicle. The skids, slides, twists, and turns he did were a wonder to watch. If the surface was dry, as was most usual during the summer season, the amount of blue smoke generated from the tyres had to be seen to be believed. I was unfortunate enough to be bidden to accompany him on such a test one morning. We had no seat belts. The way I was thrown about inside that car was almost brutal. Then, as if to cap the performance, he said he was going to check the crash gates in the boundary fence. Driving a mite more slowly over the rutted forest tracks I still had great difficulty staying in my seat. It was all right for him, he had a steering wheel to grip. I had nothing. I really thought I'd met my end when, on driving furiously down one track, he saw a spindly, dead, pine tree lying at waist height across the track. Stop and get out? Oh, no. He drove hard at it and hit it so that it bounced up off the rounded bonnet of his car and went way over the top of us to land clear behind.

There were times when he would ask me to use his car to drive some-where on the Station to deliver some document or other that needed prompt attention. I did this fairly regularly. But once, I got it wrong. Wg.Cdr. Way was in the Boss's office with him when I had to use the car. Not realising, I got into the wrong car and drove off, did what I had to, and drove back. It was only when I was parking that I realised that the Boss's car was in its usual place. I had used Wg.Cdr. Way's without permission. He was waiting for me. Using a choice of words which I can no longer remember, I wangled my way out of a dress-ing-down by somehow mentioning that he had left his keys in it when all unattended vehicles should, under orders, be immobilised. I took an enormous risk, but I got away with it. Hammer asked me what David Way had said, and I replied that I had said more to him in explanation than he had said to me.

While still on the subject of the Boss's car: at the annual Summer Ball in the Mess, after the official guests had left, and as day broke before the party ended, a near riot broke out during which Hammer West's car was lifted bodily from the car park, up the steps, and into the dining-room to be placed on a cluster of tables for all to see. The feat was executed by many hands, comparatively quietly, and with the delicacy born of drunken precision. Not a dent, not a mark was on it. There it sat on its makeshift plinth until next morning.

That morning, a little later than usual, the Boss walked to his office and, on entering, said just one thing to me "Pod, get my bloody car back where it belongs ready for Monday morning." He then retreated, probably to nurse his thumping head. This was a tall order. To attempt to get hungover pilots to remove it would have been impossible in the circumstances. Fortunately Flt.Lt. Wright, the Station MTO, who didn't drink a lot, was in his office as usual, so I phoned him for assistance, which he duly provided. He sent a group of drivers to the Mess to do the job. Unfortunately the car was dropped on being taken down the Mess steps and was dented. All credit to them, the MT Section did a cover-up job over the weekend and the car was returned, as required, for use on the Monday morning.

As to parades: for some weeks during 1955 the Station Commander had ordained that it would be good for Junior Officers (anyone below Flight Lieutenant in this instance) to have the experience of taking weekday morning working parades. If it was regarded as a nuisance to those who had to take the parades, the views of the Erks who had also to be there were unprintable. Whilst it was regarded as an absolute bind, it was admitted that it was essential experience and good for discipline. The trouble was no one knew, until their name was posted on SROs, what role they had to take, or when. I had the advantage of having studied and learned, in self-defence, as much as I could about parades and the orders to be given so, unlike others, I had no problems. Sometimes I would be a Flight Commander, sometimes a Parade Adjutant, and sometimes I had to take a parade as if I was the CO. We took these duties in turn, regardless of which Wing we came from, or our normal duties.

I well remember one morning when I was 'Flight Commander' and Fg.Off. Billy May, the Catering Officer and twice my age, was due to take the parade. He, in spite of his seniority and long RAF experience had hardly, because of his duties in the cookhouse, ever been on parade since the war. He marched on, white as a sheet and visibly trembling, and called the parade to order. Then silence. He hadn't a clue what to do next. He did, however, know of my abilities. He therefore called out my name, whereupon I left my position and marched towards him, saluted (which he returned), then, knowing full well what was wrong, and to save his face in front of the other ranks, I muttered to him what we would do. He then commanded me to take over the parade. I saluted him, he responded, and marched off back to the cookhouse. I ordered one of the Supernumerary Officers of what, until then, had been my Flight to take my place. The parade then proceeded and was concluded in the usual way. Billie phoned me when I was back in my office and was very profuse with his thanks, poor man. The matter was at once forgotten and nobody let him down.

When it came to Saturday morning Station Commander's Parades, with Flying Wing being the Senior Wing on the Station, it fell to me to be Parade Adjutant if Les Knell, the Station Adjutant, was not available. Mr. Dale, the Station Warrant Officer, was aware of what I would have to do and very kindly asked if he could come and see me in my office. On entering he tactfully explained to me why he had come and, unusually from his point of view, I asked him to sit down. I told him to dispense with formalities for the meeting and asked him to listen first to what I had to say. I ran through all the orders and moves of almost every Officer on parade, in sequence, while he listened. He was visibly surprised. I think I made two mistakes which he had to correct. That done, we understood one another the better and each had more confidence in the other for such occasions. He also passed on one or two useful hints to me.

It was daunting the first time I was CO's Parade Adjutant. Fortunately all went well. With nigh on a thousand bodies on parade, and the parade being held on an open hard-standing, I had to shout, and shout very loud, to be heard.[4] Others in my position had been known to strain their voices and go falsetto at the wrong moment. A sucked couple of nodules of Cadbury's Dairy Milk chocolate just before marching on did wonders for lubricating my larynx and I never had any such problems.

---

4   Later, towards the end of my tour at Jever, there were four flying Squadrons (Nos 4, 93, 98, & 118), three RAF Regiment Squadrons (Nos 30 & 33 Light Ack Ack Squadrons and No.3 Armoured Car Squadron), Admin Wing, and Technical Wing, all on parade at the same time.

There was another time, when on ordering the various Officers to shout out their numbers of personnel on parade, and I had mentally to add the figures so as to tell the total to the Station Commander after he had marched on, I completely lost count. At the due time, on handing over, I came out with a quick spontaneous estimate which was miles from the truth. Group Captain Prickett, on hearing this, smiled slightly and muttered to me "You bloody liar, Pod". The parade continued as if nothing was wrong. I had to buy him a drink in the bar at lunch time!

I have to mention it again. My headaches were still with me and in spite of reporting sick and them being diagnosed as migraine, no palliative or corrective treatment was offered. I had a private supply of aspirins, but they were of little use. It was either 'Doc' McBride or 'Doc' Hughes who rang my Boss to explain my situation and to tell him that at times I would not be fit for duty. On such days I had to lie in bed in my darkened room, usually until lunch time when the worst symptoms had abated. I would tell one of the pilots in my block to mention my condition to the Boss at Met briefing. I was very fortunate that he was of an understanding nature provided I never fell behind with my work.

My extraneous duties continued. I regularly visited Herr Goldbaum in the PSI Gardens. I was even able to hold stumbling conversations with him in German over the telephone when important matters arose. Speaking in a foreign language when one can't see the person to whom one is talking is not easy, it is surprising how much one relies on facial expressions and body language when conversing face to face. The gardens were prospering. The many formal displays were a blaze of colour, the three Messes were well supplied with fresh vegetables, and there was plenty, both of bedding plants and vegetables, for sale in the PSI shop. A gardening trick Herr Goldbaum taught me was that where there was trouble with moles (particularly in the garden by Station Headquarters), the best way to deter them was to bury empty beer bottles up to their shoulders in the margins of the displays. When the wind blew across the necks of these bottles a low sound was generated. This the moles could not tolerate and so would leave the area. With now working on the opposite side of the airfield from the gardens, I had a transport problem, but was able to solve this by signing for a bike from the Station Bicycle Store. The first time I got on the thing I rode off along the wrong side of the road! Driving on the right was second nature yet when mounted I had unwittingly reverted to English ways.

No harm came to me, but it did seem very strange for the first few days. A cycle ride to the gardens on a warm summer's afternoon was a very pleasant affair and legitimately took me away from the office for an hour or two.

One morning a new RAF Regiment Officer wanted to see me about Tug-of-War. I was lucky, he was keen to set up a team and wanted to know if I minded letting him take over responsibility for the sport. Trying not to show how relieved I was, I thankfully acceded to his request. I phoned Les Knell and told him of the proposed change. He agreed and the matter was promulgated in the next SROs.

My dormant Officer i/c Visits by Air Squadrons and Summer Camps job suddenly came to life. I was told of a forthcoming week-long visit by a University Air Squadron. On seeking guidance from Les Knell he quickly informed me that everything was already in hand. A full programme of events had been drawn up, and all I had to do was to introduce myself to the visitors and to be on call should any snags arise during their stay. I am pretty sure that had I still been a Squadron pilot, and not the Flying Wing Adj. with a full-time responsible job, my duties in that respect would have been far more onerous. As it happened, one of the students was Derek Needham, an old school chum of mine. We were able to have a couple of good chats about what we had both been doing since our Birkenhead School days. Although neither of us could possibly have known it, we were destined to meet again in the RAF.

One of the recently arrived RAF Regiment Officers was a lad called Mark Embry. He was a Pilot Officer and son of Air Vice Marshall Sir Basil Embry. Sir Basil, in his position, was able to fly in to see his son from time to time. The first time this happened Air Traffic phoned me to tell of his imminent arrival. I at once phoned Les Knell, Station Adj. so that he could tell the CO and, apparently, all hell broke loose as to how to handle his Sirship. In the event I had nothing to do regarding that visit. Afterwards, and now knowing that this could happen again without notice, a plan was drawn up so that, at any given time, Mark's approximate whereabouts would be known so that his father could be taken to him. Additionally, I would be the back-up for meeting Sir Basil in the event of a more senior person not being available. It so happened that on two occasions I had to drive out to Sir Basil's aircraft, collect him and take him to his son.

27. DOWN TO EARTH

~~~~~~~~ ~~~~ ~~ ~~ ~~~
by
WING COMMANDER C.S. WEST, D.F.C.,
OFFICER COMMANDING FLYING WING
ROYAL AIR FORCE, JEVER

Date..............18. 8. 55
Page........................1

Order No. 1. Duties - Duty Squadron

1.   No. 118 Squadron is the Duty Squadron for the week commencing Monday, 22nd, August, 1955.

Order No. 2. Discipline - Parade

2.   There will be a C.-inC.'s rehearsal parade on Saturday, 20th, August, 1955. Detail is to be as follows:

(a) Command

Parade Commander	Gp. Capt. T.O. PRICKETT
Parade Adjutant	Flt. Lt. KNELL
Parade Warrant Officer	W.O. DALE

(b) No. 1 Squadron

Squadron Commander	Wg. Cdr. C.S. WEST
Squadron Adjutant	Fg. Off. K.B. SENAR
Squadron Warrant Officer	F.S. SHRUBSOLE

No. 1 Flight (No. 4 Squadron)

Flight Commander	Sqn. Ldr. P.W. GILPIN
Flight N.C.O.	F.S. LLEWELLYN
Markers	Sgt. SMITH(Stn. Flt.)
	Sgt. RANDALL(A.T.C.)
Guides	Cpl. COX
	Cpl. SULLIMAN

No. 4 Squadron Standard Party

Standard Bearer	Fg. Off. BOYACK
Warrant Officer	F.S. LAYMAN
Escort	Sgt. AMOS
	Sgt. FRANKLIN

No. 2 Flight (No. 93 Squadron)

Flight Commander	Sqn. Ldr. D.F.M. BROWNE
Flight N.C.O.	F.S. SMITH
Markers	Sgt. BELLAMY
	Sgt. HART Rowbottom .
Guides	Cpl. WHITECROSS
	Cpl. BRIDGEMAN

No. 3 Flight (No. 9 Squadron)

Flight Commander	Flt. Lt. J. deM. SEVERNE
Flight N.C.O.	F.S. CROXFORD
Markers	Sgt . WEBB
	Sgt. ROSE
Guides	Cpl. DIXEY
	Cpl. LACEY

No. 4 Flight (No. 118 Squadron)

Flight Commander	Sqn. Ldr. GIBBS
Flight N.C.O.	F.S. WARD
Markers	Sgt. HORTON
	Sgt. SPENCER
Guides	Cpl. FLANAGAN
	Cpl. CUNLIFFE

The words 'FLYING WING DETAIL' at the top left are smudged out.

245

FLYING WING DETAIL

No. 1 Squadron is to be divided into 4 Flights of equal strength. Officers, W.O.'s and S.N.D.O.'s not detailed for executive positions are to fall in as supernumeraries.

Flying Wing Headquarters and Station Flight are to be absorbed in Flights 1 - 4 as required, to give Flights an equal frontage. This is to be done by Sqn. W.O.

Guides and Markers are to carry rifles and bayonets. ALL N.C.O.'s detailed for executive positions are to be available at all rehearsals until after the C.-in-C.'s parade.

(c) Guard of Honour

Personnel detailed for Guard of Honour training, are to report to F.S. Wilson at the rear of the Sergeants' Mess at 07.45 hours.

(d) Dress

Best Blue, Webbing Belts, Boots A.P. S.N.C.O.'s, Technicians, Cpls., and A.C.'s are to carry rifles with slings and bayonets. Arms are to be drawn as necessary from the Station Armoury on Friday, 19th, August, 1955, between 16.00 and 17.00 hours. Bayonets are to be drawn from Wing/Sqn. Discip. N.C.O.'s under local arrangements before 18.00 hours, 19th. August, 1955

(e) Times

Unit Arrangements.	Fall in outside barrack blocks.
07.40 hours.	Flights fall in on tarmac in front of No, 1 Hangar
07.45 hours.	Fall in the Officers.
08.00 hours	Inspection completed by Squadron Commanders.
07.55 hours.	Markers to report to Parade Warrant Officer
08.05 hours	March on to Markers.
08.20 hours.	Colour Hoisting.

(K.B. SENAR)
Flying Officer,
Adjutant,
Flying Wing

Both sides of a surviving copy of FLYING WING DETAIL, the first side being on the previous page. These orders were typed on to a Gestetner Machine waxed master which, when typed was extremely difficult to read and correct. After signing, the master was put into the hand-wound machine. The copies were distributed, according to a standard distribution list, by the Station Postal Section.

As one can imagine, I was very nervous in the presence of such a high ranking Officer. On the second time the Air Vice Marshall told me with a chuckle that he knew my nickname was 'Pod', and 'Pod' he called me. Mark had told him. He was a man who wanted no fuss and in no way wanted to disrupt the Station routine when he visited. These visits were unofficial and private. It was a privilege to have met him.

John Sutton came to me in a panic one day. He, as Officer i/c Station Flight, had just been granted powers of Subordinate Commander and, with such powers, had authority to hear a charge. One of his Airmen had allegedly done something untoward, a Form 252 had been made out, and John had to hear the case. Poor John wasn't at all sure what was expected of him, or how to go about such things. All he had learned during training had suddenly vaporised in his mind. As it happened the Boss was due to take a more serious charge himself that afternoon in his office. I asked if John could attend as Officer Under Instruction. The Boss agreed, so I was able to run through the procedure as I knew it with John and, during the actual hearing (I usually attended such events anyway), John was able to watch. John, more worried than the accused, duly took his charge the following morning. It was a minor offence and the miscreant was awarded 4 days CB.

93 Squadron went on their scheduled gunnery detachment to Sylt. What I didn't know when I was with the Squadron was that the necessary Movement Order authorising the detachment had to be drawn up by the Flying Wing Adjutant. Nobody had told me that, not even Brian Watson. Rapidly seeking out similar orders from old files I hastily drafted out the necessary document, had it duly signed, and published it to all parties on the standard distribution list. Wrong! I had totally omitted the Station Equipment Section. The Equipment Officer, Sqn. Ldr. 'Andy' Skene was not at all pleased. He said that the move could not take place without equipment (i.e. aircraft and any other items of any kind), and that he could not agree to such a move without his being informed and the required equipment summarised. I had quickly to redraft the document, cancel the previous issue, get the new version authorised and re-issue it. Panic over!

The Sylt detachment was in warm summer weather and some of the tales with which I was regaled upon the Squadron's return are hardly repeatable. Low flying over pairs of naked bodies in sand dunes, first time nudist ventures by pilots who were apprehensive about their bodily reactions in the presence of the naked opposite sex, fat Germans, and gritty intimate encounters with obliging Fräuleins in the marram grass, and so forth. Photographs were brought back and gloated over. Bare arse beach was the subject of discussion for some weeks afterwards. The majority of less randy members, although having the innate animal curiosity of all men in their very early 20s, were appalled at such behaviour. At the end of the detachment George Hickman, who had replaced me as Squadron MTO, proudly told me that he had brought the convoy back direct to Jever in a single day without the usual overnight stop at Ütersen.

I had to stand in as Intelligence Officer, in addition to my own duties, when Alan Fairfax took three weeks leave. With working in reasonably close proximity we knew each other fairly well, but I knew little of the detail of what he did. This came as a revelation when he had to brief me. He had a vast knowledge of Eastern European military hardware and maintained a locked display room of such data for use at times of special aircrew visits. He also kept tabs on the latest SOXMIS activities reported in the area and had to inform me of attempts by a 'named person' with regard to his attempted spying activities on behalf of the Eastern Bloc.[5] One thing that did strike me as particularly relevant to me personally was the log he kept of the reported sightings of Unidentified Flying Objects (later popularly but erroneously termed 'Flying Saucers'). This log showed the number of sightings and the similarity of most of these to my own earlier experience at Wildenrath during my second flight in a Sabre, and about which I had said nothing for fear of ridicule, was quite remarkable. I told Alan of what I had seen, and it was entered, with the appropriate date, in the book. He said that this almost universal fear of ridicule among aircrew about such sightings was a major deterrent to reporting such incidents. He explained that he was deterred, officially, from actively and overtly seeking such information and was therefore reliant on pilots coming to see him, in confidence, to make such reports. In all other respects I had little to do while he was away, other than open his mail, some of it classified, and file it securely until his return. There was nothing that needed my positive action on his behalf during his absence.

---

5   SOXMIS = the coded name for the Soviet Military Mission. The Soviets, being a party to the postwar agreement regarding the division and running of Germany, had authorised military access to travel in West Germany for routine inspection purposes. They were not authorised to come within a prescribed distance of certain military installations, of which Jever was one. This was ignored in practice and both SOXMIS and BRIXMIS, the British equivalent, both covertly and overtly took every opportunity to monitor and update themselves on the other's (potential enemy's) military activities and perceived intentions.

The named person also mentioned later made his escape via Lübeck to East Germany. He had been employed in Technical Wing and had been closely monitored.

Shortly after Alan came back, he came to see me and asked for my assistance. He had been briefed by the Station Commander to carry out a night time audit with regard to the after hours security of Classified files and information. The CO had authorised him to contact me, under strict security, to assist in this task. If anything went wrong during our audit, (i.e.: if we were caught red-handed carrying it out) he himself was at once to be informed. Alan chose a dark, moonless night for our task. After dinner, Alan phoned the CO to confirm that the audit was 'on' and then contacted me. It was our duty, before midnight, to enter any facility with unsecured windows or doors in which we, with justification, considered there could be a security lapse. That, in truth, gave us the right to enter any administrative, technical, or HQ building on the camp. We knew where dog patrols operated and had to evade them as well as avoid being seen acting suspiciously. Wearing denims, we commenced our task. We soon found that many unmanned (normal at that hour) buildings were not as secure as they should have been. We climbed in through back windows, went through offices – anybody's offices, regardless of rank or position – looked in desk drawers, and found many Classified files which should have been properly secured at the end of work. We had to label each file with where it was found. In fact, in one area, we found so many that we had to hide them under pine needles in the forest and come back for them later when we had completed our rounds. Laden, we arrived at the CO's married quarter and knocked on the door. He was amazed, and furious, but not with us. He signed a receipt for the list of documents. Our task was completed.

Next morning, according to Les Knell, his Adjutant, who later came personally to see us both in Alan's office, the CO played a waiting game, just to see if any of the files were reported missing. Very few were. Then the flak started to fly. Each person whose file or files the CO now had, was summoned in turn to his office for what Les described as 'a severe corrective talking to' and a warning that the security breach would be recorded on that person's personal record and would severely impair his promotion prospects. Some were awarded loss of seniority with the resultant cut in pay. Apart from the CO and, later, Les Knell, no-one knew that it was Alan and me who had carried out the check.

Once in a while, Nancy, my Boss's wife, would call in to my office. If the Boss was busy, out, or flying, and I had the time, she would stay and chat. The poor lady was lonely, the loneliness born of being a Senior Officer's wife. She was a lovely person who doted on her husband but who had difficulty with her situation. As an aside, there were times when my Boss and his wife invited me to their house for a social evening. They were a great couple and were keen to point out that not everything I did for, or with, him necessarily involved work. As a further example of the way we melded together, the WingCo, as his personal extraneous duty, was Commodore of the RAF Jever Sailing Club at Wilhelmshaven.[6]

At the time of the summer Regatta he and Nancy took me there in their private car for the day's fun and festivities. This was a very relaxed all-ranks event with greasy pole and other similar aquatic games. These were as well as the actual boat races which, because of lack of wind on this hot day, were all but abandoned. Those who fell in the murky brown water said it tasted like Coca-Cola. They weren't so happy after someone said that it was the flavour of dissolving drowned bodies from the days of wartime RAF bombing raids on the area.

My life became busier with the arrival of Nos.98 and 118 Squadrons at Jever early in May. They were commanded by Sqn.Ldr. John de Severne and Sqn.Ldr. Gibbs, respectively. 4 Squadron vacated their large hangar on the opposite side of the airfield so as to make room for the new arrivals. No.3 Armoured Car Squadron moved out of their hangar to make room for No.4 Squadron. For a while it was 'all change' until things settled down. There were new faces to get to know, larger parades to take, and a new relationship to be struck up between me and the new Squadron Commanders, both of whom shunned using my nickname and preferred to call me "Adj". Coincidentally, during this move and turmoil, an unexploded 500 lb British bomb was discovered when repairs were being done to the French drain at the edge of the Tech Wing hard-standing. A Bomb Disposal Team was called in. They defused the weapon and I watched as it was hauled out of the ground using a block and tackle and sheerlegs. One of the Bomb Disposal team was Flt.Lt. Amos Moore who I was to meet again later.

I began to get slightly unusual letters from home. Letters which had an increasing emphasis on my leaving the RAF as soon as possible now

---

6   The Sailing Club was also open to membership from personnel on the teaching staff of the British Forces Prince Rupert boarding school at Wilhelmshaven. Some of the nurses from RAF Hospital, Rostrup, near Oldenburg, were also affiliated members. RAF Jever personnel made up the majority.

that I wasn't flying any more, and saying that my headache problem
would be diminished at home. My father thought that I was wasting
the best years of my life for no purpose, and that it was time for me to
leave. He also thought that all I had to do to leave was to give the equivalent of a month's notice, pack by bags, and quit. Although he had been
in the Home Guard (as a Private) during the war he had absolutely no
concept of what it was like to be a full time serving RAF Officer, or of
the responsibilities that that position carried, neither would he listen
when I tried to explain. As an example of this, on taking leave during
the early summer, my parents met me off the troop-train in London
and, instead of taking me home by car as I expected, they drove me to
Salcombe in South Devon for a 'holiday'. It was the last thing I wanted.
I was in uniform and it was after Germany had regained its sovereignty.[7]
Officers had then signed confidential orders to the effect that uniform
was henceforth only to be worn when on, or travelling to or from, duty.
I was both annoyed and very embarrassed. I was travelling light, had no
civvies with me, and expected to change later that day on getting home.
I was stuck in a situation I couldn't handle. Worse, my domineering
father decided that I was some sort of puppet to be gloated over in
the hotel bar. I threatened to catch a train home. As I was saying this
I noticed a stranger looking hard at me; then he approached me and
mentioned my being in uniform. He was a more senior RAF Officer
in civvies, and I was up for criticism. Fortunately I was able to use this
gentleman to my advantage by getting him to have a word with my
father. Only then, but not without prevarication (and very firm insist-
ence from the stranger), did my very miffed father take me home. At
last I was able to change and then make a hurried visit to Moss Brothers
in Liverpool to buy some new kit. It was a far from happy leave and I
was glad to get back to Jever.

Additional to the arrival of new quadrons was their re-equipment
with Hunters; 98, 118, and 4 Squadrons were re-equipped first, the
latter officially changing over on the 1st of July. 93 kept its Sabres until

---

7   Germany regained its sovereignty on the 5th of May, 1955. At this time all service personnel in Germany were confined to camp for an extended weekend so as not to provoke antago-
nism with any German hotheads there may have been around. As it happened none of us were
aware of any change in attitude to us. For our part we could no longer close off a road, hold
a train up, or take a convoy the wrong way down a one-way street. It made little difference
because, in reality, we were no longer exercising this sort of authority any more.

much later.[8] Hunters had 30mm Aden cannon which used electrically fired ammunition. This meant that new armouries had to be built to store it. All of them bristled with lightning conductors as a precaution against the frequent summer thunderstorms usually experienced in hot weather.

Other building work was also going ahead at Jever. Just one item, among many, was the construction of a new camp cinema. This was sited in virgin forest to the rear of Station Headquarters and would eventually replace the now inadequate old wooden Astra Cinema at the far extremity of the married quarters. Also the old red brick pavé roads were being covered with tarmac, so changing the previous comfortable appearance of the place.

Superimposed on this period of change was Exercise 'Carte Blanche' which placed Jever on a mock war footing. My Boss wanted a bed in his office for the duration. This I duly attended to, at the same time arranging for my own bed to be transferred to my office. Thus I spent the disturbed night of my 22nd birthday supposedly asleep, but awakened periodically by photo-reconnaissance aircraft flying along the runway dropping explosive photoflashes on intruder missions. Each time that happened the Boss would leap out of his bed and brief me on what he wanted me to say in the latest SITREP.[9] I endeared myself to him the next night by sleeping right through two such raids! Give him his due, he didn't bother waking me, making the SITREPs out himself instead.

On the morning of Wednesday August 3rd, I attended Met briefing as usual but well before the briefing was over, I was called back to my office to take what could have been an important phone call. In the event, it was a routine matter and, instead of returning for the last few minutes of the briefing I stayed at my desk. I heard the meeting break up and the pilots chatting afterwards as they made their way along the corridor. There was knock on my door. I shouted, "Come in," and in walked Fg.Off. Ted Scott of 93 Squadron. As was customary he saluted. He then walked right up to the front of my desk. He stood for a moment, and before I could say anything, he announced. "I am flying

8   They kept their Sabres until after I had left Jever. I had the opportunity to sit in a Hunter and did not fit in the cockpit, neither could I have ejected safely because of my long legs being in contact with the instrument panel. I was told that had I still been with the Squadron when my tour was over that I would probably have been transferred on to Canberras.

9   SITREP = Situation Report. This was a document used to inform a headquarters of a locally changing tactical situation in war conditions.

your aeroplane today, Pod. Good-bye." With that he put out his hand, shook hands with me, saluted, and marched out. Whilst I thought his behaviour a little strange at the time, I passed the matter off and settled down to my daily routine.

A little over an hour later, the panic phone rang in the Boss's office. I ran in, but he was there and had already picked up the receiver. His face changed as he came out with some expletive or other and then said, "Thank you" to the caller. The Boss looked at me and said, "Ted Scott's bought it. He's gone into the ground at Meppen. I'm going there now. You'd better come with me because you know the way." I rushed to Alan Fairfax's office, told him the news, and got him to stand in for me until we came back. In the meantime, the WingCo had told the CO and was on his way to his car waiting for me as I had had to go back to fetch my cap. With the Boss at the wheel, and with his facility for demon driving, we arrived at Meppen in what must have been record time. There, at the range, was a dark hole in the ground, with the Range Safety Officer at its edge looking into it in shocked incredulity. It was gradually filling with brown water. Little was to be seen of my old Sabre, XB 548, 'P' Papa, or 'P' Pod as it was known when it was mine. There were bits lying around and it appeared as though Ted had flown straight into the target. He, or what was left of him, was in that hole, in the wreckage, under the slowly rising water. The Boss spoke with the Safety Officer to try and establish what had happened. Then he climbed up the Range Tower and phoned Oldenburg to arrange for a recovery crew to attend. There was little else to do, so we left the scene.

As came out in our discussion on the way back, there were several very curious events surrounding this incident. Firstly, why did Ted come into my office and behave the way he did? Secondly, there was no way he could possibly have known he would be flying XB 548 until he had been briefed to do so on his (later) arrival at the Squadron. Thirdly, although he would have known from Met briefing that there would be range firing that day, there was no guarantee that he himself would actually be doing so. The Boss questioned me closely about this as we drove back to base. We discussed whether Ted could have committed suicide, or whether he had suffered from target hypnosis and followed his bullets into the ground. Neither of these seemed likely, but both were possible. He had either just got married, or was about to be married, and had everything to live for.[10] But the overriding question that remained unanswered was "Why did Ted come into my office and say what he did when he could not possibly have known that he would be flying XB 548?" Neither of us could answer that.

Ted's body was recovered from the hole by the Oldenburg crash crew and his funeral took place in Hamburg five days later. In the circumstances, I thought it better that I should not attend. The subsequent accident investigation, to which I was not called, considered that during his pull-out after firing on the target, one of his Sabre's leading edge slats may have jammed out creating violent asymmetric lift and tipped him over, thus causing him to hit the ground. For me, there will always be unanswered questions.

Then came the day when a United States Air Force Grumman Goose seaplane entered the circuit and requested permission to land. The pilot did a low run over the runway, at which point I heard Air Traffic get in touch with the Boss and suggest that everybody goes out to piss on the runway so that the seaplane could land! Going round again, the pilot lowered the wheels of his amphibian, landed normally, and taxied to the apron in front of Station Flight.

I was given notice that my tour at Jever would end soon. This came as a blow. I had to make up my mind as to which of two options I was given regarding my future RAF career. These options were to train either as an Equipment Officer or as a Fighter Controller. I had recently seen Andy Skene, Station Equipment Officer, go down with a nervous breakdown as a result of some anomaly or other regarding equipment accounting. Also Plt.Off. Robin Sandle, EPAS Officer, had warned me of the traumas that could happen if things went wrong.[11] Fighter Control it had to be, although I knew next to nothing about the job, save for hearing voices controlling us over the R/T and knowing that radar was used in some way.

As it happened, at about this time there were a series of hush-hush meetings in the Boss's office to which I was not privy. I heard the name "Brockzetel" used in this connection several times and gathered that it was a new satellite site of some sort. But that was all.[12]

---

10 With the passage of time I have forgotten which.

11 EPAS = Equipment Pay and Accounting Section.

12 I could not have possibly known it then, but after retraining I would be regularly in touch with this, for the moment, mysterious site.

PERMISSION TO FLY

The undermentioned officer, are hereby authorised
to proceed by air in Valetta No. ???. to the United Kingdom on
1st. September, 1955.

Flying Officer C.P. Sanderson
Flying Officer K.B. Senar

(C.S. WEST)
September, 1955   Wing Commander,
                         Officer Commanding,
                         No. 122 Wing

My 'Permit to Fly' signed by Hammer West himself.

Doug Bridson, late of 4 Squadron, had been posted to the RAF 'Brat'
Apprentice School at Halton, near Wendover.[13] He chanced to hitch a
lift on a day return trip to Jever on a Communications Flight Anson.
On arrival he made for my office before having lunch with his old
squadron mates. He told me of some of the tricks the Brats got up to.
One such situation he told me he had to handle was when, one Saturday afternoon a group of them decided to have a swim, but not in a
conventional manner. They chose the upstairs ablutions of their barrack
block as their venue. They plugged the drains and toilets with newspaper and turned all the taps in the room, both hot and cold, full on.
The room flooded to a depth of three feet or so and they had a high old
time. But it was inevitable that someone would sooner or later report
the leakage of water coming out into the corridor from under the door.
The Orderly Sergeant and Orderly Officer (Doug) were both sent for.
On arrival it didn't take them many seconds to realise what was going
on. Stupidly, but understandably, the Orderly Sergeant gave the door
a kick. Already stressed to its maximum under the pressure of water
from within, it gave way. The ensuing torrent burst through, feet deep,
and washed both Doug and the Sergeant down the stairs as if they were
riding the Severn bore. Soaked, bruised, and furious, Doug summoned

---

13 RAF Apprentices were known as 'Brats' throughout the Service.

the Duty Officer who took control of the situation. Life at Halton, he told me, could be 'interesting'!

During my last weeks as adjutant I was able to take a short leave and was fortunate that, on the day before I was due to catch the train home, and my bags being already packed, I was able to hitch a flight back to the UK in a visiting Transport Command Valetta. This suited me ideally on two counts. I was able to get all my heavy gear home, including my greatcoat, and didn't have to lug it all on and off the ship, and I had an extra day's leave, even if I did have to get home from Tangmere.

My last days at Jever passed quickly. Having made my choice of new occupation, a posting notice came through for me to train as a Fighter Controller at Middle Wallop. I 'cleared' the Station, packed the last of my kit, settled my Mess bill, and left on the Blue Train for a change of RAF career.

28. Jever Reprise

MY TIME AT JEVER had been a particularly comfortable and happy one, migraine excepted. I learned a lot, did a lot, and was even able to save money.

I loved the forest, particularly in the spring when the new growth on the pine trees resembled candles, the quiet walks of an evening with the wind whistling in the tree tops and the calm down below, and the scent of the trees when the sun came out after a shower. But the forest had a disadvantage – mosquitoes. These flew into our rooms through necessarily open windows in the hot summer weather and flew round our heads when we tried to sleep. We became skilled at swatting them with a thrown book when they were perched on the ceiling, or with a damp towel (or anything to hand) when elsewhere, so much so that our walls became littered with stuck-down corpses by the time the first frosts came.

Within my limitations I enjoyed my flying immensely except, maybe, a first flight after a long period on the ground. Apart from a night flight with faulty instruments I was never lost in the air, and could see other aircraft before most other pilots. I had one or two hairy moments, but they were just a part of the risk and fun of flying.

I cannot say that I enjoyed working for Des Browne, but he could have been worse. He placed too much emphasis on the accumulation of flying hours rather than improving the abilities of his less able pilots. To be fair, when he heard that I had passed my promotion exams, and I had been one of the youngest candidates to take them, he phoned me in my office to congratulate me and wish me well. He also wished me well after I was Dined Out when my time came to leave Jever.

The Mess was well run and very homely and my room was well sited and comfortable. My batwoman, Frau Pinnau, was particularly caring and considerate. She willingly did my laundry (provided I supplied the soap powder), pressed my clothes, cleaned my shoes, and polished my buttons. I darned my own socks.

I had no major altercations with anyone. Spats, yes, but nothing that wasn't over in less than a day or two.

The one thing I disliked intensely was having to attend Courts Martial as Officer under Instruction. I never seemed to be able to follow what was going on. In one particular case the berobed civilian Judge Advocate was a garrulous individual who interrupted any witness, for defence or prosecution, when they were giving evidence, to the point of throwing them off what they were trying to say. I dreaded being nominated to take an active part in any such event. Fortunately, I was not.

The conviviality in the Mess was remarkable. Although I may have given the impression that the RAF was a branch of Alcoholics Anonymous, whilst that may have been close to the truth at certain times and for a few individuals, mostly a glass of Coke sufficed of an evening. A glass of Jever Pils and a hot Bockwurst dipped in Senf (French mustard) and eaten in a long bread roll was also the thing to do occasionally.

I travelled widely from Jever. I would never have seen Holland and East Berlin in such detail had I not played hockey.

I did my job to the best of my ability. I enjoyed Jever and look back on those two years of my life with fondness. Within the acceptable constraints of service discipline I was my own man.

I left there in September 1955.

Part 3

FROM GROUND LEVEL TO SUBTERRANEAN

29. Prologue To Part 3

NOW, AS A GROUNDED pilot, I was about to begin my new RAF career. In some respects a breath of fresh air started to blow through my life. Back at home, my father was still nagging at me to leave and could not accept that it was impossible. As a businessman running his own Company he was not used to being defied (as he saw it). Our relationship became rather thin at times, yet I had to try to put this behind me and face the new challenges which lay ahead.

In describing this section of my RAF career I have had to rely almost entirely on my crumbling memory. I have no prompts, save for my Fighter Controllers Log Book and a few unlabelled photographs, nor do I have access to any diaries, official or otherwise. Yet, in many respects, this was a more important part of my RAF career than any other. I became involved with aspects of the Cold War which, according to my advisers, have probably never been recorded from a personal or, indeed, official standpoint. Plenty has been written about the Cold War from the United Kingdom point of view, but none of those writings mention anything about the RAF involvement as part of the 2nd Allied Tactical Air Force in Germany which, without doubt, was a significant part of the defensive front line of our homeland.

I have taken time to describe something of the local German inhabitants and their activities. Whilst, at first sight, this may seem irrelevant, it sets the scene in that part of Germany and is something I would never have been able to record had I not been in the Royal Air Force.

My memories are all the more important, even at this late stage, because much of my work was unrecorded at the time, and had to remain so for very good reasons. My Log Book says really very little because Fighter Control, per se, was to be only a part of my responsibilities, much of the rest of my operational work was, at the time, regarded as being 'under wraps'. Please take account of the fact that I have only written of my own experiences. Some of them could have led to the start of World War III, and there were others of like importance witnessed by my brother Officers who were doing the same work during this period. It was a time of very strained international relations.

Without access to any official chronological order of events with which to sequence my memories, I have to point out that some of the instances I relate may appear in the wrong order. In these circumstances I can offer no excuses. It is better that they are recorded in the wrong sequence than not at all. I challenge anyone who did similar work to write up and circulate their memories, so that a fuller record of the 1950s, from an operational Signals Unit point of view, may also be placed on record for posterity before it is too late.

I must point out that, during the events to be described, the designation of my Signals Unit changed from 537 SU to 210 SU at the end of 1956. Some of the following chapters, being of a general descriptive nature, cover both Units, and necessarily cover the same period, but from different aspects.

30. Middle Wallop

I ARRIVED AT MIDDLE Wallop, from Salisbury station, in the back of an RAF truck driven by a civilian. This was a strange part of the country to me; the rolling hills of Salisbury Plain and obvious ancient earthworks were not a bit like the Cheshire and North Shropshire countryside to which I was accustomed, yet nonetheless welcoming in appearance. The day was warm and the old pre-war and Battle of Britain airfield with its roofless hangar, still unrepaired since the day it was bombed, came into view from the back of the truck as it turned left off the main road into the driveway of the Officers Mess.

I was surprised to find that I was not allocated a room in the old pre-war Mess but in a Seco hut attached to what was known as the Students Mess a short distance away. I was surprised, too, that there were a number of junior Army Officers also in the same range of accommodation. They, I quickly discovered, were on a course connected with the operations of the Joint Experimental Helicopter Unit (JEHU), run by the RAF and Army. Some were also Army AOP (Air Observation Post) pilots who had experience in extremely low flying in Auster aircraft, using trees, buildings and geographical features as cover when spotting for Artillery Units.

As was usual when arriving at a new posting, I found the Mess notice board and read everything on it. There, in one of the Details, was the information as to where, and to whom, I was to report next morning, Monday, September 25th, 1955.

At the appointed time and place I arrived to find that I was to be Course Leader of the nineteen-member, No.57 Fighter Controllers Course. This position was awarded me, in spite of there being two Wing Commanders and 5 other Flying Officers on the same course, because I was the most recently experienced fighter pilot. The rest of the students were Officer Cadets, one of whom was Derek Needham, the Old Birkonian school friend of mine, who had visited Jever earlier in the year.[1] I also discovered that Flt.Lt. Les Tweed, recently from Station Headquarters at Jever, was Station Adjutant. I had been told many times that wherever you went in the RAF, after about four years service, you would find someone you knew or, at least, someone else who knew someone you knew. I was discovering the truth of this for myself.

The Wing Commanders used me as their guide and adviser. They were not doing the full course because, whilst at Middle Wallop, they were also preparing themselves to be future Commanding Officers of Radar Units, and would shortly be posted as such. They were treated with awe by the rest of the course but, having worked closely with Wing Commander Hammer West at Jever I soon struck up a respectful rapport with them. They really only wanted to know the main theme of the course and to attend what they considered to be lectures relevant to them, usually on my advice!

No.57 Fighter Controllers Course, Middle Wallop, September 1955. I am on the front row, 4th from the left, with the two Wing Commanders to my right. Derek Needham is on the back row, far right. In the background is one of the wartime dispersal revetments.

The course instruction buildings were on two separate sites. One, the radar site, with its radar equipment, mobile control cabins, and class-rooms, was positioned on old revetted wartime hard-standings on the south-east side of the airfield. The second site was a distance away

---

1   When I was officer i/c Visits by Air Squadrons & Summer Camps. See page 244.

through the main camp, up the rise on the main road and some way to the rear of the Students Mess. Here, there were plotting tables, micro-phones and head-sets (head and breast sets comprising a standard, GPO style, breast microphone and a single earphone) all connected to various simulated and real training positions, as well as associated lecture and exhibition rooms. Transport between sites, and for outside visits, was by RAF bus driven by a civilian driver. I was not allowed to drive because I had only a Continental RAF licence and had not yet taken a UK driving test.

It seemed strange to be driven by a civilian, but this was just one of the many differences between 2ATAF in Germany and the RAF in the UK. Another significant difference was that instead of having a shared batman or batwoman, as had always previously been the case, we had to do our own laundry, with a cleaner only showing up periodically to dust and sweep our rooms. It didn't bother me greatly but it was an inconvenient let-down. I also discovered that, with recent cutbacks in funding, a permit had to be obtained to make an administrative phone call to another RAF Station. Operational calls were likewise limited to those adjudged to be essential but were otherwise not so closely moni-tored. Compared with my experience of life in Germany, life in the UK was austere and it took me some time to acclimatise.

Sqn.Ldr. 'Doug' Wilson was the CO of the School of Fighter Control. He was supported by a team of instructors, among whom were Fg.Off. Honeychurch who was a little too fond of scrumpy at times, Fg.Off. Jim (Jumbo) Cuthill who had been one of my instructors at RAF Digby when I was there, and Flt.Lt. 'Dan' Archer.[2] These were further supported by WRAFs who were telephonists, tellers, and fighter plotters, and NCOs and Airmen from the technical trades. Additional to them was a Flight of Balliol two-seater training aircraft, pilots and ground crew, whose task it was to fly for, and be controlled by, us course students when learning the techniques and skills of aircraft interception control – our prime reason for being on the course. As if further to prove the point of the RAF being one big club or family, one of these pilots was none other than Flt.Lt. Ken Knott who, as a Flight Sergeant, had been my Flying Instructor at Wellesbourne Mountford and taken me through training up to 'Wings' level on Oxfords. Ken lived with

---

2   Scrumpy = rough cider. A drink with a high alcohol content.

his wife in a caravan parked on a remote hard-standing on the side of the airfield close to the main road. I later went to visit them socially and had trouble finding my way there in the almost total night-time blackness, falling over some unidentified obstacle and cutting my shins on the way.

Our course manual, I think it was called 'The Manual of Fighter Control', covered all aspects of the task in varying amounts of detail according to the (limited) knowledge of the author – or so it seemed to me. There was one memorable statement in it which read "In flight the heaviest bomber is moved by the merest zephyr as completely and inexorably as a tuft of thistledown". Such was the prosy style of writing. At least I still remember that piece of what the man wrote.

We learned the basics of how radar worked, pulse widths, pulse rates, range, lobes, frequencies, permanent echoes, power, and much else, including the basic fact that the speed of light (and radio signals) was 186,240 miles per second.

We learned what radar was used for, the differing types of equipment, and their purpose, advantages, and disadvantages. It was only at this late stage of my RAF career, in spite of having been controlled by 'a voice over the R/T' when flying over Germany, that I was taught anything at all about how Fighter Control was done and why. It would have been of use to have been taught the basics of this during flying training. I have always thought this to have been a serious pilot training omission.

We were taught Morse code, and practised it, and again I struggled (as before) to attain a speed of four words per minute in order to pass the test. The dratted Morse code was the bane of my life, and this time I couldn't use the crib sheet I had sewn onto the leg of my flying suit!

When it came to R/T techniques and use, I was amazed to find that I was microphone shy. I had prattled away over the R/T when in the air and thought nothing of it. On the ground, in a room with other people, I found that using a head and breast set to talk to someone was a very different matter for me. I had to work really hard to overcome this totally unexpected disability. Otherwise there was little for me to learn regarding technique and terminology, except for a group of new phrases mostly concerning the control of night fighters and pertaining to their airborne radars. For instance, a failed airborne radar set was termed a 'Bent Weapon'.

Then came instruction on Command and Control organisation and how it worked, and where and when it was used. Filter room techniques were explained and practised. With our newly gained knowledge and very limited experience, we were, in turn, tasked with acting as Filter Officers so as to filter multiple plots from old plots, and identify friendly plots and hostile plots in a re-run of one of the raids of the Battle of Britain. This was a mind-boggling exercise, carried out in real time, using tellers, with plotters on a General Situations plotting table, as if it was the real thing. The plots were 'told' from timed scripts rather than actual radar sites and Royal Observer Corps posts. Plotters then placed and moved all the counters and markers on the table for us to filter out the confusion into a true(r) situation so that aircraft could be scrambled to meet each threat. Each of us had a go for 20 minutes or so, by the end of which we not only had brain fade, but were mostly more confused than when we started. The task demanded very clear thought and quick, decisive, interpretation and reactions, and a special aptitude as well. We all did better after about three attempts, and every one of us not surprisingly found it easier to criticise than to do the job ourselves. One taste of that, and I quickly realised the stress that Group and Sector Operations Controllers were under during actual wartime conditions. We, in our training, were being given an insight as to what might be expected of us should we find ourselves in similar circumstances, for this was a task very closely associated with our prime Fighter Control role.

It was during one of these sessions that, shame to say, I realised that a small number of the WRAFs did stupid things, in spite of being clearly instructed otherwise. This was nothing to do with the exercise, it was their normal behaviour, indicative of a very low IQ. One of our instructors was heard to remark that some of them would open a tin of soup at the bottom so as not to have to pour out the contents from the top! I observed, from a distance, one girl attempting to sweep a floor with a brush which had few bristles left after much previous use. Her RAF Sergeant called to this Airwoman "What are you trying to do with that? You've got more hair round your fanny than there's bristles on that brush!" She replied, "Ooh Sergeant, how do you know?" At that point I left the area.

Our use of radar was not only to be for Fighter Control, but for both Control and Reporting. That is to say, our radars and some radar

Stations could also be used both for observation (surveillance of aircraft both friendly and those of a potential enemy) and passing those plots using a system called 'Georef' to higher authority for the conduct of a war scenario, as well as for Fighter Control.[3] The combined tasks of Control and Reporting were referred to as 'C & R'.

Before using real radar for the first time we had to learn Fighter Control techniques, and practise them seemingly *ad nauseam*, using simulators or by manual plotting methods, as if we were looking at a live radar screen. Practice interceptions, or PIs (by which abbreviation they were generally known, and which abbreviation I shall henceforth use) were, in the earlier stages of the course, carried out by Fighter Plotters using Craig Computers and stop watches.[4]

Occasionally we used Dax trainers instead when they were serviceable, but these electronic devices were usually unreliable.[5] We had to be competent in all respects before being let loose on real radio with real radar and real aircraft in real time. Proficiency and written tests had to be passed before moving on.

Surprisingly, from my point of view, there were no parades to attend, but I had no doubt the National Service Cadets would have benefited from a bit of marching about. Most of them were ex-university students who thought Fighter Control would be a good skive for their two years of National Service. I had to pull one or two of them up for larking about and making a noise in the accommodation late in the evening when all sensible people wanted to get to sleep. I wasn't popular, but the RAF is no place for that sort of irresponsible behaviour.

Weekends gave us a chance to relax, go shopping in Salisbury, or explore the countryside on foot. As a 'regular' (short service) Officer I could, at weekends use the old permanent staff Officers Mess, something that was denied the National Service students. I found it to be stuffy, barn-like and, worse, the anteroom was full of blowflies buzzing around noisily at high altitude close to the ceiling where it wasn't easy

---

3   Georef = Geographical Reference. This was a simpler system than, but based on, latitude and longitude. It used a system of lettered squares subdivided into smaller numerically labelled areas, e.g. NH1247. This gave a precise enough location of a moving aircraft for all practical purposes and was very convenient and quick to transmit over the R/T or telephone line.

4   A Craig computer was little more than a draughtsman's board on the substrate of which was drawn a map of the relevant geographical area. The associated draughting instrument was graduated in degrees and nautical miles.

5   As far as I am aware Dax trainers were peculiar to the training school at Middle Wallop.

to shoot them down. As with all Messes in the UK at weekends there was hardly anyone about. The advantages of this privilege was therefore extremely limited.

Nearby was Danebury Hill topped by an ancient defensive earth work. It begged investigation. Three or four times I climbed the grassy slopes to its tree-covered summit to explore and to admire the view. At the bottom of this knoll was the winter quarters of Chipperfield's travelling circus. Some of us were shown round by the staff and were able to look 'behind the scenes' as it were. Miss Chipperfield was thought by some young Officers to be a 'good catch' but, to her credit, she remained aloof from their attentions in spite of her being invited to events in the Mess.

I only bothered to go home once during the eight week course because I didn't want to expose myself any more than necessary to further altercations with my father. Instead, I would take the bus to Andover or to Salisbury to enjoy a Saturday afternoon. Sometimes I could hitch a lift with one of the permanent staff Officers who had a car for a look round the delightful village of Abbots Ann, or to go to Middle Wallop and walk along the river and look at the watercress beds. Life was relaxing when off work. It might even have become boring had I been there for an extended period.

In passing, I must mention that there was an experimental pyrotechnics factory not far away from which all sorts of strange plumes of smoke appeared from time to time. Similarly, but on a far grander scale, on a distant hill to the south, rain-making experiments were being carried out. In what were presumably adjudged to be the right conditions of cloud type and altitude, we could see enormous clouds of some whitish chemical 'smoke' being released up into the atmosphere to mix with the airborne water droplets to 'wet' them, hopefully to make them grow and fall as rain. I don't remember hearing, or even reading in the press, that they were in the least successful.

As a necessary part of our training we made several visits, by RAF bus, to operational radar Stations. One of these was the old wartime Chain Home Low Station with its fixed aerial array slung from tall masts. It had been in operation for many years and its performance, in simple terms, relied on its geographical location at the bottom of a steep hillside to reflect its energy forwards and so improve its coverage. This was RAF Ringstead, situated on the south coast a handful of miles to the east of Weymouth. Access was down a steep track to the operations building. It was buried in undergrowth and brambles, with evidence of its original defensive barbed-wire entanglement both over and around it. On entering its dark precincts I at once noticed that it had a musty smell, and I quickly became accustomed to the necessarily dim light. We were greeted by the Duty Watch Officer and were shown the ageing equipment, the radar display on the 'A' scope, and the use of the goniometer. The radar was good for range but heights were not at all accurate. Considerable experience seemed to be required to get the best out of it. An operator told us that one of the hazards of working there was that adders would sometimes find their way inside and look for warmth near the equipment racks. These incursions caused inevitable work interruptions, some excitement, and considerable caution exercised whenever one of these poisonous trespassers was discovered and had to be eliminated. The Station had been first opened in 1940 and was to close a few months after our visit.

The radar Station at Portland was a more modern facility. Properly, this was termed La Verne and was built in the solid rock below, and within, the precincts of Verne prison on Portland Bill at the southern end of Chesil Beach. Entry was gained through the prison gates. The operations block was 70 feet deep underground in a cavity cut in the underlying Portland stone. Entrance was by lift, the top of which was accessed through a stone 'bungalow' Guardroom built to blend in with other nearby buildings. It was said to be the deepest GCI Station in the UK. Above ground, it was equipped with a Type 54, a Type 14 upper, Type 14 lower, and at least three Type 13 'nodding horror' height finding radars. The information from these radars was displayed on PPI screens and height displays down below in the bunker.[6]

This was a comparatively modern system, and was to be developed further within a short while, although we students did not know it at the time.

Working conditions at this site were far superior to those at Ringstead. The site had much more importance too because it was capable

6   PPI = Plan Position Indicator. This is a cathode ray tube on which is displayed a rotating radar trace which shows in its afterglow the location of echoes known as blips or, in more modern terminology, 'paints'. Heights could be determined accurately using nodding Type 13 radars which could be swung electrically by just turning a knob on the underground operator's console so that the radar faced in the right direction. The height of the detected aircraft could then be read off from a calibrated 'heights' screen.

of operating as a GCI Station and had a Sector Operations facility, whereas Ringstead merely passed its plots to another site for interpretation.[7] It was to a place such as Portland that anyone on our course could be posted once we had qualified. The interest factor, therefore, was greatly enhanced as we could see being put into practice the very jobs for which we were being trained.

Better still was our visit to RAF Sopley. This was a fully operational GCI Station. The operations block was underground, access to which was via an innocuous looking bungalow in the New Forest. The bungalow was the Guardroom and itself gave access, via a long sloping shaft, to the reinforced concrete underground double-storey bunker. In it was a central well overlooked by the windows of rooms housing personnel dedicated to specific tasks. In the bottom of the well were a General Situations table and a fighter plotting table; all very reminiscent of the films about the Battle of Britain seen in public cinemas. The back wall of the well carried what was called the 'Tote' on which was displayed call-signs, squadron aircraft serviceability and readiness states, weather information, and much else necessary for the conduct of an air battle. The rooms overlooking the well were occupied by the Chief Controller, civil defence, anti-aircraft control, Royal Observer Corps, and other personnel who would only be present in the event of a real war or a defence exercise. It was at this point that I saw, for the first time, a person called the Ops 'B', the equivalent of that mystical (and dreaded) individual from whom orders to 'scramble' were passed to Duty Pilots at Jever. In reality he was the Chief Controller's assistant with a rank no higher than Senior Aircraftman. What a let-down! We were shown the control cabins wherein Fighter Controllers did their job, and were able to watch as they and their support teams worked.[8] This visit taught us much more than could possibly be explained to us in any class-room. We were able to see people doing our future jobs, with modern equipment in the most modern, air conditioned, and protected environment.

Having been to Sopley and seen its facilities and beautiful location in the New Forest, made all of us on the course keen to be posted to such a place. But there was much more learning to be done before that day came, and there were many questions to be asked of our instructors arising out of what we had seen during these visits.

7   GCI = Ground Controlled Interception.
8   The support teams were usually called cabin crews.

Our instruction was far from over. At the tech site we practised the use of radar. We had nothing very new to work with. The main search radar was an old mobile Type 15 metric equipment which had seen better days. It operated on a wavelength of 1.45 metres and its rotating reflector showed its history in the form of rabbit netting patches covering holes made when it was attacked during the war. We had a mobile Type 14 centimetric (10 centimetre) search radar as well, and a mobile Type 13 height finding radar. All, as their names imply, were mounted on vehicle chassis and powered by trailer-mounted generators. To complete the set, the control cabins were also mounted in the backs of specialist vehicles. There were also classrooms, a toilet block, and a building for the technicians, together with a remote VHF transmitter. One of the instructors' party tricks was to place a neon bulb near to the twin aerial leads of the Type 15. It would glow from the power radiating from the leads. A finger placed in the same place would generate a fizzing noise caused by the electrical interference it created. No student was allowed to emulate these demonstrations.

It was on this site that we learned and practised our knob-twiddling skills, the use of IFF and how to reduce the effects of jamming.[9] Our instructors demonstrated the control of fighters by the use of Middle Wallop's own Balliol Flight, and then, under extremely close supervision, handed control over to each of us in turn. As we learned and became more adept, we were allowed to identify and separate pairs of aircraft so as to carry out controlled quarter attacks, just as I had been instructed to do from the ground when I was flying from Jever.[10]

There were times in the classroom when I was able to update my instructors with more modern thinking than was explained in the teaching manuals. Our instructors were particularly deficient in their knowledge of the handling characteristics and turning circles of jet aircraft at high altitude. This proved a useful two-way experience and meant that No.57 Course, at least, was as up to date in this respect as it could be.

I was given the opportunity to do a sortie as co-pilot in a Balliol during one of these student training exercises. Considering that the last aircraft I had flown was a Sabre, it could hardly have been more

---

9   IFF = Identification Friend or Foe. A system using an airborne transponder by which an aircraft could be identified. Modern and classified then. Old hat now.

10   Quarter, and other forms of attack, were types of PIs = Practice Interceptions.

of a contrast. I had, mentally, to revert to my Chipmunk and Oxford days, and it was quite an effort. It took a while to settle down and get used to crossing over one field at a time in bumpy autumnal air, rather than several dozen in a few seconds with the stability and surety derived of great speed. I stirred the stick as though it was a pudding spoon, and generally made a (safe) hash of things for the first half hour until I settled down. The first pilot, whose name I have sadly forgotten, watched my antics with considerable amusement and good humour. This flight, officially as a passenger, was not recorded in my Log Book, although it turned out to be the very last (unofficial) 'dual' flight of my whole RAF career.

The migraine I suffered from at Jever still bothered me, and just a couple of times, I had to leave a class and go and be sick or walk out in the fresh air. Staring at rotating traces on PPIs in the enclosed cramped space of the mobile control cabins didn't seem to bother me or make matters worse. Had this been the case my career might have been much shorter.

On November the 5th we were treated to one of the best 'home made' firework displays I had ever seen. True, some set pieces had been bought, but most of the display was made up of date-expired RAF pyrotechnics. What it didn't have in variety it certainly had in quantity. Air traffic rockets, thunder flashes, Verey lights, flares, smoke candles – all were consumed in the hour-long display not far from the Officers Mess. It was accompanied by an enormous bonfire and a barbecue (although that name wasn't in general use in 1955). The Armament Officer and Mess Catering Officer and his team did us proud that night.

By the time the course drew to its close we were well versed and practised in close and broadcast control techniques, jamming and how to counter it, bearings from, and Pigeons to, base, reciprocal bearings, R/T language and terms, and what to do if an aircraft had an emergency. We knew something of how radar worked, some of its history, and what was 'Classified' and what was not. For me, I had had 8 weeks of reasonably pleasurable enlightenment. I also knew more about GCI control than almost any squadron pilot of my age group and was all too aware of this gap in their training.

Les Tweed, the Station Adjutant, sent for me. On entering his office he told me there was a problem and that I may have to visit Jever in a hurry. He explained that there was a Board of Enquiry sitting at Jever whose brief it was to look into the circumstances as to how a Secret file had gone missing. They wanted to question me.

I discussed the matter with Les. The file had gone missing from the Flying Wing Adjutant's classified secure filing cabinet. It had been my file, and my cabinet, when I was there. Les obtained a permit for me to ring the President of the Board so that I could find out more. This I did. The crux of the matter, as far as I was concerned, was whether the file was there when I left, which it was, for I remembered it well. I was also able to explain that much of its content was routine stuff, and that I had wondered whether or not it should have been declassified due to the relevant papers being out of date, and that I had not got round to initiating such action. The President was satisfied, subject to my summarising what I had said in writing. This I did, but for speed, I arranged with Les for a Telex to be sent as well.[11] I heard no more.

Les contacted me again. I wondered what for this time, thinking that Jever might still want me. He said "Pod, where would you like to be posted?" He gave me a list of options which included the Far East, the UK, and Germany. Without a second thought I opted for Germany, and asked him why I had been granted the chance to take my pick. He explained that as Course Leader, and as he knew me, he'd give me the choice as it made no difference to him. I next enquired as to whether I had passed the course. He confirmed that I had but not to tell anybody because the results would be announced the next day. What a privilege! I was going to go back to Germany, away from UK and RAF austerity, and not to the unknown (to me) distant Far East. I was delighted.

I was granted three weeks embarkation leave before my next posting. I would be told where that would be while on leave, but I had every confidence that it would be somewhere in Germany.

---

11 Telex = Teleprinter message.

31. Germany Again

AFTER BEING ON LEAVE for almost two out of the three weeks allotted to me the inevitable O.H.M.S. envelope containing my Posting Notice arrived. Just as Les Tweed had intimated at Middle Wallop, I was to go back to Germany. This time I was going to 83 Group instead of 2 Group, and I was to report to 537 Signals Unit at RAF Borgentreich on Thursday the 8th of December.

I had not the vaguest idea of the whereabouts of Borgentreich. I had never heard of it. My travel documents instructed me to report to the RTO at Liverpool Street station, board the Harwich troop-train, and take the troop-ship to the Hook of Holland. Then I was to board the Red train for Berlin but to leave it at Altenbeken, at which place I was to catch a local train to Warburg where I was to phone for transport.

Getting to the Red train was no problem. I had seen it many times in the station at a platform by the Blue train I used to take to Jever. But where were Borgentreich, Warburg, and Altenbeken? How long was my journey to be on the Red train?

Fortunately we had an excellent atlas at home which included reasonably large maps of Germany. After a diligent two hour search, by following the most likely railway lines to Berlin from Holland, I managed to find Altenbeken, in very small print. Widening my search circle from there I found, after another quarter hour, the town of Warburg. Even knowing that Borgentreich couldn't be that far away it took me another few minutes to locate it.

So it was, that early on Wednesday December the 7th, I set off for this strange place. The journey went well. I arrived at Altenbeken, alighted, and struggled with my kit across several tracks to where the station timetable had told me the Warburg train was due to depart. It was already getting dark when I found a seat in a First Class carriage. I noticed a couple of Airmen board further along the same train. At least I was not quite alone. I reasoned that they were probably also going to Warburg and would know their way when we got there. This turned out to be true, and one of them phoned for transport, using me as an excuse for getting something better than a lorry to pick us up.

I arrived at the Guardroom at Borgentreich in the freezing cold of an early German winter at after nine o'clock in the evening. I was thankful it wasn't a tented camp, although, from what I could see as someone helped me carry my kit the short distance uphill to the Mess, it was a small Unit and the buildings looked new.

On entering the Mess hallway there was nobody about, but there were the obvious sounds of a Dining In Night in progress. Speeches were being made and it was apparent that someone was being Dined Out. Not quite knowing whether to interrupt or not I waited a while and made out my two obligatory Calling Cards, one for the Commanding Officer, the other for the President of the Mess Committee and Officers, and placed them on the hall table. I also signed the Warning In book. After what seemed like an age, but was probably less than 5 minutes, an Officer appeared from the dining-room. He was surprised to see me. He went back in and told the CO, Sqn.Ldr. 'Paddy' Ryan, who then appeared and asked me in regardless of my unsuitable state of dress. I was hungry and food was rustled up for me. I ate while most of those present, some of them quite inebriated, continued with the evening jollifications. The PMC came to me and told me, to his obvious embarrassment, that I wasn't expected until a week later and, with the Mess being so small, there wasn't a bed available for me, not even in the Orderly Officer's room, as it was occupied that night. He went on to say that there was a bathroom out in the kitchen area which I could use and asked if it would it be OK if he got a mattress for me to sleep on. In these circumstances I had no alternative but to agree. Someone bought me a large Scotch and, having downed that, and now very tired after the journey, I dragged my kit through the kitchen into my tiled cell.

I did not have a comfortable night. My 6' 4" frame didn't exactly fit easily in the standard bath. I couldn't undress, so I slept fitfully more or less fully dressed with my greatcoat over me whilst lying at an angle on a lumpy narrow mattress in the bottom of the tub, trying all the while to avoid turning on a tap with my feet when I changed position!

I woke next morning to the sounds of German staff arriving on duty to prepare breakfast and decided that, with a bit of kit rearrangement in this small room (it also sported a toilet and a wash-basin, but the floor was too small for me to lie down) to use the bath for its proper purpose and make myself presentable for the day ahead.

At breakfast, I met the living-in Officers, all seven of them; Fg.Off. John Duggan, Station Adjutant; Plt.Off. Peter Bunn, Junior Technical Officer; Pilot Officers 'Chris' Stott and Irishman 'Larry' O'Hara, both Fighter Controllers; Fg.Off. 'Mike' Rush from the Airfield Construction Branch and his Pilot Officer assistant; and the Officer who was being Dined Out the previous evening.[1] To a man they advised me to expect stomach problems for the first fortnight until my system acclimatised to the exceptionally hard water. This was quickly demonstrated, because the diluted condensed milk we used always curdled in both tea and coffee.[2] The trick was to stir it quickly before drinking, whereupon it tasted fairly normal. To fail to stir it first of all as well as before drinking could mean that the milk turned into a sticky blob which remained in the bottom of the cup.

After breakfast my kit was put in the Orderly Officer's room which I used for the next few nights until the Officer I was replacing left for the UK. I then moved into his vacated room, which became mine for the time being. There were only eight rooms in the Mess.

I spent my first day going through the usual arrival procedure, finding my way round, and learning the names of the 18 or so other Officers and what they did. I was assigned to 'A' Flight, with Flt.Lt. 'Phil' Philpot as my Flight Commander. Other 'A' Flight members were, as far as I can recollect, Flt.Lt. 'Harry' Hawker; Fg.Off. 'Doug' Breeze; Fg.Off. 'Jock' MacPhail; and Plt.Off. Chris Stott. The Operations Officer was Flt.Lt. 'Don' Crocker whose office was in Station Headquarters.

The Station, or rather the domestic site (the tech site was a distance away), was small and had three barrack blocks, Station Headquarters, Stores, Sick Quarters, Sergeants Mess, NAAFI, Airmens Mess (which doubled as a cinema), Guardroom, Boiler house for the district heating of all buildings, and a small office building for the Airfield Construction Branch personnel. Married Quarters were attached to Borgentreich

---

1 I can no longer remember all their names.

2 We did not use fresh milk because German milk came from cows that were not guaranteed to be tuberculosis free.

village about a mile and a half away as the crow flies, but about two miles through the village by road. None of the RAF buildings were more than three years old and all were painted in standard NATO colours.

Much to my surprise I quickly discovered that I was the Senior Living-in Officer. I had one more day's seniority than John Duggan, the Station Adjutant.[3] It was with some regret that, soon after I arrived, I had to use this status to call to order the junior, ex-university, Pilot Officers who were wont to lark about irresponsibly in the late evenings in the Mess, Chris Stott and Larry O'Hara among them.

---

3   John, in later life, became involved with airships and has appeared on television in this connection several times.

32. 537 Signals Unit. On Probation

AFTER THE WEEKEND I went on watch for the first time. The radar site, or tech site, as we called it, was in a classic large hollow in the countryside about three miles from the domestic site. It was ideally suited to get optimum performance from the Type 15 metric radar. To get there we, that is the entire watch, at 07.30 climbed on board two trucks for the drive to the tech site, so as to take over from the night watch at 08.00.

In addition to the Type 15 radar there were two Type 14 radars, one upper and one lower looking, and three Type 13 height finders. All were chassis mounted and capable of being packed up and moved within hours. Power was provided by mobile generating sets and there were two vehicle-mounted control cabins with two control positions in each. The Controllers rest room was also vehicle-mounted. Maintenance was done in mobile workshops. The Chief Controller, plotting table, and edge-lit vertical plotting screen, other display boards, and plotters and tellers positions were all housed in a Leyland 'Hippo' vehicle.[1] When I arrived the only permanent feature on the site, other than the perimeter fence and vehicle hard-standings, was a toilet block.

Although I was not to be fully involved with watch-keeping until I became an experienced and fully qualified Fighter Controller nearly six months later, it is worthwhile at this stage to explain the watch-keeping system.

The watch-keepers were divided into two Flights, A and B. Technical staff operated a similar, but separate, watch-keeping regime. The tech site operated 24 hours a day throughout all days of the year.

---

1   This was an articulated lorry with a trailer having sides which folded out to triple its width and thus form an almost square floor area.

Meal times in the Messes were extended to accommodate the requirements of the watch-keepers.

Whilst the changeover times may not be precise, the A and B Flight watches operated in the manner shown in the panel below, each alternating with the other, and always with a ten minute hand-over overlap to enable aircraft under the control of the outgoing watch to be handed over to a controller on the next watch for the completion of the sortie.

The C & R watchkeepers, because their duties involved overnight watches, followed their routines for one week only at a time. Personnel did night watches at intervals of three to five weeks apart, depending on manning levels, leave, and other exigencies.

	A Flight	B Flight
Monday	08.00 - 13.00	13.00 - 17.00
	17.00 - 23.00*	23.00 - 08.00 (C & R only)
Tuesday	13.00 - 17.00	08.00 - 13.00
	23.00 - 08.00 (C & R only)	17.00 - 23.00*
Wednesday	08.00 - 13.00	13.00 - 17.00
	17.00 - 23.00*	23.00 - 08.00 (C & R only)
Thursday	13.00 - 17.00	08.00 - 13.00
	23.00 - 08.00 (C & R only)	17.00 - 23.00*
Friday	08.00 - 13.00	13.00 - 17.00
	17.00 - 23.00*	23.00 - 08.00 (C & R only)
Saturday (C & R only unless there was an Exercise)		
	13.00 - 17.00	08.00 - 13.00
	23.00 - 08.00	17.00 - 23.00
Sunday (C & R only unless there was an Exercise)		
	08.00 - 13.00	13.00 - 17.00
	17.00 - 23.00	23.00 - 08.00
* If no night flying was scheduled these would be C & R only watches.		
This cycle repeated on a fortnightly basis, A & B Flights alternating each week.		

The A and B Flight Duty Watch Officers, depending on which part of the fortnightly cycle their watch fell, would, for example, do evening watch on a Monday, have 24 hours off watch, then go on night watch at midnight Tuesday, rest during Tuesday daytime, then go on evening watch, followed by 24 hours off, and so on. This, as time would tell, turned out to be a very physically and mentally wearing routine.

Half an hour was allowed for journey times. This meant that, in effect, the time away from the domestic site was a full hour longer than the actual time spent on watch.

Time off was not free time in which we could do as we liked. It was during this that we performed our sometimes onerous and time-consuming extraneous duties, but more of those later.

Travel to and from watch was usually in a Magirus Deutz truck fitted with rearward-facing seats in the back for the watch crew. Officers, if there was room, usually sat in the front, or actually drove the vehicle for the three mile journey. Once I had settled in to the watch-keeping routines I often did the driving myself, and if I fluffed a gear change (everyone did it sometimes), there would be an enormous cheer go up in the back. These trucks, in the early days of my time with 537 SU were the only vehicles capable of negotiating the extremely rough farm track from the village of Scherfede to the tech site. Indeed, in winter, that same track became impassable because the trucks slid from side to side and lurched from rut to rut and pot hole to icy pothole regardless of the competence of the driver or whether snow chains were fitted to the wheels or not. To overcome this problem, as winter deepened, it was found better to take the Lütgenede road and then travel across farmers' open arable land, which was frozen solid many inches deep and thus remained undamaged, until the thaw set in. Occasionally, just for the exercise, several of us would set off a little earlier and make our way to the tech site on foot provided the snow was not too deep or, when the snow had gone, that the going was firm. My 'Sabre boots' and a pair of Army pattern boots came in very handy, not only for these treks, but for warmth in the depth of winter.

In these early days I was not qualified for C & R work and therefore never worked nights. Night flying, when there was any, usually ceased well before midnight. Although a Watch Officer had to be present on the tech site at all times, there was very little reporting and plotting work to be done on account of the low power of the radars and the minimal after hours flying activity. In fact, the Officer i/c C & R was Flt.Lt. Hyde and he never ever went near the tech site. Instead, he busied himself very usefully as President of the Station Institutes and with looking after the relevant PSI activities and funds.

Even during watch hours there was seldom much in the way of control work to occupy us. We spent many boring hours in our rest cabin reading, smoking (I never ever smoked), chatting, catching up on sleep, playing cribbage or playing 'knock' – a rather silly, but entertaining card game. Occasionally one of us would write a letter or two, and sometimes we would do work connected with our extraneous duties. Yet, whenever anyone aimed to do that, there was usually some real control work to be done instead. We were frequent victims of Sod's Law in this respect.

As a u/t Fighter Controller my first live interceptions were closely monitored by a more experienced controller.[2] In this way I quickly learned the vagaries of the equipment, its capabilities and limitations, and many techniques not taught at Middle Wallop.

It was almost Christmas before I performed my first live real interception. On December 22nd I controlled 2 Meteor NF11 night fighters at 25,000 feet doing three 90° practice interceptions, one of which was aborted because I made a mistake, the other two being recorded as successful. The next night I did one PI with badly fading radar, again with NF11s. I was busier on December 29th when I controlled two separate pairs of NF11s. I did 3 successful PIs with the first pair and 1 good and 2 aborted PIs with the second pair in conditions of bad radar fading. All these PIs were done at altitudes between 25,000 and 30,000 feet and at night. This work, and the speeds and turning radii of jet aircraft at altitude, was vastly different to doing PIs with the slow, low altitude, Balliols at Middle Wallop. The techniques I had learned had to be considerably modified and practised in this new, operational, environment.

In the meantime, Christmas had followed the usual RAF pattern. All Officers did the usual routine of reciprocal entertainment with the Sergeants Mess and jointly served the Airmen their lunch. With the site strength numbering only a couple of hundred personnel the level of festivities was more muted but somewhat more personal than I had previously experienced. The fact that watches had to be manned throughout the Christmas period, regardless of the occasion, undoubtedly had its effect on the celebrations. With there being so few living-in Officers our own Christmas lunch was a quiet affair, but nonetheless

---

2   u/t = under training.

enjoyable. After we had slept off our lunchtime excesses, all of us were invited to spend the evening at the homes of our brother Officers on the married patch. On my walk back to the Mess afterwards, through the village, my way was lit solely by pools of yellow light spilling from the windows of the houses. On leaving the village, I continued in almost total darkness through the snow along the open lane to the main gate and the Guardroom, and on to the eerily empty Mess. Apart from the duty SP I saw no other sign of life until after I woke the following morning.[3]

During January I controlled 4 pairs of NF11s, and did 23 successful PIs with them, including one head-on interception (the others were 90°). I also controlled 2 pairs of Venoms from Fassberg in daylight (my first 2 daylight PIs). I had no failures that month.

Up to this time, 'Time under Control' times were recorded in my Log Book for me. As being still under training, I didn't keep my own log; this was done for me by the Ops team, entries being signed off by the Ops Officer, Flt.Lt. Don Crocker, and initialled by the Station Commander, Sqn.Ldr. Paddy Ryan.

On the 12th of January a group of Fighter Controllers, myself included, made a liaison visit to our neighbouring American GCI Station, USAF Detachment, Rothwesten, 4th ATAF, near Kassel.[4] Personnel from each Station were often in contact with each other on the landline link between the two sites and this was an opportunity to put faces to voices.

At Rothwesten the tech site was within the same perimeter as the domestic site. There was a typical American brashness about it. Everything was over-labelled and highly coloured, and it struck me as being very scruffy and unclean. Each serviceman seemed to own an over-large, dirty, car. Even within the confines of the camp they seemed to drive everywhere instead of walking. They were generally obese, appeared unfit, and looked as though a good long walk would kill them. We were given a welcome talk by the Commandant in his office. He sat in a high-backed chair, smoking a cigar, and talked out of the side of his mouth. The Stars and Stripes stood overbearingly in a corner. Through his window we could see, at the top of a very tall

---

3   SP = Service Policeman.

4   Borgentreich was in the far south-east corner of the British Zone of Germany. Rothwesten was in the far north-east corner of the American Zone.

pole, an even larger version of the same. After this 'Buddy Chat' we were taken to see the radars. Their performance was undoubtedly better than ours and the operators were keen to show everything to us. The working conditions were worse and much was under canvas. Heating was by large blower heaters. We asked why this was so, and were given the answer that it was to allow of rapid dismantling to retreat to a safer base in the event of hostility.[5] We remarked on the poor conditions and were told "War is hell" and then someone said, "Why should there be any difference in a non-shooting peacetime tactical situation?" We were not particularly impressed with this attitude, but envied their having more powerful radar. As far as I could tell they had an AN/FPS search radar and an FPS6 height finder. We were taken, inevitably, to their PX.[6] We had no Dollars so could buy nothing. There were abundant stocks and everything was very cheaply priced. We were also shown the Community Centre, and could see extensive rows of married quarters and barracks. The entire camp seemed unbalanced in as far as it having a very small tech site within an over-large, over-cushy, domestic 'Little America' environment. Whilst technically of great interest, my feeling was that, in the event of an outbreak of hostilities, there was far too much domestic hamper to enable them to either operate or move with any degree of efficiency.

Back at Borgentreich, in the ensuing months there was very little 'trade' for us Fighter Controllers. There was so little that, even though the work was shared fairly evenly, I did not accumulate the necessary 100 PIs to qualify until June. The performance of our radar was poor for most of the time and it took great skill to continue to estimate and plot, in chinagraph pencil on the surface of the PPI, the movements of aircraft under control when the radar was fading or had temporarily gone blank. Sometimes sorties even had to be aborted because of this. At other times signals on the Type 15 could be so strong that the paints on the PPI would appear as a full circle. Whilst the range could be read off, the location in azimuth could be very hard to determine. The paints for two aircraft at, or close to, the same range would merge and

---

5   Our own need for mobility was for us to be able to move to another site so as better to prosecute the aims of battle in a tactical situation, not 'retreat'.

6   The equivalent of our NAAFI but in supermarket style and with what appeared to be a wasteful amount of stock, including luxury items. This was taken to the point that there was no need for any off-camp shopping or mixing with the local German population.

the overall picture become meaningless. A quick change to the Type 14 equipment would sometimes solve the situation but not always. It was not unusual for us to swing a Type 13 radar across the likely area so as to pick up the aircraft and read off their azimuth location from its strobe line on the PPI. We could 'lose' fighters as they turned and therefore had to estimate their position and point of reappearance so as to keep them under our control. The pilots, of course, had no idea of the difficulties we were experiencing. Our cabin assistants, with their Craig computers, were invaluable to us estimating, as they did, the probable location of aircraft under control when we couldn't 'see' them. We had to be resourceful.

When my log book was eventually given to me I was surprised to read, as a prologue, the following statement:–

"Trained as a GD Pilot, Fg. Off. Senar became operational as a Fighter/ Ground attack Pilot (Vampires MK V & IX) and later as a High Level day Interception Pilot (Sabre Mk IV) serving on No.93 Squadron 2ATAF.

After 18 months service with his Squadron he became medically unfit for full Aircrew duties and became Flying Wing Adjutant at Royal Air Force Jever. After 6 months he was posted to No.57 Fighter Controllers Course at Royal Air Force Middle Wallop. On passing this course he was posted to Royal Air Force Borgentreich No.537 Signals Unit on the 9th December 1955.

D.A. Crocker Flt.Lt.
Operations Officer
Royal Air Force
Borgentreich."

My qualifying assessment read:–

"Throughout his training Fg. Off. Senar has shown all the keenness and aptitude required of a Controller. His reactions are quick, his R/T procedure & practice excellent and he has no difficulty in meeting changing situations. With further practice he will become an above average intercept controller."

This was signed by the Station Commander, Sqn.Ldr. Ryan.

During my qualifying period, in which I had to complete at least 100 PIs, I controlled Meteor NF11s, Venoms, F86s, F84s, and Hunters. Control heights varied from 18,000 to 40,000 feet. The longest recorded time during which I had fighters under my control was 48 minutes, the shortest was just 8 minutes. On qualifying I was transferred to 'B' Flight.

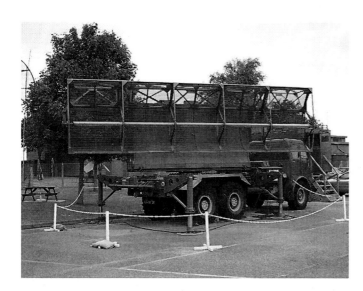

Left: A vehicle mounted centimetric Type 14 upper radar. This has a parabolic reflector as opposed to the regularly curved reflector of a Type 14 lower. (The photo was taken at the RAF Air Defence Radar Museum at Neatishead.)

Right: A type 15 trailer-mounted metric search radar. The mast to the left carried the twin aerial feeds, via the box on the top of the array, to the dipoles (just visible as dots) arranged horizontally in rows on the wire mesh reflector. (Taken from an old print.)

*Left: A Type 13
'nodding horror'
plinth-mounted
centimetric height
finding radar.
(Taken from an
old print.)*

33. Weather Conditions

D URING MY FIRST SIX months at Borgentreich I experienced weather far more severe than anything I had previously lived or worked in.

When I arrived the winter was well set in, but it was no worse than it had been at Jever and therefore caused me little concern. What none of us expected was that it would get colder – much colder. By the time February came we read in the UK newspapers (they always arrived a day or more late) that, back home, they were enduring the coldest February since 1895, and they were protected, supposedly, by the Gulf Stream. In Germany it was the coldest for 225 years.

At Borgentreich, for several days on end, the temperature equalled that in Moscow and Siberia. In those conditions, when we went outside for more than a moment, ice formed on our eyebrows from our frozen breath and even on our eyelashes, let alone our moustaches; we had to be very careful to cover all skin with as many layers of clothing as possible. Uniforms were worn, of course, and so were many 'irregular' items of clothing. I was fortunate to be able to scramble into my flying suit over my uniform trousers and jacket and, if I was due to be outside for an extended length of time, as was sometimes necessary, I made sure to put my pyjama trousers on as well. The old trick of wearing a brown paper waistcoat was also used. Ear muffs were bought in the village and worn by almost everyone as standard kit. Multicoloured scarves also appeared. The standard issue 'Airmen for the use of' woollen gloves were useless and we Officers made sure the lads kept their hands in their pockets, or wore more sensible gloves. For myself, my silk inner and leather gauntlet outer flying gloves came in very useful. Even so, I was hard pressed to keep warm, even with all this clothing and my greatcoat buttoned right up to the neck. The basic rules of wearing uniforms and being 'properly dressed' were abandoned in these conditions, and even for a quick dash between buildings we had to be very careful. Formal saluting was also largely suspended in these low temperatures.

We joked that it was so cold that even the birds walked – and then found that it was true, for no birds were to be seen on the wing anywhere. We also joked that the red alcohol in the thermometers had sense enough to huddle into a ball in the bulb at the bottom. In fact, none of these thermometers registered anything against the graduations on their stems.

The local Germans, of course, were used to these conditions. Most stayed indoors. The men wore thick clothing when doing outside tasks, and the women wore thick woollen short stockings and stout shoes or boots. Into these woollen stockings they tucked the lower ends of thick woollen trousers, and over their trousers they wore thick woollen skirts. Their upper parts were covered in heavy layers of clothing, and they always wore scarves and hats. To protect their ears they wore ear muffs or tied scarves over their hats and fastened them under their chins to stop them blowing off in the bitter wind. Elegance and chic fashion were definitely not appropriate.

When it snowed, the stuff blew horizontal in the wind, and when it stopped snowing it still blew horizontal in the wind until it had all accumulated in drifts and corners. The snow, in these temperatures, was powdery and stung on the small exposed areas of one's face. Then we would get dry sunny days and snow would disappear by direct sublimation. The ground, of course, froze hard to quite a depth.

To amuse the troops, and to get them outside in the fresh air whilst off duty, Flt.Lt. Ron Young and I decided to flood the tennis courts at the top of the camp with water from a fire hydrant, and turn them into a skating rink. It only took us a couple of hours. The canvas fire hoses (we used two) soon got a coating of ice on them and would stick to the ground very quickly if we weren't careful. We used the spray nozzles rather than the full jets. In this way the water froze and became slush in the air before it landed, and so quickly formed a layer of uneven ice. To get the surface flat enough to skate on, we flooded the water out of the hoses at reduced pressure as we retreated toward the gate. A surprising side effect was that we created a local fog which flowed down the hill and covered the rest of the camp. This fog froze into rime and covered all the buildings with hoar frost. The water we were using was comparatively so 'hot' that it steamed in the severe conditions. When we tried to take off our heavy greatcoats all the front of them was caked in ice to over ½" thick and had turned into something like armour plate. It took 20 minutes standing in front of one of the large central-heating radiators in the Mess toilet (tiled floor) before we were able to undo the buttons, by which time the water from the thawing ice was running across the floor and down the drain. The lads, who bought skates in the village, took advantage of the rink and it proved very popular, especially on sunny days when, in spite of the lack of a reading on the thermometer, they could get quite warm provided they kept on the move. There were some extremely comical scenes as beginners took to the ice for the first time and caused much hilarity among the spectators. Morale, up to this time, had been low but this episode did a lot to improve it.

MT vehicles were kept in heated garages. Our Magirus Deutz trucks had air-cooled diesel engines and coped with the conditions better than most. The fleet of air-cooled Volkswagens also stood up well to the cold. Personnel with private cars had to remove their batteries overnight and take them indoors because the acid would freeze and split the cases. All radiators had to be drained but care had to be exercised when filling them with hot water so as not to crack any metal due to sudden expansion. Engine, gearbox, and rear axle oil became so viscous that it was almost impossible to push a vehicle, even on the downhill stretches of the camp roads. The wear and tear on batteries when starting engines under such conditions was considerable. Most car owners, and there weren't many, gave up driving until the weather improved. Some laid up their cars so as not to have to drive on the polished icy surface of the local roads or in deep snow after a sudden fall.

Travel to the tech site under the tilt in the back of a covered wagon was not the most pleasant of experiences at any time. In these conditions most of us who had to do it turned away from the incoming snow, or dust-laden back-draught, and sat huddled as near to the front, away from the open rear, as possible. We had no enclosed vehicles available capable of making the journey along the rough lanes or across the open fields we used.

Once at the tech site everyone dismounted and made for cover and warmth as quickly as possible, but those radar and engine mechanics who had to service the radars and generators weren't so lucky. They were issued with special clothing and had to be extremely careful when touching metal out of doors. Bare skin could stick to any metal surfaces in an instant and have to be peeled off, leaving a very sore patch which took a long time to heal. Frost-bite was not unknown but, thankfully, was rare.

We Fighter Controllers and our immediate support personnel could stay in our heated vehicles most of the time when on watch. The exceptions were when we had to dash to, or from, one of the Ops vehicles to control aircraft, to the NAAFI wagon for a hot drink and biscuits, or to go to the toilet block. We kept these excursions as brief as possible and coped well in the circumstances. At no time did operations cease through cold alone. Constant radar surveillance was imperative.

On evening or night watch, rather than dash 50 yards to a heated toilet block when nature called, we 'let fly' from the steps of our command and control wagon. Within a very few days a mound of yellow ice built up. The practice had to cease forthwith because the mound was so slippery it became a hazard. Even so, it stood there, occasionally being added to, for several weeks until the first thaw came. Then an unfortunate Erk, as punishment for some misdemeanour or other, had to break it up and shovel it away.

When we fetched mugs of tea from the NAAFI wagon we had no tray so used a biscuit tin lid instead. There were times when it was so cold that the spilt slops of hot tea in the bottom of the lid froze to slush before we got the drinks back to our vehicles.

As February gave way to March the weather lessened in intensity. Any snow that fell was wet rather than powdery. This wet snow stuck to everything, vertical surfaces as well. Then came the first thaw when the thermometer rose above freezing for a few hours. It was then that the camp snow ploughs were put into good use. Wet, sticky, filthy slush trod into everywhere and melted in any heated space to form pools of dirty water. We had to be extremely watchful that none got near any of the electrics in our Ops vehicles.

When the short German spring arrived and temperatures rose markedly, the ice in the substrate of the German roads swelled as it thawed. This expansion broke up road surfaces and made them extremely hazardous to traffic. Many were the 'Frostschaden' signs warning motorists of the dangers until the local authority road repair teams dealt with the problem – only for it all to happen again next winter.

Summers could be very hot. Temperatures of 100°F were not unknown. By the time summer came I was fully qualified and therefore had to take my turn on the night watch rota. This was a particularly strenuous regime, especially during the very hot weather. On those days, when sleep was most needed between watches, I was kept awake by the heat, with sweat pouring off my back into the bed and light coming in through the thin curtains. Noises outside didn't help either. I rested rather than slept soundly and became fatigued by the end of the week. The batwomen, with the best of intentions, kept as quiet as possible as they went about their duties, but Frau Höhn, the little hunchbacked chatterbox, bless her heart, always seemed to be standing outside my door whispering in a stage whisper "Psssst, Misser Zinner schläft!" (Mr Senar is asleep). This, unless I was already asleep, usually had the opposite effect. I took to drinking glasses of salt water to replace that lost in sweat. Married Officers, of course, fared much better in their own homes.

On duty, in shirt sleeve order, conditions in the Ops vehicles were worse than outdoors because of the heat generated by all the thermionic valves in the equipment racks. Our rest vehicle was easier to heat in winter than to keep cool in summer. To make matters worse, everywhere seemed to be infested with white-tailed flies. These were the size of largish house-flies but had white tails in the manner of blue-bottles. We may have forgiven them if they had flown like flies but the little buggers preferred to walk, particularly on bare human skin. Trying to concentrate on the control of a pair of fast jets in this heat, and with these pestilential critters crawling all over us, was not the easiest or pleasantest of occupations. We cursed like mad but somehow kept the R/T conversations 'standard'. In the Leyland Hippo these flies would increase in numbers to the point when the Duty Watch Officer (sometimes me) would detail anyone not immediately occupied to go on a fly swatting spree to try and temporarily reduce their numbers. We didn't have DDT or aerosol sprays in those days, so we had to do the best we could. Even the MO, Flt.Lt. 'Doc' Pottinger, couldn't help us with any chemical potions in spite of our pleas to him for help.

There were periods when the weather was particularly still and hot. Back home in the UK we would have expected thunder, but not necessarily so at Borgentreich. In these conditions, at dusk or after dark, the sky would constantly flicker with high altitude, but silent, lightning. At times of no moon these electrical displays could be as vivid as they were continuous, and uncannily eerie as well.

When the rains did come the light loess soil would wash away by the wagonful. Loess is a type of wind-blown marl which had blown, it is said, from North Africa to this part of Europe over many millennia. It compacted like a light clay but would easily wash away in heavy rain or turn to dust in dry windy conditions. In the wet there would be layers of it alongside the roads where muddy rainwater had drained across. In dry winds it would pick up and blow across the land in a layer of clay-brown fog about a metre deep almost, at times, obscuring the very surface of the fields. This was weather-induced land erosion in the extreme.

When thunder came, the storms could be extremely violent with constant flashes and much noise. Most buildings, and all of those in the village, had lightning conductors. Later, after I had changed rooms in the Mess for one with a view across the open country, I watched many a bolt of lightning strike a tree or the ground, sometimes not far away. Occasionally I would be joined by a brother Officer whose room did not have such a view, and we would watch for maybe an hour or more. These storms were spectacular and, not infrequently, lasted several hours until their force was spent or they moved slowly away.

After an overnight shower of rain, or a light frost in the short spring or autumn, first thing in the morning, threads of steam rose from the land as the sun warmed the tilled soil. As the moisture evaporated it formed a low mist; thankfully we never had any serious fog.

In the late summer of 1957, and almost certainly because the weather conditions were right, we had a plague of mice. There were thousands of them. They got into everywhere, into our upstairs rooms in the Mess, into our clothes, and into every building on the camp in huge numbers. Out in the open they tunnelled in the bottom of the grass, in the dry thatch just above soil level, and had runs all over the place. At its peak these creatures could be seen openly running across and along paths, up walls, on the roofs, everywhere. The tech site didn't suffer this intrusion, only the domestic site and its environs. Something had to be done, and quick. Everyone not on essential duties was detailed for the whole of one day to arm themselves with whatever appropriate weapon they could find so as to eliminate these pests as quickly and thoroughly as possible. Even the Fire Section deployed hoses to soak all inaccessible areas, drains, ducts, drain pipes, roofs, anywhere they could get, to drown as many as possible. Pits were dug for the disposal of the corpses. The day had its effect and few mice were to be seen afterwards. Barrack inspections followed to make sure that all areas were clean and that no droppings were left about. It rained shortly afterwards, heavily enough for no more mice to be seen – something for which all ranks were very thankful.

34. The Wider Context

THE INTERNATIONAL SITUATION IN 1956 was far less than stable and the RAF was involved in several theatres of actual or potential conflict. There was the ongoing Cyprus situation with its Greco-Turkish problems. There, the RAF at Akrotiri was trying both to help stabilise things as well as protect its facilities on the island. Further away, the recent Korean conflict was still in many peoples' minds, with the border peace talks at Panmunjom still progressing intermittently and antagonistically.

In Russia, Bulganin and Kruschev were very much in charge, Molotov having recently been relieved of his post as Foreign Secretary. These two seemed to delight in goading America and its allies, taunting them and constantly probing their defences, often under so-called diplomatic cover, as though they were playing some sort of game, and a very dangerous one at that. International tensions were running high.

Only a few days after I became fully qualified as a Fighter Controller, the Poznan riots took place and there was much instability in Poland as some of the population tried unsuccessfully to lessen, or break free from, the grip of Russian Communism. This was a matter for much international concern.

The following month, July, Egypt's Colonel Nasser decided to nationalise the Suez Canal. This, in turn, led to a Royal Proclamation calling up the Army Reserve in the UK on the 3rd of August. The British Government, with some justification, was becoming worried. The number of people, it must be said, who were in the armed forces totalled almost as many as at the end of the war.

To make matters worse, the Hungarian uprising started in Budapest in October. In the same month Israel invaded Sinai, and the very next day, the RAF was bombing targets in Egypt.

On the first day of November Hungary renounced the Warsaw Pact, to be followed, the day after, by Russian military reinforcements arriving in that country. Just two days later, Russian tanks were on the streets of Budapest causing mayhem and being met by rioters. The situation was grim.

The day after this, November 5th, British and French parachute troops landed near Port Said in Egypt. That same day, Mr Bulganin threatened Russian intervention in the Middle East. On the 6th, Egypt blocked the Suez Canal. The British and French forces, under diplomatic pressure, also ceased fire. This tense situation ended with the planned but reluctant withdrawal of Israeli troops as soon as they could be replaced by a United Nations peacekeeping force.

All was far from over in Hungary, many of whose nationals were pleading for American intervention. At the same time the Russians were deporting many young Hungarian males to the USSR to face an uncertain future, whilst many others were fleeing with their families across the temporarily insecure border into the safety of Austria.

World War Three was narrowly averted by intense diplomatic pressure being brought to bear on the several combatant or potentially combatant nations.

On November 23rd, Sir Anthony Eden, the British Prime Minister, became ill and had to rest for three weeks in Jamaica. Already a sick man, the diplomatic pressures and world situation had become too much for him. While he was away, early in December, with the establishment of the UN peacekeeping force, the British and French forces began to leave Egypt.

Martial law, under the Russians, was declared in Hungary on December the 9th. Then, on December the 17th, because of the continuing Middle Eastern tensions, petrol rationing was introduced in the UK and was not lifted until the middle of May 1957.

The Egyptians, in the last days of December, allowed the commencement of the clearance of obstructions preparatory to the reopening of the Suez Canal. This clearance work, with much help from Royal Navy experts, was completed when the Canal fully reopened in April 1957.

By the end of 1956 the international situation had become a little less tense but, undercover, the superpowers, America and Russia, were still vying with one another in many different ways and continued testing each other's defences and reactions.

It was at this time that those of us at RAF Borgentreich were able to use much more sophisticated radar equipment, and ceased using our mobile radar site in the muddy field. We moved into a hardened underground bunker at Auenhausen and changed our designation from 537 Signals Unit to 210 Signals Unit. We had an increase of personnel and, with our new radar, could 'see', in clearer definition, a much larger volume of sky. It almost goes without saying, our C & R activities were largely devoted to monitoring the airspace to our east. We also continued our constant watch over the air traffic making its way along the three air corridors to Berlin from the west. With the new radar we had a far better electronic view than previously.

Sir Anthony Eden resigned as Prime Minister on January 9th. His place was taken, next day, by Harold Macmillan.

1957 was not without its tensions and shows of strength in other ways. In May and June the UK carried out nuclear tests at Christmas Island in the Pacific Ocean. Not to be outdone, the Russians successfully test-launched an inter-continental ballistic missile. This was something the USA did not yet have.

International one-upmanship continued later in the year with the Russian launch of two earth satellites, the first in October, and the second, with a dog called 'Laika' on board, on November 3rd.

Just a month later, after frenetic activity, the USA launched its own first inter-continental ballistic missile. The Americans had been wrong-footed and were playing catch-up.

Earlier, we at 537 Signals Unit at Borgentreich, with our comparatively primitive radar (although it was the best available to us at the time), were unable to undertake much in the way of surveillance work and could see precious little of any Eastern Bloc aerial activity. We were, of course, alarmed at the international situation and its tensions. Many of us wondered whether we might be posted away to other more active locations. We knew that if tensions increased, particularly during the time of the Hungarian riots, and if the Russians chanced their arm and made border incursions into West Germany, we may have to make a rapid exit from our site because we were just an hour's tank drive from the East-West border.

With Borgentreich being so close to the East German border, and just as close to the American Zone, explains why we had so few aircraft allocated to us for control. To put it another way – we were out on a limb. The nearest British Forces of any consequence were the military units at Paderborn some distance to our north.[1] Our location, though, was of significance, for had there been any form of Russian attack it was likely that they would have considered the border between the British and American forces to be a weak point at which to test the West's defences. We knew we had done our job once we had shouted the alarm. In a nutshell, we were expendable.

There is yet more. During 1956 a new bunker was being built and fitted out on a new tech site at Auenhausen, several miles away to our north. This was due to be finished at the end of the year.

On the domestic site, because of the greater manning requirements of this facility, considerable building work was also being undertaken. The married patch down in the village was being extended, too. This building work, initially under the supervision of Fg.Off. 'Mike' Rush and later, Fg.Off. 'Dave' Hattersley, both of the Airfield Construction Branch, together with their assistant Pilot Officers and German staff, impinged on our lives to a greater or lesser extent. The Messes, Guard-room, and other buildings were extended. New barrack blocks and a new Stores building were built, as were other buildings and internal roads in readiness for the eventual take-over of the site by the German Air Force. For a while we lived on what, for an extended period, was little more than a building site with all the disruption that this entailed.

Once we had our bunker and improved radar, although we consid-ered ourselves still to be expendable, we could give much earlier warning of a potential aerial attack; the West's early warning defences were thereby strengthened greatly. This though, meant that if we were invaded we would have to deny our equipment to the enemy so that it could not be used against us. This aspect had its own problems.

It was in this international and domestic context that I, as a qualified Fighter Controller, was serving my Queen and country. It was a time of tension and I, with the other Officers at Borgentreich, as both 537 Signals Unit and, later, 210 Signals Unit, had to be ready for the unex-pected. However, we had also to carry on outwardly as if nothing was of any great concern. Life, in the eyes of the RAF families on the married patch and all of the non-watchkeepers continued in ignorant bliss. At

---

1   These were army formations. Apart from the small RAF Unit at Scharfoldendorf, the nearest RAF base was even further away at Gütersloh. There was also an early 537 SU satellite unit at Waggum near Braunschweig.

work, on watch, we often saw things differently but, perforce, kept this to ourselves.

35. Other Duties

O N A SMALL RAF Station such as Borgentreich's 537 Signals Unit, with a total strength of just over 200, the 20 or so Officers had to extend their skills to doing many jobs for which they had never been specifically trained. All the tasks normally accepted without a second thought by specialists on a larger Unit still had to be carried out by others, albeit to a lesser degree in terms of time devoted to each, yet each still carried the same relative degree of importance.

As to the Officers: as far as I can remember they were as follows (I have added the names of their replacements after they were posted away, in parentheses):-

We had a Commanding Officer, Sqn.Ldr Paddy Ryan (later Wg.Cdr. 'Killy' Kilmartin) and a Station Adjutant, Fg.Off. John Duggan (later Flt.Lt. 'Sam' Weller, then Flt.Lt. Cunningham), a succession of Medical Officers, and an Accounts Officer, Flt.Lt. Roy Bertram (later replaced). We also had an Operations Officer, Flt.Lt. Don Crocker (later Sqn. Ldr. Owen Ellison), a Senior Technical Officer, Flt.Lt. 'Ray' Street, and his assistant, Plt.Off. Peter Bunn (later Sqn.Ldr. Monk and his Pilot Officer assistant), and Fg.Off. Mike Rush and his Pilot Officer assistant (later Fg.Off. Dave Hattersley), together with the Warrant Officer i/c Catering, the Warrant Officer i/c Equipment Section, and the Station Warrant Officer. All we other Officers were involved with watchkeeping duties and routines. It therefore fell to us, between us, to run all other Station activities when we were not on watch.[1] As time went on I took over three major extraneous duties, and towards the end of my stay at

---

1   The non-watchkeeping Officers were deemed to be fully occupied and most only had minor extraneous duties to perform.

Borgentreich, all three were running simultaneously. I also picked up an occasional minor one or two as well.

The Flight Lieutenants shared the job of Station Duty Officer, according to rota, on a weekly basis.[2] We Junior Officers, as on any RAF Station, did duty as Orderly Officer on a daily basis, also according to rota. The other, so-called, extraneous duties were allocated to us according to our personal abilities, interests, or basic needs. Occasionally, semi-officially, we would also help each other out or stand in for each other at times of necessity or difficulty. Somehow we ran the Station and didn't do too bad a job of it, lifting morale out of the almost despondent situation when I first arrived to, about nine months later, a thriving, reasonably content camp. This was in spite of our isolated location and the few facilities available other than off-camp shopping and German entertainment, in distant Warburg, Kassel, or elsewhere.

Within a very few weeks of my arrival John Duggan sent for me and told me that the CO wanted to see me. He discussed with me my earlier RAF and pre-RAF CCF experience as a school Cadet. He asked if I was a good shot, and what knowledge I had of field craft. He then gave me the job of Station Armaments Officer, telling me at the same time that there were nowhere near enough weapons or ammunition to go round. He told me to see to it that all personnel were capable of being armed appropriately according to rank and ability, and were capable of being issued with arms and ammunition in the minimum time.

My initial investigations revealed that there were about thirty .303" Lee Enfield rifles, a similar number of bayonets, and some two or three boxes of ball ammunition. The latter did not appear to be on any inventory. This little lot, and that was all there was, was stored in the room in Station Headquarters which was used as the Station Post Office, telephone exchange, and the Armoury. In nominal charge was one armourer, Junior Technician Thompson who, in these circumstances, was on a good skive, but was known as a bit of a tearaway. He lived with his wife on the married patch. She, I was told, was something of a red-ragger and had recently written letters of complaint about RAF life to the 'Daily Mirror'. I had to tread carefully, but someone was going to get a wake-up call.

---

2   On larger Stations this was on a daily basis.

I took over the inventory, ordered all relevant Air Publications, and started swotting up on almost anything to do with small arms and ammunition storage. My time off watch was going to be more than adequately filled, at least for the foreseeable future.

With having wholly inadequate storage there was no point ordering any more weapons or ammunition. I reported progress to the CO, and soon afterwards I was allocated the old Station Equipment Section building for use as an Armoury and explosives store, a new Stores having been just recently completed and occupied. He added that I had better put my mind to drawing up a Station Defence Plan covering both active and passive aspects.[3] Looking back, he either knew, or suspected, something of which I was not at that time aware.

I came out of that meeting as Officer i/c both Active and Passive Defence, and in charge of creating and running a full scale Armoury, including all weapons, ammunition, and relevant equipment. I was under orders, too, to report my progress on a monthly basis. I had thought, naively, that my main job was fighter control. This put a different emphasis on things.

There were no plans or maps of the local area so I bought some local walking maps from the tourist office in Warburg.[4] With tracing paper laid over them, and after several ground surveys, I planned, drew up, and had available in issuable form, the location of observation posts and defensive positions with intersecting arcs of fire.

I set up the Armoury workshop, installed weapons racks and storage shelves, and soon had them stocked with the necessary materiel to the scale appropriate to the camp establishment. This included tools, rifles, bayonets, pistols, Sten guns and Bren light machine-guns, signalling pistols, rifle range equipment, gas masks, gas capes, and protective clothing and accoutrements of all sorts. In the explosives stores, I had ammunition, hand grenades, detonators, signal flares and, after the creation of 210 Signals Unit, plastic explosive with which to blow up

---

3   Passive defence involves, among other things, protecting personnel, as far as possible, from the effects of atomic, biological, and chemical weapons, as well as creating facilities for the denial of RAF installations from use by a potential enemy, by the use of demolition charges or whatever, when all else has failed.

Active defence involves the use of appropriate firearms in the defence of a location.

4   There were no maps equivalent to the British Ordnance Survey available to me within the RAF in Germany.

at least part of it. I had charge of one of the largest inventories on the camp.

All this required an amount of paperwork. I had a small office in the building, and a telephone, but I had no access to anyone who could type. The Station Orderly Room clerks could barely cope with their own work, so they were no help. I bought an Adler 'Tippa' portable typewriter from the PSI shop (someone else's extraneous duty) and attended, thereafter, to my own filing and correspondence. J/T Thompson didn't know whether he was coming or going. His life of leisure had come to an abrupt end. His wife complained to me, and I told her that he was only doing what he was paid to do, just like everyone else. I also dropped the hint that there was a shortage of married quarters and if she cared to vacate hers, her kindness would be very much appreciated. Whether she wrote to the 'Daily Mirror' about that I didn't find out, but no-one had any more trouble from her.

Having amassed this armoury, practice weapons issues had to be organised and rehearsed. Similarly, I arranged for the use of the Sennelager range (north of Paderborn) for weapons and live-firing practice. All ranks had to have firing practice and knowledge of their allocated arms. Officers and NCOs had to be briefed as to their station defence roles and orders drawn up covering actions in case of emergency. This took much of my time. Until I was satisfied that enough Officers and SNCOs were competent to take a squad of men to Sennelager by bus and instruct them in live-firing, I had to do it myself.

By this time I was a fully qualified Fighter Controller and was on 'B' Flight. When it came to the training of 'A' Flight personnel I had to do it during my 24 hour rest periods when I was working C & R night watch routines.[5] My time off watch, at least during normal office hours, was very full, but there were advantages. I had an office in which I could hide when Officers were being sought for other tasks. I could even wangle time off camp during the day by making sure that, even if I occasionally put an hour in of an evening, everything was as up to scratch as it could be. All this activity was well under way when we heard of the Poznan riots in Poland. This news quickened the pace of training somewhat.

---

5   See the watch routine panel on page 279.

Later, at the start of the Hungarian riots, I was summoned to the CO's office again. After telling me to sit down and listen, he explained that the international situation was worsening and that he had instructions from Group to make sure that certain contingency plans were up to date. He then asked me if I had drawn up a married families evacuation plan. I hadn't because, quite simply, I hadn't even thought of it. There and then, he and I drew up such a scheme, writing it in longhand because of its secrecy. He then opened his safe and took out a Top Secret file setting out certain actions to be taken in case of war. He then summoned Flt.Lt. Ron Young but told him nothing other than to escort me to my office and stay with me whilst I took the file and read the relevant parts of it. Nothing was explained to Ron, and he didn't see the file itself. His presence was purely a security measure. I took it back an hour or so later and Ron was dismissed, doubtless wondering what it was all about.

Shortly afterwards, without raising any alarm, and without giving anyone any food for thought, the CO, in my presence, summoned to his office a small group of married Officers and SNCOs. He explained the international scene and told them than an evacuation of civilians was a distinct possibility in the immediate future. In brief, the plan was for a married, car-owning Officer, to escort at possibly no more than an hour or so's notice, the entire civilian population of the married patch, in convoy, to the west and across the Rhine to comparative safety. Easy to say.

An immediate assessment was made of how many private cars and drivers were capable of making the journey, and whether or not all women and children, with no belongings save for handbags, could squeeze into them. The BFES teachers had also to be evacuated.[6] It would be a tight fit, so additional RAF vehicles (Volkswagen Kombis) were also earmarked. The next bit wasn't so easy and demanded a certain amount of subterfuge; all petrol tanks had to be kept full for such a journey. There would be no time for top-ups, even from RAF sources, before a rapid departure.

Nothing of these plans was to be said outright by those briefed at that meeting, but every opportunity was taken to hint that, due to the worsening situation in Hungary, we could be moved away. The hint

---

6   BFES = British Forces Education Service, whose teachers ran the Primary School on the married patch.

was taken, and was reinforced when orders were given to black out all lights after dark on the tech site.[7]

Probably in view of the international situation, on November 26th, as the Russians were regaining the upper hand in Hungary, I was detached to attend No.116 ABC Course at the Inter-Service School of Chemical Warfare at Winterbourne Gunner, on Salisbury Plain.[8] We 53 students, all of us of commissioned rank, were instructed in how to protect ourselves, and others, in the passive defence role. I experienced several types of war gas in the gas chambers, and learned about the new nerve agents and their supposed antidotes. I also learned about the effects of an atomic explosion – flash, blast, and radiation, and practised the use of atomic radiation detection equipment in an area of rubble strewn with radio-active sources. I became competent in the detection of gamma radiation and beta particles. I studied the use of coloured smoke and the use of wind in its deployment and dispersal. I also learned how quickly to identify a range of war gases and what protection and decontamination measures to use.

Most of the course was of a very practical nature, although there were lectures, some from Officers who had been present at Maralinga for the Woomera atomic bomb trials. We saw films of these trials and studied the effect of atomic explosions on buildings and military installations.

Life in the wooden-hutted Army Mess was vastly different to that in an RAF Mess. The biggest difference was that there was no bar in which to congregate and chat. In the anteroom the young Pongo subalterns conversationally out-vied each other with their pretentious pseudo Oxford accents, yet the same 'far back' individuals swore like low grade barrow boys when doing practical work on the course. Drinks were ordered from the Wines Steward who was in charge of the 'wines cupboard'. They were brought on a tray to individual Officers. Worse, there were only a few easy chairs so we had to sit on upright chairs at writing tables with green leather tops and green shaded reading lamps, ranged down each side of the room. In the meantime there was usually a moustachioed half-Colonel sitting in front of the fire, in a black

---

7   Essential outside lights were replaced by those with blue bulbs

8   ABC = Atomic Biological and Chemical (warfare). Battle of Britain ace 'Ginger' Lacey was also on the course.

leather club chair, sipping his whisky and soda whilst tut-tutting over his Times newspaper.[9] Convivial it was not.

At weekends some of us from the RAF made our way into Salisbury for a drink and Saturday lunch in 'The Haunch of Venison'. On Sundays, we only used the Mess for meals, spending the rest of the day either reading in our rooms, or small groups of us going out walking to explore the nearby ancient earthworks.

I passed the final exams with an 83% overall average, Grade A2, and came 15th on the course. I was therefore qualified, for the following three years, as an ABC instructor.

Back at Borgentreich I was immediately tasked with setting up a facility for ABC training. I took on charge a range of radiation detection equipment and personal dosimeters. I also had to take on my inventory a number of radioactive sources for training purposes.

The collection of these from a Unit over a hundred miles away, was not without its humour. Ron Young and I were detailed to take a Magirus Deutz truck for the trip. We wore personal dosimeters and armed ourselves with pistols. We loaded a number of empty sand-bags from Armoury stock in the back ready for filling prior to the return journey. Before arriving at the collection point we filled the sand-bags from a sandy area at the roadside, probably putting a couple of tons of the stuff on board to make a nest, in the middle of which the sources would go. Driving off, it was obvious from the vehicle's performance that we had a heavy load. Anyway, we collected the yellow canisters containing the sources, hung radiation hazard signs on the vehicle, and set off back to base. Progress was slow, far too slow. After checking for gamma radiation we found virtually none in the back of the truck, and then discovered that Ron's luminous wrist watch was giving off more radiation than came from anywhere else! We off-loaded 90% of the sand and pressed on. We came to a level crossing with the barrier down. Coming up quickly behind us was an off-white Mercedes car which stopped close to our tail. The driver must have seen the radiation signs and immediately selected reverse and backed away at high speed. He stayed what he must have thought was a safe distance behind for the next several miles until he eventually turned off.

---

9   Ginger Lacey's remarks about this almost comic opera caricature of an individual were wholly unrepeatable.

Back at base, these sources had to be stored in a locked and protected enclosure in the open air. Fg.Off. Dave Hattersley helped me construct such a place by sinking a large, lidded, concrete drainpipe vertically in the ground. I surrounded it with coils of barbed wire on which hazard notices were prominently displayed. The regulations stated that whenever I handled these sources I had to wear white denims – as if they offered any more protection than khaki ones, or my ordinary uniform for that matter!

I initiated a series of ABC demonstrations and lectures for the now increasing number of personnel on the camp. Our new tech site was almost complete and the personnel establishment was being increased accordingly. Thankfully, the civilian evacuation plan was quietly dropped as the international situation had by now calmed.

My duties as Armament Officer and Officer i/c Station Defence and Training were to continue for the rest of my time at Borgentreich. However, with the opening of the tech site at Auenhausen, I was trained in the use of plastic explosives by Flt.Lt. Amos Moore, a Bomb Disposal Officer, who came to visit. (I had met him at Jever when he defused a 500 lb bomb). We carried out an assessment of the most vulnerable parts of the bunker, its generating equipment, and the radar heads, so that I would know where best to lay demolition charges – if there was time. This was also when I took on charge a quantity of plastic explosive and detonators.

The day before an AOC's Inspection, I discovered that, due to a minor administrative oversight, I had more hand grenades and detonators than was stated on my inventory. Inventories were also subject to random inspection if the AOC so decided. To hold too many explosives would be an embarrassment which could lead to a formal enquiry. The Equipment Warrant Officer knew of the problem and, like me, was sure it could be sorted out, but there wasn't time. Without further ado I quietly took the excess munitions to my room in the Mess and put them in my suitcase under my bed. There they stayed for two or three days. With the pressure of the inspection now gone, the paperwork was quickly tidied up.

There was no Station Cinema at Borgentreich, instead, Flt.Lt. Don Crocker put on film shows in the Airmens Mess on two nights each week, and a childrens programme on Saturday mornings. The films came from the RAF Cinema Corporation and were shown using two

Debrie 16mm projectors. Sergeant Rogers was nominally in charge of projection and he had volunteer assistants.

By the end of 1956, my 8mm ciné filming and projection hobby had become well known on the camp. I had, for instance, filmed activities on the skating rink on the tennis courts the previous winter, as well as various other events on the camp. The CO had even asked me to film the AOC's Parade and inspection. These films, after editing, were shown in the Airmens Mess on my own Specto projector which I had brought from home after an earlier leave. These shows were received, according to who or what was appearing on the screen at the time, with acclamation, cat-calls, or ribald comments. I put on several such repeat and extended performances, by popular request, before I left the camp.

With the completion of much of the building work on the domestic site, and following the doubling of the size of the Airmens Mess, while I was away on the ABC course, one of the builder's hutments was placed on stilts outside the end window of the new Mess hall. It had been adapted, with power laid on, as a projection booth. It was shortly after this that Don Crocker was posted away, his tour in Germany having come to an end. The job of being i/c Cinema fell to me. Sgt. Rogers was taken away from cinema duties, so I ran the cinema, now three nights a week, and the Saturday children's show, with the help of a group of keen Airmen volunteers. In a short time, and with the use of timber and screws from old reclaimed packing cases, some scrounged electrical gear from the tech site, and tools from the Armoury, we built a bench for rewinding films and some storage shelves. We then set the projectors up in such a way that we could show multi-reel feature films without breaks for film changes. The quality of performances was thus much improved.

Many of my evenings were spent with the volunteers in the projection box. I didn't always have to be there. I just enjoyed it. Doing this, I saw bits of many of the well known films of the time. One of the most popular was 'High Society' of which, by popular demand, extra performances were laid on and, quite illicitly, Sqn.Ldr. Ellison asked me to run it through for him in the projection box while he tape-recorded most of the popular songs.

It was probably 'High Society' and its popularity that was the catalyst for me being asked if I could give either Saturday or Sunday evening showings in the Officers Mess, rather than the Officers going to the

Airmen's Mess as had been the routine. I could hardly refuse even though I had to show these films myself, unaided.

These shows involved my temporarily removing ornamental glass from the dining-room doors so that I could rig the projectors outside in the corridor where they were less noisy. I set my own screen up on a table at the other end of the room. The Mess staff arranged the chairs for the audience. Officers and their wives and families would then come to their own private showings. I found this more than a little irksome because it cut into my free time; I was working when everyone else was enjoying themselves. I saw 'High Society', mostly right through, at least a dozen times before it was returned.

It was my job, also, to select the films and make up the shows, usually a feature film and two 'shorts', from a list sent in advance by the RAF Cinema Corporation. If the feature films were shorter than usual I might show two of these instead. Pathé Pictorial Newsreels were almost always included in each programme. According to requirements I also ordered, and sometimes projected, training and educational films. All films were delivered to me and collected on a weekly basis.

Almost as an afterthought, in November 1957, I was sent on a projectionist's course at the RAF Cinema Corporation offices in Africa House, Kingsway, London. I stayed at the Milestone Hotel, Kensington High Street, at the cost of thirty shillings a night bed and breakfast, for the duration of the course and found that evenings in London could be extremely lonely. We students were sent out to buy our own lunches at midday at local cafés, but one of our number knew the back way into the Air Ministry building (Ad Astral House) canteen. There, the food was free. No-one ever questioned us, and we were able to claim the price of the meals against our expenses.

I learned all the professional techniques of cinema projection. I was trained, with the 11 others, all in civilian clothes, in the use of Debrie and Bell & Howell projectors. (We called the latter Hell and Bowel because of their inferior nature). Film rewinds, emergency 'keep the show running' procedures, and film splicing and checking, were also covered. We used old newsreels as our material. When it came to our final tests the old films were cut about and generally mutilated before they were given to us to show. These final sessions were therefore not without some hilarity.

When the final results were announced I came first with a 92% average score and an A1 pass. A senior RAFCC manager told me that if I wished, on leaving the RAF, I would be welcome to work for the Corporation as a cinema manager.

Going backwards in time, very early in 1957 Sqn.Ldr. Monk took over from Flt.Lt. Ray Street as Senior Technical Officer. Ray's extraneous duty was to oversee the running of the Mess bar. He handed that duty over to someone who screwed it up. It wasn't long before I was volunteered for the job and refusal was not an option. Anyway it would be good experience and I would have more Brownie Points added to my record of service.[10]

I had two volunteers, officially mis-employed, Fighter Plotters as barmen. These National Service lads were respectful and capable individuals. They behaved impeccably even when dealing with sometimes extremely drunken Officers.[11]

My own duties in this respect amounted mainly to the ordering and maintenance of stocks. Supplies came both from the NAAFI warehouse and the local Warburg Brewery. Each week the brewery draymen arrived with the order, always at lunch time when the bar was open, collected the empties, had a couple of bottles of Pils, had a chinwag with those of us who could speak German, collected next week's order, and departed. Bills for all bar supplies were paid by the Mess Secretary, Flt.Lt. Colin Hanmore (his extraneous duty), or his German assistant, Karl Schrader.

I had to adjust prices of all drinks served so that the overall profit for Mess funds was no more than 15%. As an example, a 'Horses Neck' cost just 3d.[12] A 75 cl bottle of Warburger Pils actually cost more.

Stock checks had to be done monthly. This amounted to counting full bottles – that was easy. Assessing tottages remaining in partly emptied bottles was more difficult, particularly with odd shaped bottles. A valuation had then to be calculated and the figure entered

---

10 Officers' service records were written on Forms 1369 and were the equivalent of an Officer's curriculum vitae, to be examined by any superior on arrival at a new posting. Assessments were made annually.

11 Technically it was an offence for any RAF individual to get drunk. Only if some other misdemeanour (e.g. being unfit for duty) was perpetrated as a result of drunkenness was this rule actually enforced Officers, though, were supposed to use their discretion. Some didn't, and if alcohol was consumed in too great quantities on a regular basis career prospects could be very adversely affected.

12 3d = 1.25p in today's money.

in the Mess accounts. It was usual to do this work in a morning before the bar opened. That was easy as long as the task fitted into my watch-keeping timetable. Once however, it did not. I was on nights and came off watch in the morning, usually to go to bed after a light breakfast. Instead I had to stay up and, with almost overwhelming tiredness, completed the task just in time. I then went to bed, to be woken by Frau Höhn only two hours later so that I could go on evening watch. I only had to do that once.

Bar staff handled no cash. Each Officer had a bar book in which his purchases were entered. He then had to sign or initial that entry. An individual's bar account would then appear on his monthly Mess bill. There were strict maxima as to how much could be spent in the bar. Squadron Leaders and above were unrestricted in this respect. Not only did the bar sell drinks, because the Mess was too small to have a sepa-rate shop, it also sold items like toothpaste and razor blades, chocolate, sweets, and other sundries.

Predicting advance consumption when ordering fresh stocks could be very hit and miss. One month, the favourite tipple would be rum and coke, the next it might be whisky and ginger or gin and tonic. Fashions changed quickly and the problem was to not have too much stock, or to run short of anything. Wine consumption was difficult to predict, but when there were Dining In Nights or Guest Nights the port had to be decanted and presented at the right temperature in readiness for the Loyal Toast. Sometimes there would be a run on liqueurs. I remember one period when the fad was to buy 'Rainbows'. These were a selection of tots of liqueur poured into a glass, densest first, followed by a succes-sion of others of differing colour and reducing density, added very care-fully to float on top of the previous layers. These mixtures were expen-sive and the trick was to drink each layer in turn during the course of an evening. It was usual for the imbiber to have a blinding headache next morning. The bar also sold Alka-Seltzer tablets and Underborg pick-me-ups.

I also did short stints as House Member and Library Member in the Mess. The former involved control of the batwomen, the laundry, and the associated inventory. The latter meant that I was present at set times to open the library book-case and record borrowings. In this connec-tion I maintained a wish list for future additions. There were constant requests for 'Lady Chatterley's Lover', 'The Kinsey Report', and 'The

Kama Sutra'.[13] None of these was ever bought but Stephen Potter's 'Upmanship' books were, however, very popular.

There was a period, thankfully a very brief one, when I was elected Mess Catering Officer. I lasted for a week and was, admittedly, bloody hopeless at it. There was much relief all round when Flt.Lt. Bill Billing took over from me.[14]

---

13 The Kinsey Report was the result of research into sexual habits.
14 Fifty years later, as I write this, I am still as hopeless in a kitchen.

36. On Watch With 537 SU

NOW THAT I WAS properly qualified in my new occupation I had to take my turn on night watches. On these I was the only Officer on the tech site and had no more than 15 or, at the very most, 20 men on watch with me. There were a group of technicians keeping an eye on the equipment and the generators, and a couple of lads on guard duty with the anti-intruder dog patrols, but the rest were radar operators, fighter plotters, plotters and tellers. It was not expected that a night watch would ever have to carry out fighter control duties; RAF night flying was in the evenings and was usually over by 23.00 hours. Weekends were similarly devoid of RAF flying activity unless there was a scheduled exercise in progress.

Our job was the surveillance and plotting of all aircraft movements within our area of responsibility. This area was the very south-east corner of the British Zone, and over the East-West frontier as far as we could see into Eastern Bloc airspace. Usually everything was quiet, very quiet.

My position was in the Chief Controller's cabin in the Leyland Hippo Ops vehicle. I must have spent something like 6 weeks of night watches in its plywood and perspex two-person box, sweating alone in shirt sleeve order and cursing the white-arsed flies in the summer then, later in the year in the cold weather, wrapped up warmly in the underheated and stuffy atmosphere.[1] I had a corded switchboard with telephone lines to Group and to the control vehicles from which plots were 'told' on our own tech site. Lines also linked us to the USAF base at Rothwesten, and to our domestic site. There were also two outstations, one of which was at Waggum, near Braunschweig (Brunswick).

---

1   During day watches the second seat was occupied by the Ops 'B' who had charge of the switchboard.

The other was further north. Both were very small units and had their own radar. Their specific task was to monitor aircraft movements on the Berlin air corridors (and anything else they could pick up), and tell the plots to Borgentreich. Waggum, though, told its plots over a beamed radio link to a receiver located near our tech site, and thence by land line. The Waggum end of this link was far from secure because the back beam (which was found to be almost as powerful as the main beam) transmitted the data straight over the border into East Germany and was doubtless constantly monitored by the Russians.

I did not have a radar screen in front of me when on nights. All plots, from both our own radar and the outstations, were told down land lines to the plotters sitting round the GSM in the Hippo.[2] A teller, also sitting at the GSM, then told the plots to Group. The Group Ops Room also received plots from other radar Stations. Thus, Group had an overall radar picture albeit a few minutes late because of the delays of telling and plotting.[3] I was able to witness this when I was attached for a short while to 83 Ops Room at RAF Wahn for continuation training just before I became fully qualified.

Usual night time activity consisted of plotting slow transport aircraft, flogging their noisy way along the Berlin air corridors, until they faded from view below our radar cover. Occasionally we had a glimpse of activity in the Russian Zone, but these could only be high flying aircraft because other activity, if there was any, was out of sight below our radar horizon. The usual highlight of the watch was the 02.00 hours Met balloon which, although it wasn't our job, we plotted just for something to do.

Very rarely, it would rise high enough to be carried off at higher speed in a jet stream before fading from view.

Occasionally an agitated American voice would call us from Roth-westen asking whether or not we could confirm their sighting of activity over the border. Mostly we could not. We envied the Americans their equipment; ours was getting too clapped out to be of much use for serious surveillance work.

---

2   GSM = General Situations Map. Effectively a plotting table with a map of the relevant area with a Georef grid and major features (e.g. the East-West frontier) also painted on its surface.

3   This delay was acceptable in the days of slow, piston-engined aircraft. In the present jet age, as was evident during exercises, this delay could mean that fighters were scrambled too late to intercept incoming raiders.

Sleep was forbidden, and all land-lines had to be checked at least every 10 minutes so as to make sure they were still connected. At times when there was absolutely no activity, which was more often than not, the tellers and plotters would resort to telling each other yarns and holding general conversations. I well remember one of our lads on the Waggum line asking how much 'bull' there was at Waggum. He went on to say that here at Borgentreich there was so much of it that even the mice wore pads on their feet! [4] It was usual for each person to be relieved for a few minutes every hour so that they could use the toilet and have a drink. The system worked well except that for I, being the only Officer, had to stay in my cabin (except for brief toilet visits when the NCO i/c watch temporarily took my place) and have drinks brought to me. I usually had coffee every hour, sometimes with a biscuit or two, but changed to tea at 05.00 hours so that the effects of the coffee didn't stop me sleeping when off watch.

I encouraged the lads to write letters or read when on watch provided that, as soon as there was any 'trade', they immediately dropped what they were doing and got on with the job.

One night, to amuse myself, my letters home all written, and fed up with reading, I decided to clean the perspex windows of my cabin. I used 'Windolene' on a rag, as was usual. What I didn't realise was that the rag I used to apply the Windolene was contaminated with oil. On coming to polish the perspex afterwards I ended up with a smeary mess which defied my best efforts to remove it. To his credit, one of the plotters spotted my predicament and suggested that I dipped another rag in cigarette ash and tried that. It worked a treat, thus ending a two hour potentially very embarrassing struggle.

Day watches were different. The Duty Watch Officer and the Ops 'B' occupied the cabin in the Hippo. There were more plotters and tellers round the GSM and, behind the vertical, edge-lit, perspex fighter plotting screen stood two fighter plotters. These lads had lines to the control cabins and plotted, in reverse-written red and yellow china-graph crayon, the positions and identity of any aircraft under Borgen-treich control.

---

4   He was referring to the foot square pieces of old blanket on which one slithered about to protect a barrack room floor after it had just been polished. I used them as an Officer Cadet at Kirton-in-Lindsey. The mental image of mice doing the same was humorous in the extreme.

We Fighter Controllers had to wait in our rest vehicle in readiness, at all times when on watch, quickly to transfer to one of the control vehicles and take control of any aircraft allocated to us.

When it was my turn, on arriving in the cabin I donned my single earpiece head and breast set and told the Chief Controller, over a squawk box, that I was ready. He then told me the aircraft type and number (usually one or two pairs), call-sign, course, altitude, location in Georef, base, and VHF frequency of 'my' aircraft. Given this information I would at once make R/T contact and, if there was little aerial activity I might identify them very quickly on the PPI. On the other hand, given poor radar conditions and/or an amount of other air traffic, I would ask them to make a 90° turn either to port or starboard so that I could be sure that I was watching the right plots. Sometimes I had to swap radars so as to get a better picture and maybe request a further identifying turn. As soon as I could 'see' my aircraft the cabin fighter plotter started to tell the plots simultaneously to the plotter on the Craig computer, the plotter on the fighter screen in the Hippo, and the clerk who maintained a log of all calls made between the aircraft and me. Another lad, next to me on the heights screen, would then also endeavour to pick up the same aircraft on the Type 13 and confirm their altitude. I, or the NCO i/c cabin crew, would inform the Chief Controller that I had the aircraft under control.

Through my single earphone I could hear the R/T calls from the aircraft. Through my uncovered ear I could hear information over the squawk box, or the voices of the Craig computer plotter and height reader. I spoke to the aircraft via a snakes-head microphone in front of me on the radar console. Voices were kept clear but low. Information was passed between us, and (by me) to the aircraft, in a well rehearsed, standardised manner. Otherwise, unless another controller and his team were working aircraft in the same dimly lit control vehicle, all would be quiet except for the hum of electricity and faint buzz of the equipment cooling fans.[5]

When I had aircraft under control it was my responsibility to make the pilots aware of their position by informing them at regular intervals of 'Pigeons to Base', this being the course they had to steer to get to, and the distance from, their parent airfield. This was also done at the

---

5   It was not often that we worked two cabin crews in the same vehicle. It usually only occurred during an exercise.

end of a session under control, just before they were advised to change to their airfield control VHF channel.

Just four days after qualifying, during a night flying session (evening watch) I was allocated 2 Meteor NF11s and controlled them for five quarter attack PIs. They alternated between being fighter and target. On one run I put the fighter ahead of the target and another ended up as a tail chase. The other three runs were moderately successful. It was a 35 minute session and not an auspicious start. Later the same evening I was given a further pair of NF11s but, in the 11 minutes I had them under control, they only had time for one successful 90° quarter attack. All these PIs were at 30,000 feet.

Two more short sessions took place on the 29th of June. The first was when I had, for just 11 minutes, two pairs of F84 Thunderjets under control for one PI. Then, for only 9 minutes, I did a single PI with a pair of Meteor NF11s.

That same day I was allocated a pair of Hunters at 41,000 feet. This was no ordinary practice PI session. A brand new Comet II with the Secretary of State for Air and an entourage of Senior RAF Officers and civil servants on board was returning from the Moscow International Air Show. It was being escorted by a number of Mig 15 Russian fighters when I picked it up on the radar. These were scheduled to break off on approaching the East-West German frontier. It was my job to position my Hunters so as, as quickly as possible, without creating a border violation, to intercept and escort the Comet westwards across Germany. Time was tight because the Hunters were scrambled and handed over to me a little late. Nevertheless, by doing a parallel head-on interception (my first) I was able to position my Hunters at the Comet's side. They radioed to say that they had seen the Migs break away in the distance. This session lasted 41 minutes, during which other Fighter Controllers on my watch were watching and listening from the unused control positions.

The following Monday I succeeded in carrying out 4 successful PIs with two pairs of NF11s in conditions of moderate to severe R/T jamming. The next day, July 3rd, I took over control, from another GCI, of 4 Hunters already escorting a Comet en route to Moscow at 38,000 feet. I turned them back at the frontier, by which time they were low on fuel so I diverted them for a landing at RAF Wunstorf, to which place I gave them Pigeons and instructed them to change to

VHF channel 'Charlie'. During the rest of July I carried out a total of 19 PIs, all at night, in 6 sessions with Meteor NF11s.

My Log Book records that I only had two sessions in the entire month of August. The radar was not functioning well during this period. These sessions were Meteor NF11s at night. The radar picture was so poor and intermittent that I was fortunate even to be able to pick up my aircraft. Fortunately, I was able, by much use of a chinagraph pencil, to mark the deduced positions of the aircraft on the PPI. With the excellent assistance of the Craig computer plotter, all these PIs, six of them in all, were successfully carried out 'blind' by DR.[6]

I must explain DR: knowing an aircraft's track and speed, its instructions to turn, and the radius of turns at altitude, with skill and sometimes a bit of luck, it was possible to deduce fairly accurately its position for a while after it faded from the radar. It was a matter of professional pride never to tell the pilot that you were having this sort of trouble. It was usually with a sigh of relief that the same aircraft reappeared, maybe only fleetingly, in more or less the position you expected. The DR process then started over again from this fresh position. The same technique was used when aircraft were obscured by cloud responses or permanent echoes.

When controlling night fighters, it was standard practice for the GCI controller (me) to direct the 'fighter' to a position from which its navigator could 'see' on his AI (airborne interception radar) the 'target', at which point he would call 'Judy', and thence take over control of the interception by talking his pilot (over their intercom) into a position from which he could shoot the 'target' down. Occasionally the AI would fail and an R/T call announcing a Bent Weapon would be made and the session aborted. Or, there may be a call for 'More Help', whereupon it was my task again to take over the interception in an attempt to bring it to a successful conclusion. This happened to me during two sessions in September.

There were sorties in which there was intense jamming, either of the R/T or the radar, or both.[7] Occasionally this was generated by the Eastern Bloc. When this happened it paid to be on special lookout for intruders or other potentially hostile activity. Mostly though, it arose from our side of the border and was created by our own aircraft during

6   DR = 'Dead' Reckoning (deduced reckoning).

7   Jamming was also known as ECM = Electronic Counter Measures.

pre-planned exercises. Heavy cloud could have the same effect and, maybe due to aircraft aerial icing, the R/T would suffer interference.

During September I had jamming, dense cloud, and 'Bent Weapons' affect my sessions. One session involved my controlling a pair of NF11s in a climbing sortie in an attempt to get above thick cloud. Three 90° PIs were successful and one was aborted, the cloud being so thick as to jam the AI. My last session of the month involved me being given a pair of Hunters on a special purpose mission. This was to investigate the dropping of 'Window' (or 'Chaff' as the Americans call it) in Georef squares Juliet Hotel and Kilo Golf. The height ranged between 8,000 and 35,000 feet. During this session the Type 15 radar was u/s and I had to rely on the Type 14 upper and lower radars instead, swapping from one to the other in order to get the best coverage at the various altitudes. Who dropped the window, or why, I never found out. Sometimes it was better not to ask too many questions.

October was a busier month with two day and seven night sessions. All aircraft under my control were Meteor NF11s. It was this month that I was in control of freelance sorties for the first time. On the 10th I controlled a single NF11 on a search and intercept mission. The only 'trade' there was in the area, a single aircraft, was plotted while I positioned my fighter to intercept. It turned out to be another NF11 on which I controlled my first night parallel head-on quarter attack. Later in the month, on October 22nd, there was a jamming exercise during which I was allocated two separate pairs of NF11s. The jamming was so bad that I used a technique called broadcast control. This involved my giving a running commentary on the position, track, altitude, and estimated number of 'enemy' aircraft. It involved continuous talk on my behalf for a full 45 seconds with a 15 second break for receiving calls from any aircraft under control. In this way, in an emergency, a single controller could broadcast information about an enemy's activities to any number of friendly fighters and, if necessary, have his transmissions relayed from several transmitters at the same time so as to try to counter, by signal strength alone, any R/T jamming. In this instance the first pair of NF11s failed to intercept, but the second pair found, and intercepted not one, but four, R/T and radar-jamming Lincoln bombers at 22,000 feet.

Earlier in October we had Exercise Guest. My duty on the first session was to keep 2 NF11s on a patrol line. There was no trade. The second pair of NF11s were given to me for freelance work. With them I intercepted a pair of unsuspecting Venoms at 35,000 feet.

At the end of the month, again I had two NF11s and did three successful PIs and three aborted PIs with them under strange conditions. Our Type 15 radar wasn't up to scratch, neither was either aircraft's AI equipment. Two intercepts were done by DR and with Bent Weapons, both resulting in visual contact. Another was reasonably successful, but the other three were hopeless. These were the only three aborted runs I had during the month, out of a total of 16.

November was my busiest month with 537 SU. I controlled 52 PIs with another 12 aborted. I controlled Meteor NF11s, Hunters, Venoms, and a single Vampire T11. One of these sessions was with four Hunters of the 83 Group Battle Flight. In all, apart from basic PIs, these aircraft intercepted 2 Canadian F86 Sabres, 3 Hunters, 2 friendly fighters of unstated identity, 1 Canberra, and one seen but unidentified 'Bogie'.[8] As usual, there were problems with the serviceability and/or performance of both ground and airborne radar.

Some of this activity was undoubtedly part of a show of strength whilst the Hungarian Riots were proceeding and being quelled by the Russians. It was at this time, too, that the tech site was blacked out. It was also during November that I was sent to Wildenrath on a special flying mission which I shall describe next.

These were my last sessions with 537 SU because, just before the end of the month, I went on the Atomic, Biological, and Chemical warfare course in the UK. When I returned to Borgentreich, 537 Signals Unit had been disbanded. 210 Signals Unit had been created in its place at a new location near the village of Auenhausen.

---

8   A Bogie was an aircraft not identified from any known movement. It might have been an intruder.

37. An Unexpected Sortie

ON NOVEMBER 19TH, 1956, during the Hungarian riots, I was sent to RAF Wildenrath for a scheduled trip as a crew member of Lincoln bomber RF448 on a special mission. My duty was to be an Observer as I was still considered to be up to date with aircraft recognition, and official knowledge of my good long-range sight must have also been a consideration. This flight was conducted partly under wraps.

I had earlier had to hand in the bulk of my flying equipment but still had my flying suit, and thick personal flying clothing: shirts, anorak, gloves, and Sabre boots. Gone were my G-suit, hard 'bone dome' helmet and its inner helmet and oxygen mask. I took what I had with me for this sortie and dressed accordingly in the crew room. I was loaned a helmet and mask and issued with a parachute harness and a removable chest parachute.

During briefing it was explained to me that the sortie was primarily one of radar and R/T jamming during a regular Exercise Guest.[1] Our route was never announced, for it was the task of the GCIs and fighters to find us despite the jamming. The secondary objective, which was only hinted at, was to fly close to the East-West frontier and to monitor Eastern Bloc reactions to our activities. When I asked how close we were going to the border I received an evasive reply, and at the same time my role as Observer was strongly emphasised. Our crew, as I remember it, were Pilot, Flight Engineer, Navigator, nose Observer in the forward or Bomb-aimer's position, myself as mid-upper Observer (looking out through the astrodome), another Observer in the tail turret, and a

---

1   Exercise Guest was a fairly regular monthly routine during which the countermeasures for dealing with radio and radar jamming could be practised. These exercises appear fairly frequently in my Fighter Controller's Log Book.

civilian 'Boffin' who had a position towards the aft of the fuselage, near the mid-upper gunner's position, where he was surrounded by a mass of electrical equipment, oscilloscopes and radios.[2] We were introduced to him but were told neither his name nor his airborne duties.

On climbing aboard we took up our crew positions and hung our parachutes in the assigned positions in the fuselage. The intercom was checked, and start-up procedure commenced. Each Merlin was fired up in sequence and, after a pause and clearance being given from the Tower, we taxied close to the end of the runway. There, as in my Oxford days, each engine was run up in turn to test for any mag-drop. All were OK. Clearance for take-off was given and we turned on to the runway. I, in the meantime, had taken up my allotted take-off and landing position sitting atop the main spar, bracing myself with my hands as best I could. Our skipper opened up the Merlins against the brakes. The sound was deafeningly thrillingly beautiful, the whole airframe shaking like some wild beast raring to go. Then we were rolling. Soon the ground dropped below, and we turned on to an easterly heading. I judged this from the position of the sun as we climbed through, and above, a cloud layer.

A few minutes later we took up our observer positions. For my part I stood with my head in the astrodome so that I could see out and have a 360° circle of vision of everything above the horizontal. The skipper throttled back and the noise level reduced as we settled down to level flight. My first impression on looking out in the slightly bumpy conditions was that of seeing the wings flexing, and the fuselage twisting enough to put the tailplane out of alignment, first one way, then another. Fascinating as this was, I had to ignore it and concentrate on scanning the sky for aircraft. Periodically we checked the intercom but for at least an hour there was nothing to report except for either the nose or tail observer calling the sighting of a transport aircraft well below. Then I spotted fighters, 9 o'clock high, but they were minding their own business, trailing non-persistent contrails in the blue. The skipper told me to keep my eye on them. We were heading south at the time. Then more fighters appeared, too far off for identification but they had swept wings. These were nearer and not trailing. On my calling these the skipper opened the throttles and we banked hard to starboard. The

---

2 Astrodome: A perspex dome on top of the fuselage, to the rear of the main spar, and used for astro-navigation, from which place a navigator could use his sextant to take star shots.

tail observer caught sight of them, two of them, single-engined, head on to him, descending towards us, but got no positive identification. We went into a dive, engines now screaming, and I lost sight of them, the tailplane, then cloud, obscuring my view. When I saw them again they had turned away. Both the tail observer and I thought they may have been Migs but neither of us could be 100% sure as we could not make out the position of their tail-planes. We certainly didn't want them to be any closer for positive identification! Pulling out of the dive, and using the excess speed, we climbed again before settling back into a cruise at what I judged to be about 8-10,000 feet. Then we went into cloud for a while and could rest our eyes. Before coming back into clear air our Boffin called to say that he had some good information, but only he knew what he meant.

We stooged around a while longer, changing course fairly frequently, occasionally ducking in and out of cloud. I called "Aircraft 6 o'clock, level". The rear observed called "I've got 'em. Closing fast". Then I called "Two more fighters at 7 o'clock. Closing rapidly. Look like Hunters". "Roger. Hold on", replied the skipper as we immediately dived hard to port. His prompt action must have taken both pairs of fighters (they were all Hunters) by surprise, for they lost us. Better still, we lost them before they closed to within firing range. Levelling off at much lower altitude we stooged about again. Then, suddenly, we were bounced by two Meteors which came out of cloud. None of us saw them until too late. To them, we must have been dead meat. These Meteors then turned and formated on us just long enough for us to exchange traditional and impolite hand signals before they climbed away. Our sortie was now as good as over.

Debriefing was minimal and our Boffin was not present. When I asked for the pilot's name and time airborne so as to enter them into my Log Book I was at first very firmly told "Don't", then they relented and I was able to record that the Skipper was Flt.Lt. Goodenough, and the time airborne as 2 hours and 10 minutes.

I cannot say with absolute certainty that I had seen Russian aircraft, neither can I say that we had actually crossed the frontier. My view of the ground, looking out of the top of the fuselage, was limited and, in any case, I was not familiar with the topographical features of the eastern side of the British Zone, seldom having previously flown in that area. I do have the impression though, that not only were we flying as part of Exercise Guest, but that our activities also aroused more than a little curiosity on the other side of the frontier.

On returning to Borgentreich I discovered from the watches that there had been considerable radar and R/T jamming that day, and that the centre of jamming had passed over the local area.

It is only now, over 50 years later, that I have seen fit to mention this flight.

38. Domestic And Social

D URING 1956, PARTICULARLY THE second half, the domestic site was in a state of upheaval.

Our Mess, originally a single storey building, was being doubled in height and having an extension added at the front. We couldn't live in it while this was going on so we were allocated rooms in which to sleep in a screened-off wing of the recently extended Sergeants Mess. These had no toilet nearby so, unless we were prepared to skip across, hopefully unseen, to the toilet in the nearby MT Section in the middle of the night, we had two choices, stow it, or let fly out of the window. The windows were used quite frequently. Our temporary rooms had bare concrete floors. Using my initiative – and Armoury class 'B' stores – I sewed together, from material meant for warning flags, a red and green bedside mat backed with opened out sandbags. This was much better than putting my bare feet on a rough cold floor. Through a thin partition, screening off part of what would eventually be a long corridor, we could hear the SNCOs. The popular song at the time was "It only hurts for a little while" and we heard various renditions of this through that thin wall. Inevitably someone dubbed it "The virgin's song", by which title it became known across the camp.

While on a girlish sort of theme: as the new barrack blocks were completed they had to be thoroughly cleaned before being handed over for equipping and occupation. The German contractors employed numbers of local girls to do this. One had a very dubious reputation, and was known in certain quarters as 'the hack with come to bed eyes', or 'easy rider'. She was very generous with her affections, too generous, for she was known to have infected a number of Airmen with syphilis. On some evenings it was possible to see men coming back to camp divert, furtively, to the prophylactic room at the back of the Guardroom, there to try and clean themselves up after indulging unwisely. Of course, Flt. Lt. David 'Doc' Pottinger knew about this as some men had inevitably to report to him for treatment. He was left with no alternative other than to have her banned from working on the camp, and to discuss her condition and behaviour with the local village Artzt (Doctor) so that she could be 'cleaned up'. He also put out clear warnings to all ranks as to the dangers of catching something very nasty.

The Guardroom was also extended during the building programme. An extra cell was built and office space added. It was there, as Orderly Officer, with the Orderly Corporal and Orderly Sergeant, that I had to take the evening 'Jankers Parade'. At this stage Borgentreich was still a small camp and everybody knew each other. As per routine, I entered the Guardroom the parade of half a dozen Airmen formed up outside. I asked

The Guardroom during alterations.

the single prisoner in the cell if he had any complaints and inspected his kit layout. I then inspected the Key Register, initialled it, and waited a moment for the Orderly Sergeant to tell me that the parade was ready for inspection. Standing up straight and tall, possibly with my peaked cap slightly towards the back of my head, I marched out through the Guardroom door to carry out the inspection. At least that was my intention. On going through the door my cap caught the top of the door frame and fell to the ground behind me. The duty SPs saw the funny side of it, as did I, and we started to laugh. The whole darned parade started to laugh. So much for the disciplining of miscreants that night! The entire camp knew the following morning that Flying Officer Pod had created a funny. It took some living down.

On another occasion, as Orderly Officer, I was detailed to supervise a family 'Marching Out' of a married quarter. This procedure involved the checking of the inventory of the house, the condition of the house, and its cleanliness. The procedure would then be officially recorded and the records taken back to the Station Adjutant who, at that time was Flt.

Lt. Sam Weller, a sometimes prickly individual. It was usually a fairly quick routine. Not so on this occasion. The inventory was checked, everything having been laid out for examination in each room before-hand as required. The general condition of the decoration left some-thing to be desired, but was nothing that couldn't be taken care of as a matter of routine. When it came to cleanliness, I had to get the woman properly to clean the bath, toilets, and wash-basins while I watched. There was no way she would have done it otherwise because the fact that she and her two children were due to catch the afternoon train to the UK was uppermost in her mind. Then I came to the kitchen. It was a disaster. The cupboards were dirty and the stove and oven were disgusting in the extreme. They were in a wholly unacceptable condi-tion, with layers of fat, grease, and food spillages stuck to everything. The woman, now on tenterhooks because it was nearing her scheduled departure time, was getting edgy. I told her that the kitchen was unac-ceptable and she must, as was laid down in the regulations, clean it before leaving. Clearly she could not in the time available. I therefore went to the nearby NAAFI Shop to use their phone. I told Sam, and he told me, in no uncertain terms, that the woman was not to leave that day and to wait for the Marching Out process to be done again on the next available departure date, which he would fix. I had to tell her this at least three times before she understood what I was saying. I then left. The woman had to unpack and stay where she was with her children until Sam decided she could leave. In the meantime she had to get her house sparklingly clean because he was going to do the Marching Out himself next time. This was an object lesson to other less-than-careful housewives. Sam had made a point.

There was another, much later (after the creation of 210 SU), event on the married patch which, yet again as Orderly Officer, I was told to attend to. This was after the number of houses had doubled and more new Officers and other ranks had been posted in.

There was a row in the NAAFI shop among the customers (all servicemen's wives), with much pushing and shoving. The NAAFI Manageress, in desperation, phoned Sam Weller for help. That's how I was brought in to sort things out.

When I arrived the Manageress had shut the shop because she couldn't handle the situation. In front of the shuttered counter were a dozen or more women arguing and screaming at each other and threatening each other with all sorts. On their seeing me the cat-fight subsided and, inevitably, I asked what the problem was, telling them also that the shop would stay shut until the matter was cleared up. This immediately gave me the upper hand. The cause of the problem, it transpired, was that the wife of a newly arrived Squadron Leader had taken on her husband's rank and decided to throw her weight about and go ahead of the others to the front of the queue. The others, quite naturally, didn't like it. The culprit then started bridling and threatened me with reporting me, a Flying Officer, to her husband when he came home that night. I had my orders – and I stuck to them. I selected one woman at random and asked her rank. She said "Civilian", but her husband was a Sergeant (or whatever). I then turned to the culprit and asked her what rank she was. She answered that her husband was a Squadron Leader. To this I replied, "I know he's a Squadron Leader, but what rank are you?" Her expression could have killed me. I had to repeat the question. With not a little prompting from the others she sheepishly had to admit that she, too was 'civilian'. That acknowledged, I asked who was next to be served, sorted out the order of their arrival in the shop, and lined them up in that order with the culprit at the back because she had arrived last. Then I knocked on the shutter and the shop reopened. Problem solved, almost.

On returning to the domestic site I told Sam Weller what the problem had been and added that I was a little concerned as to any retribution. Sam left me in his office while he went into the CO's office next door to talk to Wg.Cdr. Kilmartin. I was called in too, and explained the situation. He advised me, there and then, to phone this woman's husband and explain to him what I had had to do, and that I was very embarrassed at having had to do it. Whether anyone else said anything to this Squadron Leader or not, I never found out. I heard no more, but admit to having been worried for a few days afterwards.

Our newly extended Mess had greatly increased accommodation. In the building as it was, I had a corner room with very little outlook. On moving back in I had a much larger upstairs room at the back with a wonderful view. I could look out across open country to the cone-shaped Desenberg knoll several miles away. This knoll had at its top the ruins of a castle dating back at least to the 100 Years War.

It was a place to visit on a nice day; the climb was very steep. It was from my new room that, one Sunday morning, on pulling back the curtains I saw a sight which momentarily panicked me. A large number of tanks and other armour was coming, cross-country, from the east, crashing through fences, crossing ditches, and ploughing up crops with their tracks. "Shit. The Russians are here" I thought. "I'm in my pyjamas. I'm the bloody Station Defence Officer. How can I get to the Armoury – but that's no good I've got nothing to kill a tank, and there's too many of them. There's no time. We've had it." Someone yelled from a room down the corridor "Wake up you lot. Look out of the frigging window". All sorts of expletives immediately rent the air of the Mess. Then I saw several army Land Rovers on the Peckelsheim road, and my senses came back to me. Only then did I realise that the tanks were British. Panic over. My tank recognition training had deserted me when I most needed it. The Pongos were enjoying one of their 'Schemes'. When we checked later, the Army hadn't bothered to tell the RAF. So much for inter-service liaison.

In 537 SU days there were so few Officers we had to make our own fun. Those of us who lived-in were often invited to the homes of those living in married quarters. We were invited for meals and parties, and maybe just for a Saturday afternoon cup of tea and a social chat. All this was very much appreciated by us. I found it just a little embarrassing because there was no way I could reciprocate; wives could come to the Mess on weekend evenings with their husbands as of right, so this was no novelty to them. I decided on another approach. To occupy myself when I had spare time I used to make up marquetry pictures from kits bought when on leave. These pictures made excellent gifts. Then there was a craze for parchment lampshades embellished with wine and beer bottle labels. I started to make these, too, steaming labels off bottles from the bar and gluing them on to thick paper cut to the desired shape. I made the frames from brazing wire and the cores of electrical connectors, courtesy of Fg.Off. Dave Hattersley's contracts and buildings repairs department. I pierced the paper, and laced the whole lot together with heavy coloured thread. It wasn't long before most houses sported at least one such shade, some being specially made to order. Later, in 210 SU days, I changed my hobby to embroidery. This was less messy and I could do it during quiet times when watching the radar on boring night watches. I could immediately drop it if there was work to do. Several households received tray cloths and table cloths as 'thank you' gifts. Throughout this entire period I continued with ciné photography but, by its very nature, I couldn't do it all the time.[1]

It was quite a walk to the married patch and involved, in early days, going through the village. One night, late on, Dave Hattersley and I were walking back along one of the village streets in almost complete darkness when, for some inexplicable reason we both started barking like dogs, varying our barks so as to represent both small and very large breeds. Within moments lights started to go on, and these helped us to see our way. When windows started to open we stayed quiet.

By this time though, the village dogs were putting on their own performance. After more married quarters were built a new road made such journeys much shorter.

Picnic at Winterberg. L-R top picture: Colin Hanmore; Paddy & Pam Ryan; myself; Irene Hanmore; Barbara Fisher; Peggy & Don Crocker.

During the summer of 1956 several wives decided it would be a good idea to arrange a car trip to Winterberg, the Services Leave Centre in the Rothaargebirge which, in winter, was a ski resort. All Officers, except the two who were on watch, were invited, as was Miss Barbara Fisher, the BFES school teacher. Sandwiches, cakes, and drinks for a picnic were laid on by the wives. We living-in Officers piled into the available cars. I ended up travelling with Paddy and Pam Ryan, the CO and his wife. Rank didn't matter, we were all off duty, knew each other

---

[1]   Films which I managed to complete, and which survived until recently, have been donated to the Royal Air Force Museum at Hendon.

well, and were intent on a good day out. The scenery was beautiful and the weather perfect. We pitched the picnic at the top end of the slalom ski slope and ate, drank, chatted, went for walks, dozed, and relaxed in the sunshine, work completely forgotten for the time being. I well remember filming Peggy Crocker eating a banana. I did it in such a way that when it was projected, it showed backwards – revolting!

Picnic at Winterberg. This picture was taken at the top of the slalom ski slope.

An Officer's wife, after far too much giggle-juice one Saturday evening in the Mess, dared another to do a handstand against the bar wall, in the manner which small girls often did in school yards. This dare was carried out and it ended up with all 'ladies' present doing the same – to the embarrassment of some of their husbands. Briefs, finger trappers, and wide legs, in various colours, stocking tops and suspenders, were all displayed that night as skirts fell to cover the participants' faces. Even bras became disoriented as bosoms fell about. It was very late and not particularly edifying.

On a different social level, Dining In Nights took place fairly regularly and were important because all Officers who were not on watch had to attend. This gave us the opportunity to meet each other and brought together those who otherwise may have not ordinarily put in much of an appearance in the Mess. Occasionally, also, there were Guest Nights when Officers and their Ladies were invited from other RAF and Army units, as well as local German dignitaries and their wives. Such occasions were always quite formal and sometimes taxing, especially when entertaining German people who had absolutely no command of the English language.

Officers, Ladies, and Guests at one of the tables at a Ladies Night held on the evening of April 13th, 1957

Colin and Irene Hanmore organised a fancy-dress party in their house one night in late June 1957. By this time there was a change of faces as some folk had been posted away and others arrived to take their places. This party was thought to be a good idea to get to know the newcomers.

Fancy-dress can cause problems for living-in Officers, as I had found out at Jever. This time I had enough notice to be able to do something about it so, on the Saturday of the weekend before the party a couple of us went into Kassel to do some shopping. There, in the Kaufhalle (a department store), I bought some plastic sheeting such as one would use to make a shower curtain. Back in my room I contrived, with scissors, glue, sticky tape, and bits of string, to make this into some sort of dress which I could fairly easily put on. I kept the secret to myself.

I made arrangements with Flt.Lt. Bill Billing (my Flight Commander) and his wife, Peggy, to go to their house so that I could change for the party. I thus turned up with my 'kit', and with my moustache freshly shaved off. I put on my PT shorts over my underpants but with the legs tucked into them, and a PT shirt inside which two rolled-up pairs of socks were suitably attached, ankle socks and gym shoes. Over this I donned my 'dress', borrowed lipstick and rouge were added, and I thus became a 'Polythene Bag' (Greek prostitute).

Left: Peggy Billing with Colin & Irene Hanmore. Right, Bill Billing and Dorothy Hogg.

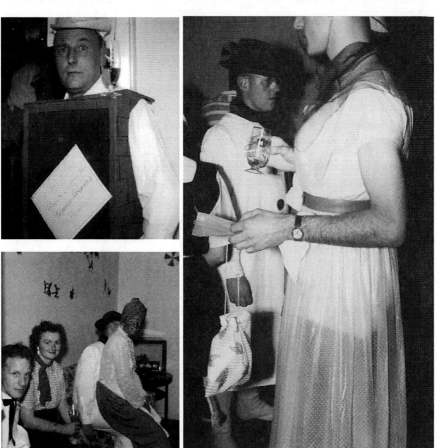

Upper left: Roy Bertram. Lower left: Fg.Off. & Mrs Taylor with Irene Hanmore sitting on David Hattersley's knee. Right: David Hattersley with a nearly headless Greek prostitute.

When we were ready, the three of us left Bill's house together, but by this time word had gone round the married patch and everyone else who lived there was already waiting outside the Hanmores. They watched all us partygoers arrive from various directions. We were jeered, cheered, politely cat-called and wolf-whistled at as we appeared. We created more jollity that night than we ever anticipated. As the party went on I became hotter and hotter in my unventilated plastic covering. The lipstick came off and the rouge disappeared in the perspiration.

Everyone had a wonderful time until well after 2 am when the party ended. After changing back at Bill and Peggy's, and drinking a cup of hot coffee, I staggered back to camp to get to bed at about three.

Sunday mornings, unless I was on watch, were always very relaxed. Breakfast was available until 10.00 after which Walter Huldt, our ancient German waiter, closed the dining-room. As often as not I, and maybe Fg.Off. George Rapley, Fg.Off. Mike Grant, Plt.Off. Clive Sabel, and sometimes one or two others, would congregate for an informal chat in the batwomen's ironing room upstairs over the front door. In this way we caught up with village and other events whilst practising and improving each other's languages. Little hunchbacked Frau Höhn, tall thin Elspeth, Frau Rust, and comely Margot, depending on who was on duty, would chat away to us while they got on with the ironing, shoe cleaning, or whatever. We heard all sorts of gossip from the village and were kept well up to date with local affairs. Our relationships with our batwomen were very informal but respectful, yet the work was always done and few, if any of us, ever had cause for complaint. They looked after us well. Frau Höhn tried to mother us. If someone had been out with a girl, and she knew of it, she used proudly to say, with a twinkle in her eye, "Wissen Sie, Mutti weis alles!" Which, loosely translated, was "You know, Mummy knows everything!" – a fact that no-one could dispute. Margot left to become bachelor Wg.Cdr. Kilmartin's housemaid when he moved into his CO's house on the married patch. Her place was taken by a Fräulein who eventually married Sgt. Rogers (previously of the cinema volunteers) and afterwards lived in married quarters.

About once a month, a visiting Church of England or Nonconformist Padre would call. There was no Chapel on camp so they both had an arrangement with the incumbent of the Lutherkirche to use his Church. The Roman Catholics were better served for they used the baroque village Church. Attendance rates of any of the faiths was fairly poor. I sometimes went to the Lutherkirche but have to admit that it was not all that often; certainly not as often as I went to the C of E Chapel at Jever.

The 'Gymnasium' (college) on the town walls of Warburg, our nearest shopping town. Battle of Britain Fighter Ace Douglas Bader was interned in a prisoner of war camp not far away in open country. It was a little distance to the left side of the road back to Borgentreich, close to Dössel. In the late 1950s the camp was occupied by displaced persons and was still clearly recognisable as an old POW camp. I passed it many times.

It was the time of Rock and Roll. I listened to it on my new Philips Philetta radio in my room. The Airmen, however, went one better. It all started with a couple of lads bringing guitars back with them on returning from leave. Others followed, and skiffle groups were quickly formed with drums improvised from buckets and dust bins. Rehearsals took place in the concrete-floored loft space above the barrack blocks. Then there was inter-barrack rivalry. Each block had its own band and, with practice, became very proficient. In the erstwhile silence of a Borgentreich evening, it was possible to hear the latest Rock and Roll and other tunes being competently rendered until lights out, or the Orderly Sergeant decided that enough was enough. One of these bands actually played, by invitation, in the village hall during one of the local festivals.

Whenever there was the option to have a Rock'n'Roll film shown in the cinema I would always choose it. Such shows were always well attended, none more so than when I was able to show 'Rock Around the Clock'.

A local German chap saw the opportunity to make a few Deutsch-marks by hiring out a juke box to the NAAFI. His idea came to naught because some enterprising Erk discovered that if he nudged the machine in a certain way at a precise moment at the end of a record, the machine would play it again at no charge. After a month the German came to collect his takings and found that the cash holder was almost empty. Two more months passed before he removed the machine.

Our 'new' Mess offered many benefits. The BFES teachers, Barbara Fisher, Dorothy Hogg, Miss Moth, and Betty Hargreaves all had rooms of their own downstairs. There was a ladies sitting-room too so that they could relax or entertain female guests in private. The bar (my responsibility), anteroom, and dining-room were much enlarged and we now had a snooker room. Our quality of life improved markedly. The number of Officers also increased, both living-in and married. This was in line with the new manning requirements brought about by crea-tion of 210 SU. Shortly after this, even more Officers arrived when the old tech site was taken over by 757 Signals Unit, a GEE station.[2] The Mess then became busier and life was not as settled or as friendly as it had previously been.

---

2   757 SU was a forward transmitting station for the GEE navigation chain. GEE = an aid to precision navigation and bombing.

39. Local Life

BORGENTREICH AND ITS SURROUNDING villages were truly rural in character. There was no industry except that derived from the land. It was inevitable that, living in an RAF camp in such a location, I had the opportunity to observe a very austere, almost medieval, way of life.

Strip farming was the norm for most people, there being very few integral areas of land under single ownership. The strips were scattered and one farmer may have three or four such narrow strips of arable land in different locations. The countryside was open, with no hedges and little protection from wind. Except in the small forests and villages there were few trees. Most roads, however, were tree-lined to provide shade and protection for horse traffic. The number of cars was minimal.

The local soil was rich loess which, given added manure, was very productive. In season, I have seen farmers spreading basic slag by hand – an extremely arduous and filthy task.[1] Both liquid manure and the more solid variety – often containing human waste (distinctive by its smell) – was spread by horse-drawn slurry barrels and discharged from a tap at the rear, or by open cart and hand-spread with forks.

Ploughing was done using a pair of yoked oxen, or two horses if the farmer was wealthy enough. I have also seen a horse and a milch cow hitched together pulling a laden, wooden, taper-sided, open cart. I think the worst situation I ever witnessed was an old farmer guiding a plough while his entire family, small children and all, pulled it up and down their little strip of land.

Corn was usually sown by hand and was harvested with sickles and scythes in Biblical fashion. Beet, mangelwurzels, and kale were

---

1   Basic slag, used as a fertiliser, is an extremely heavy and dirty by-product of iron smelting.

hand-sown in drills. From my window in the Mess I have watched women, mostly in long black clothes and white or grey headscarves, spending days on end doing this backbreaking task. Later, when the seedlings were big enough, they were thinned, some being transplanted to fill any gaps in the rows. This was done on hands and knees. Periodically, I saw the same women going up and down these rows pulling out the weeds. The distress these people suffered when heavy rain washed away the soil, or strong dry winds blew it about as dust, is almost unimaginable.

Hay, cut with sickles and scythes from roadside verges and land which was too steep to till, was carted and stored in lofts running along the entire length of the farmhouse buildings. The beet, also harvested by hand, was carted home and tipped down chutes into the cellars of the same buildings. The animals were kept in byres adjacent to the living accommodation. Poultry, including flocks of aggressive geese, were similarly housed. In this way both animals and humans, with their shared warmth under a top lagging of hay, were kept protected from the extremes of winter.

I was invited into one such house for a cup of coffee, the farmer and his wife, Herr und Frau Konze having previously been invited to a Guest Night in our Mess. I was ushered into the kitchen (there was no other downstairs room that I saw), and invited to sit on a hard upright chair at a bare wooden, scrubbed-top table. There were no easy chairs. There were dressers and cupboards round the walls, and ornaments and papers on shelves. A bare electric lamp hung from the centre of the ceiling and another lamp was on a dresser. A new radio stood alongside a vase of dried flowers on a windowsill. The room was heated by an enclosed, tiled stove, its chimney pipe disappearing into the ceiling, presumably to warm a bedroom above reached by stairs rising from the corner of the room. A small pile of wood stood by the stove. The floor was bare, apart from a mat near the door. Stark as it was by our standards, this was home to the Konze family. As to their washing, toilet, or cooking facilities, I have no idea.

Nearby, around a corner not far from the Konze farm, was a burned-out building which had been a shop long ago. This building was the sole obvious relic of the war. It had never been cleared away and rebuilt because its owner had been a member of the Gestapo. No one wanted anything to do with him (if he was still alive), his family, or his derelict property.

Tractors were to be seen in and about the village, and they were mostly horizontal-engined, single-cylinder, diesel-powered Unimogs. My understanding of the situation was that few farmers could afford to own one, and that they were owned and shared on a communal basis. The same was true of other farm machinery, although I cannot ever remember seeing a threshing machine. Occasionally, I watched as tractors and implements arrived at the village hall, there, presumably, to be reallocated, for I saw different farmers driving them away afterwards.

At certain times of the year, calves, young horses, lambs, and other animals, were taken to the undercroft of the Rathaus for inoculation, or maybe sale.[2] It was in this building, as well as the Burgomeister, that Obermeister Knoll, the local policeman, had his office.[3] He was a short, plump, individual always dressed in his pale green uniform, with leather belt, holster, high leather boots, and peaked cap. He supervised village life. He had a respect for the RAF and, for my part, I had a respect for him.

There were a number of Fachwerk houses.[4] These were survivors of pre-war days, and many had the neatest gardens I have ever seen, each totally weed-free and any bare soil neatly raked with almost unbelievable precision. Newer, post-war, houses were bare brick with walls, sometimes only one brick thick, tied in with concrete ring beams at ceiling level. These houses later had an outer layer of brick or cladding added as soon as the occupants could afford it. They had an unattractive look.

Roads were a mixture of pavé or tarmac, but sometimes little more than compacted loose chippings. Pavements in the village were marked out but not necessarily surfaced. At intervals paving stones and bricks were piled along the sidewalks so that individual householders, themselves, could surface those areas immediately outside their properties.

The people of Borgentreich, though mostly poor, were determined to make the best of what they had, and to help each other. They viewed the RAF as a useful source of additional income and were very tolerant of us. We brought trade to their shops and spent money in their inns.

---

2   Rathaus = town hall. A well-built stone building. Now an organ museum.

3   Burgomeister = local mayor.

4   Fachwerk = Frame houses rather like Tudor houses in England but with brown woodwork and buff infill.

Some newly arrived married Junior Officers even took rooms in those inns while they waited their turn for married quarters. The RAF, for its part, also employed, under the auspices of Herr Niemeyer, our RAF German supervisor, several local people and contractors.[5] Such, to an extent, was our interdependence.

---

5   Herr Niemeyer was a short, thin, wizened, busybody of an individual who spoke reasonable English but whose false teeth were prone to dropping when he did so.

40. Out And About

I N THE SPRING OF 1956, once the snow and ice had cleared, I went to a shop in the village and ordered a bicycle. They didn't have any in stock, but were agents for a manufacturer. I therefore chose a suitable model from a catalogue and paid a cash deposit. The excitement this order caused was surprising. I found later that this was the most expensive order they had handled since setting up in business.

My new bicycle gave me freedom to explore the local countryside, and freedom to visit friends in married quarters without a long walk. I had a degree of independence without the expense and hassle of buying and running a second-hand car. I could get away from camp and put work and the working environment behind me for an hour or two.

I cycled to the Desenberg and climbed it to explore the castle ruins at its summit and to admire the view of the countryside. I travelled along tree-shaded roads to Lütgeneder, Peckelsheim, Eissen, Körbecke, Daseburg, Dinkelburg, and Dalhausen. Many of these roads had crosses or crucifixes at their side, in wood, iron, or stone, to mark the spot where some poor individual had met an untimely end in a traffic accident. Speeding cars and roadside trees don't mix.

I got to know the local countryside very well and was able to organise a car Treasure Hunt one weekend for members of the Mess. I found all the clues and arranged the route purely as a result of my cycling expeditions. I put the clues to verse or disguised them so as to give reason for thought, rather than just a straight drive round the route. I was assured that all who took part had an enjoyable afternoon. I couldn't go myself so had to wait patiently for everyone to return with their answer sheets. Ray and Daphne Street were the winners.

Dalhausen fascinated me and I visited it many times. It was a village with an industry. Situated on a very minor tributary of the river Weser, it nestled in a valley with the stream running alongside the road to Beverungen. There was a railway station, a veneer works and, more interesting from my point of view, it was a centre for the weaving of willow baskets. Over the period of almost a year I took my movie camera there to film the various stages of basket making: the growing osiers, the cutting of them, their soaking in bunches in the stream at the roadside, the stripping of the bark, the trimming, and finally the weaving. When exploring the osier beds there were times when I couldn't film because of the attentions of the horse-flies which wouldn't let me alone. Otherwise I filmed in detail and, in so doing, got to know many of the villagers, at least by sight. Usually I dropped in to a Konditorei for coffee before cycling back to camp. I never finished the film because my stay at Borgentreich was cut short before I had completed the final sequences.

Sam Weller, our Adjutant, lived in the Mess and, like Plt.Off. Clive Sabel, who also lived-in, enjoyed walking. Both would set off, quite independently, on their long hikes at Saturday lunchtimes to reappear tired and weary on a Sunday evening. Sam told of the time when he stayed at a farm and was kept awake most of the night because of the sounds of scraping and clanking chains. On investigating next morning, he found that on the other side of his bedroom wall a big, rather restless, bull was chained up! Then there was an occasion when I was weekend Orderly Officer and I got a phone call, in German, from miles away. Clive Sabel had walked nearly 30 miles, to close to the East German frontier where, in growing darkness, he was looking for an inn at which to spend the night. The man on the phone was a member of the Grenzschutzpolizei (Border Police) who had arrested him because he looked suspicious! It took some words of explanation from me to explain that I knew who he was and that he was probably lost, and could they please help find him a bed for the night. Speaking German on the phone was never my forte, but somehow I managed to rescue Clive from his predicament. He took a while to live it down after he returned the following evening. Clive was noted for carrying a small haversack whenever he went out, even for a short stroll. Someone became curious as to what was in it and decided to investigate, and checked more than once. The contents were nothing more than either an apple or an orange and an English dictionary!

It was not too unusual to go out for an evening meal instead of staying in the Mess. Several of us, in someone's car, would drive to a favoured restaurant, very often the 'Zum Grünen Baum' in Beverungen, there to enjoy a glass of Pils or share a bottle of Hock. One of our favoured foods was a good fluffy omelette stuffed, according to season, with either Steinpils, Pfifferlingen, or ham.[1] Wiener Schnitzel and juicy Rumpsteak were other favourites. The omelettes were huge, but we always had room for some sort of delicious Torte and cream. It made a change from Mess food.

While at Borgentreich our leave allocation was altered. It had previously been two periods of three weeks of UK leave for which travel was paid, and 10 days Continental leave which could be spent anywhere but travel was at our own expense. Continental leave ceased as an entitlement. Not many of us ever took it; I certainly never did, but all of us missed the option of it now it had gone. It was almost in frustration that three of us, Flt.Lt. Phil Philpot, Fg.Off. Slim Rose, and I decided to have a weekend away. Using Phil's car we went to a Gasthof at Hardehausen, on the edge of a forest where wild deer and wild boar could be seen. Karl Schrader, our Mess Clerk, arranged for us to stay in the

The 'Gasthof zur Egge' at Hardehausen where we stayed.

'Gasthof zur Egge' not far from where he lived.

We spent two nights in Hardehausen, and the Frau who ran the hotel (it was little more than a pub with several bedrooms to let) did so with a rod of iron. Meal times were strict; food was put on the table at the due time whether you were there or not, and stayed there until you came and ate it. The rooms were adequately furnished with very

---

1 These were varieties of fungus which grew in the forest and were very tasty.

heavy furniture but a little austere. The beds were comfortable, of the shake-up variety, with huge feather-filled bedding of the type we had seen everywhere airing out of upstairs windows on fine sunny days. None of us ever thought we would ever sleep in such beds, but we all admitted that they were very warm and comfortable. The upstairs toilets were a little strange, for when any of us went to use them we usually had to shut the doors of other cubicles because, more often than not, at least

Left to right: Myself, Phil Philpot, and Slim Rose.

one, if not two of the three, would be occupied by a woman, sitting there with knickers round her knee caps. For ourselves, we were much more careful.

We rose early on the Sunday morning for a walk in the forest to try and see some deer. We had been told the previous afternoon where the best place was to go, and where there was a good deer hide. We took cameras with us. We found the hide, a tall structure on stilts, climbed the ladder, and sat and waited. Our patience was soon rewarded and we watched, fascinated, as many deer came out into a clearing to graze. As the light grew stronger and the sun came out they disappeared into the trees. On our way back for breakfast we stumbled upon a dead wild boar. Then, a very aggressive live one came into sight

The deer hide.

and charged at us. Never have three fellows climbed three trees so fast! This swine kept grunting and squealing at each of our trees in turn. We were kept very uncomfortably aloft for at least half an hour until the aggressive porker made off. On returning to the Gasthof we reported the matter. Later in the morning after breakfast we went back into the

The dead wild boar.

forest with the local Forstmeister to show him the dead pig.[2] For reasons we could not have foreseen it was a memorable weekend.

There was one Saturday afternoon that two of us were walking through Borgentreich and, on rounding a corner, could hardly believe our eyes. There, ahead of us, was one of our Sergeants (a very Irish Sergeant) sat, bareback, and very drunkenly, atop a large grey bridled mare – the horse's rightful owner tagging along behind. Sergeant Trigg was shouting orders to his mount in what we could only describe as vernacular Erse while heading it towards the front door of Lappe's bar.[3] On nearing the door he was last seen by us

Karl, Ursula & son Thomas Schrader outside their home in the old Hardehausen monastery.

2   Forstmeister = head woodsman (literally 'forest master').

3   Lappe's had another name but was known to us only by the innkeeper's name. It was Out of Bounds to Officers.

trying to get the horse to mount the steps. At that point, we decided to use discretion and withdraw around the corner from whence we had come. No doubt the matter resolved itself and was surely better for us not having been seen.

There were times when I had to go out and about on duty. As Officer i/c Armoury I had responsibility not only for the weaponry at Borgentreich, but also for the small armoury store at RAF Scharfoldendorf, home of 646 Signals Unit, to our north-east. I had to make six-monthly visits to this outpost to retrieve its weapons and replace them with newly serviced ones. The journey involved a pleasant drive in a Borgward truck along a winding road by the banks of the Weser, through Höxter and Holzminden, and on through beautiful forests to our hilltop destination. Scharfoldendorf did not look like any normal RAF camp. It was a small Unit which blended well into the countryside and occupied buildings identical to those in the surrounding area. The Officers Mess, where I usually had lunch, had been a Gasthaus and was often mistaken as such by German tourists. The business aspects of the trip were usually handled by the Station Adjutant and involved logging the quantity and serial numbers of the weapons exchanged. Apart from this, the visit was largely social and a good day out. At the time I never asked the purpose of the Unit, but by its blending into the surrounding scene, I suspected that it was some kind of monitoring establishment.[4]

In May of 1956 I was sent on a midweek liaison visit to RAF Celle. My job was to discuss fighter control matters with the Squadron pilots. This didn't take all that long and I had time to spare. Using the transport I had been given, I took time out to visit the very pretty town and went as far as the gates of Bergen-Belsen, that horrendous concentration camp. I have to admit that the racks of funerary urns, the gates, and the railway line, filled me with mixed feelings of total horror and deep sympathy for those families who had lost loved ones or were entirely wiped out by disease and starvation in that awful place.

Another official journey I had to make in autumn time, was to deliver and fetch new cypher materials from Group HQ at Wahn. Three of us made the journey, a Corporal Service Policeman, an SAC driver, and myself. Our transport was a Volkswagen beetle. I had the locked leather bag containing the cypher material chained and locked to my wrist and,

---

4   It was much later that I was told that it was a 'Y' station: a listening post for eavesdropping on Eastern Bloc transmissions.

if we stopped for a toilet or refreshment break, I was to be escorted by the SP. Our route was clearly defined, with nominated Services establishments at which I could seek help should anything go amiss. We all wore holsters with Smith & Wesson revolvers and six rounds of ammunition. It was serious stuff.

We set off immediately after lunch and made very good progress. We arrived in the area of the Ruhr in good time and navigated our way along an Autobahn, as briefed, and soon found ourselves driving in a dirty sort of mist. The nearer the Rhine we got, the thicker the mist became until it was dense fog. By this time the SAC was getting tired. We had a break, and I took the wheel. Speed dropped to a crawl. With windows open and all eyes trying to see where we were and read the road signs, I suddenly found myself driving with nothing ahead but with streams of slow moving traffic coming towards us on both sides! It was now dark and the headlights of the oncoming traffic illuminated the fog so as to make forward vision all but impossible. Panic was welling in me, but I was sure I was on the right road. What had happened was that I was at one of the sometimes very complicated Autobahn interchanges. Thankfully, a confirmatory sign loomed out of the fog. Speed was down to 10 miles an hour and still there was a distance to go. The route we had been given was straightforward and clearly described so we pressed on, our eyes out on stalks like snail's. To divert to some other unfamiliar Unit down side roads which we couldn't see was not an option. One of us noticed that there were, unusually, no other military vehicles in the traffic (we had seen many up until then). Eventually, and very late, we reached our destination. We checked in at the Guardroom. I summoned the Orderly Officer who, in turn, summoned the Duty Officer who, after signing a receipt, relieved me of my bag, and arranged for our weapons to be stored safely overnight. He then told me that all military movements had been banned for some hours because of the fog, and that there had been some concern as to our whereabouts and safety. The traffic Polizei had been alerted to look out for us, but in that pea-souper had little chance of finding us unless we had broken down. The fog didn't lift until very late the following morning. It was only then that we were permitted to depart. Our return journey took half the time.

In late summer of 1957 I heard that RAF Fassberg was due to close. I also was told that there was furniture available for collection. It wasn't on any inventory as it had been captured from the Luftwaffe. Not one to miss an official trip off camp, and in need of a break from watch-keeping, I sought permission to go and see what was available for the benefit of Borgentreich. So it was that I drove to Fassberg in a Magirus Deutz truck. Sure there was furniture, so I filled the truck with what I thought suitable. I stayed overnight. Again, as when I was at Jever, I occupied Hermann Göring's old room – and his ghost still didn't appear. During conversation that evening I met the Station Armaments Officer who had the task of disposing of all munitions. I happened to mention aviation pyrotechnics and his eyes lit up. "Have you got any?" I asked. "Do you want to take them off my hands?" he offered. I had November the 5th in mind and asked for all that would be suitable for such an occasion.[5] Next morning I drove round to the Armoury where I was met by a Sergeant who helped me find space for several boxes of pyros and Verey cartridges on my already laden truck. No signatures were needed. I set off back to Borgentreich rather pleased with my haul.

I shall finish this tale by saying that the furniture found good homes throughout the camp and, come November 5th, two volunteers and myself, all wearing tin hats, put on a firework display fit for sore eyes. We let off, to a sort of ad hoc programme, dozens of flares, Verey cartridges of all colours, parachute flares, thunderflashes, and rockets. All at no expense. Afterwards there was a huge bonfire and roast potatoes and other food laid on for everyone who cared to attend – all ranks and families.

Late in 1957 there was a tragic fire at a farmhouse in the village. On hearing of this our RAF Fire Section turned out to attend. They arrived before the local volunteer Feuerwehr could get itself organised. The RAF, as was usual practice, went to search the house for anyone who may be trapped but the Burgomeister forbade them from entering, possibly doubting their motives. Minutes passed before the majority of the Feuerwehr turned up with their equipment, by which time the RAF had its hoses deployed and in action, but only from the street. The German Fire Chief turned up and just watched. He did absolutely nothing until someone brought him his fireman's hat, at which point he started to use his authority and give orders. Only then did his

---

5   All firearms and ammunition had to be returned through Stores channels, but these pyros were close to the end of their storage life and, as such, were not returnable and would have had to be set off to dispose of them anyway.

firemen attempt to enter the building which, by this time, was engulfed in flames. Owing to this delay, and the prevention of the RAF from entering the building, the farmer's wife perished, trapped in an upstairs room.

At Borgentreich we were all very much aware of the German tradition of Christmas. Snow always came early, usually before Advent, and lay thick on the ground. All houses had Advent Wreaths (Adventskräntze) on their front doors, often with a single candle burning in the centre, in the cold, still, evening air. There were shrines on the approaches to the village, each with a candle or lamp burning within, and carefully decorated on the outside.

The festive season was marked with much religious (Roman Catholic) celebration. Regardless of how cruel the weather, the Priest, carrying a crucifix, and his choir, could be seen at Christmastide in their surplices (over thick clothing) singing and holding services at each of the candle-lit shrines placed where each road entered the village. To see and hear them, their lanterns hanging on crozier-like staffs, hymn books in hand, loudly singing 'Heilige Nacht' and 'Adeste Fideles' ('Holy Night' and 'Come all ye faithful'), their steaming breath rising in the crisp air, snowflakes falling the while, is something which impressed me greatly. They visited and sang at all the significant houses in the village, crunch-ing in the snow as they made their way in temperatures a long way below freezing, some dropping off for a few minutes into a local Kneipe for a Bier and a warming Schnapps. It was the prettiest of pictures – deep snow on the roofs and under foot, no traffic, lights glowing in the windows of the brown and ochre timberwork medieval houses, and through the windows, the sight of a Christmas tree with white burning candles could often be glimpsed. They never had coloured lights on the Christmas trees, only white ones. They didn't use coloured paper deco-rations in their houses, only greenery, and those who could afford them would adorn the greenery with coloured baubles from Czechoslovakia. Any villagers I met always greeted me with "Grüss Gott" or "Fröhliche Weinachten" ("God greets you", or "Happy Christmas"). If there was a gap in the weather, the moonlight and bright starlight contributed greatly to the beauty of such evenings.

Borgentreich Church was a sight to see; I remember it being candle-lit and with someone playing Bach on its baroque organ. Even as Prot-estants we were always welcome. In those days, not ten years after the war, the farmers and many villagers were still very, very, poor. They were grateful for any money we could spend with them. We invited many of them into our Mess around Christmas time and they were always very appreciative. These things I shall never forget.

41. Auenhausen

WHEN I RETURNED FROM the ABC Course at Winterbourne Gunner in December 1956 I found that all the 537 SU radar equipment had been dismantled and was parked, as a convoy of vehicles, along the roads of the domestic site.[1] Never again did I visit the site from which it had come. This old tech site was later, in mid-1957, to be occupied by 757 Signals Unit, a mobile GEE station, the personnel of which were based with us. Other than getting to know the Officers, and it being entered on the defence plan, I had nothing to do with this Unit.

My Unit was now 210 SU and our tech site was in an R3 reinforced concrete bunker deep underground, a short distance to the north-west

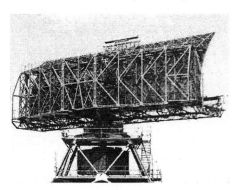

of the small hamlet of Auenhausen, itself some miles to the north of Borgentreich along narrow country lanes, about 20 minutes drive away.[2]

This new site was equipped with a Type 80 search and control radar mounted on a fixed 25 feet high gantry. There were also several Type 13

The rear of the rotating head of a Type 80 radar.

---

1   It was some months later that this was driven away to be relocated at RAF Sylt for use as air-air firing range surveillance radar.

2   R3 was the designation of the type of bunker. It was similar to several bunkers built in the UK when the whole air defence radar system was updated to counter the Russian Cold War threat of the 1950s. The building of these bunkers was coincident with both organisational and communication improvements, and the introduction of vastly superior radar. This was termed the ROTOR plan in the UK, but BOOKLET in Germany.

'nodding horrors', but these were mounted on 10 feet high concrete plinths rather than on trailers.[3]

Power came from three power stations, one of which was within what was now called the radar garden, within the site perimeter. The other two were at remote locations, each about two miles distant, and connected by ring main to a sub-station at the inner end of the sloping entrance corridor to the bunker. These power stations were equipped with heavy MAN diesel engines direct-coupled to large alternators. The previous 24 hour mobility standing order to which 537 SU had to adhere could clearly no longer apply. It was therefore for the potential destruction of these generators, and the denial of other equipment in the event of invasion, that I had been instructed in demolition, and held a stock of plastic explosive and detonators in the Armoury.

Outside the main gate was a turning area for vehicles where the lane had been widened. Entrance to the site was via a Guardroom housed in an innocuous German-looking building situated almost at the road-side. All personnel had to prove their identity to the SPs on duty before entering this building. Access to the bunker was from the back of, but within, the Guardroom, down several flights of stairs leading to the sloping entrance corridor. In this corridor were shoe racks where all personnel, except SNCOs and Officers, took off their outside footwear and changed into plimsolls. Also in this area was a vertical ladder rising to a surface manhole atop a narrow shaft where cabling rose to the surface. Beyond were several dog-leg, blast protection, turns to nego-tiate before entering through heavy steel blast doors into the corridor running the length of the upper floor of the bunker proper. At each end of this corridor was a stair well leading to the lower floor. At the far end of this same corridor was another set of blast doors, through which were two enormous air intake fans drawing fresh air down a vertical 20 feet square shaft, which also served as an emergency escape route. This shaft ended in a louvered building on the surface. Exhaust air left the bunker via the usual access tunnel (this gave it a smell not dissimilar to that of a London Underground station). The square ventilating shaft had, rising within it, a series of iron stairs and platforms which gave access to security doors at the surface. These had to be checked during the night watch when the Duty Watch Officer had the opportunity. Whenever

---

3   I am uncertain as to whether there were four or five Type 13s.

it was my turn, it was a blessed relief to go up this shaft on an early summer morning and briefly see the sun rise. On one such occasion someone down below extinguished the lights and I had to grope my way down in the blackness and past the fans, where there were several awkward concrete steps, to find the handles of the blast doors so that I could get back into the bunker. It was my duty, also, to climb the narrow cable-shaft ladder to ensure that the ground-level manhole was still properly secured.

The bunker could be sealed, and the air conditioned and recirculated in the event of a chemical or biological threat or attack. The plant rooms capable of doing this were along the right side of the corridor, as well as toilets, crew rest rooms, a small canteen/kitchen, and an emergency lighting accumulator room. On the other side of this upper corridor were the C & R surveillance room, control cabins, training room, Chief Controller's cabin, and other necessary offices.

The lower floor had a similar corridor but, in my time, many of the facilities available (air raid warning, civil defence, Army liaison, Ack-Ack control, and other communications facilities) were not used, even under exercise conditions. Those that were in regular use were, the GPO/Deutsche Telefon equipment room, the radar office, the radar workshop, and store rooms.[4] Most important though, with access from this floor, was the Operations well.

The well extended the full height of the bunker and was surrounded on most of three sides by the windows of the various command cabins. The Chief Controller's cabin was centrally situated on the upper floor from which place he overlooked the Tote on the far wall.[5] In front of this was the General Situations Map table and the smaller Fighter table, both of which were manned by plotters. Behind, almost against the back wall, was the Tote which stretched from floor to ceiling. On this was displayed, for viewing through the tilted internal windows of the control positions, the whole air picture as far as 210 SU was concerned. This included the tracks and altitude of relevant aircraft, airfield states, readiness states, Duty Squadrons, serviceability, call-signs,

---

4   The GPO = General Post Office (telephones) wired the bunker under contract, but the German telephone service provided all the landlines. The radar office was where the radar signals were processed for distribution to the PPIs and other equipments throughout the bunker. The radar workshop was part of this facility.

5   The Tote was named after the familiar runners and riders display commonly seen at racecourses. It was similarly slatted but was far more complicated.

radio frequencies, weather information, and much else (including the cricket score!). The Chief Controller, the Operations Officer, and others were thus able to see all the available information. It was updated continuously.

The Tote operators worked from galleries behind the Tote, from which they could change the display. In the corner behind the Tote was a small table at which a volunteer signwriter sat when altering or making new indicator boards. There always seemed to be a good sign-writer available among the Airmen even though this post was not on the Establishment.

The Chief Controller, as well as having the full radar picture on a console in his cabin, had, via his switchboard (usually manned by his Ops 'B') contact with the rest rooms and all cabins and facilities throughout the bunker, as well as the domestic site switchboard. He had direct lines to neighbouring radar stations at Rothwesten (USAF), Brockzetel (near Jever), and Üdem (near Goch on the Dutch border), and, of course, to Group HQ. The communication system was designed so that almost any facility within the bunker could be 'patched' through to almost any other, or to Group and elsewhere. The site operated in the 'Zulu' time zone and all colour clocks displayed this.

Each of the four fighter control cabins had two separate sets of radar displays, comprising PPIs and height displays, so that two control teams could operate in each, giving a maximum capacity of eight control positions on the site. Each cabin crew (one per controller) was in the charge of an NCO who monitored the activities of: the Craig computer/plotting board operator, the height finder, the log-keeper who recorded all transmissions between the Fighter Controller and the aircraft in abbreviated longhand, and the controller's assistant. The latter sat at his own screen alongside the cabin switchboard, radio channel selector, and squawk box connected to the Chief Controller. All the cabin crew, save usually for the NCO in charge and the fighter plotter, were connected by the same audio network and wore head and breast sets with single earpieces. The Fighter Controller spoke to the aircraft via a snake's head microphone and transmit switch on his Type 64 control console. There was also, during exceptionally busy periods, a supernumerary Airman who could take over any of the tasks when relief was required. On each PPI was superimposed an electrically lit video map showing all places within radar range, as heretofore described when discussing the mobile operating cabins of 537 SU, but at Auenhausen the range and coverage were far greater.

The top (desk section) of an old and very dilapidated Type 64 PPI display console. This one survives in the RAF Air Defence Radar Museum at Neatishead.

As can be gathered from the foregoing, there was a mass of electrical wiring connecting all aspects of power supply, radio and radar signals, and communications. This wiring was carried in underfloor ducts throughout the bunker. The floors all had varnished wooden removable panels for access to a deep mezzanine area through which the wiring was laid. Air-conditioning and cooling trunking was mostly placed overhead. The heat from the equipment racks could be considerable as each contained access drawers full of thermionic valves. If the chillers and air-conditioning failed, as it did once in my experience, as much equipment as possible had to be shut down to prevent too great a build-up of heat and stagnant air. Fortunately, in this one instance, the problem lasted only about half an hour. In that short time the heat and stuffiness became almost unbearable even though all but a dozen or so essential personnel were evacuated from the bunker.

As can be understood, this facility took many more people to run than were needed by the old 537 SU. It was at this time, therefore, that the new buildings on the domestic site were being finished and occupied as additional personnel were posted in.

The site had to be kept secure and, to this end, as Station Defence Officer, I had to issue the SPs in the tech site Guardroom with weapons.

Accordingly, each duty SP was issued with a Sten gun and a full magazine of ammunition, both to be kept separate, but close at hand, and signed for in a register at watch change-over. After a while the SPs tended to become lax about their responsibilities regarding these weapons. On one occasion, when coming off watch I found an unattended Sten gun so, with full authority as Armament Officer, I openly removed it and took it away with me to the Armoury on the domestic site. I awaited developments, but an hour passed before the loss was reported. The responsible SP was duly charged and brought before the Station Commander (whom I had informed of my actions as soon I had returned the weapon to the Armoury) and was severely punished. The SPs were more careful with their weapons after that. The point here is that it could have been snatched by anyone coming in off the road and used to threaten the SPs and cause them to hand over their other weapons, thus leaving the tech site open to an aggressor. We could not be too careful and never had to forget that a Russian tank, provided it could cross the Weser, might only take about an hour to get to us from the border.

42. Tech Site Travel

ON ACCOUNT OF THE increased number of 210 SU personnel on watch, we had to use transport, other than the usual Magirus Deutz trucks, to get to work at the tech site. In this piece I shall describe some of the incidents which took place en route.

Our journey was via normal narrow roads rather than the rutted track of old. There were two favoured routes. Both left Borgentreich by route 241. One of these took the first lane left to Natzungen, on through a stretch of forest to Frohnhausen, and then to Auenhausen and the tech site. The other took the slightly longer route by continuing a little further along the 241 before turning left to Borgholz, then to Natingen, then Auenhausen and the tech site. Both routes were hilly. For day watches, we Officers usually travelled by Volkswagen Kombi, with one of us driving there, and another driving back. But when it came to evening and night watches, it was more usual for the entire watch to travel in a Ford Köln bus. Travel, at times, was not without its interest.

Coming off watch one dark evening after a night flying stint, I was driving the Kombi and was overtaken by a speeding Mercedes car, its headlights blazing. Some distance ahead, maybe a mile or more further on, on a tree-lined stretch of road I saw lights ahead shining nearly vertically. Slowing to investigate, that same car had hit a big roadside apple tree on a corner and was now pointing up it, in a crumpled state, but with lights still on. Stopping, I went to investigate, and on forcing open the door the very dead driver fell out almost on to me. He stank of alcohol. At this, those who were travelling with me decided that it was better to leave things as they were, for there was nothing we could do other than cover the body with some coats from the back of the crumpled Mercedes (we were unable to extinguish its lights) and press on to Borgentreich. There, I got in touch with Obermeister Knoll and told him what we had found. The car was still there next morning but the body had gone. At lunch time when we passed the spot again, the car had gone. We heard nothing more. Later a roadside memorial cross was erected at the spot.

On another occasion, when returning at night with the evening watch in the bus, our driver hit and killed a young deer which ran out in front of him from the forest. Not knowing what to do, because there was no one around to tell at that time of night I, the only Officer present, made the decision to load the animal into the bus and take it back to the Airmens cookhouse as 'loot'. I was summoned to the CO's office next day and had to offer an explanation because, he said, a forester claimed that he had seen the RAF lift the deer from the road and remove it. Someone had told Obermeister Knoll and he had contacted the CO. I was given a smiling admonition for my attempt at enhancing the Airmens menu, and advised to keep out of sight of the Borgentreich policeman for a few days until the matter blew over. In the meantime the carcass was returned to whomsoever came to collect it.

I was involved with Obermeister Knoll again later in the summer. This time I was again driving the Kombi to the afternoon watch and making my way through Auenhausen village when, down a steep side-road, a child on a bicycle came hurtling towards me. I did an emergency stop, nearly throwing the other Officers out of their seats. I was stationary when the child hit. His body dented the front of the vehicle to the extent that the bulge nearly came in as far as my shins. We all jumped out fearing the worst, but the child got up and started crying. What a relief! His old, brakeless, bicycle was completely wrecked. Dazed, he started to wander off. Then one of the locals came over, said they had seen what had happened, and took the boy away. Somewhat shaken, I drove the dented vehicle to the tech site, and phoned our Station Adjutant (now Flt.Lt. Cunningham) at the domestic site, who reported the matter to Herr Knoll. To give the policeman his due, the next time he saw me in the village he was eager to tell me that the lad was OK and that, when he got home, he was given a good "Schinken cloppen" (bottom smacking) by his father who was no less a person than the Burgomeister of Auenhausen!¹

There was the time when, as a bus passenger, I saw, at a small building site, a workman climb an electricity pole with what looked like a pair of jump leads in his hand. He connected one to an overhead wire, but when he touched the other there was an enormous blue flash and he dropped to the ground. Within seconds he was on his feet and was dusting himself down having connected his equipment to the mains!

While mentioning travelling by our Ford Köln bus, which had a V8 engine, in the heat of high summer the engine frequently spluttered or failed due to fuel starvation because the petrol vapourised in the fuel line before it got to the carburettor. To circumvent this it was usual practice, although highly dangerous, for the driver to remove the engine cowling and to feed neat petrol from a Coca Cola bottle direct into the carburettor. Fortunately this practice was limited only to the hottest days on the steepest hills en route and no harm ever came of it, except possibly to the engine.

On another journey, this time to morning watch, and in winter, our driver was making his way cautiously on the treacherously slippery packed snow covering the roads when we came upon a farmer's wagon loaded with milk churns abandoned in the middle of the lane. It was totally blocking our progress on a downhill stretch. Tyre tracks showed that the farmer had abandoned his attempt to pull the wagon up the hill by tractor, and had used a gateway to turn round and pass the wagon, with the tractor wheels almost overhanging the edge of the ditch on one side. Our driver tried reversing, but the hill was too steep under those conditions. Flt.Lt. Colin Hanmore was on the bus and i/c watch so, with no alternative, and in order to get to the tech site on time, he ordered the whole watch off the bus and told everyone to manhandle the wagon down the hill and into a gateway over a ditch (there were ditches on both sides) and thus out of the way so that we could pass. It goes, almost without saying that we failed miserably. The wagon was too heavy to hold once the farmer's wheel-chocks were removed and it ran away from us, our feet sliding on the icy surface as we tried to hold

---

1   Schinken = ham (literally). Cloppen is self-descriptive. No serious mechanical damage was done to the vehicle save for a huge dent in the front. As was usual in such circumstances I had a number of forms to complete. Fortunately the passenger sitting alongside me was Flt.Lt. Billing, my Flight Commander, so I couldn't have wished for a better witness.

it, some of us falling over. It accelerated away and quickly moved to one side before turning turtle in a ditch, milk spilling from the churns and flowing downhill. We did get on watch on time – just.[2]

Farm tractors could be hazardous in themselves, especially the Unimog single-cylinder variety. These would bounce up and down on their tyres if left on slow tick-over. Sometimes this bouncing was sufficient to actually move the vehicle, bounce by bounce, when on a slope. There was one occasion when such a tractor was parked in a field gateway on a slope leading at right-angles to the road along which I was driving. This tractor bounced itself on to a patch of mud and promptly slithered into my path, causing me to swerve violently to miss it.

In the early winter before the Christmas of 1957, I was on night watch and was waiting for the relief crew to arrive and take over in the morning when, instead, I received a phone call from Sqn.Ldr. Ellison, the Ops Officer, who was still on the domestic site, to tell me to hang on and stay on watch because the road was totally blocked with snow at Frohnhausen. There, it went through a defile which had filled level to a depth of over 10 feet. The alternative routes were also impassable. In the event, with a very tired crew we were able to keep the tech site running until relief finally got through some 26 hours later. The bad weather, fortunately for all of us, also prevented any flying so I did not have to man a control cabin solo without anyone but a scratch crew. Group was informed and apparently put great pressure on the Station Commander to get a full watch on duty as soon as possible. He did his best, as did the RAF snow plough and snow-blow drivers. We kept the radar working and a surveillance watch was maintained continuously throughout this period. We also, out of curiosity periodically phoned, or I sent someone up to, the Guardroom to find out what the weather was doing. The SPs were not normally given access down into the bunker, but in these circumstances I had to arrange for each one of them, in turn, to come below for a break, while one of the radar watchkeepers did a stint as his replacement for an hour or two.

On travelling back, having been eventually relieved by a new watch, we went through several places where the snow had drifted many feet deep and where our lads had cut their way through it with their equipment. In areas sheltered from the wind, the telegraph wires were

2   I believe that the farmer was compensated for the loss of the milk.

stretched and sagged low with the weight of snow on them, and tree branches had broken off. The normally very timid wild deer were openly foraging close to the villages.

It had been quite a storm. Fortunately for us the high, constantly rotating, search radar antenna had kept itself sufficiently clear of snow for us still to get good signals. If the Eastern Bloc had got up to any tricks, even in those conditions, we would still have seen them.

Once back in the Mess, I was extremely pleased to get a hot meal and go to bed after, like the rest of my crew, surviving on hot drinks and biscuits until supplies ran out.

43. Personal Problems

BEFORE I GO ON to describe my activities on watch I must tell of certain things which, with others, were to have a considerable cumulative effect on me and ultimately, shortened my RAF career.

I still suffered from migraine fairly frequently. Strangely, staring at a radar tube, the trace rotating as it did, four times a minute, and contrary to some people's predictions, had no adverse effect on me. Increases in my radar activities were certainly not paralleled by any increase in the frequency of my migraine headaches. Fortunately for me, most Chief Controllers had an understanding of my problem and would leave me alone if I was suffering an attack while on watch. This was true for both 537 SU and, later, 210 SU. If I had problems in the bunker I would, on occasion, retreat into the dark and comparative quiet of the standby battery room and sit there until the worst had passed, or until the end of the watch. The attacks, as far as I could tell, were entirely random but I have to say that I never had one when I was Duty Watch Officer on night surveillance duties. I suffered from migraine, and I had to live with it.

In mid April 1957 I was on night surveillance watches for a week. On returning to the domestic site just before midnight on Wednesday the 17th, and on entering the Mess, I was met by Plt.Off. Clive Sabel who was Orderly Officer that day. He said "Pod, I've got something very important to tell you, can we discuss it in your room?" On going upstairs and closing my door he said "Look, this is serious, please sit down". Clive then went on to tell me that, earlier that evening, he had received a signal from Air Ministry to say that I was to go home immediately on compassionate grounds. I was stunned and puzzled. He then told me that my father was dangerously ill in the War Memorial

Hospital in Wrexham, that I was to leave Borgentreich at once, and that I had better start packing up some kit ready for the journey. He told me that there was a meal waiting for me in the Airmens Mess and that I must leave as soon as I had eaten. Not quite taking in all of this, and while beginning to get some kit together at the same time, he informed me that all travel arrangements had been made while I was completing my watch. He gave me a large envelope containing my travel documents and authorisations. He also said that if I needed to be away for more than a week I was to contact an office in the Air Ministry.

Within minutes I had packed a bag with clothes for a week and was on my way to the Airmens Mess where I was met by the duty cook and served my meal. As I was finishing it an MT driver came and said that he had a Volkswagen waiting outside for me, and that he was taking me to Frankfurt airport. The time was now nearly 01.00 hours. Later in that journey, as dawn broke and I could see to read, I opened the envelope and found that I was to go to the Lufthansa desk.

After some difficulty finding the airport, and after having taken turns at the wheel, we eventually arrived. My driver dropped me off and, on contacting Lufthansa I found that I had a seat on the early morning plane to Heathrow. I had the ridiculous thought that a German pilot would be flying me – was he safe – had he been bombing my home on Merseyside? Anyway, I took my seat on the plane and dozed off as I had had little more than three hours sleep in the last 24.

At Heathrow I was met by a taxi driver bearing a card with my name on it. He took me to Paddington station. I gave him a tip but there was no fare to pay. At Paddington I showed a Travel Warrant and was issued with a ticket to Wrexham General station on the old Great Western Railway line. I lunched in the dining-car.

All the time I was travelling I was worrying as to what was wrong with my father. I came to the conclusion, wrongly as it turned out, that he must have met with some sort of accident; maybe he had crashed his car because I knew that he would drive when under the influence of drink, he thinking that his reactions were made sharper after imbibing a whisky or three.

At Wrexham I was met by another taxi and taken to the hospital. There, I was shown to the private wing and met Sister Edwards and my mother. My father lay in bed, heavily sedated and with tubes stuck into him in several places. At least he was still alive.

My father, due to his excesses, had had stomach problems which had turned rapidly into peritonitis. His condition was critical, so much so that mother and I slept in the hospital for three nights before moving to the Wynnstay Hotel after the 'crisis' was over.

Mr John Spalding was the Surgeon in charge and he suggested that I stay in the UK for at least a fortnight. Accordingly, I contacted the Air Ministry and arranged to take that year's leave allocation to give me time to sort matters out concerning the family business. As it turned out, this was a serious error because, although I could not have foreseen it at the time, the lack of any leave later in the year was to have its consequences.

My time was spent either at my father's bedside or travelling to Birkenhead with my mother (I had no UK driving licence) to attend to matters at the family engineering business. I must explain that we had two homes at that time. One was at Upton on the Wirral peninsula, near Birkenhead. The other was at Welshampton in Shropshire, and it was at the latter that my father had been taken ill. My time was thus spent between these two houses. Mother was a Director of the business. I was not, so could only advise, although my appearances (occasionally deliberately in uniform) in the workshop let the work-force know that there was supervision, even though the 'Chief' was ill. Fortunately for us all, we had a very reliable foreman and a superbly competent office manageress. They, between them, took over the day to day running. In the midst of this I was still dealing with my own migraine attacks. It was a stressful time. My father, meanwhile, still thought that I could take off my uniform, leave the RAF there and then, and stay at home. He was most voluble about it.

I have to admit that it was almost a relief, after I knew that my father was going to recover, albeit with a colostomy, to get back to Germany and start watchkeeping duties again. Had things turned out differently, during my discussions with the Air Ministry I was told that there was a possibility that I could have been granted a compassionate posting to RAF Hack Green, another GCI radar site some 11 or 12 miles from Welshampton, but an awkward distance from the business in Birkenhead. Had this happened I would have had to take an almost immediate UK driving test.

My father, after a long illness, eventually made a full recovery and his colostomy was reversed.

44. Down The Hole On Fighter Control

WE SOON NICKNAMED OUR brand new R3 bunker 'the hole'. It was a more friendly, less formal, name for it, or so we thought. After working in it for a while, the rumour went round that some of our number had grown an increased amount of body hair on their backs arising from our new troglodytic lifestyle!

The coverage of the new Type 80 search radar was vastly superior to the old Types 14 and 15. The performance of our new Type 13 height finding radars, with which we were already familiar, remained the same, but we were now able to use their full range and height potential. These radars complemented each other very well.

The new radar picture, as displayed on the PPIs, was far clearer, and the paints were sharper, with more precise definition. We were now able to pick out individual aircraft flying in loose formation. The range was far superior, to the point that we could see, at 50,000 feet (the assumed maximum combat altitude), in a clockwise direction from the north, well into Denmark, some of the Baltic Sea, just past Stettin across the Polish border, round to well past Prague into Czechoslovakia, just to the Austrian and Swiss borders with Germany, over Basel including the Black Forest, and continuing round to cover eastern France, almost the whole of Belgium, and all of Holland. We could off-centre and adjust our view of any of this area so as to look at any one part in much closer definition. It was claimed that, at higher altitude, the coverage extended over the UK coast and as far as Warsaw to the east but we, at Auenhausen, had no way of proving it. Our coverage at lower altitudes was, as ever, limited by our straight line radar horizon over the curving surface of the earth.

In mentioning the radar horizon, there were rare times, usually early in a morning, that we experienced what we called 'anoprop' or, to give it its proper title, anomalous propagation. This was caused by a temperature inversion in the lower atmosphere. It effectively split our radar beam so that a part of it hugged the surface of the earth. In these conditions it was possible to see, many miles away, such things as radio masts and tall buildings. On several occasions I was able to identify the wireless masts on the north German coast and the tower of Jever Schloss, the locations of all of which I knew well. When this happened I would normally tell the Senior Technical Officer of the watch so that, if necessary, he could micro-adjust the position of the video-map display on our PPIs. It was unusual for anoprop to last long, maybe only an hour or so.

We could see cloud and heavy precipitation as on almost all centimetric radars, but we now had ECM equipment which could reduce this interference and enable us to see aircraft through it.[1] Our Permanent Echoes (reflections from local high ground and nearby fixed edifices) were, because of our higher position, much less in area than at the old tech site. We also had the advantage of more effective IFF equipment. This enabled us quickly to identify any aircraft allocated to us for control or other purposes.

It took a while for us to acclimatise to our new working environment and equipment. Although the fighter control task remained entirely unchanged it was now made much easier. With eight potential control positions, and our increased radar coverage, the number of aircraft allocated to us for PIs and other activities increased enormously.

We had a training room wherein were two synthetic interception trainers. These machines enabled us to track real-time radar plots and to control a synthetic paint as if it was a fighter intercepting the real-time plot. Before going 'live' I had two such sessions. On the first I selected a target whose speed was calculated to be 500 knots and generated an artificial 'fighter' pulse with a speed of 550 knots with which I carried out two 90° quarter attacks. The second training session was a week later when, selecting real and 'artificial' aircraft, both of lower speeds, I concluded 6 successful attacks and aborted another because the 'live' target disappeared. This session was under the supervision of Flt.Lt. Billing, my Flight Commander.

---

1   ECM = Electronic Counter Measures. This, in effect, was sophisticated anti-jamming equipment which enabled us to counter both interference and potentially hostile jamming of various sorts.

My first real use of our new radar (other than playing with it for training purposes) was the next day, Thursday, January 17th, 1957, when I was allocated a pair of Hunters on a freelance sortie. I had them under control for 26 minutes at an altitude of 40,000 feet and, using 90° quarter attacks, intercepted a USAF F86F Sabre and a pair of Canadian F86s. Such a mission would never have been possible using the equipment on the old site. Four days later, I was allocated another pair of freelance Hunters with which I was able to intercept two other pairs of unsuspecting Hunters, whose pilots could not have been keeping a good look out because they didn't break away to 'mix it' with mine. My pilots had been looking forward to a good old dog-fight but were disappointed.

I was in Fighter Controllers' Utopia. This was what fighter control was really all about, and it would have been the same in wartime. To be given fighters with which to 'bounce' any other (hopefully) unsuspecting aircraft, was a thrill and very satisfying for all concerned.

Then came the boring bit; pairs of comparatively slow Meteor NF11s for my next four sessions before the end of the month. These were night PIs. The first, an hour-long session, which included six PIs, of which one was a successful, very tight parallel head-on attack. This was a new technique to practise both for me, the pilots, and the radar navigator of the attacking aircraft. With a head-on closing speed of near 1,000 knots it took some guts and no small amount of skill to pull it off. In the next session of an hour and four minutes, seven 90° quarter attacks were successfully completed before the aircraft returned to Ahlhorn. The last two sessions were not as good. The aircraft suffered Bent Weapons and the aircraft R/T was pretty duff.

In February I completed no less than 50 PIs, of which only one was aborted because, during a practice head-on PI, I turned the attacking aircraft on to the target just a second or so too late. This was the only 'Controller Error' to be recorded in my Log Book since qualifying. With the amount of practice and experience I had now accumulated, I could, without any pause for thought, come up with the reciprocal bearing of any 5° angle on the compass rose, even when under the strain of extreme concentration. This quickened my R/T responses and increased my efficiency as a controller. I also found that I could, in extreme circumstances, control two independent pairs of aircraft doing separate sets of PIs at the same time. In these instances R/T transmissions were longer because almost every call had to be preceded by the appropriate aircraft call-sign.

It was an interesting month. There was a mix of PIs, five sessions with NF11s at heights varying from 4,000 to 35,000 feet, with 9 parallel head-on attacks and 14 ordinary quarter attacks. There was another session, also with Meteor NF11s, during 'Exercise Skittle' when I had five aircraft under control for an hour and five minutes on patrol duties only. In the middle of the month, for the first time, I controlled a Swift, the pilot of which intercepted a Hunter and a USAF B45 bomber.[2] All the other sessions were with Hunters. All were either during specific exercises or freelance. To sum these up: apart from intercepting other Hunters, they successfully intercepted 4 Belgian Meteors, 2 Dutch Meteors, 4 F86 Sabres, and 4 Canberras. Two sessions involved handovers to and from 'A' Flight controllers, at the end and start of watches.

A remarkable thing about controlling Hunters was that I suspected that I was, on occasion, controlling some of my own old 93 Squadron pilots. One of them confirmed this by calling "Papa Oscar Delta, do you read me?" My nickname. I acknowledged "Papa Oscar Delta reading you loud and clear." From that day on there were several non-standard, but brief, R/T messages between me and my old pals. Knowing that the Russians monitored all our calls, as we monitored theirs at Scharfoldendorf and other locations, I wondered what interpretation they put on this unique Papa Oscar Delta call-sign.

If I thought February was busy, March was even busier. With eight controllers on a watch (say seven on average, allowing for leave and other duties), and I had 24 sessions, then there is a probability that some 150 sessions were completed by 'B' Flight alone. Including the activities of 'A' Flight in this estimate, there may have been 300 sessions comprising possibly, some 1000 PIs in all for the Auenhausen GCI. The equivalent maximum for 537 SU would, using information from the previous November, with four active controllers per flight, have worked out at something like 120 sessions and 450 PIs. Clearly, our combined workload had more than doubled. No longer did we have watches of total boredom hoping for aircraft to be allocated to us.

Of the 82 PIs I controlled during March, 6 were aborted. Of these, one target went below our radar horizon, 3 targets turned away at the

---

2   The B45 was also called the Tornado. There were less than 150 built, so this was quite a rare catch.

last moment when I was setting up freelance attacks, 1 NF11 had a Bent Weapon, and the last was when one of the Hunters under control had u/s R/T. The shortest session, just 11 minutes, ended when I handed over control to the Brockzetel GCI, No.101 Signals Unit.

As far as targets went, my aircraft intercepted 4 F84s, 1 Meteor Mk 8, and 1 F84F Thunderjet in a single sortie; 2 NF11s and two Hunters in one sortie; a pair of NF11s, a B45 Tornado and then 3 PIs in another sortie (the best session of the month) using 2 NF11s at night; then 4 Venoms, a formation of 4 Hunters, another 4 Venoms, and then another 4 Venoms, all in one sortie with a formation of three Venoms under control; 2 B57s (USAF Canberras), with 3 Venoms; 1 Vampire T11 and a formation of 4 F84s, with 4 Hunters; then 2 sorties when 4 Hunters under my control intercepted 2 other pairs of Hunters.

On March 22nd, during the early part of an evening watch when on a week of night watches I, with 2 Hunters, at heights varying from 12,000 to 37,000 feet intercepted a formation of 3 Hunters, 2 single Hunters, and a Viscount airliner. That must have given its passengers a thrill! In the final days of the month, 4 Sabres intercepted 3 separate F84s; 3 Hunters then 'bounced' a formation of 6 other Hunters I had found for them; and finally, at 45,000 feet I had under control 4 Hunters which intercepted a pair of Canberras.

From these seemingly dry Log Book entries it is apparent, from the types of targets intercepted, that I took some of our fighters over the American Zone of Germany. There was nothing that our fighter pilots liked better than to 'bounce' a few unsuspecting Yanks. They treated it as good sport and were pleased to let the USAF know that, for all their American blah, the RAF frequently bettered them. This love/hate of Americans was evidenced in the Station Cinema when American war films were shown. These, as a matter of course, were referred to mockingly as "How the Americans won the war" films, and during which cat-calling was the norm.

March was noteworthy for something else. On the twelfth, in the brightness of a completely clear afternoon (as verified with the Guardroom), we were observing responses which we called 'Angels'. We had seen them at times before and passed them off as some sort of electrical interference, but on this occasion there were a lot of them. Each of these paints was separated by about a mile in azimuth, and they varied in altitude between 3,000 and 7,000 feet. We could also easily pick them up on our Type 13 height finders, so that ruled out electrical interference on the Type 80 or the PPIs. Fascinatingly, these paints were travelling east-west into the prevailing breeze. Suspicions aroused, our Chief Controller checked with Brockzetel, and Üdem, our other main RAF GCIs. Both had seen migrating cranes at times, but nothing like we were describing. The Chief then checked with the USAF at Roth-westen – nothing there either. Concerned at the persistence of these paints, and their apparent origin in the Russian Zone, after discussions with Group, a formation of three Venoms was allocated and I was given the job of using them for investigation. They saw nothing. They were fed up with orbiting around in a comparatively small airspace at slow speed and differing heights, and straining their eyes for the invisible. In the meantime, the Chief sent other controllers to stare at the sky to see if they could see anything with their Mark One eyeballs. Nothing. I gave the Venoms Pigeons to Base and thanked them for their trouble. This phenomenon recurred from time to time, and we just passed it off as more Angels. As far as we were concerned it was harmless and posed no threat. I was told not to put any entry in my Log Book about that specific sortie, but I remember the circumstances well.

This was a time when new controllers were on probation under training. I had several sessions with them in the Training Room, and supervised and advised them while they were doing synthetic intercep-tions. This training continued for some months and was a feature of my watchkeeping activities, to the point that I was not actually controlling aircraft myself.

The first week of April was spent on nights, thereafter I was actively involved with fighter control on only three days, the 9th, 11th, and 12th. Then I was on nights again from the 13th, but this was the week of nights interrupted by my being called away on compassionate leave as already described.

I only controlled Hunters this month, three sessions of which were occupied with another Exercise Guest. Aircraft intercepted were, a Canberra (the fighters got close enough to report that its number was WE169), 4 more Canberras, several other Hunters, 4 Belgian Air Force Meteors, and a Meteor 7. In spite of the problems of jamming as a result of the Exercise, the interceptions went ahead without diffi-culty except in areas where there were cloud responses as well. In these, I had to resort to the use of the chinagraph pencil and do a bit of dead-reckoning. I lost one Canberra target as a result and couldn't conclude the interception. All sorties were between 3,000 and 35,000 feet, an unusually wide height range.

In May I was only 'on the scope' during the period 9th to 17th, from after my return from compassionate leave until the start of another week of nights. During those nine days doing my 'proper' job I did 12 sessions controlling NF11s, Hunters, and Venoms. The only targets of note were a formation of 6 Sabres during Exercise Argus, and then a formation of two Canadian T33 Shooting Stars some days later. One session, during another Exercise Guest, with a pair of Hunters at 45,000 feet was totally without any targets within their area. A most unusual circumstance.

Then came a period of concentrated work on training and attending to pressing work in the Armoury, organising live-firing practices at Sennelager, Station Defence matters, and a stint as Orderly Officer.

While attending to defence matters I took a Gamma Ray detector to Auenhausen at the behest of Sqn.Ldr. Monk, the Chief Technical Officer, as he wasn't sure what sort of radiation emanated from his high power transmission equipment. On touring the equipment racks the Geiger counter started clicking, even before we got close. The levels were not high, but high enough to give us some concern. When he opened the doors to some of the equipment the counter went berserk. The mercury rectifier was one of those items, but there were others. The levels reduced with the doors shut. As a result of this visit all significant equipments had radiation hazard labels affixed to them and he altered the maintenance procedures accordingly. We had previously known of the power of the Type 80 when, one evening back in January the head inadvertently stopped so that it faced the centre of Auenhausen village. It was noticed, by chance, that its transmissions were powerful enough actually to light up any unlit fluorescent lights in the buildings. Fascinated by this, the NCO in charge inched the head round to prove the point. After this it was always parked facing west, and not aligned with any nearby habitation.

There was also a visit by a group of Americans from their GCI Station at Rothwesten, with which I was involved. The tables were turned on them for, when we had visited them 17 months earlier we were envious of their radar equipment. This time they were extremely envious of ours. We showed them round the bunker and they saw all our control facilities as well as watching and listening to fighters under our control from one of our cabins. They were impressed, too, with the cleanliness and neatness of all our facilities, and particularly so when we took the Officers into what they termed our "Lounge" which was, to us, only our rest room down in the hole. We also, above ground, showed them the Type 80 radar head and allowed them to climb the gantry and ride in the rotating transmitter room below the reflector. In there, one of them inadvertently pressed an emergency stop button so when we came to step out, the head had stopped, much to the concern of all as it was facing the village. After their visit to the tech site we took our guests back for lunch in the appropriate Messes at Borgentreich before bidding them farewell.

From my controller's standpoint June was a poor month. I was on nights for the second week, and then I only had four control sessions; the first on the 17th, the other three on the 25th. I had three pairs of NF11s on PI missions, and a formation of three Hunters freelancing. Papa Oscar Delta led them to intercept a pair of NF11s and a T33 Shooting Star. Of the NF11s under control, one of these pairs, while doing five PIs transited from Wahn, their departure point, to Ahlhorn. On two of the missions the R/T was very poor, poor enough in one instance to require a channel change.

July was a far better month. Most of the aircraft I had under control were Meteor NF11s; 11 sessions with them. The others were two separate Canberras, a pair of Hunters, a pair of CF100 Canucks of the RCAF, and two sections of 4 Canadian F86s doing PIs together.

On July 16th I was extremely fed-up. My Log Book records that I did 3 PIs with a pair of NF11s and "Video map display intermittent, AI dubious, R/T horrible, radar needed imagination". Later the same day, with another pair of NF11s: "2 x 90° runs. R/T p.p![3] Heavy background howl." The next entry for the day, with another pair of NF11s reads "2 x 90° runs. Everything good but type 80 goes off for servicing – I can't win!" Clearly, the 16th was not one of my best days.

The first July Canberra sortie was for radar calibration purposes. It was under my control for 43 minutes at 45,000 feet under very cloudy conditions.

---

3   p.p. = piss poor! I must have been thoroughly disenchanted to put that in my Log Book.

With the Canadian Canucks I completed 8 'scissors' interceptions. This was a technique, favoured by the Canadians, for getting the maximum number of PIs done in a single sortie. Eight in this case. The second Canberra sortie was most unusual, it was under my control as if it was a fighter. Under conditions of poor R/T, involving a channel change, and poor radar, it intercepted a single NF11. I reckon the Meteor pilot must have had quite a surprise. During this month I also had a session during which I was instructing a u/t controller.

August was a comparatively busy month, even though it included another week of night watches. Hunters, F86s, NF11s, Canucks, and Venoms were allocated to me for a variety of tasks including PIs, scissors PIs, freelance work and, new to me, a range monitoring session. This involved my monitoring the aircraft doing ciné attacks on a towed drogue target at a practice air-air range newly set up at Ahlhorn. Two of the NF11s previously mentioned were Danish. The pilots spoke perfect English and were no trouble. Four good PIs were completed with them.

Sometimes I was allocated Belgian aircraft. Belgian pilots were reluctant to speak English, the standard NATO language, except during an actual interception. Otherwise they went off into what, to me, was utterly incomprehensible gobbledy-gook. It was neither Dutch nor French, both of which I could recognise. It was their own dialect, said by some to be Walloon. Many were the times when I had to interrupt their gabble and tell them to "Keep the R/T standard". This they would obey – until after the next interception.

Exercise Counterpunch was held in September. For this I was temporarily posted to the GCI at Üdem. I shall briefly describe this detachment in the next chapter. Otherwise, during the month, apart from a week of nights, I only had three control sessions. One was a daytime radar calibration sortie with a Canberra. The others were with single freelance NF11s. The first intercepted two Canberras at 36,000 feet, and the second intercepted a pair of CF100 Canucks and a single NF11, both at 25,000 feet. Both these sorties were at night. My Log Book records that further control activities were precluded because of an Exercise Stand Down until the end of the month, although night watches were not affected.

It was during this autumn that, one weekend when I was Orderly Officer, I had an unusual experience. I had a few minutes to spare before I was due to meet the Orderly Sergeant and Orderly Corporal in the late afternoon before going to inspect the Airmen's tea, so I walked from the Officers Mess, a short distance up on to the sports field for a moment's breath of fresh air after having been indoors for a while. Standing there, I heard the sound of an approaching jet aircraft. This was unusual for two reasons. The first was that the RAF, although on standby, did not normally fly at weekends and, secondly, the RAF had never been seen to overfly us since I had been at Borgentreich, it being too far into the south-east of the British Zone. The sound was getting louder and approaching from the south. Suddenly it appeared below a fairly low cloud base. It was a twin engined jet. It approached from over the old tech site where 757 SU's GEE Unit was now established, to over my head at no more than 1,000 feet. It was Russian. I could clearly see the red stars on it. It was an Ilyushin 'Beagle' light bomber. Dumbfounded, I watched it disappear towards Auenhausen. I ran to the Mess and phoned the tech site to tell them to see if they could see it. Then, out of sheer frustration and absolute annoyance at this blatant border violation, I phoned the CO in his married quarter. When I told him what I had seen he said "Well, Pod, what do you expect me to do – get my bloody peashooter out?" I could have throttled the man! With hindsight, that Beagle had probably been a photo-reconnaissance version and almost certainly would have followed a track over Rothwesten, Borgentreich and its tech sites, and very probably Scharfoldendorf, before heading back east at low level in the one border incursion.

October was busier even though I was spending time supervising u/t controllers. Two of my own ten sessions were in the evenings when I was officially on night watches. I only controlled RCAF Canucks and RAF NF11s with, unusually, no Hunters. The month saw the longest control session I ever had. It was on the night of the 16th when I was allocated a pair of CF100s for PIs. I had them under control at 35,000 feet for an hour and seven minutes, and completed three 90° scissors and four head-on interceptions, the last two of which were aborted because of u/s AI. R/T conditions were difficult with questionable airborne radios transmitting and receiving at only strength 1.[4]

Earlier, on the 11th, with another pair of CF100s I had a very busy session. In just 52 minutes they completed 4 x 90°, 1 parallel head-on, and 2 scissors PIs as well as intercepting an RAF Javelin and two other

---

4   R/T transmission and reception signal strengths were graded from 5 (best) to 1 (poorest workable).

CF100s at 35,000 feet, and this when the radar was poor due to the coverage being split because of anoprop.

Javelins had just come into RAF service. I intercepted a pair of them with an NF11 in daytime, the only day session, later in the month.

From my own personal control standpoint, both November and December were poor months. I was only on the scope for nine sessions and did only 29 PIs in the entire period, and three of these were aborted. All December sessions were in the evenings when I was on surveillance watch.

Embarrassingly, one of these aborted PIs was when my own performance was being assessed and monitored by a Categorisation Board examiner, Flt.Lt. Archer, who had been one of my instructors at Middle Wallop. This was on Monday, November the 4th, following a week of nights. With him breathing down my neck I had two Canadian CF100s under control at 35,000 feet for an hour and six minutes in poor radar conditions. I messed up one of the PIs because the attacking pilot turned late onto the heading I had given him, and I failed to give him sufficient correction. The result was a tail chase. My score was 73%. I knew I could have done better.

The last Practice Interception of my Fighter Control career was on December 12th. It was a parallel head-on PI with two Canadian CF100 Canucks at 30,000 feet at night.

I have to emphasise that, whilst my control activities were very limited in some months I was, at the same time, when on watch, monitoring and supervising the activities of u/t controllers both 'live' in the cabins, and on the simulators in the Training Room. I also stood in, maybe only for a few minutes at a time, as Chief Controller while the Chief himself took a short break. I also maintained the leave chart for the watch and did the duty rosters. I have to add, regrettably, that there were watches when I suffered from migraine and was incapable of any control activities. Watchkeeping was also interrupted when I did my turns as Orderly Officer and attended a Court Martial as an Officer Under Instruction. Similarly, there were times, through pressure of work in the Armoury and its related training sessions, when these took temporary precedence over watchkeeping. I was busy also with the Mess bar and the Cinema. I valued my time off – when I could get it.

I needed a break as I was getting very tired, but my annual leave allocation had all been used up by the compassionate leave I had taken earlier in the year. During a routine medical examination the MO, Flt. Lt. Martin Clarke (in civilian life a gynaecologist from Bournemouth), suggested I take a break, but that was impossible. No-one had the power to authorise it.

On December the 18th I was promoted to Flight Lieutenant, but I didn't know it at the time. The information took a while to get to Borgentreich, by which time other things had happened.

45. Üdem Detachment

ÜDEM, NEAR GOCH, WAS the home of 348 SU, another GCI Unit, and situated close to the Dutch border. I was there from the 16th to the 23rd of September during Exercise Counterpunch and never personally got to control any aircraft the whole time! It had facilities similar to those at Auenhausen and was being used as an international centre for this major NATO exercise. The bunker became quite crowded and we were tactfully advised that we should perform certain aspects of our ablutions before going on watch, lest we might overload the sewage system.

Our accommodation was in standard NATO two storey barrack blocks. It was the first time I had slept in a barrack room since I was a Cadet at Kirton-in-Lindsey and it seemed strange to be in one again. In our room were two French Officers, some Dutch and some Belgian Officers, along with the RAF, about 14 of us in all. We English, Dutch, and Belgians got on very well together. The French, in their fancy embroidered kepis, stuck to their own language, would not mix, held themselves aloof and looked down their large Gallic noses while doing precisely nothing useful during the whole time they were there. Worse, one of them was a sleepwalker who woke most of us up at least twice during our stay. On one of his somnambulations he walked down the room, penis in hand, and headed straight for my bed. Not wanting a shower of that sort, I leapt up and steered him out of the door. Where he got to I don't know. His bed was still empty in the morning.

Üdem was a mixed Unit. It had a normal complement of WRAFs and, for the exercise, a small number of Volunteer Reserve WRAF Fighter Control Officers were drafted in as part of their summer camp obligations. One of the reasons I did not officially control aircraft myself was because, as an experienced controller, I was given the task of supervising two of these ladies when they were allocated aircraft. One, I remember well, was a Flight Officer in her late 30s.[1] When she was allocated a pair of fighters I had to sit by her in the control cabin. She was very nervous, and told me so. I first identified and took over the aircraft while she watched. They were two NFIIs. Our call-sign was 'Bedmate'. Handing control over to her, as was usual she called "(aircraft call-sign) this is Bedmate how do you read me?" The reply came loud and clear "Strength five darling, I hope I don't suffer a Bent Weapon". I grabbed the microphone and replied sternly "This is Bedmate, keep the R/T standard". The poor lady couldn't cope. The mixed cabin crew were in stitches, and it took me a moment or two to restore order. I then gave the aircraft a course to steer to keep them occupied. I turned to the lady and, because the safety of aircraft was involved, stressed to her that Bedmate was only a call-sign, and she had better ignore its meaning for the purpose of fighter control. Steeling herself, she continued the session and concluded several very satisfactory PIs with almost no guidance from me.

While I was at Üdem there was an Asian 'flu pandemic. The Station MO realised that if anyone succumbed and was working in the crowded environment underground, the 'flu would spread quickly, to the point that the operational efficiency might be severely compromised and, when the exercise was over and we all returned to our bases, we stood a good chance of carrying the virus there, with similar potential consequences. To this end he had everyone on the camp – domestic and tech sites – take two large tablets the size of small marbles, three times each day.

WRAFs were given supplies of these to administer to us and took a great delight in going round all the Officers, one at a time, to give us our medicine. Whether they were placebos or not is of no consequence, for none of us caught the 'flu.

At Üdem I met a Belgian Fighter Controller who spoke perfect English. Chatting, as all service personnel do, I quickly discovered that he had had a reputation as a saboteur with the Belgian resistance during the last war. Some of the tales he told about derailing ammunition trains during the Allied advance through France were almost unbelievable. Another Belgian verified his stories. He was a brave man

---

1   Flight Officer = nowadays a Flight Lieutenant.

who, because of his clandestine anti-German activities, always kept one bullet in whatever weapon he was carrying – just for himself if capture appeared inevitable.

For part of the exercise I was involved with surveillance and plot reporting and analysis. This was an interesting facet of air defence and, apart from during training at Middle Wallop, I had never done it before.

My over-riding impression of my work at Üdem is that I did nothing, yet I was occupied working at something or other the whole time. There did seem to be too many bodies in the bunker and I wondered whether we were all needed, and whether the Unit would have run more efficiently with less of us. Maybe this was one of the lessons learned from the exercise.

46. Down The Hole On Surveillance

AT NO TIME, TO my knowledge, was there any break in night surveillance work, not even when the changeover from 537 SU to 210 SU took place. Neither can I remember any instance, when I was in charge of a surveillance watch, when the radar was, even temporarily, taken off the air through malfunction or for maintenance. Occasionally, though, a technician would, during his routine rounds, find a valve that had gone 'soft' in one of the consoles or equipment racks. In this case he would seek permission to take that particular PPI or Height Display out of service for the few minutes it took him to replace the valve. In these rare instances the aircraft plotter or operator would temporarily move to another console, his work otherwise uninterrupted. Even during normal day watches our surveillance work continued and was interrupted only during periods of routine maintenance.

I was responsible for maintaining the 'B' Flight watchkeeping roster, so can positively state that, subject to leave and other commitments, night watches came round every five weeks or so. Controllers who were still under training were not qualified for night watchkeeping duties. Also, sickness could have its effects on the frequency of one's watches. On checking the gaps in my Log Book, it appears that during 1957, I did maybe eleven such watches, with two in October.

There was only one instance when I was alone on nights that I was allocated fighters. I shall describe the episode fully a little later on. However, when on nights, and doing the evening watch, it was often the case that a full (day) watch would also be present when there was night flying control work.[1] If there was enough trade for us, then I

---

1   In this case the day watch on night flying duty in the evening would already have done the morning watch.

could be allocated fighters and do a session or two. All these sessions have already been mentioned in a previous chapter, only a few of which were recorded in my Log Book as 'surveillance control'.

Most evening and night watches were boring in the extreme. Even when things became frenetic, as they sometimes did, we had orders not to write anything down other than in the plotter's logs, and to say nothing to anyone who did not need to know. Discussion of such events, within hearing range of those who didn't already know, was strictly taboo.

It is for this reason that I am wholly reliant on my memory for what I am about to relate in the rest of this piece; some events, therefore may be recorded in the wrong order, but I hope at least to give an overall impression of night watch work and tell of some of the, as far as I am aware, unrecorded happenings in which I was involved. I shall not describe events on a watch by watch basis.

As did any Officer i/c night watch I had complete responsibility for the whole tech site during my watch. All personnel had their orders. The radar technicians and the Service Police in the Guardroom all knew what to do without any special attention from me. Only if there was an unusual technical problem did the NCO i/c the Radar Office bother me, or me him. I had my security checks to do, as already described, otherwise my attentions could be almost entirely devoted to the surveillance crew who were usually about a dozen in number. As a watch crew, we were responsible to 83 Group for passing plots to them of all aircraft and any other phenomena observed during the watch. Watches were organised so that all watchkeepers (except me) had rest periods. No-one could stare at a PPI or other display the whole time.

The surveillance crew worked in the C & R room, to the left of the bunker upper corridor. The remainder of the bunker, save for the rest rooms, toilets, and the Radar Office, was not used at night, although it was kept fully operational. Nothing was switched off. Apart from the sound of the air conditioning and the dull electric hum from the equipment cabinets and their cooling fans, all was eerily silent in the areas not in use.

During night watches it was difficult to maintain concentration watching a radar screen, its trace rotating four times a minute, for much more than an hour without one's eyes becoming glazed. Most Watch Officers had their own ways of dealing with this. Some, quite wrongly, had a kip in the rest room and relied on an NCO to wake them up if any unusual paints appeared. This was, of course, not the official way to behave, and it certainly didn't set a good example.

As at the old tech site, I encouraged the Airmen to write letters, darn their socks, read a paper, or whatever, provided they also kept an eye on the PPIs and, (this was important) whatever they were doing could be instantly dropped, literally, when the need arose. Some lads brought knitting or other handiwork. Fortunately, down in the bunker there were no white-tailed flies to bother us, only the rare gremlin which sometimes crept into the equipment.

For myself, I was able to sit in a corner of the dim C & R room where there was a small spotlight. I usually took something to read. It was also a chance to catch up with correspondence relating to the Armoury and the Cinema. I even did two Correspondence Courses on Estate Management whilst on night watches.[2] When I had finished these courses I took to doing embroidery as a constructive therapy. As was my routine, I went to the rest room every hour or so until 05.00 and had a cup of coffee, then I changed to an hourly cup of tea for the remainder of the watch. Biscuits were available if I wanted any – at a nominal cost per packet. I always told the NCO i/c the surveillance crew where I was going so that he could call me if anything unusual showed up.

Night watch highlights usually consisted of watching and plotting aircraft flogging up and down the Berlin air corridors, and the progress of the Met balloon launched somewhere to our northwest at about 02.00. We could see these Berlin transport aircraft much more clearly than previously, and we could see the Met balloon to a far greater altitude. Very soon after watches commenced at 210 SU the Unit at Waggum and our other satellite Station were both closed down as they had now become redundant.

With our much improved radar visibility we were able to watch Eastern Bloc aircraft more effectively. They, like the RAF, tended not to fly after midnight but just occasionally there would be some sort of exercise and we would watch as paints formed up into formations, usually on summer evenings and during weekends. All these paints

---

2   This was an extension of my previous agricultural interests. The course was free and organised for me by the RAF Education Service whose representative at Borgentreich was Fg.Off. Alan Calderwood.

were plotted, recorded, and 'told' to Group straight from the PPI. Our own plotting facilities in the well of the bunker were not used during surveillance watches; there was no point. Sometimes we saw aircraft doing night aerobatics when there was a full moon and a clear sky. We also saw them doing practice interceptions but these were rare. Such activities gave us something to study and helped pass the time. Most nights there was nothing beyond the predictable and time would drag.

We had a scare one summer morning, just as day was breaking, when there was obvious jamming from outside our coverage to the east. I phoned Brockzetel and they could see it, so could the USAF at Roth-westen, whereas Üdem couldn't. It grew more intense by the minute. We checked again with each other and all radars were reporting it on a parallel heading (the exact same bearing), with no calculable point of convergence. Comparing notes again, we Duty Watch Officers thought that each of our Stations was being jammed by some clever Russian system which none of us had experienced before. It was only when we realised that the source of jamming was moving slowly towards the south that it dawned on us that we were picking up the sunrise! As the sun rose, Üdem picked it up, then it faded from our screens. After this we came to expect it during clear summer mornings.

In August, during the hot weather, when it was almost impossible to sleep during the day because of sweat trickling across my back, it was a pleasure to go on evening watch into the cooler conditions down the hole. On one watch, I was actually sitting at a PPI myself when, at the far north-east of our coverage, at what must have been great altitude, I watched as a series of paints headed across part of the Baltic Sea and over Denmark at a speed far in excess of anything I had seen before. I was not able to pick up the track on the Type 13 so could not get a height. My estimate of the speed was in thousands of knots. I thought it was interference, but the heading was steady. I checked with Brockze-tel. They had seen it, too, and it was too high for them to pick up on a Type 13. Our theory at the time was that we had seen some sort of meteorite as it was entering the earth's atmosphere.[3]

On later watches we started to see tracks over the border which were moving rather more quickly than we would expect, and behaving

---

3   With the benefit of hindsight, this may have been a test firing of one of the experimental Russian inter-continental ballistic missiles which had maybe gone wrong. The Russians announced the successful firing of an ICBM later in the month.

peculiarly. These interested us. Sometimes they were at great altitude, and were beyond our understanding. Group became interested too, and arranged for a visit by a gentleman in civilian clothes whose name and status we were not told. He questioned us about these paints and tracks. A short while later one of our PPIs was fitted with a cowl to which was attached a time-lapse camera. The film cassette had to be exchanged each morning for a new one. The completed films were sent away. This was one of those times when so-called flying saucer activity was appearing in the press.[4] It was evident to us that someone at a higher level of authority was taking an interest in what we could see.

Weeks later we had a return visit from this civilian gentleman. He brought with him one of the films, and arrangements were made for it to be projected on our rest room wall. Those Officers who had regularly been on nights were shown it but all others were excluded. The film was definitely 'ours' because we could recognise the shape of our PEs. It seemed that one picture was taken after each four sweeps of the trace, thus the afterglow of previous paints was still visible and provided data from which course and speed could be determined by analysis. When projected at normal speed these paints appeared as very fast-moving aircraft tracks. Even though the film was run through several times it was difficult to get a grasp of what we were looking at. Certainly none of us saw anything interesting. We asked questions, but were given evasive replies. After the gentleman left we had the impression that something was being kept from us, and that we had been conned in order to assuage our curiosity. We felt dissatisfied, but this was spiced with a determination to pay even more attention to anything we thought was unusual or couldn't understand.

One night when it was Plt.Off. Clive Sabel's turn on watch, the usual Met balloon rose up in its normal way and must have entered the jet stream to be carried off eastwards at a great rate of knots. He told me next day that the Russian response was quite extraordinary. Apparently, all sorts of paints appeared across the border and climbed to intercept it! He also said that Group became quite excited as the interception point was not that far east of the frontier.

In October the Russians launched the first 'Sputnik' earth satellite. It was at about this time that the Russian Beagle overflew us, presumably

---

4   Flying saucer was the popular term for UFO = Unidentified Flying Object, into which category our sightings of 'Angels' also fitted.

taking photographs. When we spoke to them on the tie-line the Americans were very edgy about what the Russians were doing. For everyone doing our class of work it was a time of extreme tension.

Later in October, as I recall it, there was a night which I shall never forget. My watch commenced in its usual boring way and, with nothing unusual to see, I took a break for a cup of coffee. No sooner did I put the cup to my lips than the Duty NCO came rushing in shouting "Sir, you'd better have a look at this!" So 'Sir' went into the C & R room and sat himself in front of a PPI. There, clear as crystal, were several clusters of aircraft climbing from areas where we suspected East German airfields to be. As I watched, more joined them, and more still. I opened another telling-line to Group as these plots were too many for one person to tell. The Duty NCO fetched in the lads who were on rest just to watch. Rothwesten came on the phone, so did Brockzetel, we could all see them. By now these clusters were in tens and, worse, all turned west at the same time. Group came on and wanted to know more. I told them what I could and estimated that there were over 100 aircraft heading our way, possibly many more. They were approaching on a broad front. Group rang again and asked me to wait on the line to be connected to someone else. On this crackly line I heard a voice saying, "You're through to the forward radar station now, Sir." I was asked by this voice to state the situation quickly and briefly. This I did, giving position, top and bottom altitude limits, and Georef limits of the still growing aircraft numbers. He then rang off. Group came on again, so did Rothwesten (who I had to tell to hold), and Group asked if I could take fighters under control. I said I was alone and hadn't got a cabin crew. "Are you a controller?" they asked. I said "Yes." They told me to call out assistance and then said that two pairs of night fighters were being scrambled for me to control! I told the Duty NCO to get the Duty Officer at Borgentreich on the line and to ask him to get the CO to call me PDQ.[5] Rothwesten were swearing at me and started to sound off about what they were going to do in a very trigger happy fashion. The voice said he was a Colonel and asked what I was going to do. I said "Nothing, these plots are on the other side of the border where the Ruskis can do what they want." The man exploded in a cloud of extremely fruity American vernacular and rang off.

---

5 PDQ = Pretty Damned Quick.

In the meantime the 'raid' started to drop 'window' to make it look bigger than it was, and to try and confuse our radar, but my lads were able to ignore most of these false plots. Group came on again and told me to go to a cabin as they were about to hand over fighters to me. The CO came on. I very briefly explained the situation and told him (I didn't mince my words) to "Get a watch up here bloody quick." I took a scratch cabin crew into the Chief Controller's cabin where I had maximum communications with the outside world and left the Duty NCO in charge of plotting. I put one lad as my Ops 'B' to take phone calls (he had done it before) and others took up control cabin positions. After patching phone lines through to me from the C & R room I spoke to Group who at once handed over two pairs of night fighters. I picked them up easily as they were the only aircraft in our Zone. I took both pairs east and then turned them on to north-south patrol lines comfortably on our side of the border. The Ruskis kept coming. Everyone on watch was beginning to sweat because we were central in the potential line of attack. We all knew that once we had said they're coming, and they had crossed the border, we would be their first target and, our job done, all we could do then would be to head west as best we could and await orders. We thought we were going to go west, in another sense, within the next 15 minutes. The 'raid', now no more than 20 miles from the border, as if it was a single aircraft, turned through 180° and headed back east whence it had come. Once I was sure this wasn't a feint, I told Group and they allowed me to give the fighters Pigeons to Base and stand them down. Relieved, we watched the 'raid' break up and its individual elements fade from our PPIs. It was as the last paints disappeared that the CO and a motley group of watch keepers arrived down the hole. I closed down the Chief Controller's cabin and asked one of the newly arrived Officers to take over C & R duties from me for a few minutes while I went into discussions with my rather short tempered CO.

Still in a sort of shock from what had just happened, I did my best to explain the situation to the Station Commander. Clearly, I couldn't describe everything and politely suggested that he, in the morning, examine the plotters' log books. He still didn't seem to grasp the gravity of the last 45 minutes or so and summed everything up by saying "Pod, for your sake, I hope you're bloody right. I'll see you when you come off watch." He stalked out and took his scratch team with him back to the domestic site, presumably to go back to bed. On returning to the C &

R room, my plotters were still plotting the falling 'window' and it was drifting slowly in the wind over to our side of the frontier. I told them to make a careful and separate note of where they estimated it would hit the ground. I went for another cup of coffee, which I was able to drink this time. Then I got on to Group and told them my CO's reaction towards me. The rest of the watch was quiet.

On coming off watch next morning I returned to the Mess for a quick breakfast and, instead of going to bed as usual, I reported to the CO's office as ordered. He was still not in the best of moods. He had on his desk a Telex from Group giving him a rocket for not having any contingency plans for a watch call-out in a situation as had arisen during the night. He questioned me again about what had happened and how I had handled it, and was grudgingly satisfied that I had done the only things possible in the circumstances. I told him about the 'window', and where it was estimated to have landed. With that, I left his office and made my way to bed to try and sleep in readiness for the evening watch. The following day when, apart from extraneous duties, I was supposed to have 24 hours off, I was told that search parties had been out and were able to bring back samples of the Russian window. I was shown some and kept a strip in my office as a souvenir.

Very soon afterwards, on my next week of nights, I had a similar event to that just described. This time, though, it was a single aircraft that headed our way and, within a short distance of the border, commenced radar jamming. With our sophisticated ECM I was able to tune out most of its effects and to track the transmitting aircraft as it patrolled up and down parallel to the frontier. To us, it was no threat, and little more than a nuisance. We would clearly have seen if the jamming had been masking any other activity. Group took a relaxed attitude towards it and said that if the Ruskis want to play, let them get on with it. No fighters were scrambled, which must have been a disappointment to the other side.

It was when I was on nights in the first week of December that we had a severe snow storm when, as already described in Chapter 42, we were snowed up and ran short of anything to eat.

I had done four weeks of night watches in three months, all of them involving more or less serious events either due to Russian activity or, more recently, the weather. This was an above average number of night watches for anyone to do. With running short of food when snowed up, and with the only food available away from normal meal times being the standard RAF greasy fry-ups, coupled with a degree of stress as described in Chapter 43, I began to get stomach pains and to feel generally unwell. As previously stated, I had seen the MO and he could do nothing for me. He fully understood my situation and condition, but said no more.

Everyone knew that I needed a break, including my Flight Commander and even the Operations Officer, Sqn.Ldr. Owen Ellison. The migraine was bothering me again too. I had a letter from my parents telling me that my old home where I had been brought up at Upton, Wirral, was to be sold and that my new permanent home address would be our cottage at Welshampton in Shropshire. I had no say in this. My parents wanted me home for Christmas but that was totally impossible, and I had to write and tell them so. I got a very acrimonious letter by way of a reply. My father never understood or accepted that orders were orders that had to be obeyed. Everything seemed as though it was ganging up on me.

I was desperate for time off so I tactfully struck a bargain, fortunately to everyone's satisfaction. The arrangement proposed was for me to work nights during the Christmas period so that others were relieved of that duty and could enjoy themselves. Afterwards, by way of unofficial compensation, I would be granted a whole week to myself in which to do what I wanted without any duties whatsoever. I agreed, also, to take a bed up to the little used emergency accommodation in the wooden building above ground at the tech site. Breakfast cereals and snacks would be brought to me by the morning watch so that I could spend longer time in bed (and get more rest) during the day without having to travel back to the Mess.

In due course, with small kit packed, and books to read, I arrived for the evening watch on Christmas Eve. The watch was quiet, as expected. On schedule, Flt.Lt. Bob Myers came to relieve me for the midnight stint. I went above ground, had a snack, washed, and prepared myself for bed. I had just changed into my pyjamas when I got an urgent toilet call. The motion was black with a lot of blood in it. I felt faint, but didn't faint, and was able to stagger to a phone and call Bob down in the hole. He came up at once, took one look at me, and said "SSQ for you, I'll phone them."[6] Then I went dizzy and the lights went out.

---

6 SSQ = Station Sick Quarters.

The next thing I remember was being stretchered into the local village Doctor's room, and him talking in broken English with a Medical Sergeant and Orderly.[7] The words I hazily remember being said were: Blut. Geschwür. Krankenhaus.[8] I next remember being in SSQ and being told that I had a bleeding ulcer. The lights dimmed and went out again.

Although I didn't know it at the time, I was no longer a Flying Officer, I had been a Flight Lieutenant for seven days.

It was a hell of a way to start a Christmas Day.

---

7   The MO, Flt.Lt. Martin Clarke, was on Christmas leave.
8   Blut = blood. Geschwür = ulcer. Krankenhaus = hospital.

47. Out For The Count

AN ARMY MEDICAL OFFICER was bending over me, and the Queen's Christmas address was being broadcast on the radio when I regained consciousness. An Army Sister and the RAF Medical Sergeant from Borgentreich were there, too.[1] I was in bed somewhere. Almost as soon as I realised who was around me I faced a barrage of questions. The one that was asked several times was "How much did you have to drink last night?" Each time I replied "Nothing. I was on watch." The RAF Sergeant then substantiated my replies. The MO then bent low over me to check my breath. The Sergeant then explained that I had collapsed after coming off duty, had been seen by the local German Doctor, diagnosed as having a bleeding ulcer, been taken to SSQ and put to bed until daylight, and then brought by ambulance to wherever I was now. At least I found out what had happened. The MO, not in the best of humours, because my arrival had upset his Christmas activities, then suggested that the Sergeant and his Orderly had better get back to Borgentreich. Only then was I given a full medical examination. I asked the Sister, whose name I later discovered was Sister O'Day (that's how it was pronounced), where I was. She said, "You're in BMH Rinteln."[2] "Where's that?" I asked. "Near Minden," she replied. At that, the greyness set in again.

I was diagnosed with having a bleeding peptic ulcer, brought on as a result of overwork, anxiety, and too much greasy food. No operation was thought necessary. On enquiring how long I might be in hospital I was told, "Several weeks."

---

1   The Army Sister was in the Queen Alexandra's Royal Army Nursing Corps, as were all the nursing staff. The RAF hospital Sisters were in Princess Mary's Royal Air Force Nursing Service.

2   BMH = British Military Hospital.

Just before New Year's day a Flight Lieutenant with a broken leg arrived in my ward. He was none other than the Station Adjutant from Scharfoldendorf whom I had met before when changing weapons in their Armoury. He had fallen over on the ice outside the front gate of his Married Quarter on his way to work. Having previously been on my own in the small ward in the Officers Area I now had someone to talk to. We both had phone calls from our respective camps. Flt.Lt. Bill Billing came to see me a couple of times and brought me books, clothes from my room, and my radio. It was he who told me that I was now a Flight Lieutenant. I couldn't put my new rank up because I had no spare braid. On listening to one of the BFN Sunday morning request programmes I was surprised to hear a tune dedicated to me, wishing me a speedy recovery, from my colleagues at Borgentreich.

As I recovered I was allowed up and was slowly weaned off my milky, low roughage, diet. Then I suffered several migraine attacks which gave the medics some concern because I vomited during each one. These passed and I recovered sufficiently to be discharged back to Borgentreich, sick, with no duties.

Just 48 hours later I was sent home on sick leave pending further instructions. I was at home for about a fortnight when orders came for me to return to RAF Hospital Wegburg, near Wildenrath, in Germany. By this time, though, I had bought braid and shoulder tabs and was now visibly a Flight Lieutenant. This gave me the privilege of better sleeping quarters on the troop-ship, and, joy of joys, a cup of tea brought to me in the morning!

On arrival at Wegberg on March the 11th I was put under observation and stayed there until interviewed by a Medical board. I had suffered more migraine attacks and was warned that I may be invalided out of the RAF. I occupied myself as a walking patient by reading, chatting to others, helping out in the ward, and weaving woollen scarves using a hand loom borrowed from, and wool bought from, the Red Cross based in the hospital. I made over half a dozen scarves, plain, white angora, banded, and two complicated tartan ones. I used these as gifts for past hospitality received back at Borgentreich to which I returned, Medical Category A4GT, on March 22nd, to pack my kit.

I got two good packing-cases from the Equipment Section and four empty ammunition boxes from the Armoury which fitted snugly in to one of the crates. I packed almost all my kit into these: tape recorders, radio, ciné projector, editing gear, films, camera, marquetry tools and woods, books, and several small gifts from friends, as well as my winter-weight and spare clothes. I painted my name and address on the crates, screwed down the lids, and had them taken to the Stores. They then started their journey home to Welshampton, without charge, courtesy of the Military Forwarding Organisation. I sold my bicycle.

Whilst doing this I was interviewed by Sqn.Ldr. Routh whom I had met when he was the MO at Wellesbourne Mountford. He was on a fact finding mission. He wanted to know what had happened to me, the hours I had been working down the hole, my other duties when not on watch, and other personal matters. He explained that he had been sent to see me, and the other watchkeepers, because others in my position had also become unwell. Food and meal times at small Signals Units appeared to be his main concern. I heard no more from him.

One thing about my duties must have registered with higher authority because a full time Armament Officer and Station Defence Instructor from the RAF Regiment had been posted in while I was in hospital. I didn't meet him because he was on leave when I arrived back. My life could have been quite different if I had not been Armament Officer and had its associated duties.

During these last days at Borgentreich I was introduced to Hauptman Bartels, an Officer of the new German Air Force which would eventually take over Borgentreich from the RAF. He was living in our Mess. We both had occasion to go to Paderborn by train together and, on stopping at a station en route, a crowd of German women saw him in the carriage and started pelting him with tomatoes from their shopping bags. They left me alone. So much was the hatred of any idea of German rearmament at that time.

I returned to Wegberg on March 31st for a couple of days for further medical examinations before being flown, on April the 2nd, from Wildenrath to RAF Lyneham in a specially fitted out CASEVAC Valetta.[3] It was my last flight in the RAF. It lasted 1 hour and 45 minutes. The pilot was Flt.Lt. Jones. I was classed as 'walking wounded'.

From Lyneham I was transferred to RAF Hospital, Wroughton, for a meal and an interview. Then, the same afternoon, I was transferred by ambulance (I sat in the front alongside the driver) to the RAF

---

3   CASEVAC = Casualty Evacuation.

Hospital at Halton, near Wendover. At the same time, I was administratively posted on the strength of No.1 Personnel Holding Unit, RAF Innsworth.

During my stay at Halton the crew of a Canberra were admitted but were kept apart from each other. One was put in the same ward as me. They had abandoned the aircraft at the then highest altitude for a successful bail-out. They were severely frost-bitten during their free-fall descent to a lower altitude at which they could use their parachutes. The chap in my ward was in a bad state but was visibly recovering during the short time I was there.

Several other things also happened. We must have had the windows in the ward too tightly closed one night because, when the Sister arrived next morning she announced, in a broad Scottish accent, "This ward smells like an Armenian Brothel." We wondered how she knew! We all helped each other in the ward, fetching bottles, and so on. One lad filled not one, but two, pee bottles in one session, telling me to hurry up with the second one. I know, I emptied them in the sluice room.

While at Halton we saw the second Russian earth satellite go over. It was the one with the little dog 'Laika' on board. Also, some of us volunteered to pose in white coats, as doctors, in a room where there was a brand new prototype kidney dialysis machine, for press photographs to be taken. Kidney dialysis was a new development in medical treatment at the time, and the RAF Medical Branch was involved in the work.

I stayed at Halton until April 16th when I went before No.1 Central Medical Board by which I was categorised as A4GP and returned to my home address pending instructions.

On May the 15th I had to report to No.1 Personnel Holding Unit at Innsworth, Gloucestershire, for my final discharge and civilian documentation. Later, on July 11th, I received my last RAF pay, and on the 12th I relinquished my Commission. On the 14th of January 1959 I received my Commission Scroll signed personally by Her Majesty Queen Elizabeth II.

I had left the protective environment of the Royal Air Force. I was now working for my tyrannical father and confronting the ill-disciplined turbulence of civilian life.

48. Epilogue

AFTER LEAVING THE RAF, and following a difficult discussion with my father, I joined the family engineering business, of which I was later to become a director. My pay, initially, was less than a third of my RAF emolument. That hurt. I still suffered from ulcer problems and had to watch my diet carefully. I lived at home where we also ran a smallholding

I became a Life Member of the Royal Air Forces Association, but otherwise had no contact with the Service for many years. I sought, and was granted, a further medical and was found fit, which, of course, I wasn't.

My interest in flying was still there so I joined the Shropshire Aero Group based at Sleap airfield near Shrewsbury. Having been found 'fit' at one medical, I sought another with a view to applying for a Private Pilot's Licence, and passed. At the Aero Group I took the necessary refresher lessons and flew the Auster which the Group owned, dual. The CFI was satisfied.[1] I then flew it solo, once only. I found during that trip that my tall frame limited the full and free movement of controls in the small cockpit, to the extent that I could never have recovered from a spin had I ever got into one. I saw a red light. I never flew the aircraft again. Nor any other.

It was at that Aero Group that I first met my wife who was learning to fly. She never went solo, but was very close to it. It was because we had other things on our minds that she decided to conserve money and not take any more lessons so that we could afford to marry.

The migraine persisted. It came in waves of attacks. Some weeks I could only work for two or three days. I even volunteered for psychiatric

---

1   CFI = Chief Flying Instructor.

analysis and became a voluntary patient, so desperate was I to find a cure. Nothing was found. The attacks continued until we had been married for 14 years and moved house. The attacks reduced, and then almost ceased. We came up with the theory that it might be a chocolate allergy, because no longer was there a sweet shop close to home from which to buy the chocolate that I loved. I mentioned this to our Doctor who said, scoffingly, that I should have known that chocolate can give people migraine. It was his last consultation with me. My new Doctor suggested that I also consider red wine and oranges as possibilities. He was right.

Looking back, at a Dining In Night, the menu would usually have on it a melon boat with a slice of orange for a sail (which I ate), a pudding with chocolate of some sort in, or on it and, of course, there was port wine for the Loyal Toast. What a mixture!

I had been poisoning myself and no Doctor, at any time, had told me.

My home-built 'Puff Duck' hovercraft. It was powered by a 650cc BSA motorcycle engine which drove two twelve-bladed centrifugal fans for lift. A Villiers invalid carriage engine drove, by belt, a cut-down Airscrew-Weyroc wooden aircraft propeller for thrust. Hover height was about 6" and top speed about 40 mph – faster than the official hovercraft speed record at the time.

I must add that my interest in flying machines led me to build, in my garage at home, a light hovercraft to my own design. I even took out a patent on hovercraft control which I later sold to the then Ministry of Technology at absolutely no profit. I also competed in the first ever European Light Hovercraft Rally and came second – or last – whichever way you want to look at it. I am, I believe, still the only person to travel from King's Gap, Hoylake, Wirral, to Hilbre Island (in the river Dee) and back, with the tide out and across the quick sands, in his own home-built hovercraft. That was within 10 years of leaving the RAF.

So I really was a low level pilot!

APPENDICES AND GLOSSARY

Appendix 1

ESCAPE AND EVASION

THIS PIECE RELATES TO an exercise which took place during a Friday night and Saturday of the course described in Chapter 7 (page 63). It was, in its way, a significant enough event for it to be described separately and in detail.

As aircrew it was not unreasonable to expect, in the circumstance of our being involved in hostilities, that we would fly over, and conceivably be shot down over, enemy territory. The Air Ministry, with this in mind, sought to ensure that all trainee aircrew were given practical experience of evading those forces which could be expected to find and capture them.

At Desford, as mentioned in Chapter 6 (page 46), I had been on the defending side and became thoroughly cold and bored having been on look-out duty all night and seen nothing. In this later exercise I was an evader in a foreign land.

The rules were quite simple. We were to be considered caught and captured if a defender laid a hand on anybody and gripped his clothing. There was, officially, to be no violence. Common trespass was permitted but any form of damage to property, theft, or use of vehicles without permission was taboo and would be treated as a criminal offence. The start and end times of the 25 hour exercise were clearly defined. Our dress was any comfortable clothing, whether uniform or not, under a pair of khaki denims. Footwear would be of our own choice. The denims were not to be removed as they were effectively a form of recognition. We had also to carry identification. Money was not permitted. Many of us chose to carry bottles of water and a bar or two of chocolate.[1]

About 21.00 hours, an hour before the start of the exercise we, as 'downed aircrew', were assembled for briefing in the main hall of the Ground School. Because we were in the building in a potentially 'enemy' country it was searched, including the roof spaces, to ensure that there were no eavesdroppers before briefing commenced. Some of us, like me, carried small electric torches, others carried compasses. There was not enough of either to go round so whatever we had, if anything, was decided at random. We wore a variety of footwear, from gym shoes to heavy boots. I wore boots. Some of us blackened our faces, as did I. Listening intently, we were told that we would shortly climb aboard crew buses which had their windows obscured so that we would not know where we were going. We would be dropped, two at a time, as if we had bailed out, at various intervals after a journey of at least half an hour. We were to confine our movements to within the county of Warwickshire (excluding the City of Birmingham), which represented enemy territory for the period of the exercise. Looking for us would be our own Airmen and Station personnel, those of other unspecified RAF Stations, Civil Defence personnel, Army personnel, and the county Police Force which had had all leave cancelled for the period.

Only when all this had been explained to us were we told that, in the darkened vehicles we would each, at the very last minute, be given a local Ordnance Survey map and be told the addresses of two 'safe houses' (which we had quickly to memorise) to make for, and hopefully arrive at, whilst evading capture.

So it was that, after last minute use of the toilets, we boarded the vehicles, pair by pair, and set off, into what was soon to become enemy territory, so as to arrive at about 22.00 hours, the time the exercise was due to start.[2] If captured we were to go 'quietly' with our captors who would be expected to interrogate us, and we were only to divulge our individual Service Numbers, Rank, and Name.

I must explain that in 1952 there were no motorways, there was comparatively little vehicular traffic, street lighting was dim to

---

1 Sweets were still rationed and we were advised in advance to save our coupons for this event.

2 I am ashamed to admit that I have since forgotten the name of the student with whom I was paired that night. I shall therefore hereinafter refer to him as 'Ginger'.

non-existent, there were many more branch line railways than exist today, and trains ran throughout the night.[3]

The journey to our dropping zone took about an hour and we were worried that our vehicles might be seen and recognised before we were even set down. We also thought that we had been driven round in circles in order to mislead us. As it happened, neither opinion was borne out in fact.

Ginger and I were dropped off about 3 minutes after the previous pair and dashed for cover into some bushes in case we had already been seen. We lay low, listening to see if anyone was about. We also listened to find if our vehicle dropped anyone else close by so that we might team up, but its engine droned on into silence without stopping. Cautiously we emerged and attempted to get our bearings on our hitherto unseen maps. Warwickshire is a big county and we could be anywhere.

There was occasional light drizzle but there were gaps in clouds, sufficient to let through a little moonlight. It was a good night for evaders and at the same time sufficiently unpleasurable and demoralising for defenders who, under those conditions, we hoped would soon lose their enthusiasm.

On looking around there were two features which caught our attention. One was a railway line, and beyond it on a slight rise, a square water tower. We were in farmland but there were houses about as though we might be on the edge of a suburban area. The position of the moon initially helped us to get a sense of direction but it was some time, using closely shaded torchlight that we found the water tower on the map. The presence of the railway helped us, but at first we had no idea which railway. Goods and passenger trains passed fairly frequently so we deduced it was a main line. Eventually we were happy we had the right spot. We were north of Nuneaton and the nearest safe house was not far from Rugby some 20 miles off. The other was about twice the distance away so was at once discounted as an option. We needed to make rapid progress as early as possible before defenders captured any of us and found in which directions we were all heading and thus concentrate their forces in areas where they assessed our destinations to be.

---

3   This is being written over 50 years after the event. Even after this time some memories are very vivid.

We made our way along the road towards Nuneaton, but quickly had to dive into a ditch when a heavy vehicle approached. It was an Army wagon. It didn't see us in its headlights and drove on slowly. We decided to walk in the fields alongside the road but found that tough going, and very slow, because we had to get through fences and hedges. It was far too slow. Then we came to a wide stream, so back to the road we went. Making sure that no-one was about, we crossed the bridge using, as far as possible, the grassy road edges because our footfalls were quieter than on the tarmac.

Only half a mile was travelled in over an hour. We had to speed up to gain sufficient ground to allow us time to lie up somewhere and rest for a while during daylight. We reasoned that there were houses on roads and with them, a much greater chance of being seen, whereas there are no houses on railway lines. The railway it was to be. After crossing two fields, we were negotiating the tight wire trackside fence when a passenger train passed, its carriage lights illuminating us as it went by. That was another lesson learned; lie down whenever a train came. It was a four track railway so trains were not infrequent. Progress, however, was much faster but we were soon to find it, in its way, to be somewhat more hazardous than being on a road. Each overbridge had to be approached with caution in case it was guarded. We went forward, one at a time, using whatever cover was available, until the last minute before having to quietly make our way under. We developed a series of whistles; one simulating an owl meant all was clear. We managed about three miles an hour for a while and never saw a soul. Then we came to a bridge with obvious guards on it, silhouetted against a sky reflecting the lights of Nuneaton. There was nothing for it but to leave the tracks and cross a field to one side to approach, and quietly cross the road away from the bridge, and then regain the track several hundred yards further on. But we got it wrong. We chose the side where there was a canal or river which thwarted our plan, so we had to retrace our steps and go past the guards from the other side. Time was lost.

We came to a small station. No one was about. It was closed for the night so, somewhat daringly and brazenly, we walked along the platform and continued on. We came to a junction and a large area of sidings as we approached Nuneaton. Making our way, necessarily across some tracks, I tripped and stumbled over some signal wires. The noise I made was heard by someone who shouted at us. We didn't know who, but took no chances and decided to run towards a line of trucks in what we thought was a siding. I stopped under the trucks while Ginger went on out of the other side of them and waited for me in the shadow of a large coal dump. In moments the trucks over me started to move. There was no way out without risking being guillotined by the wheels, so I lay between the rails, but to one side because the coupling chains were coming perilously close above me. I have never lain so flat in my life. The clatter of the trucks as the engine took up the slack was enormous. Worse, I didn't know whether the engine was pushing or pulling the train and dreaded it going over me. About 20 trucks passed over at increasing speed, the ground moving under me as each heavy truck passed, all the while realising that the sound of the engine was getting closer. It was backing the trucks in some shunting manoeuvre or other. Then, unnervingly, it tooted when it was almost over me. I was first sprayed with hot water from some pipe or other, then the hellish hot ashpan separating the firebox from my head passed over, followed by all the mechanism and steam as the rest of the engine nearly machined me to death. The steam was my saviour because, before it could disperse in the damp air I rolled over the top of the rail nearest Ginger, and into a hollow between pairs of rails, and stayed there, flat, until the train was a hundred yards or more away. Only then did I crawl to him by the coal stack. He said he wouldn't have been surprised if I was a 'goner'.

After a few minutes to recover, we headed, in the shadows and taking care to avoid signal wires, to the edge of the goods yard, picked up the main line again and cautiously continued towards Nuneaton station. On nearing it we could see that there were too many people about for us to climb a platform ramp, walk along through the waiting passengers, and disappear off the other end. That would be too risky. On pausing to consider which way to avoid the station, we heard a low whistle as though someone was trying to attract our attention. We risked a reply. The whistle was there twice this time. We replied twice. Then we saw someone crawling in our direction from not far away. We waited, prepared to do a runner, and then just made out someone whom we recognised. He made another whistling noise and his mate duly crept over and joined us.

We agreed to split up and make our individual ways through the streets by the station and to try and meet again, using our quiet whistle codes, on (if possible) the left side of the tracks a couple of hundred yards further on, or in the nearest available shadows beyond. It sounded OK.

Finding my way on my own down to street level from the raised tracks was not easy. I found it impossible on the left side so, using a passing train as a distraction, I crossed to the right side where I had better luck and slid down the sloping wall supporting the embankment at an underbridge. No one saw me, but there were people about. I took a chance on them not knowing about our exercise and walked as nonchalantly as possible along the streets by the station, sticking as close to the railway as possible and all the while keeping in the shadows. Had I been seen with blackened face and filthy denims I am sure the very sight of me would have aroused suspicion even in the most unsuspecting of minds.

I decided to make use of a road bridge under the tracks so that I would be on the proper side to meet Ginger and the others further on.

Just ahead of me, not 30 yards away, a helmeted policeman appeared from a turning I hadn't seen in the dim street lights. Before he turned to face in my direction something caught his attention and distracted him long enough for me squeeze into a vertical channel which had once held drain pipes in the blue brick retaining wall. I could hear his booted footsteps getting nearer. I squeezed myself back as far as possible into that filthy damp groove and held my breath. He was within a yard of me when a heavy lorry passed and he never noticed me. The lorry turned off and I stayed put, listening for Mr. Plod's footsteps seemingly taking an age to fade into the distance. Only then did I emerge and regain as casual a gait as possible whilst finding my way towards our rendezvous. Little did I know it, but one of our number saw what had happened to me while he himself was skulking in the recess of a dark doorway. We exchanged whistles and made our way forward, a distance apart, to a place where we could clamber up on to the railway.

We waited long enough in the shadows to convince us that we had lost the others, and decided on our own plan of action. Not too far ahead of us there lay a fairly major junction. Near it was an overbridge which looked as though it might be guarded. Worse, there were a lot of lights both on the road and the railway in that locality. Logic told us that people in lit areas are not going to be able to see well into the darker gloom. Uncomfortable as it was, drizzle started to fall again, but that was advantageous. The junction itself bothered us, as we didn't want to make the mistake of following the wrong line. That problem solved itself when a passenger train passed and we saw on the carriage destination boards the name 'Rugby', and watched which way it went. We now had to 'follow that train'.

As we approached the bridge we came to a platelayers' hut and paused for a while by it. We heard voices inside. It was Ginger and the other of our foursome. Having got together again we held a brief council of war as we sheltered from the drizzle. Our plan was for the four of us each to shoulder either a pick or a shovel from those within the hut and to walk, quite openly, in single file as we had seen gangers doing, under the bridge to the next hut which we could see dimly in the gloom beyond. We saw people looking at us but disregarded them, as they did us, and reached our destination, left the tools there, and ran on for quite a distance before we reckoned we had got away with it.

We were back to the routine of coming to a bridge, assessing it, and if necessary by-passing it through the adjacent fields or houses, then regaining the railway until we came to the next obstacle, always avoiding the bright beam of light from the modern colour-light signals, and from the light from trains which, in the early hours, were now fewer in number. Fairly good progress was made for several miles, although we had trouble crossing a bridge with gaps in its deck, over a fairly large watercourse.

We came to an overbridge with houses along the road on each side. They were big detached houses with long gardens, and extended as far as we could see. We took no chances. Ginger and I went to look for a way through past one end of the bridge. The other two took the opposite side. Again we would rendezvous at the next platelayers' hut, or the one after that if the first happened to be too close.

We had an additional problem. We weren't sure how far along the railway we had come. One bridge looked like any other in the dark and, with all the delays, we had no idea of what average speed we had been doing. We weren't sure how soon we would have to leave the railway and make our way cross-country towards our safe house. In fact, we were miles short of that point but didn't know it at the time. The night was now darker and the ability to pick out worthwhile landmarks to check against our map was diminished to the point of virtual impossibility. Wherever we were we still had to get past the bridge ahead.

There was nothing for it but seriously to trespass through someone's back garden, work out our next move, then sneak past the house and hide before regaining the road. We picked a house without any side gate or obstacle to getting to its front garden. Ginger climbed the fence and landed quietly. I climbed over and as I landed, crashed through the glass of a cold frame on the other side. I was lucky not to cut myself, but I'd made a lot of noise, so both of us froze where we were. No dogs barked. No windows opened, so we ran, avoiding a gravel path, into a shrubbery at the front. A car came in the drive – someone was arriving home from a late night party – but no-one saw us. Slowly, I raised my head over the front garden wall and saw guards on the bridge. Our caution was justified. Another car approached towards the guards from our direction. As soon as it had passed us we dashed across while its headlights were too bright for the guards to see us. The extensive garden we had now entered was that of a very large house. On going to the back we saw a light on upstairs. Quietly, very quietly, and slowly, we crept towards the back fence and climbed over into a field. We heard a noise behind us and looked back to see someone open the back door and let a dog out. Nothing else happened. Silently we walked towards a hedge and followed it back to the railway but couldn't get through because of barbed wire. Someone coughed behind us; thankfully it was only a curious cow.

We saw a platelayers' hut while we were still in fields searching for a way back to the railway, but were too far away to risk a whistle signal. Eventually we came to a stile where a footpath crossed the line and used that to get over the fence. The next platelayers' hut was a considerable distance ahead, and there were signs of dawn in the sky. On nearing it we saw wisps of smoke from its chimney. A whistle revealed that our friends had got there first and had lit a fire in the grate. There was coal available, so the four of us decided to stay and dry our clothes.

We all went to sleep. When we woke it was broad daylight. A recce was made outside. It was immediately obvious that our location was very exposed and that to move away in broad daylight would invite observation from anyone within a mile who had a pair of binoculars. We had to stay where we were until it grew dark again, or until it rained heavily enough for any guards to lose interest and take cover. It didn't rain. The sun came out so, after at last finding our position on the map, we went back to sleep to ready ourselves for the next part of our journey later in the day – and that was going to be further than we had anticipated.

It was fortunate that no gangers were working that part of the line that Saturday for we were undisturbed the whole time we were there. Towards evening, we heard lorries on a lane some distance away and, on cautiously investigating saw that they were hostile Army lorries heading in the general direction we would be taking. It seemed to us that they may have discovered, maybe from captured evaders or from observing their (hopefully not our) movements, where many of us were making for. We hadn't been seen so, for the time being, but having taken our observations as a warning, we were safe to proceed but with great caution once it grew dark enough to leave our hut.

We left in pairs advancing, wherever possible, using bushes and any other cover near the fence at the side of the track. We lay down as each train passed. We were still in countryside and the going was comparatively good. We knew we had to leave the railway shortly and move to the west, on our right, away from it. In the dark we hadn't noticed a deep stream on our left and what we took to be a wide canal only 50 or 60 yards away on our right. We saw a bridge ahead at a rise in the ground and realised we had come too far, but the canal had prevented us leaving the railway earlier. We were in effect in a funnel, with the only way out being forwards past the bridge, or retreating far enough to cross the canal and regain open ground. Ginger and I decided we would approach the bridge very cautiously to see if it was guarded. We couldn't bypass it because of the water features. If it wasn't guarded we would use the road that crossed it, which, on our map, also crossed the canal. We would then, as the crow flies, be about a mile from our safe house. If it was guarded, there was no alternative but to retreat. Success was tantalisingly close.

Immediately before the bridge the railway entered a shallow cutting and we crept our way along, halfway up the cutting, on the left side. Thorny undergrowth made progress difficult. A passenger train passed very slowly and as it left us there was a shout "There they are – grab them." We were caught in a carefully laid trap, for the defenders were not only on the bridge, but lying low along each side of the railway. For us there was no way out and we had to concede capture.

I was taken up on to the bridge where a Police Constable took charge of me and told me to sit at his feet. A mobile fish and chip van arrived and someone bought him a helping. Ginger, by this time, had joined me and was sitting by me on the pavement. The Constable taunted us about being hungry while he had food. This annoyed me somewhat. I wasn't being held in any way so escape was fair game. I waited until he was looking away and had his mouth full, nudged Ginger, and all in one action sprang to my feet, tipped the Constable's helmet forwards over his eyes, and ran like hell down a slope towards the railway on the other side of the bridge to that on which I had been captured. No luck. One of our Squadron's Corporals jumped out and caught me.

I was frog-marched back to the Constable who promptly handcuffed me and gave me a good talking to, which I was perfectly entitled to ignore. Not long afterwards a Police patrol car came along and stopped. I was bundled in and whisked off to Rugby Police Station.

I was man-handled into the Main Bridewell and pushed behind an iron gate leading to the cells, where I was 'collected' by a burly Sergeant who put me in a cell where there were piles of other captives clothes. He ordered me to strip naked. I could hear the shouts of familiar voices and was soon to join them in a cell where a CID man was doing his best to carry out interrogations – with little success in the riotous, abusive, not to say distinctly smelly, atmosphere. It was about 8 o'clock in the evening and we were held in a passageway and the adjacent cells, but no cell doors were ever locked.

One of the captives decided to be 'helpful' and volunteered to be questioned. We were a bit surprised when he said he had been making for the locks. "Which locks," he was asked, "Bollocks," he replied. The Sergeant had been listening and let out some verbal abuse at us where-upon, quite spontaneously, a number of us set on him and debagged him, telling him at the same time that if we were naked he was bloody well going to join us.

The keys to the iron gate were extracted from him, the gate was unlocked, and some of us, me included, opened it and lifted it off its pintles and set it against the wall. Simultaneously, there was a surge of cheering male torsos out into the office part of the Police Station. Some of them made for the toilets and managed to climb out of a window into the yard outside. They were quickly rounded up and brought back. Those in the offices caused mayhem by cavorting about but without doing any damage. I think every policeman in the building rounded us up back into the Bridewell. A very Senior Police Officer appeared and told us to shut up and listen. He was quite fair, said we had had our fun and, as it was now only an hour until the end of the exercise, and if we behaved and rehung the gate, he would let us get dressed and would arrange transport for us to be taken back to Wellesbourne Mountford, to arrive just as the exercise ended. If we did not comply, we would be held for another hour and be taken back late. We complied.

Just as we were leaving some Saturday night drunks were marched in and banged up in the cells we were vacating. It has to be said that the police handled our behaviour with an amount of good humour. Several of their number shook hands with us as we left.

On arrival back at base, we checked in and then made our way back to our accommodation to shower and go to bed. Food was available but I don't think anybody bothered with it.

After being given a chance to recover on Sunday, we were debriefed on Monday morning. Less than half a dozen of us had arrived at the safe houses. Most of us had been captured and a very few had neither been captured nor reached safety. We were certain that the location of the safe houses was known to the defenders before the exercise began, but that was denied.

Those who were caught, and taken back to base, received rough treatment. They were incarcerated in the decontamination building, had fire hoses turned on them periodically and, just to liven them up, thunder-flashes were thrown in among them. This, it was said, was done because some evaders had given themselves up, thinking that, once captured, the exercise would be over for them. If that was true, they had been very wrong.

It took almost a week before most of us went about the camp without first wanting to look round corners or keep an eye open for other people. Only gradually did we lose our furtiveness.

Appendix 2
EAST BERLIN

T HE PICTURES SHOWN IN this appendix were bought
during a Sunday afternoon visit to East Berlin on the 8th of
November 1953.[1]

*Unter den Linden, now called Stalin Allee, lined with apartment
blocks. (More recently Unter den Linden again.)*

---

1   See Chapter 13, page 119.

The Brandenburg Gate with the Russian flag above.

Alexander Square with its HO store (Handels Organization), the Communist-run department store. An unglazed station concourse stands down the side street.

The Russian cemetery with the red marble draped flags at the entrance. A statue of Mother Russia bowing her head is in the left foreground.

Looking back towards the entrance of the cemetery.

*A view in the opposite direction showing the inscribed memorial
stones lining the edges, with the mausoleum beyond.*

One of the inscribed memorial stones. It has Lenin's face on the centre of the flag on the side.

A closer look at the mausoleum on its mound.

The statue of a Russian soldier holding a child and striking a broken swastika with his sword. The bronze sculpture was cast in Moscow and brought to Berlin in five sections.

The illuminated ceiling of the mausoleum depicting The Order of Victory.

This photograph was taken against the instructions of the Commissar who was accompanying us and without him knowing. It is typical of what was to be seen behind the facade of buildings in the main streets of East Berlin. In it one can just make out the shells of buildings. The circular object is the top end of an air raid bunker toppled on its side by demolition explosives. To its right is another, square, blown up bunker. We were told that this stood at, or close to, the site of the Reichs Chancellery and that of Hitler's underground bunker. Some new buildings are in the distance to the right of the picture.

Appendix 3
AIRCRAFT INFORMATION

I flew at the controls of the following aircraft types:

Tiger Moth	"Digby jets"
Chipmunk*	"Chippies"
Oxford*	"Ox boxes"
Meteor Mk T7	"Meat boxes"
Vampire Mk T11	"Bananas" or "Wheel barrows"
Vampire Mk 5*	"Kiddie-cars"
Vampire Mk 9*	"Kiddie-cars"
Sabre F86E*	"Blowlamps" or "Swords"
Balliol	

* Qualified as First Pilot.

I flew as crew or passenger in the following aircraft types:

Prentice	
Anson	"Faithful Annies"
Valetta	"Flying pigs"
Lincoln	

I controlled the following types of aircraft:

Balliol
Meteor NF11
Venom
F86 Sabre

F84 Thunderjet
Swift
Hunter
Vampire T11
Canberra
CF100 Canuck
Javelin

The aircraft I controlled intercepted the following types of aircraft:

Balliol
Meteor T7
Meteor NF11
Meteor (undentified mark) RAF, Dutch, and Belgian
Venom
F86 Sabre (RAF and Canadian)
F84 Thunderjet
Hunter
Comet MkII
Lincoln (jamming aircraft)
Canberra
B45 Tornado (USAF)
B57 (USAF Canberra)
Viscount airliner
T33 Shooting Star (two seat version of the F80)
F80 Shooting Star
CF100 Canuck (Canadian)
Javelin

The above were all recorded in my Log Books.

During my RAF service I also came into contact with other aircraft types, of which Tempests, Mosquitos, and various marks of Meteor were the most common.

In civilian life I soloed in an Auster and designed, built, and 'drove' my own single-seat hovercraft.

GLOSSARY

Glossary of Terms used (all were valid in the 1950s decade)

2ATAF	Second Allied Tactical Air Force (of which the RAF in Germany is a part)
2TAF	The RAF element of 2ATAF
ABC	Atomic, Biological, and Chemical (warfare)
Adj.	Adjutant
Admin	Administration
Admin Wing	Part of Station organisation responsible for support aspects of a mostly non-technical nature
AFN	American Forces Network radio station
AI	Airborne Interception radar
Aldis Lamp	Signalling lamp
ALO	Army Liaison Officer
AOC	Air Officer Commanding
AOP	Air Observation Post
AP	Associated Press
APs	Air Publications
ASI	Air Speed Indicator (essential flying instrument)
A-scope	An oscilloscope with a rectangular or linear display
Astra Cinema	RAF cinemas were almost always called 'Astra'
Authorisation Book	See Duty Book
AVTAG	Jet engine fuel
AWOL	Absent WithOut Leave
BAOR	British Army of the Rhine

BAFSVs	British Armed Forces Special Vouchers
Bang seat	Ejection seat
Battle Flight	(Usually four) aircraft, fully armed, waiting for take-off in readiness to counter any perceived threat (scrambling)
Bent Weapon	Faulty airborne radar equipment
BFES	British Forces Education Service (schools)
BFN	British Forces Network radio station
Blighty	England
BMH	British Military Hospital (army run)
Bogies	Aircraft selected by a ground radar controller as a target for a practice interception or investigation
Bounced	Intercepted or attacked (usually unexpectedly)
BRIXMIS	British Military Mission
C & R	Control and Reporting (radar watch keeping duties)
CASEVAC	Casualty Evacuation
Caterpillar Club	Club all of whose members had baled out by parachute in an emergency
CB	Confined to Barracks
CCF	Combined Cadet Force
CFI	Chief Flying Instructor
Chain Home	Type of radar
Chance Light	Unidirectional landing-strip floodlight
C-in-C	Commander-in-Chief
CO	Commanding Officer
CO2	Carbon Dioxide gas
Craig Computer	Mechanical device similar to an architects drawing board, used for calculating an aircraft's track and ground speed
CRDF	Cathode Ray Direction Finding (Control Tower equipment)
Cu-nims	Cumulonimbus clouds (thunder clouds)
Dalton Computer	A simple, manually operated, hand-held mechanical device
DCO	Duty Carried Out
Dead stick	Engineless (landing)
Detail Board	Notice board in a crew room showing the flying schedule
DI	Drill Instructor

DI	Direction Indicator (a form of gyroscopic compass)
Dining In Night	Formal evening and dinner for Officers – a compulsory gathering presided over by the Station Commander (CO)
Dining Out	Formal Officers Mess occasion at which a farewell dinner is held for an Officer about to leave the Station
Dinner Night	Slightly less formal dinner only for living-in Officers (unpopular)
DNCO	Duty Not Carried Out
DR	Deduced (Dead) Reckoning
Duty Book	The authority to fly and the duty to be carried out, signed by all pilots prior to take-off and on return
Duty Squadron	Squadron on a higher state of readiness for operations, etc.
ECM	Electronic Counter Measures
EPAS	Equipment Pay and Accounting Section
Erk	Slang for Airman
ETD	Estimated Time of Departure
EWS	Emergency Water Supply
FFI	Freedom From Infection
Fg.Off.	Flying Officer
Field Rank	Squadron Leader equivalent, or higher, in all armed services
Finals	Final approach to landing
Flight	A number of RAF personnel, similar to a Platoon in the army
Flight Officer	Nowadays a Flight Lieutenant (female)
Flt.Lt.	Flight Lieutenant
Flt.Sgt.	Flight Sergeant
Flying Wing	Part of Station organisation responsible for all flying and aviation matters
Form 252	A disciplinary charge sheet (used for miscreants)
Form 540	An official diary document
Form 700	Aircraft servicing and serviceability log book, to be examined and signed prior to take-off and on landing, listing any faults found whilst airborne
Form 1369	Officer's Service assessment and record
FWHQ	Flying Wing Headquarters

'G'	Measure of the force of gravity. EG: 4G is four times normal weight on earth
'G' suit	A suit, pneumatically activated, worn under flying clothing; automatically inflated to assist a pilot to overcome the affects of high 'G' forces
GCA	Ground Controlled Approach (radar talk-down almost to the point of landing)
GCI	Ground Controlled (radar) Interception
GCI Station	An RAF Radar Unit from which interception instructions are given
GEE	An aid to precision navigation and bombing
Georef	Geographic Reference (a navigational grid system)
Goniometer	Device used to determine the azimuth of a response on some types of radar
Goosenecks	Paraffin flares
Gp.Capt.	Group Captain
GPO	General Post Office (pre British Telecom)
Grant	Officially sanctioned time off work
Groupie	Group Captain (slang)
GSM	General Situations Map (usually a large plotting table)
GSO	German Service Organisation
Guest Night	Formal Officers Mess event at which invited guests are present
HQ	Headquarters
IAS	Indicated Air Speed
i/c	In charge (of)
IF	Instrument Flying (blind flying)
IFF	Identification Friend or Foe
INS	International News Service
Interdiction	Interfering with enemy supply columns and trains, tank-busting, etc.
ITS	Initial Training School
JEHU	Joint Experimental Helicopter Unit
J/T	Junior Technician
JTC	Junior Training Corps

LAA	Light Ack-Ack = anti-aircraft guns/gunfire
Mach Number	A measure of the speed of sound (Mach 1 is the speed of sound)
Machmeter	Instrument showing the aircraft speed in relation to the speed of sound
Mae West	Inflatable life jacket
MAFL	Manual of Air Force Law
Mag drop	Mag = Magneto. Two are fitted to each piston engine. When one is switched off the revs will drop within prescribed limits, hence mag drop (test)
Malcolm Club	Civilian run All-Ranks canteen and social welfare club
Mayday	Call used in dire emergency (Mayday Mayday Mayday)
Meppen Range	Air-to-ground firing range for guns and rockets, close to the Dutch border
Met	Meteorology (weather)
MO	Medical Officer
Movement Order	Document listing responsibilities for a major move to another location, timings, transport, materiel, logistics, personnel, and much else
MT	Station Mechanical Transport (vehicles) Section
MTO	Mechanical Transport Officer
MTSS	Mechanical Transport Servicing Section
NAAFI	Navy Army Air Force Institutes
NATO	North Atlantic Treaty Organisation
NCO	Non-Commissioned Officer
NF11	Meteor Mark 11 night fighter
No.2 Home Dress	Usual daily working uniform
OHMS	On Her Majesty's Service
Ops	Operations
Paints	Radar responses
Pan call	Level of emergency second only to Mayday (Pan Pan Pan)
PDQ	Pretty Damned Quick
PEs	Permanent Echoes
Pekol bus	The local Jever town bus service
PFO	Physical Fitness Officer

PI	Practice Interception
Pigeons to Base	Information to a pilot regarding course to steer and distance to base (Pigeons)
Plt.Off.	Pilot Officer
PMC	President of the Mess Committee
Pongos	A derogatory term for army personnel
PPI	Plan Position Indicator (a circular radar display)
Press tits	Initiate engine start procedure
PSI	President of the Station Institutes, who oversees a myriad of welfare and official support organisations
PSI Gardens	On-Station market gardens
PSI shop	Shop in which produce from the Station farm and gardens, and other giftware, etc. is sold to all ranks and their families
PT	Physical Training
PTI	Physical Training Instructor
Pundit	Flashing airfield identification beacon easily seen from the air
PX	American forces on-camp supermarket
QGH	Radio controlled procedure for descending to within a short distance from base (from an old Q code)
QNH	Airfield barometric pressure at time of take-off (from an old Q code)
QRs & ACIs	Queens Regulations and Air Council Instructions (a law book)
Radio Compass	Instrument which indicated the direction from the aircraft of the radio transmitter to which it was tuned
RAFCC	Royal Air Force Cinema Corporation
Recce	Reconnaissance
Red Shield canteen	All-Ranks canteen run by the Salvation Army
Regiment Wing	Part of Station organisation responsible for all matters concerning the RAF Regiment and its activities
RN	Royal Navy
RNAF	Royal Netherlands Air Force
RNZAF	Royal New Zealand Air Force
R/T	Radio Telephone (ground/air and air/air radio)

RTO	Rail Traffic Officer
SAC	Senior AirCraftman
S.Ad.O.	Senior Administration Officer
SBA	Standard Beam Approach (passive radio homing system)
SBAC	Society of British Aircraft Constructors
Sector Recce	Sector Reconnaissance. Familiarisation with the local area or sector of operations
SHQ	Station Headquarters
SITREP	Situation Report
SNCO	Senior Non-Commissioned Officer
SOXMIS	Soviet Military Mission
SP	Service Policeman
Sprog	Junior (of any rank) with little experience
Sqn.Ldr.	Squadron Leader
SROs	Station Routine Orders
SSAFA	Soldiers' Sailors' and Airmen's Families Association
SSQ	Station Sick Quarters
Station Flight	Unit responsible for visiting and non-squadron aircraft
Station Signals (section)	Station organisation responsible for the maintenance, etc., of all communications services, radio and landline
Streits Hotel	Transit hotel for Officers passing through, or in, Hamburg
SU	Signals Unit (there are many types)
SWO	Station Warrant Officer
Tannoy	Loud speaker public address system
Tech Wing	Part of Station organisation responsible for in-depth technical maintenance of aircraft, vehicles, and other mechanical items
Telex	Teleprinter message
Thunderflash	Hand launched exploding pyrotechnic with an extremely loud bang
Trolley-acc	Battery pack on a trolley. Used for engine starting then immediately afterwards disconnected and pulled away
Tote	Large vertical, constantly updated, information display (as on a racecourse)
Tower	Airfield control tower (Air Traffic Control)

Travel Warrant	Document to be exchanged for a travel ticket
Type 13 (etc.)	Types of radar antennae
UN	United Nations
UP	United Press (agency)
USAF	United States Air Force
USSR	Union of Soviet Socialist Republics
u/s	Unserviceable
u/t	Under Training
VD	Venereal Disease
Verey Lights	Coloured flares fired from a special pistol
VHF	Very High Frequency (a band of radio frequencies)
VHF/DF	VHF Direction Finding
Vic	V-shaped formation
VIPs	Very Important Personages
VSI	Vertical Speed Indicator (essential flying instrument)
Warn in	Formal notification of arrival at a Mess
Warn out	Formal notification of departure from a Mess
Window	Short strips of foil, air-dropped to confuse radar. Also 'Chaff' (American)
WingCo	Wing Commander (slang)
Wg.Cdr.	Wing Commander
White Card	An instrument flying qualification
WRAF	Womens Royal Air Force
Zulu time	Greenwich mean time